Caliph of Cairo

Caliph *of* Cairo

Al-Hakim bi-Amr Allah, 996–1021

Paul E. Walker

The American University in Cairo Press
Cairo New York

First published in 2009 by
The American University in Cairo Press
113 Sharia Kasr el Aini, Cairo, Egypt
420 Lexington Avenue, Suite 1644, New York, NY 10170
www.aucpress.com

Dar el Kutub No. 13275/09
ISBN 978 977 416 568 9

Dar el Kutub Cataloging-in-Publication Data

Walker, Paul E.
Caliph of Cairo Al-Hakim bi-Amr Allah, 996-1021 / Paul E. Walker.—Cairo: The American University in Cairo Press, 2009
p. cm.
ISBN 978 977 416 328 9
1. Al-Hakim bi-Amr Allah I. Title
923.1

2 3 4 5 6 29 28 27 26 25

Contents

Preface

Readers who come to this book with special regard, perhaps even affection, for the Fatimid caliph and imam al-Hakim might recoil at the title 'Caliph of Cairo', sensing that it belittles the broad scope of his authority and the vast extent of his domain, both politically and religiously. In truth he governed an empire that stretched from North Africa and Sicily to Syria and the Holy Cities of Arabia. As spiritual leader his province was greater still, covering, in theory, the whole realm of Islam itself. To assert that he ruled Cairo, if it implies thereby that his position in the medieval Islamic world was confined to that city, is analogous to Christians speaking of the Pope as the 'Pope of Rome', a locution used not infrequently by detractors who wish to demean his status vis-à-vis the Christianity of competing groups. It is true, moreover, that enemies of the Fatimids – their Abbasid rivals in particular – routinely employed phrases of the kind, for example 'the one who rules from Cairo', 'the person who appeared in Egypt', as a way of deriding Fatimid legitimacy. Many modern adherents of the line of imams descended from al-Hakim rightly view that as offensive both then and now. For them an alternate title, such as 'The Caligula of Cairo' or 'Nebuchadnezzar on the Nile', two examples of those sometimes suggested, which those less sensitive to the issue might see as offending, actually carry less sting. Some personal peculiarities of an individual imam will not impugn the sanctity of the dynasty as a whole. The authority and status of the imam-caliph is crucially important. Any attempt to diminish his exalted rank, or to suggest that it is confined to a given region and does not apply to others, one territory but not the rest, constitutes an affront not to be accepted lightly.

That implication, however, is certainly not what is intended here. Rather it is the intrinsic connection between al-Hakim the ruler and the city of Cairo, which was founded by his own grandfather. He was himself, moreover, born in that very city, the first caliph of any dynasty to have that honor. Growing up there, he never strayed far beyond its outskirts. His forefathers all had come from elsewhere. They were not Egyptian but he was. During his adulthood, over the more than two decades of his reign, although at the height of his power, he rode incessantly in, through and about Cairo and its older urban sibling Fustat, by night and by day, often all but alone, as if it belonged to him and he to it. In a sense this caliph haunted his city, this city and its people, in a way no other ruler has ever done. To speak of him as the caliph of Cairo, understood in this latter way, is therefore certainly appropriate.

Acknowledgements

It is essential first of all to acknowledge with my most sincere thanks the Guggenheim Foundation for a grant in support of this project in its earliest stages. A year of fellowship allowed me to investigate in detail the full range of sources required for a comprehensive understanding of al-Hakim and his reign, the controversies he engendered, the fables and myths surrounding him, and, in so far as it is now possible, the truth behind them.

Over several decades of studying both the Fatimids and the Ismailis, many colleagues and friends have contributed much to enlighten me about either subject. Not all can be named here. Best to limit myself to those who had a direct part in the writing of this particular book. They include Michael Bonner, Robert Dankoff, Carl Petry and Everett Rowson, who deserve special mention for crucial assistance and support at the very beginning. Ahmed Hashim for various consultations along the way. And, when nearly finished, three others volunteered to read parts or the whole of the text with a critical eye for its mistakes and flaws. Shiraz Hajiani went through the early chapters and kindly told me where I seemed to have drifted into an impenetrable density. He pointed out several sections that, as the text stood then, his niece, who would have otherwise been interested in the subject as a whole, but having become lost, surely would give up and quit reading any further. Although I have never met his niece, her guidance proved most helpful. The remaining two readers were Bruce Craig, Director of the Middle East Documentation Center at the University of Chicago and editor of *Mamluk Studies Review*, and Alyssa Gabbay, who is currently a visiting scholar in the Department of Near Eastern Languages and Civilization at the University of Washington. Both went through the entire work carefully and provided a check against errors and infelicities of many kinds.

Finally I must express my gratitude to an old friend, Eric Ormsby, who generously granted permission to reprint here his poem 'The Caliph.' The maps were prepared by Olaf Nelson of Chinook Design, Inc.

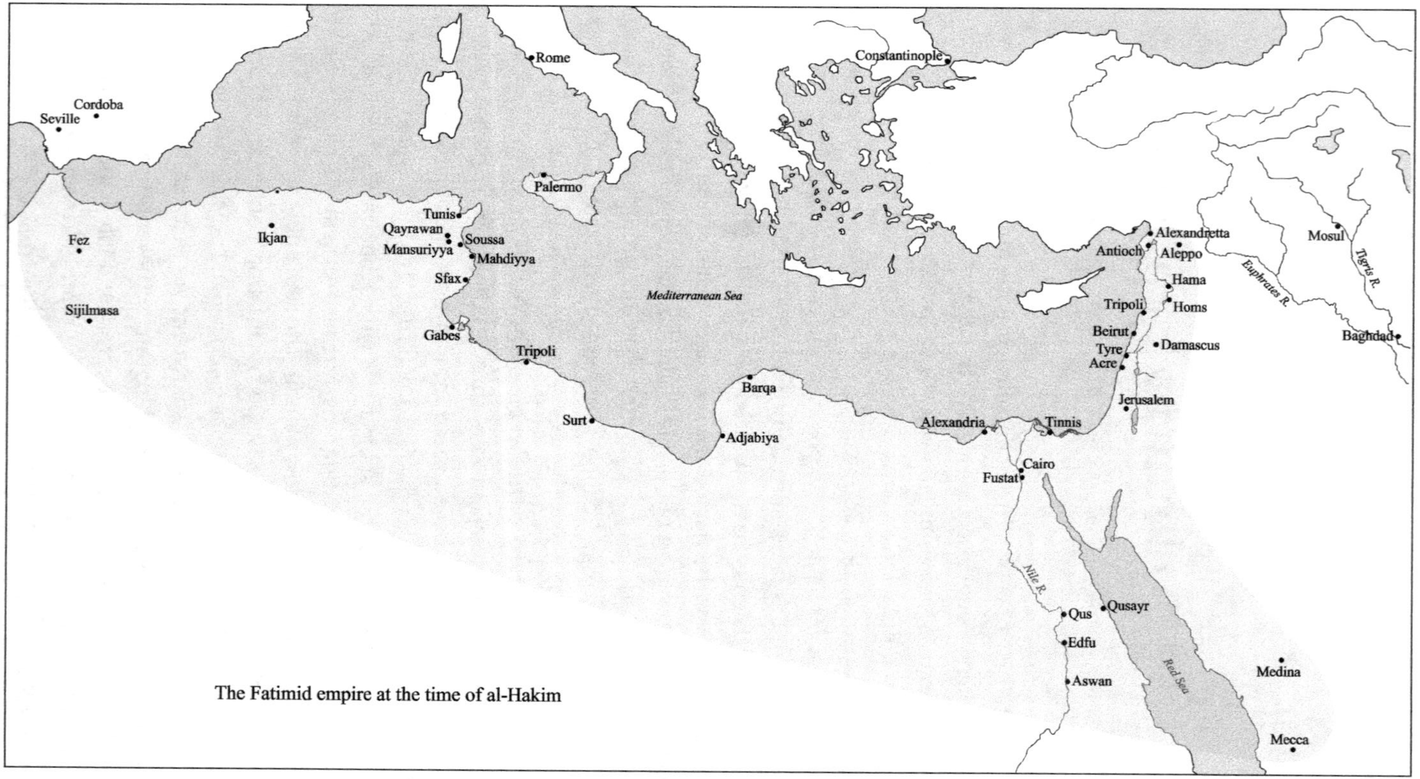

The Fatimid empire at the time of al-Hakim

PART ONE

1

Writing the Biography of an Enigma

The night it all came to an end was otherwise ordinary. On the 27th of the Islamic month of Shawwal, in the year 411 (Monday, 13 February 1021), with only a faint sliver of a moon overhead, the caliph al-Hakim rode out of his palace accompanied by two grooms. His small party next exited one of the southern gates of Cairo and set off into the uninhabited foothills along the low slope between the much higher Muqattam plateau to the east and the Nile river to the west. By that time in his career, his nightly forays into the desert had become almost as common an occurrence as his ramblings in other directions, at times into the heart of markets and the habitations of the common people, at times toward the river and the gardens on the flat valley floor along its shore. So frequently did al-Hakim mount his favorite riding animal, a grey donkey named, perhaps with irony, Qamar (the moon) and depart the comfort and safety of his royal abode for the silent darkness of night, none of his staff would have thought much of it. Riding into the blackness of the evening was for him almost an obsession. Nor, though constantly risking the imminent danger of assassination, did he allow an armed guard of men on horses to escort, or even to follow, him. He had long before ceased that practice which would have been customary for any other ruler. Although, like most others, he certainly had many enemies, he seemingly feared nothing. The police captain in charge of the southern gate of Cairo duly opened it for him and closed it behind without regard for what might happen next. One of the most powerful men in the world simply wandered out, as was his custom, to circulate however whim should strike him, on this occasion to the area of the southern Qarafa cemetery, riding nearly alone among graves and the stars, the monuments and the sands.

At the first light of dawn, the caliph and his two servants found themselves at the tomb of al-Fuqqaʿi (the beer merchant), not far from the mosque of Sidi ʿUqba. There they encountered seven men of the Bedouin clan of

Suwaydi from the Banu Qurra, an Arab tribe with many reasons to hate al-Hakim. These men requested money. Whether it was robbery or extortion by threat of harm or not, al-Hakim accepted their demand and consented to pay them. Over recent years he had become well known for most generously rewarding such requests, much to the alarm of those responsible for the maintenance of his finances who felt he was too easily giving away all of his wealth and holdings. Having no funds with him, however, the caliph could only offer to send one of his grooms back to the treasury with these men, there to arrange the agreed-upon payment. He remained with the only other groom, whom he soon also dismissed, telling the boy to leave him at the tomb where they were. That was the last contact with al-Hakim; no one ever saw him again.

As was their standard practice, the servants and others of the palace went out over the next days bringing with them processional mounts in expectation of his return. They kept that up until Thursday and the start of the new month. Finally, on that following Sunday, a large party consisting of several members of the royal entourage and some of the most loyal members of the Berber and Turkish guards proceeded south from Cairo along the path the caliph was thought to have taken. They passed by the monastery of Qusayr and spread out, moving into the hills beyond it. There, eventually, they spotted al-Hakim's distinctive grey donkey on the top of a ridge, two of its legs run through with a blade, hobbling it, but with its saddle and bridle still in place. The search party observed traces of two men on foot, one of whom had walked in front of the donkey and the other behind. Following these tracks, they came to a pond eastward of the town of Hulwan, in which they found the caliph's robes, seven pieces altogether. The buttons on them had not been unfastened and yet, even so, the cloth itself revealed evidence of several thrusts of a knife.

Whatever the exact truth of this story, it is based on the most widely quoted version of these events in the earliest sources. It thus appears to account best for what might have actually happened, although parts of it, surely, need to be viewed with skepticism. However, the story itself served an important purpose. The claim of having found al-Hakim's clothes showing signs of knife wounds proved to those responsible at the time that he was in fact dead. But, all the same, it also confesses that he had quite unexpectedly disappeared and that the authorities were unable to produce his body, or a better account of the event, to confirm that fact. Other versions of what took place exist, some more explicit as to the manner of death, who arranged it and how it was done. Conspiracy theories were as prevalent then as they are now. Not unlike the first, these other accounts betray the interest of one party in portraying another as guilty of the caliph's murder. All of them are thus, for one reason or another, even more suspect than the first. But was al-Hakim really deceased, murdered somehow, or could he, as yet another possibility, have chosen instead to abandon his royal life, wandering off to live as a reclusive ascetic, a dervish monk alone and anonymous?

Regardless of the answer to that question, the plainest truth was that the caliph had literally disappeared into the desert, never to return, thus ending one of the strangest careers and most puzzling eras in Islamic history, so bizarre and irregular that, despite modern scholarship and an array of source materials unusual for a period so long ago, it continues to defy explanation. Al-Hakim has, however, never been forgotten. To the Druze, who form an important religious subgroup within the modern states of Israel, Syria, and Lebanon, al-Hakim was (and is) God. His disappearance merely indicated His reversion to non-human form. For Ismaili Muslims, al-Hakim was the 16th imam of a continuing sacred line that descends from the prophet Muhammad's cousin and successor ʿAli (and his wife Fatima, the prophet's daughter). They are now represented by at least two branches with significant numbers in India, Pakistan, and lately in Europe and North America – one branch constitutes the followers of the Aga Khan. As the Shiite imam as well as caliph, al-Hakim was, in the view of the Ismailis, absolutely infallible and incapable of error or sin. His actions and decrees were (and are) beyond question. In his time he was the sole arbiter of religion and religious law or of the interpretation of scripture.

Christians and Jews, by contrast, long remembered al-Hakim as their persecutor, a man who made them wear large crosses and bells in public places, and who ordered many of their churches and synagogues destroyed. One of these churches was, in fact, the Holy Sepulchre in Jerusalem, the destruction of which sent shock waves throughout all Christendom. Muslims within al-Hakim's realm who were not of his Shiite Ismaili faith were likewise threatened by him in odd ways. At one point in his reign, for example, he forbad women from leaving their houses or appearing in public for any reason at all. And, to make certain they did not, he commanded that shoemakers cease making footwear for women. He also outlawed the game of chess and the consumption of various foods that were staples of Egyptian life. His campaign against alcoholic beverages, including an attempt to restrict commerce in any produce that could be fermented, was a model of excess and ultimately of futility. But, he also, paradoxically, rescinded many of these same measures himself and allowed the churches and synagogues to be rebuilt (one rebuilt synagogue was to house in its lumber room the famous Cairo Genizah, a massive treasure trove of documents from the Jewish community of the subsequent two centuries or more). And, despite a lengthy record of cruelty, al-Hakim remained popular with the masses and a figure of legendary majesty and awe to the very end. He also must be credited, for example, with the founding of a rare public library, supplied with books from his personal collection and endowed with his own funds, and with providing employment for two of the most distinguished scientific minds of that time, Ibn Yunus, an astronomer, and Ibn al-Haytham, a mathematician and physicist. His was a mixed record indeed.

It is obvious that al-Hakim was not normal, either as a person or as a ruler, not even by the Shiite standard for an absolutely infallible imam in its most extreme form. None of his ancestors or his descendants displayed the same characteristics or adopted similar policies. He was unique, unpredictable, and his actions simply inexplicable. Contemporaries confessed as much, as did even his most ardent supporters. His enemies never knew what to make of him. One of them was a Melkite Christian scholar and historian, later a bishop of Antioch, who once resided in Egypt and suffered persecution there under al-Hakim. In Egypt he had personally known al-Hakim's physician who had reported to him that al-Hakim suffered from melancholia, a form of madness that, according to this doctor, required treatment by soaking the patient in a large tub of violet oil in order to bring it under control. (This same physician was a noted singer and musician, especially at parties to which he was often invited for this reason. He drowned late one night tangled up in his own clothes which, in a thoroughly inebriated state – quite in violation of the imam's law against the drinking of alcohol – he was trying to take off in order to go swimming. Unfortunately, therefore, he did not live long enough to effect the cure he had prescribed.)

The notion that al-Hakim was certifiably insane has long served as an explanation of his odd behavior. It reappears regularly in the historical reappraisal of his rule. It is a concept, however, that is highly offensive both to the Druze and to the Ismailis, for understandable reasons. Their views of the period, though quite different one from the other, are thus not those of most other observers, medieval or modern. But there exist, in fact, enough eyewitness accounts of events of the time, and of the consternation they engendered, to create a history of al-Hakim's life and times that is full of validly conflicting views even of the same evidence.

One group argues that al-Hakim was infallible; what he did was therefore correct. Another insists that he was God. Modern historians frequently point out that his actions actually violated Islam. The destruction of churches and synagogues and the persecution of Christians and Jews, as but one example, are not now, and were not then, 'legal' in Islam. Yet others say that there was no such thing as an Islamic law to which the imam was accountable. His interpretation was the law; the law was, so to speak, accountable to him. How then is what he did to be explained except as an aberration, the result of madness and tyranny, both together in a lethal combination?

When he disappeared that night in February, the dynasty to which al-Hakim belonged was at the height of its power and fortunes. The empire he ruled from its capital in Egypt comprised a vast territory stretching from North Africa and Sicily, where the local rulers recognized his overlordship, to the holy cities Mecca and Madina in the Hijaz and to much of Syria and Palestine. Outside the domain of his direct political control, other regions, especially in the eastern Islamic lands, contained pockets of adherents and secret sympathizers, who on occasion proclaimed their allegiance to him.

The dynasty itself was known from late medieval times by the name Fatimid, a term used to indicate that its caliphs claimed descent from the Prophet Muhammad and from ʿAli b. Abi Talib, his cousin, adopted brother, and chosen successor. ʿAli was also the husband of the Prophet's daughter Fatima, who was to bear with him two sons, Hasan and Husayn, the only offspring of the Prophet to live to produce their own progeny. The name 'Fatimid' affirms descent from one or the other of the Prophet's grandsons, in this case of a line stemming from Husayn and not from Hasan (nor from additional sons of ʿAli from another wife than Fatima).

In Islam the caliphate denotes supreme leadership of the Muslim community as a whole. For the Shiʿa, the caliph inherits all of the authority once held by the Prophet except for the reception of revelation. Direct messages from God to His people have, with the completion of the Qurʾan, ceased. Nonetheless, the Divine guides those who serve Him through the institution of the imamate, which is, in this sense, the equivalent of the caliphate. The imam is the caliph, the caliph is the imam. In Sunni Islam the matter is much less clear. The term 'imam' for them implies leadership: the imam of a mosque leads prayers, for example. The founder of a school of legal doctrine and interpretation is its imam. The very earliest caliphs were certainly also imams, both politically and religiously. But, in later periods the religious authority of the caliphs declined substantially, as eventually did their political power. By contrast the Shiʿa have always regarded the imam – that is, their imam – as the repository of religious knowledge and ultimate authority concerning all matters. He holds the supreme position in Islam, governing in theory all its adherents, in fact all humans everywhere. The imam is the ultimate representative on earth of all of God's people.

The rise of the Fatimids in 909 and their assumption of the caliphate meant that the imamate had joined with the caliphate in the person of the first of them, al-Mahdi, who ruled from the formal announcement of his reign in January 910 until his death in 934. For his followers political governance had now returned to the appointed imams descended from ʿAli, who had been the only one of the earlier caliphs with any right to this office. Al-Mahdi represented the restoration of true Islam; the wrongs of the previous centuries were in him redressed. But the line of imams immediately prior to the new caliphate, from ʿAli to al-Mahdi, while partially clear and well known, is also partially obscure and hotly disputed. Husayn's great-grandson Jaʿfar, according to nearly all accounts, designated his second son Isma'il to succeed him. When this son died quite unexpectedly before his father, confusion ensued. A majority of the Shiʿa eventually upheld the rights of another, younger, son, Musa, who produced his own line, which subsequently ended with the disappearance of the imam reckoned to be the 12th, hence the name of these Shiʿa, the Twelvers. Others insisted that the imamate had passed from Ismaʿil to his son Muhammad, and continued from there. The Fatimids in general claimed that al-Mahdi descended from this Muhammad son of Ismaʿil, but they were hardly forthright about the imams who filled the generations in between the one, who was born in the first half of the eighth century, and the other who died in 934, nearly 200 years later. They preferred to speak of the missing imams cryptically as those who were forced to conceal their identities in order to survive hostile persecution instigated by evil men who had wickedly usurped the imamate. From al-Mahdi onward, however, the imamate passed openly, son succeeding father by explicit designation, one to the next, coming, in the sixth generation, to al-Hakim from his father al-ʿAziz.

Al-Hakim was thus the sixth of the Fatimids. He was also the third to rule from Egypt and the first actually born there. As the Shiite imam he inherited the full divinely sanctioned authority that the Shiʿa believe resides in the imamate. And yet he governed an empire in which the Ismaili Shiʿa were a minority. The term 'Ismaili' (*Ismaʿili*) – a supporter of Ismail (*Ismaʿil*) – denotes a person who follows an imam descended from this son of Jaʿfar, and not therefore from any other son of his. However, the word seldom appears in early sources. Not until much later did it have any currency. Nevertheless it is useful as a name to indicate those who accepted the Fatimid caliph as the imam in the sense just described. For Ismailis, once al-Hakim had received the designation of his father and had succeeded him, temporal and spiritual authority depended solely on him. He was the single infallible arbiter of Islam, of its law and its ritual. The prior imams – his ancestors back to ʿAli – retained an important degree of authority, but, as the living imam, the final word was his.

Expectations for each new imam were naturally high. And al-Hakim's five predecessors had all achieved noteworthy successes during their reigns. His grandfather in particular had expanded the empire, first westward to the Atlantic, and then, second, eastward to Egypt, Syria and the holy cities in Arabia. Cairo itself was his city. There were still other regions left to conquer and the main rival for the caliphate, the Abbasids, continued to rule from Baghdad. The way was thus open for him to surpass his immediate ancestors, to enlarge the empire to include, as his most ardent followers certainly felt it must, all of the Islamic domain (and perhaps all of the known world). It was no small task, nor light a burden, for the imam-caliph who both lost his father and came to power as a boy of only 11.

Modern scholarship first encountered al-Hakim in the masterly study of the Druze by the great early nineteenth-century French orientalist Baron A. I. Silvestre de Sacy, whose *Exposé de la religion des Druzes* (Paris, 1838) remains a classic. This work inspired several generations of French investigators and even a continuing tradition of imaginative literature that has used al-Hakim as a theme, the prime examples of which are some wonderful but quite fanciful pieces by Gérard de Nerval. Closer to our time, there has been considerable work done on sources that Silvestre de Sacy could not have known, among them many Ismaili texts that were unavailable prior to the middle of the twentieth century. Moreover, despite the persistence of both myth and misinformation concerning al-Hakim and the Ismailis, it is possible now to study his reign on the basis of a variety of sources, both Ismaili and not, and from several perspectives. The oldest Druze epistles, for example, copies of which Silvestre de Sacy had but which had never been published earlier, have finally appeared. The important *History* by Yahya of Antioch, the Melkite contemporary of al-Hakim, a *History of the Fatimids* by the fifteenth-century Egyptian master historian al-Maqrizi, and the Coptic *History of the Patriarchs of Alexandria* are readily obtainable and often consulted.[1] Although a few relevant Ismaili texts remain unpublished, manuscript copies exist and can be investigated.[2] The secondary historical literature has grown as well. We have important studies of al-Hakim and his era by J. van Ess,[3] H. Halm[4] (both writing in German), Th. Bianquis[5] and D. De Smet[6] (in French). It is possible therefore to contemplate a thorough, detailed re-examination of the era of al-Hakim, both as history and as religious legend and myth.

The book that follows presents the history of al-Hakim and the Islamic Middle East at the beginning of the last millennium, roughly from 996 to 1021, the dates of his reign. It constitutes in one sense a biography of the man and provides a detailed account of his strange actions over the course of his life. In addition it explains him on the several levels that he represents to his followers and to his detractors. The religious meaning of al-Hakim ranges far wider than the ordinary history of his deeds. He was God; he was an infallible imam; a caliph; a divine king; an heir to prophecy; a messiah (he disappeared while riding a donkey exactly 400 years after Muhammad's own departure from the world); he was a woman-hater; a heretic; an arch demon; a despicably evil and capricious tyrant; and more. Yet he ruled an empire at the height of its power and he was generous to a fault, loved by commoners, patron to scholars, marked by such an awesome personal majesty he never required a military guard during his frequent, at times almost daily, public appearances.

Here is as definitive an account of al-Hakim as is presently possible on the basis of all of the evidence in the sources but in a form accessible to a general readership. The subject itself has its own inherent interest quite apart from the broader context of medieval Islamic history. Nevertheless this aspect of the study adheres in the first instance to the normal rules of academic history. In addition, however, it renders al-Hakim, in general, sympathetically in his various religious roles – as Ismaili imam, for example, or as a humanoid manifestation of the One True God, as another – and as symbol and legend, in political polemic and in fiction (as with de Nerval).

Fortunately, there exists a fairly rich store of information for each of these purposes. One observer of al-Hakim's era was the amir al-Musabbihi who lived through it and kept a detailed record that is reported to have contained well over 26 thousand pages by the time he stopped writing. It is now lost except in parts but was heavily consulted by later compilers whose works are still extant. Several other contemporary accounts survive more or less intact. But sorting all of this information, separating myth from fact, bias from reality, for a figure of such complexity, replete with ambiguity built into his very character, the subject of obvious and not-so-obvious hostility, from both medieval and modern writers, friend and foe, is not simple, and perhaps is not even possible. Al-Hakim was condemned and derided, his actions often held up as representing the worst excesses of autocratic and theocratic rule. Yet few, even among those who censure him most harshly, do not also admit to other traits in him and his governance that were quite admirable. Where he was quite ready to shed blood, executing far too many of those who worked in his regime, he was incredibly generous with goods and money, a fact spread far and wide. Excesses of religious intolerance under his authority were matched by a general sense of the prevalence of justice in his domain. The following judgment of him, and the paradoxes he represented, by the thirteenth-century Sunni historian Sibt Ibn al-Jawzi, who was normally quite hostile to the Fatimid cause, is not untypical:

> His caliphate was a contrast between boldness and audacity and cowardice and restraint, a passion for learning along with a loathing for scholars, and a penchant for rectitude with the slaughtering of the righteous. A tendency to generosity predominated in him and yet on occasion he was miserly in regard to some thing no one else had ever been. He continued to dress in woolens for seven years and abstained from entering the bath; he persisted for seven years holding sessions night and day in candlelight. Then it occurred to him to sit for them in the dark, which he did thereafter for a time. He executed scholars, government clerks, and notables too many to count; and he had written on the [walls of] places of worship and congregational mosques a cursing of Abu Bakr in the year 1004. Then he had it erased in the year 1007. He ordered the killing of dogs and [forbad] the selling of *fuqqa*ʿ beer; he eliminated the *mukus* taxes from the land and from what was sold in it. He outlawed astronomy yet studied it himself; he banished the astrologers and yet used to make observations [of the stars], waiting upon Saturn and its rising with Mars. That was the reason for his readiness to shed blood. He built the mosque of Cairo, and the Rashida mosque on the Nile at Fustat, and many other mosques. He sent to them Qurʾans adorned with silver, and curtains of silk, and candle holders of gold and silver. He forbad the *tarawih* prayers performed during the nights of Ramadan for ten years. Then he allowed them again. He cut down the grapevines and prohibited the selling of grapes; no grapevine remained within his territory. He poured five thousand jars of honey into the river out of fear that it would be made into mead. He prohibited women from leaving their houses either at night or during the day. He decreed emblems for the protected peoples [Christians and Jews] by which they were to be

> distinguished. Jews were made to wear black turbans. They were not to ride with Muslims in boats, nor to employ as servants Muslim youths, or use as riding mounts the donkeys of Muslims, or to enter the public baths where there were Muslims. He set up baths for them separately. No monastery or church remained in his domain that he did not destroy. He proscribed the kissing of the ground in front of him and asking for God's blessing for him in the *khutba* sermon and in correspondence. In place of the personal blessing, he had substituted: 'Peace be upon the Commander of the Believers'. But later he went back on that. A multitude of the protected people converted to Islam in fear of him but then recanted, and he restored the churches to their original condition.

The history of al-Hakim must allow for all of these many paradoxes. It should depict him as those who witnessed his reign saw him, for better and for worse, both fancifully, if that accurately conveys what a given witness's words express, or with the concrete detail of mundane reporting, if that is the nature of the facts related by another. There will be, it seems, more than one al-Hakim and yet who is to say they are not merely different aspects of the same person, possibly aging and changing over time. This caliph did not write his own memoirs; all that is known to us depends on the words of others, not his. Some, such as the contemporary historian al-Musabbihi, actually knew and spoke to him in person, but most repeat the accounts they found in the various sources available to them, adding here and there judgments and opinions about what happened, why, and what it all meant. A biography of this kind is not entirely fair or accurate. It can never be that. Parts of it are real and historically verified, parts myth and fiction, occasionally a combination of both. Hopefully readers who expect a confirmation of what al-Hakim may mean to them personally or to their religion will find it, even if it appears as one among many other views of the man which they might reject and consider distasteful.

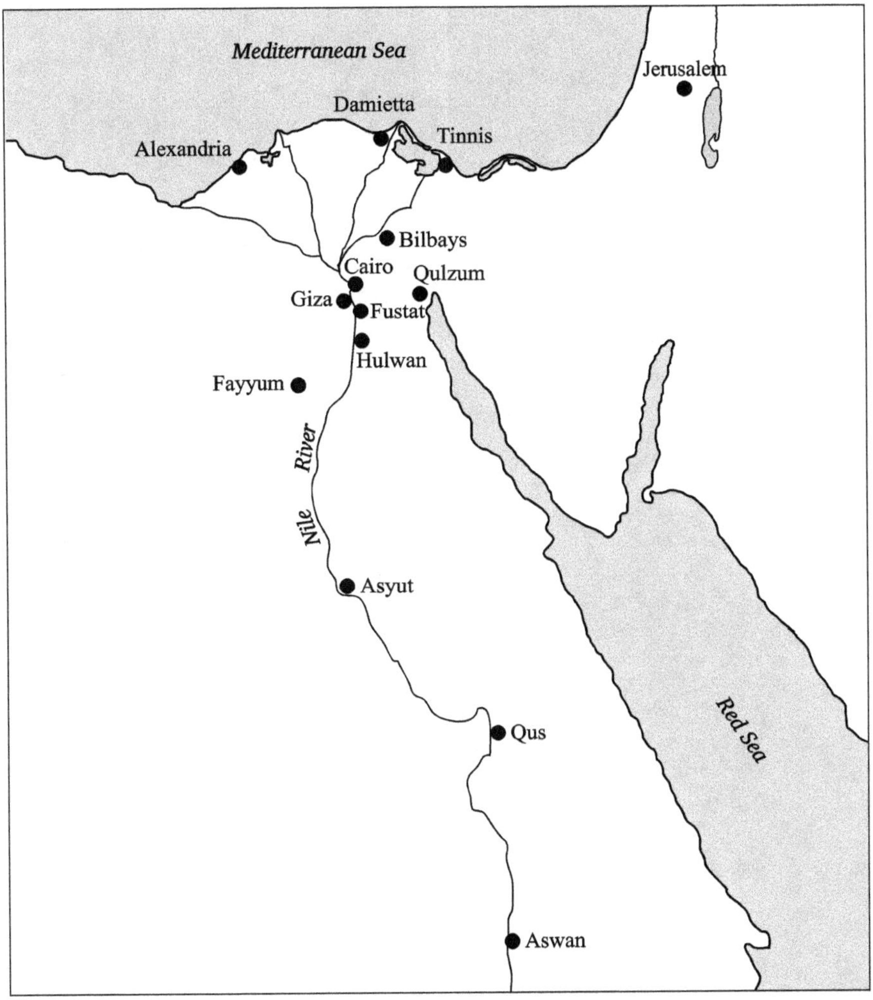
Mediterranean Sea
Jerusalem
Damietta
Alexandria
Tinnis
Bilbays
Cairo
Qulzum
Giza
Fustat
Hulwan
Fayyum
Nile River
Asyut
Qus
Red Sea
Aswan

2

The Father, the Dynasty, Childhood and Regency

While at Bilbays, the Nile Delta staging area where al-ʿAziz had been assembling a grand army for a major campaign into northern Syria, the caliph took sick beginning the latter part of the month of August in 996. Although he experienced short periods of relief, his illness also came back and grew in intensity. Finally, on a Sunday near the end of Ramadan of that year, he rode to the baths of the city, leaving them only to stay at the house occupied for the duration by the chief of his palace treasuries, the eunuch Barjawan. The caliph was there Monday morning, and his pain and suffering, the result of a combination of gall stones, gout and colic, increased throughout the day. Early Tuesday he summoned the chief justice, Muhammad b. al-Nuʿman, and the commander of his most loyal Berbers troops, Abu Muhammad al-Hasan ibn ʿAmmar, and spoke to them about his son and about the coming succession. Next he called in the son, the 11-year-old Abu ʿAli al-Mansur, and conversed with him a while. Hoping perhaps for some relief, he returned to the baths, but matters only became worse. Between the time of the noon and the evening prayers, he expired. It was the 28th of Ramadan (14 October 996).[7]

Normally the death of one Fatimid caliph and the succession of the next would have been kept secret until the situation had been tested and any potentially disturbing factors brought under control. Not so in this instance. The news of al-Aziz's death spread within the hour. Barjawan, who was also the tutor and caretaker of the child Mansur, went immediately to find the boy. He located the son of the dead caliph playing high in a sycamore tree near one of the houses of Bilbays. When he saw him, the eunuch exclaimed apprehensively, 'End your game and come down'. The boy responded, 'I won't come down for a while.' But the servant insisted, 'Come at once! Woe to you;

may God be with you and with us.' Mansur then descended and Barjawan placed on his head a special jeweled turban, kissed the ground before him, and said to him, 'Greetings to the Commander of the Believers.' It was a salutation reserved only for a caliph.

Already the new caliph's much older sister, Sitt al-Mulk, had departed for Cairo with her personal escort of the palace guard. Other leading members of the government, who all had been at Bilbays, left with her including the chief justice, Raydan, the royal parasol bearer, and others. They hastened to the capital to prepare for the funeral and for the mourning in the palace. In Cairo the populace showed proper restraint, with no agitation on the part of anyone; still there was no street or quarter but was full of loud crying and wailing. The following day the people went out of the city to meet the new caliph as he approached at nightfall. Banners and bugles preceded his arrival. He came riding beneath the royal parasol, which was borne over his head by Raydan who had gone out in advance for this purpose. Mansur wore a soldier's cloak of a single color and a jeweled turban. He carried a lance and was girded with a sword. The entire army accompanied him. The body of the deceased caliph was conveyed at the front in a litter borne on a female camel with his two feet protruding from it. Criers shouted through the land as they came, 'No burdens or impositions will be imposed; God has made yourselves secure; anyone who claims or tells you otherwise has forfeit his own life and property.'

The litter carrying the body entered the palace and the chief justice commenced the ritual washing of it, after which it was placed that evening in the same crypt within the complex that held al-Mu'izz, the father of al-'Aziz, and their immediate predecessors. All then passed the night of the feast of the fast-breaking. On the morning of the feast – the *'id al-fitr* – the chief justice went out to the festival square to lead the people in prayer. As he mounted the *minbar* (pulpit), he kissed the spot where al-'Aziz would have sat. The audience began to weep and sob. The judge delivered his sermon over the tears of those in attendance, lamenting al-'Aziz himself and bewailing his loss, but also issuing the appeal for the new caliph, Abu 'Ali al-Mansur, now to be known by his throne name, al-Hakim bi-Amr Allah, 'he who rules by the command of God.'

Though at the time only 11, al-Hakim would himself remember many details of those moments. In later years he recounted the story to the historian Mukhtar al-Musabbihi. 'Mukhtar,' he said, 'my father summoned me to him just prior to his death. He was wearing hardly anything, some tattered rags and bandages. But he reached out for me, kissed me and hugged me closely. He said, "I am worried about you, O dearest of my heart." And his tears began to flow. Then he said, "Go, my boy, and play. I am in good health." So I left and went to amuse myself with the games young people play, while God the exalted and highest took al-ʿAziz away to Himself.' Al-Hakim also recalled Barjawan coming to find him, his being in the sycamore tree, the first words they exchanged, the jeweled turban, the eunuch kissing the ground, and the first ever salutation to himself as caliph on that very day. Barjawan, he reported, also presented him to the people then and there and they likewise all kissed the ground and saluted him as caliph.[8]

Given the trauma inherent in the loss of a popular ruler, one moreover who died relatively early – al-ʿAziz was only 42 – the transition to the new caliph, especially a boy so young, passed, despite the lack of immediate secrecy, with relatively little fuss. Several of those involved in these events also continued to play major roles in the life and the early reign of the child who had just become caliph and, for his religious followers, the supreme imam of all Muslims. Sitt al-Mulk, 15 years older than her brother, was at the age of 26 a wealthy woman of significant power and determination. She had been a favorite of their father, who rarely, if ever, denied her a request. But, though she may have tried to influence her brother over the subsequent period of his minority, she later stayed largely on the sidelines until the end of the reign. The chief justice, Muhammad b. al-Nuʿman, enjoyed a status accorded by prominent lineage. His father was the eminent legal scholar and author Qadi al-Nuʿman, whose writings, especially on law, retained a revered place in the literature of the Ismailis long, long after his death. As chief judge of the Fatimid empire, his son Muhammad continued in his office under al-Hakim. Raydan, the bearer of the royal parasol, remained a trusted palace servant, close to the caliph. Barjawan likewise preserved his position as tutor and caretaker of the young imam. Ibn ʿAmmar, the leader of the Berbers in the army, was, at their insistence, assigned the major role of regent, taking thus charge of all institutions of the government concerned with military affairs and with the perquisites and privileges connected with them. These figures will all enter the story of al-Hakim again, some many more times.

Al-Hakim himself was born in the palace on the eve of Thursday 23rd of the Islamic month of Rabi'a al-awwal in 375 (13 August 985). The Egyptian historian al-Maqrizi, atypically, insists on greater specificity in this one case. He reports that it was the ninth hour [of the night], the morning of which was the 13th of the Coptic month of Ab, the rising of Cancer had reached the 27th degree, the sun was in Leo at 25°, the moon in Gemini at 11°, Saturn in Scorpio at 24°, Jupiter in Libra at 8°, Mars in Libra, 13°, Venus in Libra, 19°, and Mercury in Leo, 10°, and the head in Aquarius, 5°.[9] Why he provides such detail is an open question. At the time of his birth, the infant al-Mansur Abu ʿAli had an older brother who was then regarded as the likely heir. The future al-Hakim did not move up until the later, premature death of that brother during their father's lifetime, but at a date uncertain.[10]

Al-Hakim's mother was, if we accept the only direct testimony available, a Christian, most likely a concubine. According to the *History of the Patriarchs,* in a section composed originally in Coptic by Michael, Bishop of Tinnis, later translated and preserved in Arabic, that concubine, who was the mother of al-Hakim, was Melkite, a member of a rival Christian sect.[11] Using her influence, this text claims, she had her own brother, by name Arsenius, appointed Melkite metropolitan for Cairo and Fustat. The Copts harbored considerable resentment against the Melkites. Suggesting that part of their troubles in that era were caused by the caliph's Melkite mother's intervention against them may have been purposeful and is therefore suspect. There is no doubt, however, that one of al-ʿAziz's women was Melkite and that this lady used her position to arrange the appointments of two of her brothers to critically important patriarchates, one over Jerusalem and the other in charge (metropolitan) of Cairo and Fustat, and then later patriarch of Alexandria.

Better information comes from Yahya of Antioch's *History*, which is, in general, a more accurate source, particularly here as it involves the Melkite church in which its author was an important figure. Under Yahya's entry for the year 375 (985–86), the very year of al-Hakim's birth, in the month of Ramadan – al-Hakim would have been six months old – Aristos, the maternal uncle of the daughter of al-ʿAziz, was made patriarch of Jerusalem, a post he would hold for 20 years before eventually dying in Constantinople. Arsenius, his brother, was appointed metropolitan of Cairo and Fustat. He was patriarch of Alexandria from 1000 to 1010. Thus it was Sitt al-Mulk, not her half-brother al-Hakim, who was related to Arsenius.[12]

Additional evidence confirms the relationship between Sitt al-Mulk and the two Melkite priests. Yahya himself reports that when the churches of Alexandria were rebuilt after their destruction by al-Hakim and after he had disappeared in 1021, Sitt al-Mulk sent the new patriarch vestments, books and silver objects that she possessed because of her maternal uncle Arsenius.

Sitt al-Mulk was born in North Africa in 969, three years before the caliph of the time, her grandfather al-Muʿizz, and his court moved to Egypt. Her mother was also a concubine, an *umm walad*, 'a mother of a child', that is, a consort who has given birth to a child. That a woman in such a position, a mere concubine, not in Egypt but in the Maghrib, would have been Melkite is not impossible. That the same woman had two brothers later to become patriarchs is less understandable. Nonetheless, the testimony of Yahya seems clear enough and therefore decisive.

One remaining possibility, finally, is that Sitt al-Mulk and al-Hakim shared the same mother. That, however, appears quite unlikely. Her mother, who was the favorite companion of their father – a situation fairly well attested in our sources, and confirmed by her title al-Sayyida al-ʿAziziyya (ʿAziz's Lady) – died in December 995, while the government and army were being assembled at Bilbays. The report states that 'the mother of al-ʿAziz's child, who was his wife, died [at the army's camp] in Mina Jaʿfar. She was carried back to the palace and al-ʿAziz himself said prayers over her. The material used for her shroud had a value of 10 thousand dinars. The woman who washed her body received the bedding under her and the clothes she wore [at the time]. The value of what she received was 6 thousand dinars. Two thousand dinars were given to the poor [on her behalf] and the readers [of the Qurʾan] who recited at her tomb were paid 3 thousand dinars. Afterward al-ʿAziz returned to his encampment but the lady's daughter remained at the tomb for a month in mourning. Al-ʿAziz would return to her each day.'[13] There is no mention, in this otherwise detailed account, of al-Hakim; Sitt al-Mulk's mother was obviously not his. Moreover, the Melkite historian Yahya mentions the caliph's mother in a report covering the year 1009.[14] She was thus still alive at that time, long after the death of Sitt al-Mulk's mother. The two women are simply not the same.

The Christianity of his mother became a part of his legend even so. A Christian writer in Europe in the first half of the eleventh century, Rodulfus Glaber, who possessed scant real knowledge of the east but a fervid polemical imagination, not necessarily against al-Hakim but the Jews of Lyon, who he insists put the caliph up to the destruction of the Holy Sepulchre in Jerusalem, claims to have known that she was called Maria and that she was instrumental in the rebuilding of the church, in part to make amends for her son's destruction of it.[15] William of Tyre, the great medieval historian of the crusades, comments that al-Hakim ordered it torn down to prove his *bona fides* as a Muslim against the Christianity of his own mother.[16]

But, if this confusion yields the only evidence that al-Hakim's mother was Christian, are we to conclude otherwise, that she was Muslim? It would appear safe to refrain from a judgment although one story about his being treated for an illness at his mother's behest by a physician who used the text of the Qur'an in his remedy suggests that she was.

To have more information about al-Hakim's mother would be highly useful, but, as is far too often the case, Fatimid royal women rarely appear in the histories. His sister is an exception, notably so. Other bits of information relate that his father's mother, like the mother of his sister, was an *umm walad.* Two names are recorded for her: Durzan[17] and Taghrid. She died shortly after her daughter-in-law in the first few days of 996, also while at the same encampment, near Bilbays. As with Sitt al-Mulk's mother, the caliph returned her body to Cairo, arranged her funeral, distributing alms, and then rejoining his army.[18] Two of al-Hakim's paternal aunts, daughters of the caliph al-Mu'izz, are also known. Both died long after him in 1050, at the age by then of about 90. The first, called al-Sayyida Rashida, left an estate worth an astonishing one million seven hundred thousand dinars, a figure well beyond that for most rulers and kings of the time. The lady's wardrobe contained 30 thousand silk gowns, 12 thousand robes of unmixed colors, and 100 glass jars full of camphor. She was, says one historian who reports this, even so quite devout, living off her spinning and not from funds of the government. Her sister, 'Abda, died three days later. Both were born in Raqqada in the Maghrib. The second sister also left such a massive estate it took, says the report, 40 Egyptian pounds of sealing wax and 30 reams of paper to complete the inventory of all items found in it, among which were 1,300 pieces of silver, each weighing ten thousand dirhams, 400 swords embossed in gold, 30 thousand pieces of Sicilian cloth, gems of which there was an *ardabb* [24 *sa'*] of emeralds. And yet throughout her life she ate nothing but bread mixed with some meat broth.[19]

The evidence for the wealth of Fatimid royal women includes more examples but mainly, as in these cases, in connection with the obituary notice of their deaths. One more obituary of the same type concerns the daughter of al-Hakim himself. Known as Sitt Misr (the Lady of Egypt), she died in 1063 long after her father, leaving again an impressive estate, among which were eight thousand female servants, over 30 thousand Chinese vases all full of musk, unique gems, one of which was a piece of ruby weighing ten *mithqals*. Her landholdings yielded an income of 50 thousand dinars annually. Yet she, like her great-aunts before her, was noted for virtue, in her case for generosity and munificence.[20]

For the long run of Fatimid history, there are other examples of the kind but the women just mentioned have a direct connection to the story of al-Hakim. What is rarely stated, however, is that all the estates in question, as fabulous as they were, became the property of the government. These women had no heirs; none had ever married. And, because they lived so long, their brothers and other immediate family were deceased. In the case of Rashida and ʿAbda, whose wealth obviously engendered the envy of each successive caliph, it would be al-Mustansir who eventually benefited. But it is most curious that we have no evidence of any of these women marrying or producing offspring. Although no written policy exists to confirm it – there is in the literature no discussion of a rule to that effect – evidently Fatimid royal women, here mainly the daughters of the caliphs, were not permitted to marry. In contrast to the royal families elsewhere, whose fathers regularly contracted marriage alliances through their daughters to enhance their prestige or solidify treaties of mutual association, the Fatimids never engaged in such a practice. The reason for this attitude eludes us. Since dynastic succession and the transference of the imamate occurred strictly by designation, not by primogeniture or any other means that allow either the automatic inheritance of the caliphate by the oldest son, or by any member of the family not explicitly chosen by the preceding imam, the possibility of some daughter spawning a contender was unlikely in the extreme. And in fact it never happened.

But also, if none were married, their estates can have only derived from personal inheritance, gifts, and the careful management of their holdings. By law, these women, as daughters, like the wives of the caliphs, would have inherited a portion – less than that of males but not apparently negligible in these cases – of the estate of their fathers and husbands. If the father was the Fatimid caliph, such estates might have been enormous. The size of his daughter's holdings may thus provide some indication of al-Hakim's own estate, remembering that she would have received substantially less than her brother, the caliph al-Zahir. The holdings of the two aunts hint likewise at the extreme wealth of the dynastic family as a whole.

And these examples cover only the women. The men of the dynastic family, those who did not become caliphs – the brothers, uncles, and great-uncles – might equally be of interest. Again the information about them is scant. Apparently none were ever appointed to positions of authority; they did not figure among the officials of the government, nor the commanders of military units. And, unfortunately, there exist for them almost no obituary notices. Because they could and did marry and produce offspring, their estates were inherited by their children. Accordingly, there was no reason for a government audit of their holdings, as was the case with the women. Thus the matter was private and remained so, and no record of these inheritances entered the public domain.

By the time of al-Hakim's accession to the caliphate, five generations of earlier imams had, even without the participation of the female members, produced a burgeoning extended royal family. Al-Mahdi left seven sons, including his successor al-Qa'im, who had himself seven more. Al-Mansur produced five sons; al-Mu'izz four. Those who lived to adulthood might well have in turn generated progeny, as is clear in several known cases involving the descendants of these same sons. The first three caliphs had between them 16 daughters in all.[21] There were thus potentially also many unmarried aunts and great-aunts, even prior to Rashida and ʿAbda.

To this point all members of the family were born in the Maghrib, in the cities of Ifriqiya, what is the modern Tunisia, where the dynasty first rose to power. From the beginning, the Fatimids hoped to move eastward, back to their ancestral center in the Islamic heartland. The overthrow of the Abbasids in Baghdad was always uppermost in their ambitions. Several early attempts to conquer Egypt as a first step failed, but the dream remained. It was al-Hakim's grandfather, the caliph al-Muʿizz, who finally achieved that success. Noted for his perspicacity and wisdom, the fourth Fatimid caliph carefully prepared the way. Reforms undertaken in his reign brought into government service three remarkable men: the majordomo of the palace establishment, the eunuch slave Jawdhar; a slave of Sicilian origin, Jawhar, who advanced from the position of clerk to become the commander of the armies; and the judge and legal scholar Qadi al-Nuʿman. In early 969, following a long period of detailed preparations, al-Muʿizz dispatched Jawhar toward Egypt with a large force backed by a generous supply of funds. The conquest this time proved easy; most Egyptians welcomed the Fatimid general.

Once in control of Egypt, Jawhar set about creating an enclave suitable for the royal court, a walled cantonment designed to grow eventually into the city of Cairo. Four years later, with a new palace nearly finished, Jawhar advised his master that all was ready. Al-Muʿizz gave the order for the whole of his court – the entire royal family, uncles, aunts, sons and daughters (including a three-year-old Sitt al-Mulk), Jawdhar – now like Jawhar a freed man – with his personal retinue, Qadi al-Nuʿman with his family, and many, many others – to commence the shift east. Even the bodies of the previous caliphs joined the party, a sure indication of the finality of this transfer. Some members of the party died en route, among them the old eunuch Jawdhar, and the famous poet Ibn Hani', but most completed the move and took up residence in Cairo. So massive was the influx to Egypt of members of the previous establishment that, for a long time afterward, those who had come from the Maghrib constituted a majority in the new capital. The Westerners (al-Maghariba), as they were known in Egypt, included the soldiers of the occupying army, who were mainly Kutama Berbers, easily identified by their ethnicity. The Kutama, in contrast to other Berbers, had converted in large numbers to the Ismaili version of Islam. They were thus especially loyal and devoted to the imams in the true religious sense. Still, of those born in the Maghrib, the non-Berbers, including the sons and grandsons of Qadi al-Nuʿman, the son of Jawhar, various Slavic army commanders, and others, constituted, among the new elite of Cairo, a distinct bloc. Al-Hakim, who was born in Egypt long after the conquest and a full decade after the death of his grandfather, was not among them. Throughout the earliest years of his rule, when he was still too young to act on his own, members of that same elite sought to play a central role. Later, despite signs that their influence might have been resented, some continued to obtain high positions. But, by the end of his reign, hardly any of them were left.

The four sons of al-Muʿizz traveled with him to Egypt. The eldest was Tamim. He had once been regarded as the likely successor. As he attained puberty, however, it had become obvious that he could not produce offspring and he was then passed over. The exact cause of his impairment is unclear but in Shiite theory an imam must engender a male child, or be at least capable of doing so. For the Ismailis the line must continue; an imam who fails to produce a successor cannot have been the true imam. With Tamim out of the way, the choice fell on the next oldest, ʿAbdallah. As the court moved to Cairo, he was the presumed heir. Nizar, the future caliph, and his even younger brother, though honored members of the royal family, were out of the picture. Obviously ʿAbdallah was to succeed; and he was groomed for it with such responsibilities as leadership of the army sent to repel an invasion of the Qarmatians that threatened Cairo as late as 974, a year prior to the death of al-Muʿizz himself. ʿAbdallah's victory over the invaders was much celebrated. On the threshold of succession, however, ʿAbdallah sickened with little or no warning and died shortly afterward. In that situation al-Muʿizz decided on his third son, Nizar, whom he formally designated to succeed only days prior to his own death in 975. Thus, quite unexpectedly, and with a minimum or, possibly, no preparation, this third son assumed the responsibilities of caliph and imam, adopting the regnal name al-ʿAziz.[22]

The new caliph was himself only 20 years old, but, if he lacked experience in leadership, he was nevertheless in good hands. Al-Mu'izz left behind a prosperous realm, well managed by a talented staff of experts. One among them, the converted former Jew Ya'qub b. Killis, rose shortly to the highest rank, that of wazir, a position not previously used by the Fatimids. Ibn Killis proved exceptionally adept at both administration of governmental affairs and the role of advisor to the caliph. By augmenting and insuring the flow of funds, he allowed al-'Aziz free reign to opt for the lavish court life he favored. He loved pomp and spent great sums for it. A writer characterized his era as an endless succession of festivals and weddings. He indulged his passion for horses and hunting, being notably skilled at handling riding animals and birds of prey. A favorite activity of his was hunting lions, a sport then, as at other times and places, of kings.[23]

A trait always cited about al-'Aziz, even occasionally as a weakness, was his ready willingness to forgive and a reluctance to shed blood. He seldom imposed a severe punishment on those who crossed him. Transgressions against him frequently ended with clemency. A Turkish adventurer named Alptakin, with a small band of troops, opposed him in Syria at Damascus. An army under the caliph's father's old commander Jawhar failed miserably against this man. Many months of effort and a massive expenditure of money eventually brought the Turk into captivity, but at great cost and loss of prestige. Once within his control, however, al-'Aziz chose to honor his former enemy and to enlist his help in creating a regiment of Turkish soldiers to serve the Fatimids. Such leniency was typical of him; there are many other instances of it from his years. Over time it came to be expected, possibly even anticipated, by those around him. And eventually the tolerance and thoughtful compassion of the caliph – he was also notably open to the participation of Jews and Christians in his government – was taken by some as a fault. That the rule of his son was to be, in this regard, the opposite of the father was often pointed out by medieval historians. Could the son have perceived some lesson from observing this overly lenient tendency in his own father?

Yet another obsession of the father was the conquest of Syria. From the beginning of his reign to the very end, he fretted over the details of various planned campaigns. He led one himself into Syria fairly early on. And he died at Bilbays in the midst of orchestrating another. A key for him involved establishing effective control over the north of Syria and thereby opening a route down into Iraq. Fatimid hegemony so far north, however, encountered natural resistance from local Syrian groups as well as the Byzantines, whose empire extended into the region. Al-ʿAziz's hope of controlling all of Syria was never more than a reverie. His vast wealth and resources were simply not enough. The domination of southern Syria and Palestine alone was in itself a constant struggle, with Damascus often in rebellion and the loyalty of the Bedouin tribe of the Tayy constantly in doubt. The Tayy predominated in southern Palestine and their chieftain, Mufarrij b. Daghfal b. al-Jarrah, cultivated an ability to switch allegiances whenever he sensed an advantage in joining the other side. Al-Hakim would inherit many of these same problems, particularly of having to deal with the Tayy and their leaders, but he, in contrast to his father, appears to have harbored no obsession about the status of northern Syria, which, however, was often, although not always, beyond his grasp in any case.

About al-Hakim's childhood prior to becoming caliph, we have a few items of information. One report describes him as being particularly interested in literature and studies, with a predilection to investigate the fine points of the sciences as in, for example, the study of the stars and observations of them, alchemy, incantations, talismans, and all the exact sciences.[24] Precisely when such a description might have applied to him is not exactly clear. The earliest dated notice about him personally mentions his having taken ill during November of the year 991, a matter quite obviously of great concern to his father, who responded by distributing ten thousand dinars as alms to the poor. It must have worked. When, two months later, his grandfather's old commander Jawhar took sick with the illness that killed him, Mansur himself, even though a child of five, is said to have personally sent the former slave five thousand dinars. His father also sent five thousand, as well as himself riding to visit the aged general.[25]

The next report is two years later in 993. About mid-year the annual gift from the Zirid ruler of North Africa, a vassal of the Fatimids and of al-ʿAziz, arrived in Cairo. As usual it included many items of great value among which were prized horses and mules, some with fittings of the finest type, but also hunting dogs, gold and servants. In this particular lot, there were five horses with their saddles designated especially for the caliph's son.[26] In Ramadan of that same year, al-ʿAziz, as was his custom, delivered the Friday sermon in his mosque. With him on this occasion was his son the prince Mansur, who rode to the mosque underneath the royal parasol. Al-ʿAziz went uncovered, evidently preferring that his son, who was only eight at the time, have it.[27] Was it a sign that Mansur was to be considered the successor? Several accounts insist that al-ʿAziz made Mansur his heir apparent in that very year.

Presumably his older brother Muhammad had died by then, or possibly had just died.[28] Whatever the exact intention of al-ʿAziz, the symbolism of the moment was likely obvious to all who witnessed the event. For the *ʿid* festival following the close of Ramadan, Mansur also accompanied his father to the festival square for the public prayers and for the sermon.[29]

From early in the next year, a report states matter-of-factly that the young Mansur held an audience in the library.[30] No additional details are mentioned. Two months after that, when a party of Fatimid sea raiders arrived in Cairo with 100 captured prisoners, the caliph celebrated their victory by festooning the capital and nearby Fustat. He and his son rode through the streets and then returned to the palace in a grand procession. It was, says our source, 'a magnificent day the like of which Egypt had never seen before.'[31] The poets composed and recited verses especially for the occasion. In that year also the son rode with his father for the ceremony of opening the canal, signifying the commencement of the annual flood season.[32] In Ramadan al-ʿAziz gave the sermon and led prayers on Fridays also with Mansur beside him.[33] At the end of the year the caliph set up a review of his troops on the outskirts of Cairo. A tent made of Greek brocade, furnished with royal finery, was set up there for him, and another specifically for his son.[34]

By the end of Ramadan of the following year, the army and most of the government had moved to the staging area at Mina Jaʿfar near Bilbays. There, for the festival of breaking the fast, Mansur himself, though only ten, led prayers and delivered the sermon, as his father would have done. The young Mansur was dressed like him, was covered by the royal parasol, and wore the caliphal gem.[35] Clearly al-ʿAziz was at the moment suffering and unable to attend in person. Nevertheless, he thereafter resumed his duties, among them leading prayers, which he did by giving the sermon two months later on the feast of sacrifices.[36] But, less than a year after that, he was dead. The medical conditions that ended his life were likely already in evidence several months before. Eventually they worsened gravely, bringing about his death.

Once back in Cairo, with his father laid to rest, the young caliph sat the following day for an audience of his subjects. Those who had not been involved previously now flocked to the palace. The great hall held a throne of gold set up on a platform also decked in gold. Al-Hakim departed his part of the massive palace on horseback wearing the jeweled turban. The people stood at attention in the hall, then kissed the ground and passed in front of him as he took his seat on the throne. Thereafter those who normally stood continued to stand; those ordinarily allowed to sit, sat. All extended their salutations to him as the imam, using the name that had been selected for him, al-Hakim bi-Amr Allah. He was, at that moment, exactly 11 years, five months and six days old – a fact the Arab historians insist on repeating.[37]

A prominent group of Kutama Berber chieftains, however, refrained from attending this initial ceremony, instead gathering together in the festival square just outside the northern gate of the city. It was a serious act that indicated their displeasure, and possible resentment, even rebellion. Hasan ibn ʿAmmar, the same man that al-ʿAziz had called upon in his final hours, along with the chief judge, to manage the transfer of the caliphate to his son, went out to them accompanied by another group of their leaders. Ibn ʿAmmar remained with them, striving to quiet the unrest, until at last they agreed to present themselves. They complained bitterly about ʿIsa b. Nasturus, the head of the bureaucracy at the time, and asked that he be removed from office. The chief executive officer of the state, they argued, should be one of their own. No one else, in any case, should supervise matters pertaining to themselves.[38]

The threat posed by these renegade troops had its effect. To calm the situation it was decided that Ibn ʿAmmar should be appointed chief executive to run the government and see to the complaints of the Kutama.[39] He in turn readily agreed to their demands, increasing to eight the disbursements made to them in a year, each man to receive eight dinars. In the presence of al-Hakim, they were also to be given a bonus that very day of 20 dinars. The funds were brought out and the bonuses given as specified, and in front of the young imam. A possible rebellion on the day that al-Hakim's reign began was thus quickly averted.

The conditions leading to this incident were, however, long in coming, a result of festering animosity between the Westerners and the Easterners. The Kutama Berbers had supplied the major contingents of the Fatimid army going all the way back to the first rising in the Maghrib. The army of Jawhar that conquered Egypt was largely Berber, mainly Kutama. In contrast to many other Berber groups, moreover, the Kutama from the earliest days were converts to Ismaili Shiism. They had accepted the Fatimid caliphs with some passion and religious devotion. Their loyalty was unquestioned. But, as the Fatimids had pushed from Egypt, where they encountered little or no resistance, into Syria, their successes were mixed with failures, particularly in any conflict with Turkish soldiers, who proved to be much better trained and equipped. A relatively small force of Turks under the command of Alptakin in Damascus inflicted a humiliating defeat on the army of Berber troops led by

Jawhar. The Fatimid general then reported to al-ʿAziz that the Kutama had been disappointing in the confrontation with these Turks. Thereupon the caliph turned against them and began to create for himself regiments of Turks and other professional soldiers from the east. Unlike the Kutama who came to the army as ethnic recruits, thus retaining their tribal allegiances, the Easterners entered the Fatimid military as individuals, or as small groups, each having accepted the patronage of their employer, in this case the caliph. Their motives were thus more mercenary than religious. But their skill in combat, honed by youthful professional training and advancement in accord with merit, gave them a decided edge over the clan affiliated levees.

Over the long course of al-ʿAziz's reign, the standing of the Kutama diminished steadily and that of the Turks rose. At the accession of al-Hakim, the commander in charge of Fatimid forces in Syria was Manjutakin, a Turk. There were now many Turks in Egypt, along with other Easterners. Another non-Berber force consisted of the slave soldiers, a separate regiment formed of Sudanese and other sub-Saharan troops that had been purchased. The Westerners, having come from the original home of the Fatimids, resented the influx of the others, these Easterners, including both the Turks and the Sudanese. The two sides grew increasingly suspicious of and hostile to each other.

Ibn ʿAmmar, though often said by later historians to have been a Kutama chieftain, was of Arab descent, a member of the old Arab nobility transplanted to North Africa. His family came from the Kalb, a Yemeni tribe. Ibn ʿAmmar's grandfather had served the first Fatimid caliph and died fighting for him in Sicily. His son Hasan became the Fatimid governor of Sicily. A second son, ʿAmmar, provided al-Qa'im and then al-Mansur with key military support against the rebel Abu Yazid. He was later, under al-Muʿizz, commander of a flotilla sent to raid Byzantine territory but drowned tragically returning from it to Sicily when a severe adverse wind trapped and destroyed his entire fleet. Subsequently, the son, Ibn ʿAmmar, accompanied his uncle Hasan in 962 on a campaign against the Christian held city of Taormina and then the fortress of Rametta in the far north-eastern corner of Sicily. Taormina surrendered but Rametta held out. As the siege wore on, Hasan left his nephew in charge and returned to his home base. Meanwhile the Byzantines prepared and dispatched a large force, by sea and by land, to relieve Rametta. An army landed at Messina and marched inland. A much smaller force under Ibn ʿAmmar confronted and defeated it decisively. The Byzantine commanding general died in the battle and his army was thoroughly decimated. It was a tremendous victory for the Muslims, much to the credit of Ibn ʿAmmar.[40]

Later Ibn ʿAmmar returned to North Africa and to serve with al-Muʿizz, eventually playing a part in the conquest and move to Egypt, where he himself remained through the last years of al-Muʿizz and the whole period of al-ʿAziz. For the dying caliph to have called for him must indicate both the high esteem he had earned from long years of service and the reputation of his military victories won on behalf of the Fatimid dynasty. But it is also likely that Ibn ʿAmmar, like others of his family and some of the Sicilian nobility, had converted to Ismaili Shiism in earnest. The chief judge, Muhammad b. al-Nuʿman, the other man summoned to take responsibility for the succession, was head of the *daʿwa* – the Ismaili appeal – in addition to being chief justice. To entrust the fate of the dynasty to these two, and they are the only ones named in this connection, makes special sense if both were Ismailis. Thus Ibn ʿAmmar began his period of regency merely as the trusted confidant, in part the result of his Ismaili devotion, to the dying caliph. As representative of the North African Westerners, he then assumed a greater status, regent not merely for the transition but for the affairs of government at large.

Even before Ibn ʿAmmar was accorded such status, the government recognized another of the Slavic eunuchs, Abu'l-Hasan Yanis, as supervisor of the palace staff, a position that would, whether intended or not, make him a potential rival of Barjawan, a situation he would not long tolerate.

On 23 October, the feast for breaking the fast, the golden throne in the great hall was furnished with a fabric of silver thread. Al-Hakim rode to it on a black horse, wearing the jeweled turban, girded with a sword. By his right stirrup walked Husayn b. ʿAbdallah al-Rahman, the horse trainer, and on his left was Barjawan. The people stood and then kissed the ground, offering prayers. Ibn ʿAmmar said to the chief qadi Muhammad: 'Our lord commands you to leave for the festival square and lead the people in the prayer, and initiate the appeal for the Commander of the Believers.' The qadi stood up to set out. Barjawan girded him with an ornamented sword that had belonged to al-ʿAziz. He proceeded, led prayers, established the *daʿwa* in the name of al-Hakim and returned. Next a golden throne was set up on a bench in the hall and silver tables of food were arranged around it. Al-Hakim again went out of the palace, which he had re-entered meanwhile. This time he rode a light red horse. He sat for the feasting. Those who normally came were present and they ate and departed.[41]

On the 25th, Ibn ʿAmmar received honors in recognition of his new position. He was girded with one of al-ʿAziz's swords and brought a horse with a golden saddle. Al-Hakim then granted him the honorific title: Amin al-Dawla

('The Trustee of the State'). The caliph said to him, 'You are my trustee over my state and my men'. He led away the horse carrying 50 colored robes of the finest cloth and marched in a grand procession to his own house.[42]

In the next days other measures followed, most by the issuing of royal decrees. One among them formally announced the elevation of Ibn ʿAmmar to the position of *wasita*, the chief executive of the state, a rank less than but almost as high as wazir. Al-Hakim, in contrast to his father, never entrusted his government to a wazir, a step that implied turning over nearly full control. The *wasita* was more a go-between, the executor of caliph's orders, rather than someone who had been delegated an authority all but equal to the caliph himself. As with the other decrees, this one was read out publicly in the central mosque by the chief justice. It repeated Ibn ʿAmmar's title, Amin al-Dawla, and stipulated that all persons must dismount in his presence, a high honor indeed!

Additional favors were shown the Kutama; most of their chieftains received gifts of horses as well as money. In the middle of the following month, a ceremony of honor was arranged for Salman b. Jaʿfar b. Falah, the leading Kutama commander, who was girded with a sword embellished with gold, presented with a horse with a golden saddle, along with four other horses with their equipment, and much fine cloth, all in anticipation of his departure with an army for Syria. Commanders under him were also honored in a similar fashion. Funds and arms in large amounts were assembled to travel with his army.

Yet another month later, on the feast of sacrifices, al-Hakim rode to the festival square for prayers. He gave the sermon himself. Those who mounted the *minbar*-pulpit included, most significantly, the qadi Muhammad b. al-Nuʿman, Barjawan, and Ibn ʿAmmar, the three most important officials of the new administration.[43]

Another of the decrees served to proclaim to the general public that al-Hakim had inherited the dominion of his father and that he intended to care for his flock in the best manner possible. As a first step he was canceling the taxes on commerce applied at the point of entry. This tax, the *mukus*, although it supplied useful revenue for the state, was not recognized in Islamic law. In part because of its irregular status, doing away with it was always a popular move and caused much rejoicing.[44] A proponent of this tax, the pragmatic Christian chief financial officer of the bureaucracy, ʿIsa b. Nasturius, who had always been able to count on the support of al-ʿAziz, was now the brunt of attacks by Muslims, who resented a Christian so high in government, by the Kutama, who blamed him in part for their previous decline in status, and by those who were to benefit from the cancellation of the *mukus*. Although he was now confirmed as head of the bureaucracy, his days were obviously numbered. Early in the following year he was arrested and hung, the first of the old government to fall.[45] Ominously more were to come.

Ibn ʿAmmar and the Kutama regarded Manjutakin, the Fatimid commander in charge of the armies in Syria, and a Turk, as a major opponent of theirs.[46] Preparation of a new force under Salman, consisting at its core of Kutama horsemen, had as its principal aim the removal of Manjutakin and his replacement with one of their own. Of the new measures in Cairo designed to raise the status of the Kutama, one involved reading a decree praising them and cursing Manjutakin. Like the others, it was read out from the pulpits of mosques in Fustat and in the palace. Salman's army was suitably equipped not only with arms and money but also with goods symbolic of association with al-ʿAziz. The horses and other riding mounts, swords and textiles sent with them were a legacy of the dead caliph. Turks that remained in Cairo had their stipends and privileges either diminished or denied, and in many cases turned over to the Kutama. Anticipation of what was to come spread fear among the Turks, some of whom left for Syria individually or in small groups.

Salman set out also toward Syria. Manjutakin, resolved to block his advance, came southward to Ramla. At Rafah the two fought a major battle, which Manjutakin lost. Further struggles between the two parties eventually resulted in the capture of the Turkish general, who with a promise of safety was sent back to Egypt, where Ibn ʿAmmar extended him the courtesy due a former commander but without his previous rank and honors. With the fall of Manjutakin and the elevation of their own in his place, and the respect shown them in Cairo, the Kutama should have been pleased. Ibn ʿAmmar took to his new status with a vengeance. He began to remain mounted when he passed through the palace. He insisted that those who came to see him arrive at his abode earlier than necessary, where they would congregate en masse at his door or in his waiting entryway. Meanwhile the door was locked, while he sat in his receiving room not allowing anyone to enter for the space of an hour. Then he granted permission for the most important, such as the chief justice, the elite of the Kutama, and the commanders of military units. Finally he permitted the rest to come in although they entered in such a throng that none of them could actually reach him. Some merely offered a gesture of kissing the ground, although he returned a greeting to no one. When he rode out the same thing happened; only the highest elite could kiss his hand. Others kissed the ground or his stirrup.

Ibn ʿAmmar emptied the royal stables of its horses, bestowing on the Kutama two thousand five hundred of them. Many more went with Salman. He sold so many of the remaining horses, mules, dromedaries, and donkeys that prices fell so far that a female camel sold for six *dinar*s, a donkey that had once fetched 50 now went for four. The Turks and others lost their privileges; the palace staff likewise. There were ten thousand slave girls and eunuchs in the palace. He ordered those that wanted to be sold, sold, and those that asked to be freed, freed, all in an effort to raise funds and curry favor.

As the younger Kutama were given commissions, they began to play the role of grandees, laying hands on married women in the street, plundering people in the alleyways and elsewhere. Complaints against them multiplied, but no one reined them in. Finally matters reached the point where they attempted to interfere with some of the young Turks with the intention of seizing their clothing. The evilness of this act led to a fight in which one of the Westerners and one of the Turks were killed. Leaders of each side quickly assembled their men, two factions ready to fight. Ibn ʿAmmar backed the Westerners. Each invoked harsh language against the other and the situation only grew worse. A number were killed and others wounded. With the conflict gaining in intensity, Barjawan rode from the palace to mediate, but the Turks meanwhile set out to plunder the house of Ibn ʿAmmar, eventually taking from it more than they had recently lost to the Kutama.[47] In the end Ibn ʿAmmar realized that he had been wrong, and that he had lost control of the government in the process. Giving up, he departed Cairo for his home in Fustat. After slightly less than 11 months, his tenure as chief executive was over. A month later al-Hakim graciously summoned him back to Cairo and restored many of his privileges – back to the level he had attained in the days of al-ʿAziz – and his house there, but he no longer rode in processions or met with anyone other than his personal servants and he did not govern again.[48]

The Turks, however, neither forgave nor forgot. Ibn ʿAmmar remained confined to his house in Cairo until three years later when he was at last given permission one day to ride to the palace where he dismounted with all the other people and waited as they did. A group of Turks used this very opportunity to kill him.[49]

The fall of Ibn ʿAmmar meant the rise of Barjawan.[50] Al-Hakim quickly turned over to him supervision of all affairs once under the former regent. The eunuch tutor and caretaker was obviously close to the young caliph and presumably easily able to influence him. Raised in the palace of al-ʿAziz, Barjawan first achieved a high rank in the bureaucracy, becoming the chief supervisor of the palace, and then later also the person who raised the prince from his earliest years. He was thus a consummate insider in an establishment largely restricted to females and eunuchs, the latter being the only males outside the immediate royal family allowed access to the inner sanctum. The exact degree of his hold over al-Hakim, even as a child, however, is uncertain; as the caliph grew older, however, he sought more and more to escape from it.

Was Barjawan complicit in the events leading to his appointment as *wasita*? Did he engineer the fall of Ibn ʿAmmar for his own benefit?[51] Some sources claim as much. They suggest that Barjawan planned and then fueled the conflict with Manjutakin, aiming, by sending a large contingent of the Kutama under Salman to Syria, to rid the capital of their influence. With so many away, those that remained would be weakened. Ibn ʿAmmar could hardly fail to lose thereby a substantial portion of his support in Egypt.

Whatever the truth of such reports, Barjawan's initial measures restored order and harmony.[52] He forbad the Turks from interfering with the Kutama and the Westerners at large, took steps to reclaim many items previously looted, and at the same time restored stipends and privileges cancelled by Ibn ʿAmmar. To better run the government, he selected the Christian bureaucrat Fahd b. Ibrahim as his secretary, the person who would handle his paperwork, seeing to petitions and grievances, and other matters, brought before it in a timely manner. Steadily the two put the affairs of the palace and the populace in good order, relieving in the process the distress and disruption of the recent period. Barjawan characteristically refused to allow anyone to dismount for him. He would meet the people at his house and then, when he went from it to the palace, all would proceed in front of him together. He gave Fahd the title *raʾis*, meaning the man-in-charge, the 'Executive', and that was how he was to be addressed in correspondence. When the people arrived to see these two at the palace, Barjawan sat in the innermost entryway, with Fahd in the outermost. As matters arose, they first went to Fahd, who examined the case and decided, either on his own, or with more important items, which to pass on to Barjawan. The response then came back to Fahd for final resolution. He thus shouldered the greatest share of the daily responsibility.

In the first months of the new arrangement – that is, early in 997 – al-Hakim would often ride each day to the central square and sit there on a throne in a special kiosk, reviewing passing horses, listening to recitations of the Qurʾan, and to the readings of various poets.[53] He would then return to the palace. Barjawan and Fahd meanwhile took up positions there to receive the letters of those with grievances or other needs. The two would remain in place until all cases had been presented and only then re-enter the palace. When al-Hakim had completed his meal, the table would be removed and the two would come in. Fahd sat facing the caliph with Barjawan standing next to him. They presented to him the letters and petitions they had just received and al-Hakim would sign each in his own hand at the top of it to indicate that he had seen it, after which it was sent out for distribution to the appropriate bureau of the government.

If, during al-Hakim's sitting in this kiosk, poetry of note was read, Barjawan would obtain a copy of it. Later, in the evening, when the work of the petitions was finished, he would read again those odes in the presence of a person knowledgeable in the subject of poetics. Although only 12 when these sessions occurred, al-Hakim was himself usually perceptive and proficient in this area. If a particular poem contained an especially fine verse or remarkable allusion, he would comment on it to Barjawan and ask him to repeat it, after which rewards commensurate with his impression of its value would be sent to the poet involved.

In August of that same year, Sitt al-Mulk gave her brother a gift of 30 horses with saddles, one studded with gems, another with rock crystal, and the rest with gold, 20 mules with saddles and bridles, 50 eunuch slaves of which ten were Slavs, 100 wardrobes of clothes, an embellished crown, a decorated hat, many baskets of scents, and a toy garden made out of silver planted with a variety of trees. This information comes with no indication of what prompted it, or if she often sent al-Hakim gifts of such extravagance.[54] From the following year another account mentions the gift to al-Hakim of horses and arms presented by the Turks and their leaders and a group of Ismailis. The occasion was the observance of Nawruz, the Persian new year. The caliph thanked them sincerely but accepted little of it, returning most to them.[55]

Another piece of information lets us know that for the festival of breaking the fast, al-Hakim himself led prayers and delivered the sermon. Those who mounted the pulpit with him included specifically Husayn, the son of Jawhar, the chief judge Muhammad, and the eunuch Barjawan. Two months later, on the festival of sacrifice, the caliph again gave the sermon. At the end of the year he wrote two decrees to be sent with his emissary to Abu Manad Badis, the Zirid ruler of the Maghrib who was his vassal. One confirmed the Zirid's appointment over North Africa and granted him in addition the title 'Nasir al-Dawla'. The second formally announced the passing of al-ʿAziz and the succession of al-Hakim, and it requested of him an oath of allegiance from the Zirids. On arrival the Zirid ruler honored the emissary appropriately and he administered an oath of loyalty to al-Hakim from all the clans belonging to the Sinhaja Berber confederation, to which the Zirid family belonged, and any others. The long delay between the actual death of al-ʿAziz and the taking of this oath by such an important vassal is odd but may have waited for the chance to send an ambassador of a suitable rank.[56]

The year 998, in which al-Hakim would turn 13, began with a series of formal honors granted one by one to various commanders and others of the government. But the first item reported is the observance of Epiphany, the Christian feast of baptism on 6 January, by the number two man in the government, Fahd, Barjawan's secretary. Tents, pavilions and banners were set up in a number of spots along the banks of the Nile. Special seats were erected for Fahd, with lit candles and lamps. Singers and musicians attended. He sat there with his family drinking until the time of the baptism, at which he was immersed and left.[57]

Honors were bestowed on Fahl b. Ibrahim, a Kutama chieftain, who was put in charge of the city of Tyre. Others honored included ʿAli Abu Saʿid, who was given the job of market inspection (*hisba*), and ʿAli Abu'l-Hasan Yanis, a Slavic eunuch, who received a sword, a lance, and much more as well as five thousand dinars, horses, clothes, and 100 youths. He was sent to Barqa. Khawd, another Slav, received a similar set of gifts and was appointed to command of the police for the lower district, i.e. Fustat; Qayd, a black eunuch, was given command of the Cairo police. Maysur, a Slavic eunuch, became governor of Tripoli; Fa'iq another Slavic eunuch, was put in charge of the fleet. For Easter of that year Fahd received honors, as did, about that time, the brother of Barjawan, Abu Sa'ada Ayman, who was like him a eunuch. He was put in charge of Ghaza and Askalon.[58]

This small snapshot of those who held important commands in the early years of al-Hakim provides evidence of diversity. Fahd was a Christian; many of the others were Slavs, religion unspecified; some were eunuchs, some not; and one among those named here was black. Yet all received important commissions with major responsibilities. That the majority of these appointees were eunuchs does not necessarily indicate the hand of Barjawan, but it might.

About mid-year news arrived in Cairo of the recapture of Tyre. It had been the scene of a nasty rebellion of the locals against the Kutama garrison, many members of which were killed. The main instigator was a man known as al-ʿAllaqa. Once his revolt was under way, he had appealed for help to the

Byzantines, who promptly dispatched a fleet of ships carrying fighters. Cairo responded with its own fleet, which scored a victory over the Byzantines. Al-ʿAllaqa and his supporters were eventually confined to one of the towers of Tyre and from there surrendered. He and his band were transported to Cairo. There he was paraded through the city wearing a large, heavy dunce cap made of lead that threatened to fall down to his neck, after which he was executed and crucified.[59] This was not to be the only incident during that period in which the Byzantines opposed the Fatimids. Others followed, though they occurred further north in Syria. Preparing and sending troops in that direction was, in those years, a constant necessity.

In Ramadan al-Hakim gave the sermon and led prayers in the mosque of Cairo, wearing, it is reported, a cloak, a sword, and with the royal scepter in his hand. The main part of the dome over the pulpit was closed around him when he delivered the sermon, which was itself brief and only those near him heard it. It was the first Friday that he prayed in public as caliph.[60] But then he did the same again on the following Friday, as well as leading the prayer on the festival of fast-breaking at the festival square, at which he gave the sermon in the more customary manner, and was present himself at the feast table. On the feast of sacrifice he again led prayers and offered the sermon.

For the year 999, the major event was the death of the chief justice Muhammad b. al-Nuʿman, on 25 January, but a month before al-Hakim turned 14.[61] This judge was the same one who had accepted the trust of arranging the succession from al-ʿAziz. He was well regarded, known for his knowledge of the law and for his care in administering it. By the time of his death, he had held the post of chief justice for over 14 years, although he suffered from chronic bouts of gout and colic that were often so serious that he had to delegate his court duties to his son ʿAbd al-ʿAziz. While ill and confined to his home over the last year, Barjawan himself, despite his exalted position, would come to see him every Thursday. Muhammad was reputed for his good character, for his poetry – although there was some disagreement about its quality – and his willingness and quickness to give generously.

Nevertheless, upon his death, in a review of his estate, a sum of either 20 thousand or 36 thousand dinars – both figures being recorded – were found missing that should have been available for transfer as the funds that had been deposited with the judge for orphans. Al-Hakim then ordered Barjawan to investigate. He dispatched his secretary Fahd to inventory what was left and to seize and sell the possessions of the judge to settle the claims of those whose money was missing. Portions of the debt had been placed with the judge by notaries and they now insisted that the qadi had seized it from them. Those of them who could provide a document written by the qadi to prove their claim were absolved; those who could not were fined. In the end the authorities managed to raise from the estate of the judge and from these fines only half of the missing amount, which they paid to the claimants accordingly, forcing them to accept a reduced amount.

Accounting for the funds of orphans and of those whose heirs who happened to be absent, all of which became the responsibility of the qadi, created a continuing specter of possible corruption, if not of the incompetent keeping of records. While a qadi lived his funds came and went. Those belonging to others were always a temptation; many borrowed from these funds, fully intending to repay what they had taken. If death intervened, the original intention of the judge might become a lost opportunity turned into a charge against his estate. To prevent just such problems after the scandal visited on his judge, al-Hakim issued an order that no judge or notary should henceforth hold the funds belonging to an orphan or those who were absent. Instead the government leased a storehouse in the Zuqaq al-Qanadil (the Lamp Maker's Alley) where all such moneys were to be held. It was kept locked and sealed by each of four notaries; and it was not to be opened except in the presence of all four.

The empire waited 17 days for the appointment of the next chief judge. Finally Barjawan summoned Husayn b. ʿAli b. al-Nuʿman, nephew of the deceased judge, into an audience with al-Hakim. There he was granted a salary, bonuses and fiefs double those of his uncle with the warning that, as the new judge, he should not be tempted in any manner by the funds of other Muslims. He was then accorded honors with the bestowal of a white robe, a cloak with gold thread, a turban likewise with gold, a mule to ride and two to carry many other gifts. The decree of his appointment was read out in public. A copy of it survives. He was, among other of its provisions, to assume responsibility for the administration of justice throughout the empire, including the supervision of subordinate judges in all the territories belonging to the Fatimids, as well as control of mosques, the mint, weights and measures, and matters of inheritance. In due course he appointed a number of subordinates, even for duties in and around Cairo, a few of whose names are listed in our histories. In addition he was to direct the Ismaili *daʿwa*, its appeal, and the agents who taught and propagated its doctrine. Like his grandfather, father and uncle, he thereafter read the weekly lesson to the faithful in the palace as part of the Ismaili Sessions of Wisdom, the *majlis al-hikma*.[62]

Later in that year, during Ramadan, al-Hakim led prayers on two Fridays and on the festival of fast-breaking, at which he also gave the sermon. When he mounted the *minbar*-pulpit, the new qadi went up with him, among others. The caliph also led prayers and delivered the sermon on the feast of sacrifice. At the start of the next Islamic year, 390 (December 999), he sat in open session to receive the new year's greetings of those who presented themselves.

On Thursday evening 7 April 1000, one month beyond al-Hakim's 15th birthday, the caliph summoned Barjawan to join him and a party assembling in the palace to ride out to the port of Maqs on the edge of the Nile. As had become typical of the all-powerful eunuch by then, he arrived late, having delayed as long as he thought he could get away with. The others were waiting at the gateway from which they would all exit. Barjawan entered the palace and went to find al-Hakim in the inner garden that was called the 'Little Garden of Figs and Grapes'. There he saluted the caliph and stood next to Raydan, the bearer of the royal parasol, who was attending al-Hakim at the moment. At that the caliph started for the exit and, as he did, Raydan drew a knife that he had hidden in his shoe and thrust it into Barjawan. Immediately, others ran over brandishing knives and daggers. Bent on killing Barjawan, they inflicted many more wounds until he died, after which they severed his head and buried him on the spot. Meanwhile, as the riding party formed up at the gateway to leave the palace complex, Raqiq, another of the eunuchs, burst on the scene crying and shouting, 'My master has been killed'. Raqiq had been Barjawan's spy inside the palace, and at one point in charge of his storerooms. The news created instant confusion, uncertainty, and no little anxiety. A throng of people quickly gathered at the gateway to the palace, waiting there for information. Al-Hakim himself then appeared on a parapet above and Raydan stood up and shouted to them, 'Let he who is in obedience depart now for his home and return to the palace tomorrow.' All promptly left.[63]

If the populace of the Fatimid capital were caught off guard by the suddenness of Barjawan's demise, signs of what led to it are not hard to find. The young caliph was growing older. The tutor and guardian of his extreme youth persisted in thinking of him as the little boy of former times. The more Barjawan gained in control and rose in status, the less attention he spent on the niceties and protocols of his service, either to the caliph or to the state. He shut al-Hakim out just as the caliph wanted in. Barjawan's increasing assumption of independence fit a changing situation poorly and he failed to realize how his high-handed rule rankled his young master.

In addition, with fewer and fewer limits on his power, Barjawan began to devote more of his time to his favorite pleasures. He was passionately devoted to music and to musical performances. It consumed him. He would gather groups of singers, both males and females, at his house and there consort as if he were one of them. So enamored of these musical sessions was he that he remained at home listening to the performance through the morning hours, while those in need of his services as chief executive of the state had to wait outside his door. The better part of the day gone, he would finally emerge to lead the assembled group off to the palace to take care of business. Yet, even there, he paid attention solely to those matters that interested him, and made decisions without consultation, thus excluding al-Hakim from the administration of his own government as much as possible. Later, after ordering his execution and having it carried out, al-Hakim spoke of some details of Barjawan's insolent behavior in this period. He remembered in particular an incident when he had called upon Barjawan while the two were riding. The eunuch approached him with his leg up over the neck of his mount, the bottom of his shoe pointed at the face of the caliph, a major lapse of etiquette, a sure mark of bad character, and, most serious of all, lack of proper respect![64]

About Barjawan odd discrepancies exist in the sources. He was called Abu'l-Fath Barjawan al-ʿAzizi, the last term meaning that he belonged to the caliph al-ʿAziz. Al-Maqrizi and others insist that he was white and a Slav, although yet another report claims that he was black[65], which seems unlikely. The length of his tenure as chief executive was exactly two years and eight months less one day.[66] Immediately after his death, the head of the treasury, Jaʿfar b. Muhadhdhab, went to audit his estate, which, naturally, as that of a eunuch, had no heirs. The auditor found 100 scarves for turbans of fine colored linen with 100 skullcaps, a thousand pairs of trousers of *dabiqi* linen with a thousand waistbands of Armenian silk, and much more, including 33 thousand dinars in cash, 150 riding horses, 50 mules, and more mounts for his servants, all with saddles, ten of which were worked in gold, plus a considerable library of books on the sciences and literature. Transporting it all to the palace required 80 donkeys.[67]

One curious story about Barjawan engendered an enduring legend. Al-Hakim called him, for some reason, 'the gecko'. But somehow the facts were turned around and we have a report stating that it was Barjawan himself who referred to the young prince as the gecko and, when that last final reckoning took place, the caliph is reported to have sent for Barjawan with the message, 'Tell Barjawan that the gecko has grown into a large dragon and now wants him to come.' Though false – it appears only in quite dubious medieval sources – this story persists to the present, repeated often in modern accounts.[68]

Within hours after the killing, al-Hakim summoned Fahd, his secretary, to assure him of his personal safety, saying to him, 'You are my secretary and your master was my servant, the *wasita* (intermediary) between me and you. Things I disapproved of were done by him and he got the punishment he deserved, but you are in your role as secretary secure as to your self and your property.'[69]

In the morning the people came to the palace and stood at its gateway. The general al-Husayn, the son of Jawhar, went out to them and allowed them to enter into the presences of the caliph, who came out riding a cream-colored horse. He stood in the courtyard, with Raydan on his right and the tutor Abu'l-Qasim al-Fariqi on his left, the people standing in front of him. He spoke to them directly. 'Barjawan,' he said, 'was my servant. I made use of his services. He advised well and I was good to him. But then he behaved badly in what he did and I had him killed accordingly. Now, you are the chieftains of my state' – and he pointed to the Kutama – 'and you are in my regard more excellent than you were previously.' Turning to the Turks he said, 'You are the disciples of al-ʿAziz bi-llah and have the place of sons. For each one in my esteem there is nothing but affection and love. Be as you have been accustomed to be. Go to your homes and adopt my resolve for those of you who have none of your own.' They to a man then saluted, kissed the ground and departed.[70]

Sensing that more was needed, al-Hakim gave an order for the head of the chancery, Mansur ibn Surin, to draft a decree to be read in all the mosques of Fustat, Cairo and Giza. Minus the opening formulas praising God, it said:

> From the servant of God and His deputy, al-Mansur Abu ʿAli, the Imam al-Hakim bi-Amr Allah, Commander of the Believers, to all those who witness the Friday prayer in the mosques of al-Qahira al-Muʿizziyya, Fustat, and Giza: Salutations to you, O Muslims assembled for prayer on this day of ours in these places, and to the rest of the people in their entirety. The Commander of the Believers thanks God on your behalf, He other than whom there is no god, and he asks Him that He bless his grandfather Muhammad, the seal of the prophets and lord of the apostles, and his most pure family. And now, praise be to God who said (and His word is the plain truth): 'If there were in them [the heavens and the earth] gods other than

God, they would fall into corruption; so hallowed be God, the Lord of the throne, above what they attribute to Him; He cannot be questioned about what He does but they will surely be questioned' [21: 22–23]. The Commander of the Believers thanks Him for what He gives him of his caliphate, and allots to him in respect to it, beyond creating him, of grasping and seizing, of setting up and tearing down. O people assembled, Barjawan was previously a servant and sincere advisor. He pleased the Commander of the Believers at one time and so he employed him as he saw fit. He did with him what he wished, as was previously well established in what is known and approved and was permitted according to settled precedent. God the exalted and glorious said: 'If God enlarged the provisions for His servants, they would become oppressive on the earth, but He sends it down in measures as He wants; He is with His servants most knowing and watchful' [42: 27]. Most certainly was the Commander of the Believers the owner of him and so, when the fellow went bad, he inflicted on him punishment. For the words of God the exalted are: 'So when they provoked us at length, We took revenge on them' [43: 55], and His words: 'Is it not so that man transgresses, in regarding himself as independent' [96: 6–7]. The Commander of the Believers forbad him doing what he was inclined to do and tried to pull him out of what he had fallen into. But the will of God, the all-high and glorious, ran its course; His rule was carried out and executed on him. 'That was in the Book recorded' [17: 58]. Accordingly, O assembled merchants and citizens, devote your attention to your livelihood and busy yourselves with your own work. It will be of greater benefit for your affairs. Do not over step the proper bounds in the matters that concern you. The Commander of the Believers is watching out for it and for you. For those of you with a case or need that wants attention, let him take it to the Commander of the Believers. He is himself certainly the manager of such a matter for you, and his door is open between you and him. 'And God will designate for His mercy whomever He will; He is the master of unbounded grace' [2: 105]. You are the subjects of the Commander of the Believers. The gateway to his justice, his beneficence and favor is open. God wants what he wants; He authorizes good for those of the people who obey him, and protection for he who protects Islam. 'I put my trust in Him and to Him will I return' [11: 88]. Peace be upon you, and the mercy of God and His blessings. Written on Friday 11 April 1000. God bless our lord Muhammad and his pure chosen family, peace unconditional.'[71]

From the one master copy, many were made and sent to all the other districts and provinces of the empire.[72] Although this decree was formally composed by the head of the state chancery, what it says matches well the words of al-Hakim to those who had come to the palace. He is obviously its real author, if not in its exact phrases then certainly in its message. Most of all it represents a declaration on his part of full and conscious responsibility for the act it explains. The caliph himself announces thereby that he has taken over, in no uncertain terms, the duty of governing and of leading as imam and caliph; no longer will he be, even nominally, under the authority of either regent or tutor. By killing Barjawan, al-Hakim had put an end, both in theory and in practice, to his childhood and to the minority status that had come automatically with accession to the caliphate at the age of only 11. The perception that he remained no more than a mere youth under the supervision and tutelage of his handlers ceased with this dramatic step. The decree issued to explain it confirmed this fact boldly and directly.

It is worth noting, moreover, that with the execution of Barjawan, added to the fall of Ibn ʿAmmar and the death of the qadi Muhammad, all three of the men al-ʿAziz had asked to assume aspects of the regency over his son were out of the picture. (Ibn ʿAmmar, though still living under house arrest, was to be murdered five months later.)

The personal image of the young caliph in the period that had just come to a conclusion is necessarily limited. The information available in the historical record reports only sparse details: when and where he led prayers and delivered the sermon on the one or two Fridays in Ramadan and on the two annual *ʿid* festivals, what were the occasional audiences he sat for, how he accompanied his father for various ceremonial duties, gifts from the sister, his riding in processions, approving decrees and appointments, and signing the documents and petitions of government. Yet it is perhaps more than we normally get for a period so long ago, especially for a caliph emerging from childhood and in the first years of a reign that was to be as fraught with drama and controversy as his became.

PART TWO

3

al-Maqrizi's Chronicle of the Middle Years

> *A woman arrived coming from Syria riding in a box the height of which was one cubit without extras. She had traveled from Khurasan. With her was a brother of hers who looked as if he were a grown man. She was settled in the palace and provisions were ordered for her and those with her, of which there were many. [She was so small] in a single sitting [with a seamstress], 100 heavy garments and silks were cut for her. Her speech was quite agreeable and refined. She remained just over 30 days and then died. Her funeral was an immense affair.*[73]

This terse and yet tantalizing slice of information pops up suddenly without explanation in al-Maqrizi's account of al-Hakim's reign in the year 998, between a report of the caliph's participation in the ritual ceremonies of the feast of fast-breaking and the departure of the annual pilgrimage caravan. The historian offers us nothing more about the woman or her circumstances, just these few facts, which add up to a touching curiosity amid the serious business of the comings and goings of the ruler and the matters of state in which he was involved. Yet it is impossible not to wonder what it all means. Were the two, the sister and the brother, midgets, small people, so tiny as to elicit such a reaction, a generous reception and unforgettable funeral? What was the box or cask that carried her and why did she travel in it? Was it for her privacy, and the modesty of a woman, however small, having to travel in public? If she was given a place in the royal palace, surely the caliph himself arranged it. Was he, too, captivated by her charm?

In the kind of history that al-Maqrizi wanted for the work he called *Lessons for the True Believers in the History of the Fatimid Imams and Caliphs* (the full title of the *Itti'az*), like that of most medieval Arab authors, chronology rules. But, whereas many other histories of that era observe the events of a given year briefly with greater attention to a list of important men who died in it, al-Maqrizi hoped in this instance to capture as much of what had happened as he could locate, both the grand and the less grand, even bits of the mundane, little events from the realm of the strange and curious that his sources had thought interesting enough to report. He wrote about the Fatimids two and a half centuries after they had ceased to exist. To recapture their era he relied on much older materials, earlier histories, some even from the time of their rule. Not all of al-Maqrizi's historical works have this intention and, for certain periods of the Fatimids, a detailed chronological scheme proved impossible. To set out to record what happened year after year, even month after month, depended on the availability of sources that supply such information. For many years of Fatimid rule, nothing of the kind either exists now or existed then. The reign of al-Hakim, however, is a fortunate exception.

Our historian, according to several sources, also believed that he himself had descended from the Fatimid line. The connection would have been remote by al-Maqrizi's time but friends and associates nevertheless say that he and his family could, and occasionally would, claim a Fatimid ancestry. As well some suspect that he went too far, that he favored them accordingly and that he either ignored or forgave their Shiite heterodoxy, at least in so far as he could in a later age of strident Sunnism. The problem that bothered al-Maqrizi, however, was the bias, obvious to him, of non-Egyptian authors against the Fatimids and things Egyptian. He trusted his Egyptian sources almost exclusively for matters pertaining to Egypt. For him the major histories by Syrians and Iraqis had to be consulted sparingly and with great caution for what they reported about events in Cairo. Again, for the years of al-Hakim, he found himself in good hands with the work of al-Musabbihi, who had been a contemporary observer and one who lived in and wrote from the perspective of Cairo and Egypt.

The amir al-Musabbihi enjoyed the advantages of a high rank while even so aspiring to record, as a historian, a complete account of the years he lived through. He participated personally in the government under al-Hakim and then his son al-Zahir. But, at 26 thousand pages, his legacy was too enormous to survive intact. As the original suffered the deterioration of passing time and use, only recopying would have preserved it, and that must have seemed a task not lightly undertaken, particularly for an era regarded later as one of heresy and unorthodox rule. Nonetheless, one small section of the original text and scattered passages from his work remain even now. Later medieval historians sought out his account, which they summarized in their own. Comments by al-Musabbihi here and there reveal that he himself spoke to al-Hakim on occasion, that he attended major events and ceremonies along with the elite of the notables, and that he actually witnessed personally many of the events he recorded. It is likely that it is he who reports the arrival of the small lady from Khurasan and that he himself heard her speak so agreeably. He would also have attended her funeral.

For fairness' sake and to create as complete a picture as possible, it would be a shame to lose the history that al-Maqrizi – and al-Musabbihi before him – gathered for the reign of al-Hakim by focusing exclusively on its highest drama and the themes most germane to the affairs of state. Moreover, for the middle years of al-Hakim's reign – from the execution of Barjawan through events of the following decade and a half – al-Maqrizi's history of the Fatimids is, far more often than not, the principal source. His account even with its flaws is better than anything else we have. Best, therefore to begin with it, and trace, as he did, those years of al-Hakim, as a series of events, a chronology of what happened year by year, little events running amid the momentous, related as neutrally and without bias as was his intention. Therefore, let us re-enter the path laid out by al-Maqrizi, commencing at the point when al-Hakim, by asserting his right to have Barjawan executed, assumed sole responsibility for his own rule. We will follow our medieval historian's lead as closely as possible, adding only the information required to flesh out his reports to achieve a minimal understanding of them. What follows is, therefore, most often based on a translation of his Arabic original.[74] Later we will return to the major events and discuss the important issues separately and there explain them in greater detail. First, it is necessary to return to the beginning and catch up on a few items he mentioned that have been left out of our account thus far.

A cautionary note is in order. The Islamic calendar of our Muslim authors depends strictly on lunar months and allows for only 12 of them, no more, which means that its year is 11 days shorter than the solar year used by Christians and others. The Islamic year moves a third of a month relative to the Christian. Accordingly, a given Islamic year may commence in the middle of our year. Islamic months do not correspond to ours. And yet our sources almost all employ an Islamic dating system. Therefore, when al-Maqrizi provides a summary of events in, say, 395, that corresponds to the period October 1004 to October 1005. In what follows we have attempted a simplified notation. Otherwise the importance of the original chronology could be lost. For dates given precisely in the Arabic record, those that include day, month and year, a precise common-era equivalent is available, but for months and years the latter, when used here, is somewhat imprecise. Al-Hakim ruled either as a minor under a regent or on his own for 25 years, from 386 hijra (996 Christian) to 411 (1021). Since he ascended the throne late in 386, the first full year of his reign would be 387 (997).

Information about the years before the killing of Barjawan concern less al-Hakim himself than general affairs. The government appears to be anonymous; those in charge remain largely hidden from our sources. Nevertheless al-Maqrizi found a stream of facts to relate.

> In the earliest days of the reign beginning in the year 996, the general Husayn ibn Jawhar, suitably honored, resumed supervision of the mail system and the chancery. Ibn ʿAmmar appointed as his personal clerk a certain Abu ʿAbdallah al-Mawsili and delegated him to receive the petitions submitted by the people and to register them. ʿIsa b. Nasturius was confirmed as head of the Privy Purse;[75] a number of others received honors in connection with appointments, all of which were announced in decrees.
>
> Near the end of the year the pilgrimage caravan departed in late November carrying with it the covering for the Kaʿba, and various gifts and charitable donations for the Meccans as had become customary.

At the beginning of the next year, 387 (997) – year one of the reign – the caravan returned to report that it had completed the pilgrimage and that the prayer-blessing had been said in the name of al-Hakim in the Holy Cities. That would have constituted the first time for the new caliph. For him to be recognized as the supreme leader of all Muslims in the holy cities carried special importance.

> That same month the price of wheat rose excessively and its existence became scarce, high prices causing much hardship. As well there was a serious scare caused by the movements of a thief during the night, and his entering the houses of people. They began to take precautions at night; women disappeared from the streets; and the whole matter generated great alarm. The next month the remnants of the pilgrimage caravan finally arrived back. Subuktakin, the commander in charge of it, received special honors and rewards. The price of bread reached four pounds to the dirham.

Al-Maqrizi's tendency to mix the information available – the price of bread, a thief in the night, news of the annual pilgrimage caravan, miscellaneous appointments to office – with little regard for its general importance is, in these examples, quite obvious. We do not even know in every case how to break it up (or add it together?) to form paragraphs. Do we, perhaps, simply treat it as a list? Nevertheless, his purpose, which is to lay out a firm chronology and to let us see the real flow of events, is admirable. He thus allows us to judge for ourselves which of them are most important. His narrative resembles a series of newspaper clippings rather than a coherent story; it lacks form and structure, but feels even so more authentic. It is a digest of what happened, a summary of the news recorded day by day, perhaps in al-Musabbihi's diary.

From this early period our historian reports more details of the fighting in Syria and of the movements of various forces and commanders there.

> In the month of September the inhabitants of al-Qulzum were forgiven the *mukus* tax due on goods in vessels coming into the port.[76] On 13 November the pilgrimage caravan left Birkat al-Jubb, the point where it assembled to the north-east of Cairo. It carried the covering for the Kaʿba, decorations, flour, wheat, wax and scents for Mecca and Madina. The general Jaysh b. al-Samsama departed for Syria to replace Salman, who moved from Damascus to Ramla. A terrible storm of thunder and lightning, rain and hail, hit the upper Egyptian town of Qus hard, spreading destruction the like of which was until then unknown. Violent convulsions brought down date palms and sycamores, uprooting totally 500 of the palms. Afterward there was nothing green still standing in Qus and its dependencies. A number of boats fully loaded sank with loss of crops worth a great deal. The pilgrimage caravan arrived back on 18 February, 998. At the beginning of June, Salman and his brother came in from Ramla. In August news arrived about Jaysh and his battle with the Byzantines at Apamea and Antioch in Northern Syria, events and movements of Fatimid troops and commanders being reported at length, including a major victory over the Christians. At the end of the year Khawd arrived, coming on behalf of Jaysh with a number of prisoners and many heads of the slain enemies. All were paraded through the city and then the prisoners forgiven and released.
>
> As the next year, 389 [999, year two] commenced, the advance party of the pilgrimage caravan returned with the news that all of Adan in the Yemen had burned with the loss in the fire of property and goods of a value

> so great no one knew how much it had been. The main caravan traveling by land reached Cairo on 10 February. Ten months later the next one set out with the covering for the Ka'ba and the regular donations. The local Shiite community celebrated the festival of Ghadir Khumm as usual with a procession of the faithful through the palace complex.
>
> Early in 390 [999] the price of bread was 16 pounds to the dirham and a stable belonging to Fahd, Barjawan's secretary, suddenly collapsed killing upwards of 60 mules that had been housed in it. The pilgrimage caravan returned in January without having been able to visit Madina.

These reports, added to those already discussed in the previous chapter, provide a more complete picture of what the chronicler recorded. Note that everything centers on Cairo-Fustat, the cities of the Fatimid capital. Our reporter lived there and he treats us to a summary of the news of what happened locally or arrived from elsewhere, not quite daily but usually monthly or better. Syria seems far away, as do Mecca, Madina and the vassal states in Sicily and North Africa, but he certainly knew with more intimacy what transpired in the palace and among the elite; and he tells us about what seemed important to him at the time, as if we too were present. From it all, however, it is hard to extract a sound picture of al-Hakim. Which of the events reported relate to him and his activities, either personally or in his role as caliph? Unfortunately, there exists little else. His biography is bound up with the account of his rule for better or worse, or whether we like it or not, and the greater part of it consists of details only some of which we have the means to appreciate now. Others, although they might frequently suggest an intriguing event or issue, are lost on us; we simply do not know the full story or what it means.

The last news from the year 390 (1000, year four) was of the demise of poor Barjawan and al-Hakim's proclamation to defend the necessity of his execution. The subtext of the event offered evidence of the emergence of the young caliph from under the domination of those who previously attempted to control him and administer the kingdom in his stead. The next event in al-Maqrizi's account is the bestowing of robes of honor, 11 April, on the general Husayn ibn Jawhar.[77] He says:

> He received a red brocaded robe, a blue scarf with gold thread, a sword embossed in gold, a horse to ride complete with golden saddle and bridle, and three horses to carry an additional 50 robes of every sort. Al-Hakim

delegated to him the handling of petitions and the supervision of the affairs of the people and of the state, and the hearing of grievances. At the same time honors were granted to Fahd, including a mule to ride and another to carry 20 robes. Following this ceremony, the general departed the palace trailed by Fahd and the rest of those in attendance. He went to his house. He put Fahd in charge of dealing with the petitions of those who presented them as he had done previously, working hand in hand with Husayn, assisting him in the job of administration, and acting in his place if he was absent.

The next morning the general presented himself at the palace along with Fahd. They began to look into the affairs of the people and to keep al-Hakim informed about them. The general would position himself in front with Fahd behind. If the two went in to al-Hakim, as they presented letters and petitions to the caliph, the general sat, with Fahd standing to his rear.

Husayn gave an order that no one having business to bring before him should attempt to meet with him in the street or ride to his house. If the need arose, he was to be sought at the palace. He also forbad anyone addressing him in correspondence or the like as 'Our lord and master'. In letters and other correspondence, he should hereafter be addressed only as 'The General'. And Fahd similarly was 'The Executive' (*al-ra'is*), and nothing more.

Fahd conveyed a gift to al-Hakim that included 30 splendid mules of various colors, 20 horses of which ten came with saddles and bridles, ten were spectacularly colored, 20 thousand dinars, a basket with a suit of clothing brocaded with gold thread whose like had never been seen, a drawer of gems, many baskets of the finest linen cloth, and an oil-rubbed treasure box.

Once, when the general Husayn was riding, he came upon a group of Turkish commanders standing in the street waiting for him. He stopped and said, 'All of us are the servants of our master, may the blessings of God be upon him and his kingdom. I continue to hold my position, by God, or would you remove me from it? No one is to meet me other than in the palace. Leave at once!' Thereafter he stationed two Slavic eunuchs in rotation on the street to prevent the people from going to his house or meeting him other than in the palace, which was where he regularly held sessions to receive them.

Husayn directed Abu'l-Futuh Mas'ud the Slav, who was keeper of the curtain concealing the caliph, to have the people admitted to al-Hakim without exception, no one being excluded, and that he make known the proper protocol governing those who presented themselves and those who entered

> sessions for receiving petitions if one occurred. The people then came in to him and he accepted their letters and accounts and commenced to examine them. Meanwhile al-Hakim remained in his own place, sitting as those who had various needs went in to him and conferred on important matters.

Information of this kind is crucial in determining what role the young al-Hakim actually played in this relatively early period. Our source reports more about Husayn, how he performed his duties and guarded his own dignity and rank as intermediary between the caliph and those who would court his favor. In the following report we hear about the order of seating at a session with al-Hakim. The men mentioned are those holding the highest offices, one the equivalent of prime minister, others commanders in the military, the head of the Aliid nobility (descendants of the Prophet), the caliph's personal physician, and more.

> A group of those who were accustomed to visit al-ʿAziz at night came to al-Hakim. They were ordered to frequent the palace at the time of his audiences, which then extended into the evening. The first such night was Wednesday, 16 February 1000. Those who came included the general Husayn, the general Fadl b. Salih, and Husayn b. al-Hasan al-Bazyar, who took up seats to the right, first Husayn, next Fadl and then Ibn al-Bazyar. After them was Abu'l-Hasan ʿAli b. Ibrahim al-Rassi, followed by the qadi ʿAbd al-ʿAziz b. Muhammad b. al-Nuʿman. On the left sat Rajaʾ and Masʿud, two sons of Abu'l-Husayn, beyond them the physician Abu'l-Fath Mansur b. Maʿshar, and the clerk Abu'l-Husayn b. al-Maghribi and his brother. Placed close by were a number of relatives of the caliph and a group of commanders, among which were Manjutakin and some others. Next, another group including Ibn Tahir al-Wazzan came in. This same order remained in effect until 20 May.

From this period al-Maqrizi reports that 'al-Hakim rode several times to the district of Sardus, to the Birkat al-Jubb, and to 'Ayn Shams, and Hulwan for the purpose of hunting and other activities.' The places named are outside of the Egyptian capital but not more than a day's ride. Nonetheless, this is the only account of him traveling to any of these towns to hunt, an activity his father loved but which he seems to have stayed away from for the latter portion of his life. It might be evidence that in his youth al-Hakim tried to follow the example of his father, either that or the men, such as the courtiers named above and those who sought to control him, attempted to guide him in that direction. Significantly on 4 June a decree read from the pulpits of all the congregational mosques announced that the general Husayn would now have the lofty title 'Commander-in-Chief'. His status had risen even higher than before.

For each year of the reign al-Maqrizi tried to indicate what had happened in Fatimid Syria, most especially when important information about events there reached Cairo. Control of the regions remained crucial both offensively, in the hope of further conquest in eastern Islamic lands, and defensively, as a buffer against encroachment of enemies from the north and the east. The following report suggests that the situation in Syria was not good and that al-Hakim's representative in Damascus abused his office, although not for personal financial gain.

> In Syria, the condition there of Jaysh b. al-Samsama's control of Damascus became increasingly difficult and tenuous because of his tyrannical attempt to extract money from the inhabitants through various schemes. By conscripting through tricks those who could bear arms and then taking their funds, he denuded the area of fighters and caused great harm and distress to the population. Most of its market closed as a consequence. His dire threats of punishment forced many to flee. At that, news arrived that the Byzantines were approaching. Jaysh tried to enlist the Bedouin Arabs. Meanwhile the Greeks took Shayzar and Homs, the latter for the third time. As winter wore on, however, their strength diminished, eventually causing them to retreat to Armenia. Jaysh's repressive policies continued unabated until he was struck by leprosy, which thereafter intensified, removing the hair on his body, oozing from his flesh and turning it black until the expression on his face disappeared and his body began to smell badly. His torment was obvious and he cried out for death until it finally arrived in March. He had governed Damascus 16 and a half months.[78]
>
> Having collected what possessions he had left, a son of his then arrived in Cairo. Al-Hakim honored him. But Raydan brought to the caliph a registry in the hand of Jaysh that contained his will, which noted exactly what he had left with details, and that all of it was for the Commander of the Believers. None of his sons had any right to a single dirham of the estimated value of two hundred thousand dinars for both cash and goods. Al-Hakim took the registry and went to the two sons of Jaysh. He honored them and said in the presence of elite Ismailis of the state, 'I have examined the will

of your father, may God have mercy on him, regarding the cash and goods he has bequeathed. Take it all, a blessed goodness for the both of you.' They then departed with the whole of the bequest.

In this same year, that is 999, still quite early in the reign, Sitt al-Mulk was granted fiefs, land holdings, rents and fees for properties in various parts of Egypt valued in excess of a hundred thousand dinars per year. It represented a gift to her of enormous size. Was it evidence of her brother's regard and generosity? Repayment for her lavish gift to him earlier? Certainly it would appear that relations between brother and sister remained to this point quite amicable.

One major disadvantage of a strict chronological record is that it often obscures a story that took place over many months and years. Al-Maqrizi had to adjust for this problem, in part by occasionally inserting a report covering a longer period somewhat arbitrarily at a given date. In a few cases he also repeated bits of information by adding a second notice of it at a later time. The following account of problems in the west begins under Barjawan but then ends with the alienation of the Bedouin Banu Qurra and that has implications for troubles that continued long after. This is how our historian first brings it up.

Once Barjawan had assumed direction of governmental affairs, the rivalry for leadership between himself and Abu'l-Hasan Yanis, the Slavic slave of al-ʿAziz, who had been given responsibility for the palace staff immediately after the death of the former caliph, grew more serious.[79] Barjawan conceived of the stratagem to send Yanis off to Barqa as its governor, which was done early in his tenure. Later Tamusalt ibn Bakkar, then in charge of western Tripoli, requested via letters to be relieved of that post so he could come to Cairo. Barjawan used them as an excuse to move Yanis further afield. He ordered Yanis to take over Tripoli, which he did, and Tamusalt then departed for Cairo, leaving many of his troops behind. They clashed with Yanis and left going back to the Maghrib to complain to the Zirid ruler about what had happened. The latter in turn sent a second commander with another army toward Tripoli. Yanis tried to stop it but was defeated and killed. A colleague of Yanis then went to and rallied the forces in Tripoli against the new commander. Al-Hakim wanted to extend help but the person he sent, Yahya b. ʿAli, quarreled with his associates and returned a humiliated failure to Cairo. The caliph had decided to kill him whereupon he produced a letter written by Raydan, the royal parasol bearer, stating that the money from Barqa was to be paid to him, thus taking it away from the caliph's own funds, leaving no money to spend on an army in Barqa. Accordingly, it was Raydan who was executed for what he had done.

A part of the force with Yahya had been a group of the Banu Qurra. However, they had abandoned him and returned home. Al-Hakim invited them to Cairo but they were fearful and refused. He ignored them thereafter for a while and then dispatched to them a formal statement of amnesty. In return they sent some of their number as hostages. He commanded them to come to Alexandria to take up what he had ordered them to do. Most of them were wary but a group did come to Alexandria where they were killed and their heads taken to Cairo. The hostages were also killed. The Banu Qurra thereupon conceived a decided aversion to al-Hakim, which was to play an important role later in the revolt of Abu Rakwa.

In order to complete his account and cover the rest of the same year, al-Maqrizi adds the following miscellany of information, parts of which are of minor significance but others portend conflict to come, as was to happen in the dispute between the two grandsons of al-Nuʿman, one of whom is the subject of the first item below.

On 9 June, Abu'l-Qasim ʿAbd al-ʿAziz b. Muhammad b. al-Nuʿman, nephew of the chief judge and his sometime rival, received a robe of honor and he went down to the Old Mosque in Fustat with robes carried on two saddled and bridled mules. A decree announced that he was to take charge of the court of grievances and to hear cases brought before it.

The effects of Barjawan were transported to the palace on 80 donkeys and a decree read there stated as follows:

> O people who hear this appeal, truly God, who is most great and powerful, requires that the imams have singular obligations that no one else in the community shares. Those who, after the reading of this public decree, have the audacity to address in correspondence or communications to anyone other than the Hallowed Presence by the term 'our lord' or 'our master,' the Commander of the Believers has declared his blood lawful. So let those present inform those absent, God willing.[80]

In Ramadan (August) al-Hakim broke the fast with a group arrayed to his right and his left. He led prayers in it on two Fridays and he rode in procession for the annual ceremonial opening of the canal that gave access to Nile flood waters.

Tamusalt ibn Bakkar the black, mentioned previously in connection with the misadventure of Yanis and the Banu Qurra, arrived in Cairo at this time. He had been a slave of the Zirid ruler and had been the latter's governor of western Tripoli. However, Tamusalt had also acted tyrannical to his own people, taking from them a great deal of money, after which he fled in fear of his own master. He came from Tripoli accompanied by over 60 children of his, males and females, and a large army, after having passed by Barqa, where he had given Yanis, its governor, 30 thousand dinars for his own use. He also spent a large amount on his army and men. Al-Hakim sat for him and honored him by having him sit as well. Tamusalt said to al-Hakim, 'I have come into the presence of our master the caliph with family and funds and children, bringing with me what suffices me and the offspring of my offspring. But the troop who are with me are men belonging to my former master and he was good to them as is apparent.' Tamusalt presented to al-Hakim a hundred thousand dinars and a hundred thousand dirhams, more than 50 loads of linen and fringe, 80 horses, 40 horses with their saddles and bridles, 40 mules, 50 Bactrian camels with their camel saddles, and 200 ordinary camels. In return robes of honor were bestowed on him and on those of his sons present. He marched then to a house that had been prepared for him in which there were 35 rooms, each one with its utilities and furnishings. Five thousand dinars had been spent on that house.

For the festival of breaking the fast, al-Hakim led prayers with the people and delivered the sermon as was his customary practice. The judge Ibn al-Nuʿman mounted the pulpit with him along with a number of commanders. He and they sat on the stairs. On 8 September, permission was given for Ibn ʿAmmar to ride to the palace, which he commenced doing, and which led eventually to his being killed. The pilgrimage caravan departed on 14 October. Khawd was removed from command of the police force of Fustat and Masʿud the Slav was given it in combination with that for Cairo. He marched down to the Old Mosque with his robe of honor and drums and banners for the reading of his decree from its pulpit. On 4 November the people were commanded to attach lamps on all shop-fronts and the doors of houses, and in all locations and in both side and main streets. They did that. Al-Hakim led prayer and gave the sermon on the feast of sacrifice at the festival square and then performed the actual sacrifice at the palace as was his practice. He sat for the feast table.

> The people suffered serious harm and misfortune in the struggle between ʿAbd al-ʿAziz and the chief qadi Husayn. ʿAbd al-ʿAziz accepted the testimony of a group he had chosen himself. A litigant whose opponent had gone before Husayn might then decided to take the case to ʿAbd al-ʿAziz. When ʿAbd al-ʿAziz sat to hear a case of grievance, his witnesses would be there and he would hear their testimony, having them testify concerning what was happening and what had transpired. None of them attended Husayn or came near his house. Testimony at the latter court was confined to the old witnesses who testified for Husayn but who were not present at the court of ʿAbd al-ʿAziz in connection with the case and who had not ridden with him to the sessions he held.

The Fifth to Eighth Years of His Reign

To this point we have a provisional record for the period 996 to 1000, those years when al-Hakim ruled under some form of regency, predominantly that of Barjawan. From April 1000 onward, following the execution of his old caretaker, he governed more independently, although still relying heavily on Husayn ibn Jawhar and his Christian clerk Fahd. One report about an evening session of his court and the order of seating hints at the ranking of the elite. We see also how Husayn ibn Jawhar conducted his affairs, and how he and Fahd presented matters to the young caliph whose exact role, however, is less obvious. In the next period from the Islamic year 391 to the end of 394 (December 1000 to October 1004), al-Hakim emerges more and more in the record. Note that the first report from the later period comments that the frequency of his nightly riding had already reached once each night. The pattern of his unusual behavior, at least in this one regard, was thus evident almost from the beginning. What are the other signs that his character was to be uniquely at odds with that normal to Islamic rulers and how much of it shows up in these years: acts of uncommon generosity, concern for public welfare, fearless contact with the ordinary citizen, frequent unexplained killing of personnel of his government and of the elite, sudden shifts in mood and policy?

Over the long period that remains of al-Hakim's rule the little details of routine activities – departure and return of the pilgrimage caravan, the many appointments to lesser offices, the caliph's participation in the annual rituals or prayer, fast-breaking and sacrifice – need not be observed as carefully and completely as al-Maqrizi recorded them. We have seen already the wealth of this kind of information he had at his disposal. The record for the next 14 years or slightly more is similar. Where and when such minutiae become important, either singularly or collectively, we will return to them.

The Fifth Year[81]

Though just turning 16, this year al-Hakim's riding at night begins to happen with noticeable frequency.

For December of the year 1000, which corresponded with the beginning of the Islamic year 391, al-Maqrizi comments that:

> the occasional nightly riding of al-Hakim had reached once each night. He would ride to one place after another, one street after another, and from alley to alley. He ordered the people to light lights and then add to them in the streets and alleys. The markets and bazaars were adorned with various decorations. The people sold and bought. They lit many candles throughout the night and expended much money on food and drink, music and games. Men walking in front of al-Hakim prevented any of the people from approaching too close to him, thus driving them back. But he said not to prevent them and so he was surrounded by people, frequently pleading to him. The arsenal was decorated and the people went out at night to observe. Of those going out at night, women outnumbered the men. Crowds in the street and roads increased. The large number of them who were intoxicated became evident. The matter was especially acute from the night of 19 until 24 December. When the people had exceeded the proper bounds, al-Hakim ordered that women not go out from evening time onward.[82] If they did, they were given an exemplary punishment. He also forbad the people from sitting in the shops.[83]

The information supplied here pertains not only to al-Hakim's penchant for riding at night but also, possibly, to his attitude to women in public, both of which we can thus trace back to the earliest days of his independence following the execution of Barjawan. Once free of supervision by handlers, the young caliph quickly took up a habit of nightly excursions that, with some interruptions, persisted until the end.

Another problem al-Hakim, or any other of the Fatimid caliphs, had to address often enough concerned the anti-Shiite sentiments of their Sunni subjects. However the following incident early in his reign raises the issue in a more radical form.

> A Syrian man was arrested; he maintained that he did not acknowledge ʿAli b. Abi Talib. 'I hold,' he said, 'that the Prophet, may God bless him and keep him, is the one who was sent, but I do not acknowledge ʿAli b. Abi Talib.' He was imprisoned, then checked again, but he persisted in maintaining that he did not recognize ʿAli. The general Husayn treated him gently but he would not admit to the acknowledgement of ʿAli. The matter ended with an order for his execution; he was hung and crucified.

This report hints at a broader policy and provides key data about the struggle between the Shiism of the Fatimids and the anti-Shiism of elements of the population they ruled. In this instance, however, this man's unforgivable sin was to reject the authority of ʿAli totally, a stance by this time quite uncommon even among ardent Sunnis who by and large accepted ʿAli as one of the four Rightly Guided caliphs. Although becoming rarer, some supporters of the Umayyads then ruling Spain, and some Syrians who continued to favor the Umayyads who had once long before ruled their homeland, declined to acknowledge ʿAli in this fashion. Fatimid policy with respect to this infraction, as applied by al-Hakim, was, as is apparent in this incident, unrelentingly severe.

As already noted the two cousins, both grandsons of Qadi al-Nuʿman, the founding father of Ismaili jurisprudence, were rivals. A further chapter in the struggle is described below.

> The conflict between ʿAbd al-ʿAziz and the chief qadi Husayn grew more intense. Al-Hakim wrote a note in his own hand and sent it to Husayn, the text of which follows here:
>
> > O Husayn, may God be good to you. I have been appraised of the nasty rumors running about among the people and those up to no good, and their spreading lies. We renounce anything of the kind in regard to one who occupies the position you hold in our service, for you are our qadi, our *daʿi* and our trusted friend. We propose to put an end to that. We will appoint no one other than you to supervise matters pertaining to cases and the judgment of them, or for anything else that we have hired you to do, and no correspondence of any one of your deputies

> here or otherwise and in all other districts, that we not correspond with anyone other than you. Anyone else who is called a judge, is merely figurative that not actually. Since we have forbidden others than you issuing decrees in any matter, it behooves all notary witnesses and jurist adjuncts not to bear witness in the decree of anyone other than you. If two litigants dispute and one of them appeals to you and the other to someone else, the one who appeals to the person other than you must came back to you voluntarily or involuntarily. He will accept what you decide as to the execution of cases and judgments, seeking the help of God the mighty and glorious, and then from us. The fine opinion we have of you will provide you felicity in this world and in the next. We authorize you that all correspondence addressed to the qadi be to the Qadi of Qadis, which is what we appointed you to be. You will use that in correspondence you write and write it in your decrees. Understand that well! Spread our order to all those to whom this rescript applies so that they will take heed of it and not transgress. May God bring you into His pleasure and ours as well; may He support you in that and aid you to that end, if it is the will of God most high. May God bless our lord Muhammad and his family, with peace unconditional.

The qadi read it to all the notary witnesses accordingly and commanded that the title 'Judge of Judges' be written in his decrees. And that was ordained and prescribed.

Although the caliph may have hoped he had resolved the dispute, the story was then long from over. His dissatisfaction with either man, or with many others who served him, would soon become apparent. First, however, we read the following notice.

In the same year al-Hakim executed his tutor Abu'l-Qasim Sa'id b. Sa'id al-Fariqi while he was walking alongside him by motioning to the Turks with his eyes after having contrived with them to kill this man. The fellow was then cut down by their swords. It was he who had introduced al-Hakim to the affairs of state and read to him petitions. He had been allowed into such matters as if he were a wazir. In December al-Hakim also executed Ibn Abi Najda who had once been a green grocer but later rose in status until he was appointed to the market inspection wherein he got involved in matters

> he was not supposed to and behaved quite badly in his dealing with the people. He was first arrested, then had his hand cut off, next his tongue, before being paraded on a camel and hung.

Inevitably the record of such executions cannot go unnoticed, not simply because later Muslim historians insist on keeping track of them, even al-Maqrizi, but in order to understand exactly what happened and why. Here we have an explanation at least for one of the two reported. Still al-Maqrizi also comments that in this year 'a number of person were executed' which is surely an indication that more than these two men were put to death.

The Sixth Year[84]

In it the 17-year-old caliph orders Fahd 'The Executive' hung.

The major event of this year was yet another killing, the execution of the Christian executive Fahd. Al-Maqrizi says:

> On 24 April, Fahd b. Ibrahim was hung. The length of his administration as director was, in all, five years, nine months, and 12 days. Fahd's brother Abu Ghalib transported to the arcade of the palace out of the stipendiary funds of his brother five hundred thousand dinars. When al-Hakim appeared, he asked about it and was told what it was for, but he left it there. It remained where it was for some time and then the caliph ordered it turned over to the children of Fahd, saying, 'I did not kill him on account of money.' The money was accordingly taken to the children. Later, those charged with informing brought news of comments that Abu Ghalib had uttered, for which he too was executed and his body burned.

Evidently no one knew, most especially the family of Fahd, why he had been put to death or what prompted the anger or disfavor of the caliph in his case. The matter is clearer, however, with respect to the brother Abu Ghalib. At least we have a word of explanation.

An additional killing about the same time is also explained. 'On 30 May, Abu Tahir Mahmud b. al-Nahwi, who had been the supervisor of districts in Syria, was hung for having tyrannized excessively and oppressed its people.'

To this information, al-Maqrizi adds in typical fashion the following bits of miscellany:

An order was issued to complete the building of the mosque that al-ʿAziz had begun through his wazir Yaʿqub ibn Killis. It lay just outside the Bab al-Futuh, one of the northern gates of Cairo. Forty thousand dinars were allotted for construction and the work commenced.[85] On 15 June, there was an assembly in the new mosque just outside the Bab al-Futuh. Al-Hakim ceased riding at night. He restored to the children of Fahd their ornamented saddles and ordered them to ride with them. He released from jail some of the Christian clerks. During Ramadan, al-Hakim prayed with the people after having given the sermon. He led the *ʿid* festival prayer and delivered the sermon as usual and he was constantly in motion during July and August to Damanhur and the pyramids and other places.

In Syria, when Jaysh died, one of the western chieftains, by name Fahl b. Tamim, took over as governor but he lasted a month only and died. At that ʿAli b. Jaʿfar b. Falah came over from Cairo and settled in Damascus at the end of August. There he remained without laying a hand on its funds. That was July 1002. About that time a *daʿi* called Khatkin al-Dayf came also on behalf of al-Hakim. Baraza Ibn Falah and he stayed on the outskirts of Damascus. Khatkin wanted to reduce the stipends of the troops. They made trouble and went to find Ibn ʿAbdun the Christian who was in charge of administering the finances and paying salaries. Khatkin stopped them, using crude rough language in doing so, not being given to flattery. They turned away and plundered the houses of clerks and the churches. The Westerners then allied with the Easterners in the army to act as one party in seeking their pay. ʿAli b. Falah swore that he was with them in that resolve. That reached al-Hakim who exclaimed, 'This man has become blind.' And so he sent to have him removed from Damascus and Ibn Falah departed with a small group of his associates in August. The army remained in Damascus until Tamusalt b. Bakkar arrived there on behalf of al-Hakim. There he stayed until Muflih the Bearded was appointed governor in October 1003. This man was a eunuch but with hair on his face.

In this year, Abu ʿAli al-Hasan b. 'Usluj was executed in November and burned, as was ʿAli b. 'Umar b. al-'Addas in July, and Abu'l-Fadl Raydan, the parasol bearer, in the latter part of October, was hung.

That year also ʿAbd al-Aʿla, son of the prince Hashim, who was a son of al-Mansur the third Fatimid caliph, received permission to leave town to visit one of his estates. Al-Hakim himself gave this permission to his cousin, who went out with a group of his boon companions. Al-Hakim sent with them a spy to report on their activities.

With this latter piece of news and the account that follows we begin to discover the possible seeds of a rebellion against al-Hakim from within the royal family. To that we will return in a later chapter with greater detail. Suffice it to note that many of those involved were eventually executed.

Here ends al-Maqrizi's report for 392 (year six), which he followed with that for 394 (year eight) leaving out 393 (year seven). What happened to 393? We do not know. Our historian was evidently either at a loss or perhaps confused. Possibly the events of 392 include some from 393 and vice versa. Obviously his reconstruction of the chronology was not perfect; it is likely that his sources also failed to cover everything adequately.

The Eighth Year[86]

The year the chief justice Husayn b. ʿAli fell from grace and his cousin ʿAbd al-ʿAziz took over.

On 7 July Husayn b. ʿAli b. al-Nuʿman was removed from the judiciary.[87] He had once been stabbed in the mosque and so al-Hakim had allocated to him a detachment of leading members of the *adyaf* corps to ride with him to each session of court he sat for and another group to walk before him every day with swords drawn. When he was present at the Old Mosque and began his prayers, the group of *adyaf* stood in a row behind him in order to shield him. None of them said prayers until he had finished his and returned to his court session. When he sat in court they would stand to his left and right. He was the very first judge for whom that was done. As well he was the first to have written into his decree of appointment the title Judge of Judges. His status with al-Hakim rose quite high and the caliph relied on him privately. A group around al-Hakim would speak his praises and go to lengths in extolling him. One among them was Rayhan al-Lihyani, another Zaydan, and yet another Muflih al-Lihyani. The judge's influence spread and his importance became great. He allowed an oath of condemnation between a drunken man and his wife, and he treated the people sternly. If a notary witness was slow to arrive at his house and ride with him on a day when he sat in the mosque, which he normally did, he would note it and fine him an amount as a reproach. He forced his clerks into a constant attendance at his house. The Ismaili *daʿwa* was also under his control. He was thus both Judge of Judges and *Daʿi* of *Daʿis* and, in that, he attained a higher status than a group of the scholars, literary experts and respectable families. The length of his supervision of the judiciary was five years, six months and 23 days. He was born in 969. He was the first judge to be burned after being executed. Al-Hakim had him burned after killing him on 23 October, as will be seen.

On 7 July, Abu'l-Qasim ʿAbd al-ʿAziz b. Muhammad b. al-Nuʿman was appointed judge, in addition to the duties he already held in the court of grievances. A robe of honor was given him; he was girt with a sword embossed with gold, and carried on a mule with a basket of clothes in front. He went out in a great procession to the Old Mosque, where he sat beneath the pulpit as Abu ʿAli Ahmad b. ʿAbd al-Samiʿ mounted it and read out his decree of appointment. Then he departed for his house, settled into it and commenced judging. He delegated to Abu'l-Hasan Malik b. Saʿid al-Fariqi the judgeship for Cairo, in addition to the similar position he already held as deputy. Abu Yusuf Bayan was given the job of court clerk and recorder. Shortly thereafter another decree had ʿAbd al-ʿAziz receive the two fees, the *fitra* and *najwa*, paid by those Ismailis who attend the Sessions of Wisdom at the palace. He was also to administer the appeal to the people and read what was read to those who entered the *daʿwa*.

On Thursday, 13 July[88], he was present and read what was normally read in the palace and he collected the *fitra* and *najwa*. He suspended all of the notary witnesses that Husayn in his day had accepted and he removed some of those deputized to act in outlying districts.. Confined to his house, Husayn b. ʿAli's fear intensified. The records of the judiciary were moved from his house to that of ʿAbd al-ʿAziz.

That month Sahl ibn Yusuf, the brother of Yaʿqub ibn Yusuf ibn Killis, the former wazir, was executed because of his greed and excessive covetousness. As he was being brought to his execution, he asked to pay on the spot three hundred thousand in cash to ransom himself, a request that was refused. Also killed was the general Abu ʿAbd Allah al-Husayn b. al-Hasan al-Bazyar because he used to enter the Bab al-Bahr with his leg up over the neck of his mount and it happened once that al-Hakim was sitting in the belvedere atop this gateway. This man's foot thus was in the face of the caliph. Ibn al-Bazyar was also afflicted with a painful gout. Al-Hakim counted that as a debt against him for which he killed him in July for poor settlement.

The Decade from Year Nine to Nineteen

Events of the preceding period reveal a caliph who had become personally active in the administration and control of his government and they contain hints of things to come, of his deeper involvement, of a compulsion for change and reform. However, nothing quite prepares us for the flood of legislation about to descend on the subjects of the realm imposing one restriction after another. The Islamic year 395 (year number nine, October 1004 to October 1005) was to be unlike any other of the reign, and quite possibly any in medieval Islamic history. And yet, we know little or nothing about what prompted al-Hakim to act as he did then, rather than later or earlier, to stipulate by decree the long string of measures intended to reform the social order most of which began in that year.

The Ninth Year[89]

The year of a great many new rules and proclamations, creation of the House of Wisdom, and the birth of al-Hakim's sons.

The details in the report that follows are crucial for assessing both exactly what happened and when. Al-Maqrizi's account for this particular year is the prime document from which to reconstruct al-Hakim's legislative agenda. He apparently issued no explanations for the new laws, at least none that have survived.

> On the 24th of October a decree read in the mosques ordered the Jews and Christians to fasten on the *zunnar* [a waist band], and wear the *ghiyar* [a badge], and to make them black, the symbol of the seditious Abbasids. That year there was quite a bit of disparagement and vilification of the right of the two Shaykhs Abu Bakr and 'Umar, may God be pleased with them both. A decree was issued concerning foodstuffs. It forbad eating *mulukhiyya* [a green leafy vegetable], which had been much loved by Muʿawiya b. Abi Sufyan, and another green leaf called *jirjir* that was associated with ʿA'isha, may God be pleased with her, and *mutawakkiliyya* [exactly what this was remains a mystery] connected to the Abbasid caliph al-Mutawakkil. It also stipulated that bread dough should not be kneaded with the feet, that a small fish without scales called *dalinis* not be eaten, that cows that had not produced offspring not be slaughtered except during the festival of

sacrifice, on other days none were to be slaughtered unless they were not suitable for plowing. Slave dealers selling slaves and bondmaids to the protected peoples [Christians and Jews] were reprimanded, with harsh measures taken against them to prevent the practice.

Another decree set the time for the call to afternoon prayer at the beginning of the seventh hour, and the call to evening prayer at the commencement of the ninth hour. Weights and measures were to be corrected and tampering with either was forbidden. It also outlawed the selling of *fuqqa'* beer or making it at all because of the evidence that 'Ali, may God be pleased with him, detested the drinking of *fuqqa'*.

Bells rung in the streets announced that no one should enter the baths without wearing a loincloth (*mi'zar*), no woman should show her face in the street, or follow behind a funeral, or adorn herself. No part of fish without scales were to be sold, nor was any of the fishermen to fish for them. The baths were watched and persons caught in them without loincloths were beaten and paraded.

An army formed up to fight the Banu Qurra and it set out.

In the month of November, there was written in the other mosques as well as the Old Mosque, inside and outside, on all walls, and on the doors of shops, cornerstones, tombstones and cenotaphs curses and insults directed against the Companions of the Prophet. They were inscribed and painted with a variety of colors and gold; that was done on the doorways of the bazaars and the doors of houses, having been forced to do so. People came from the outlying districts and estates to join the Ismaili *da'wa*. One day was set up for the men, another for the women. The crowds grew so large that in one session a number of persons died in the crush. When the pilgrimage caravan returned, those in it were assaulted and cursed by the masses, who asked them to insult and curse the Companions even while they refused.

A cry went round Cairo that no one was to go out into the street after sundown, nor was there to be any buying or selling.[90] The people obeyed that order. In December homes were searched to find out who was making intoxicating beverages and a great quantity of vessels were smashed. The same year al-Hakim ordered that a storehouse at the foot of the mountain be filled with thorns, thatch and reeds.[91] People at large began to be gripped with fear, but especially those connected to government service, including the Ismailis, the commanders, clerks and the rest of the ordinary people, who thought the storehouse was meant for them [al-Maqrizi evidently intends us to understand that the content of the storehouse would have been used as fuel to burn the bodies of those to be executed]. Word to that effect spread on the street and agitation became that much stronger. A group of clerks and those involved in public affairs, both Muslims and Christians, set out together on 20 December to a place inside the Bridge Gate in Cairo. They kissed the ground all the way to the palace and then stood at its door calling and beseeching, imploring and asking to be forgiven. They carried with them a letter composed on behalf of all of them. This group entered through the doorway into the great palace all the while asking for forgiveness but not to deal with a mere messenger. They handed over their letter to the Commander-in-Chief Husayn ibn Jawhar himself and he passed it to al-Hakim, who agreed to it. The caliph forgave them and ordered them, via the Commander-in-Chief, to leave and return in the morning to hear the reading of the decree granting them amnesty. Accordingly, they departed. The decree was promulgated on the following day, one copy of it for the Muslims and one for the Christians, another for the Jews, each specifying clemency and forgiveness for them.

During the night of 24 December, a son was born to al-Hakim. That morning he sat to receive congratulations. He ordered the storehouse to be burned and it was. On the seventh day of the birth, the boy was brought out in the arms of the Commander-in-Chief and handed over to the barber for the shaving of his hair. The Sharif Abu'l-Hasan al-Rassi slaughtered the *ʿaqiqa* with his own hand. ʿAmmar, the chamberlain, carried the blood and *ʿaqiqa* . For that he was ordered given a thousand dinars, a bridled horse, and several robes. The barber received 100 dinars and a horse. The boy was called al-Harith, with the patronymic Abu'l-Ashbal. The Commander-in-Chief rode out to the rest of the Turks, the Daylamis and other authorities to announce that our master extends greetings of peace to you and reports that your new master has been named al-Harith with the patronymic Abu'l-Ashbal. All then kissed the ground with much expression of good wishes. They left. The city was festooned for four days.

In that month al-Hakim suggested to a group of youths that they jump from a high point in the palace, offering each of them a reward. A group presented themselves and jumped. Upwards of 30 of them died because they fell outside the water of the pool onto the stone floor around it. Money was paid to those who jumped.

In January fear of al-Hakim among the general population intensified. A number of decrees of amnesty were written for the young Turks of the private guard and their officers, and those among them who were from

> units called the Hamdaniyya, the Bakjuriyya, the pages of the higher authorities, the *mamluk* slaves, the youth of the royal household, holders of fiefs and the mercenaries, and al-Hakim's foot pages. Decrees of amnesty were written for a group of those who served the palace especially designated for the service of the caliph after they had assembled together and gone to the crypt of al-ʿAziz clamoring in tears and uncovering their heads. A number of decrees of safekeeping were written for the Daylamis, the cavalry, the drink pages, resting pages, good news pages, the Persian *mufarraq* pages, and others, the heads of corporations, and Greek mercenaries. A number of others were written to extend amnesty to the following groups: the Zuwayla soldiers, the flag bearers, the drummers, the Barqiyin, the ʻUtufiyin[92], the ʻArrafa al-jawwaniya [inspectors],[93] the Jawdhariyya, the Muzaffariyya, the Sinhajiyin, the purchased slaves of al-Husayniyya company, for the Maymuniyya, and al-Farajiyya. Another decree of amnesty was written for the *mu'adhdhins* of the palace gates, and yet another for all of the keepers of game animals[94], and other amnesties for a number of groups, each of those following their asking and begging for it.

Al-Maqrizi reports in this and several additional passages that fear of what the caliph might do spread widely among various groups and yet he provides no direct evidence of the cause for the panic, which was nonetheless obviously palpable. Had al-Hakim by this time executed so many the rest had begun to anticipate something similar could befall them as well? Was it the irrationality of it all? Or merely unfamiliarity with the unusual actions of a ruler unlike any previously known? Certainly his behavior was already not predictable by any standard set in an earlier era. Government policy – assuming that the changes instituted constituted a policy and were not based on a haphazard whim or momentary inclination – clearly lacked precedent. In these circumstances officers of the regime obviously had no assurance of their own safety.

> Also that month an order was given for the killing of the dogs. An uncountable number were slaughtered until there were none at all in the alleyways and streets. They were dumped in the desert and along the shore of the Nile. Another order was issued for the cleaning of the alleys and streets and the gateways to houses all over and that was done.
>
> In March the House of Wisdom was opened in Cairo. Scholars took up residence in it. Books were brought to it. People entered to copy those books and to read them. Scholars of law, recitation, grammar and other

subjects were assigned to it. It was furnished and servants provided to maintain it. Stipends were set up for those of the scholars and others who worked there. The ink, paper and pens required were also provided.[95]

That month the search for the grooms belonging to the Rukkabiyya intensified after 50 individuals from it had been killed over two days and the remainder went into hiding. No one was to have a page or groom walk in front of him. Commanders, and those whose status was the equivalent, used to have them proceed in front of them when going out alone. If they stopped and dismounted to extend greetings, that person's servant grabbed the reins of the mount. But then they were forgiven and an amnesty was issued for them.[96] Several others were written for a number of people.

All of those who rode were precluded from entering through the gate of Cairo mounted. The Makariyya were prevented from entering on their donkeys. People, merchants and others, were prevented from sitting on the Zahuna gate. Then the Makariyya were allowed to enter and an amnesty was issued for them.[97] The people grew more fearful. The personnel associated with the markets went each group separately to request the writing of an amnesty decree. Over a hundred were written for the people of the markets in particular, each read in the palace by Abu ʿAli Ahmad b. ʿAbd al-Samiʿ al-Abbasi and then handed over to the leaders of that group. All these came from one original. Following the invocations it said, as one example of it:

> This letter is from the servant of God and his agent al-Mansur Abu ʿAli, the Imam al-Hakim bi-Amr Allah, Commander of the Believers, to the people of the mosque of ʿAbd Allah. You are among those secure through the security of God, the King, the Truth most plain. He gave security to our grandfather Muhammad, the seal of the prophets, and to our father ʿAli, the best of legatees, and to our forefathers of the prophetic rightly guided lineage, may God bless the messengers, the legatees, all of them. The Commander of the Believers provides security for persons, status, blood and property. Have no fear. No hand will bring evil upon you other than for an infraction that requires a penalty, of a right taken for one who deserves it. Be assured of that and depend on it, if God so wills.
>
> Written in the month of Jumada al-Akhira in the year 395 [March 1005]. God be praised! May He bless Muhammad, lord of the messengers, and ʿAli, the best of legatees, and the rightly guided imams, the progeny of prophecy. Peace unconditional without end.[98]

On Wednesday 20 June, a male child was born to al-Hakim. He sat on Thursday for congratulations. The seventh day was Tuesday. Shakr the eunuch carried the child; Abu'l-Hasan 'Ali b. Ibrahim al-Rassi came and performed the *'aqiqa* slaughter. The barber came and cut the boy's hair; he received the customary sum for it. Al-Hakim called this son 'Ali with the patronymic Abu'l-Hasan. It was he that succeeded to the caliphate and was named al-Zahir.

In the same month the mosque of Rashida was furnished. Al-Hakim rode the day of the festival of fast-breaking wearing an unpatterned yellow robe, an indeterminate kerchief on his head, with a turban *muhannak* style with a tail, and a gem between his eyes. Six horses with saddles adorned with gems were led in front of him, and six elephants and five giraffes. He prayed with the people the *'id* prayer and delivered the sermon to them. In his sermon he cursed his oppressor as his due and those spreading false lies about him. The Commander-in-Chief and chief qadi mounted the pulpit with him.

In that year the qadi Husayn b. al-Nu'man was killed. He was hung and then burned in fire. It was because of a complaint lodged by a man in a letter passed up to al-Hakim in which it mentioned that the man's father had died and left him 20 thousand dinars, which were held in the office of the judge. A stipend used to be drawn from it as if it was a regular trust. But the judge Husayn b. al-Nu'man had informed him that his money had run out. So he appealed to the judge and let him know of his complaint by letter. The latter replied as he would have to a man whose money from rents had been paid in full. Al-Hakim ordered the bureau of the judge to be presented and it was brought within the hour. It was then discovered that the amount the man had received to date was the least part of his money. The amount the judge had short-changed was compounded against Husayn and applied to the favor of the plaintiff. And the judge was not excused by his illnesses lest he persist in doing what he was forbidden from doing of this and other types of irregularities. He asked for forgiveness, expressing repentance. But al-Hakim ordered him hung and burned.[99]

A number of other people were put to death, the exact number exceeding 100 persons. They were hung and crucified. The caliph killed 'Abd al-A'la b. Hashim among the royal family because it was said about him that he sought the caliphate and that he had met with a group and promised them various governorates. His news was reported earlier.

We are certainly allowed to wonder at this point what it must have been like to live through the year just finished and to suspect, judging from the number of killings, new laws and regulations promulgated, and the growing fear of the caliph both within the administration and the general populace, that al-Maqrizi has not told us everything. Or, perhaps, it was al-Musabbihi who held back in apprehension lest writing more would have put himself in personal jeopardy. He was after all a ranking member of that same administration; presumably what transpired also applied to him as well.

The Tenth Year[100]

The year of the tufted planet and the revolt of Abu Rakwa.

For this year – the Islamic year 396 – al-Maqrizi comments that this is where al-Musabbihi put his account of the rebellion of Abu Rakwa, although the whole story occupied more than this one year. From the information in his report, especially its specific detail about the reactions of the population of Cairo and Fustat during the height of Abu Rakwa's threat, and their treatment of him when he was finally brought to the capital as a prisoner, suggests strongly that most of this material comes from an eyewitness, most likely from al-Musabbihi himself. He was all but certainly present when these events happened.

Although the full report given by al-Maqrizi is highly useful and remains important, it, in contrast to many other details of the middle years, is not alone. This revolt drew the attention of many medieval historians and often they supply additional facts that must be considered. Best therefore to delay a complete description of the affair of Abu Rakwa to a later chapter and here only note where al-Maqrizi and al-Musabbihi before him first brought it up. The timing might have played a major role as well in the progress of al-Hakim's agenda of reforms. In the preceding year he appeared bent on changing society, perhaps by instilling among his subject aspects of Shiite practice. His command to curse the Companions is the most radical example but several other measures begun then may have had a similar purpose. The year that followed saw the rebellion of Abu Rakwa grow from a disturbance far to the west of Egypt into a dire threat on the very doorstep of the capital. In response did the caliph alter course, allow relaxation of his new laws and even give up the campaign to vilify the Companions?

We resume with al-Maqrizi's account once the revolt of Abu Rakwa has ended.

> Rumors began to spread among the people that General Fadl b. Salih [the hero of the battle against Abu Rakwa] would begin to administer the affairs of state and its governance in the place of the Commander-in-Chief Husayn ibn Jawhar. Between the two in private there was a separation caused by rank and envy concerning it. General Fadl had become arrogant; his haughtiness and snobbery increased toward the Commander-in-Chief in both his words and actions. Al-Musabbihi reports that 'al-Hakim bi-Amr Allah said to me while recounting the story of Abu Rakwa, I did not intend to kill him, but what happened to him was not by my choice. I said to him, 'O Commander of the Believers, your servant Fadl b. Salih did not fail in his service.' He replied, 'What? Do you suppose that it was Fadl who caught him?' I said, 'Yes, O Commander of the Believers, this is what the people report.' He answered, 'No, by God, the magnificent, Fadl was not successful in his attempt to do that and he would not have succeeded had I not expended a million freshly minted dinars. It was only that the king of Nubia captured him and sent him to me.' I said at once, 'You are right, O Commander of the Believers.' I then knew that this was part of what the Commander-in-Chief Husayn ibn Jawhar had decided himself in order to make false the actions of Fadl and his service. And so that is how it remained.
>
> As for the news of Cairo, the order in regard to observing 'Ashura' in the customary fashion involved closing the markets and singers and mourners gathering at the mosque of Cairo. They manifested during it the cursing of the Companions openly. A man was arrested and the call against him said, 'This is the punishment for he who curses 'A'isha and her husband.' He was hung. An order was then passed to the police that no one should curse the Companions publicly. Should someone do that, he should be arrested. The rabble thereafter desisted from the cursing.

The Eleventh Year[101]

The year of the first edict of tolerance; al-Hakim's physician drowns after drinking too much.

On 2 January, al-Hakim commanded that what had been written on the mosques and doorways and other places cursing the Companions be erased. Accordingly, it was all erased. The superintendent of police passed around to make sure that nothing of that remained. A decree was read out to prevent the involvement of anyone in matters that did not concern that person, and that all persons should occupy themselves with their own livelihood and not be distracted by the actions of the Commander of the Believers and his orders.

That year the Christian Ya'qub b. Anastas, who was al-Hakim's physician, died thoroughly drunk in a pond of water. After passing his body through the town, he was carried to the church in a coffin, but then returned to his own house and buried in it. All the notables of the state were there at his funeral and for it a great many candles were lit and there were also many censers of incense. He was the physician of the age, a master of medicine, a prodigy of memory. There was no melody sung for him he did not retain. Were a hundred singers to perform for him in a single session, he would have memorized all of what they had sung and could discuss its harmonies and poetry. He was also a skilled musician. In medicine he devoted himself to the service of al-Hakim and thus grew to be wealthy, leaving an estate worth more than 20 thousand dinars in cash not counting clothing and other items.

The Twelfth Year[102]

Salih b. 'Ali replaces the Commander-in-Chief Husayn ibn Jawhar and Malik al-Fariqi becomes chief justice.

On Friday 27 March, Malik b. Sa'id al-Fariqi was appointed chief judge. The honors bestowed on him in the treasury consisted of a plain shirt, a golden turban, a shawl with seams of gold thread. He was girt with a sword. Ahmad b. 'Abd al-Sami' read out his decree as he stood by. He left preceded by a basket of clothes, he on a mule preceded by two others. When his decree was read, Malik b. Sa'id was standing on his feet. Every time a mention of the Commander of the Believers came up, he would kiss the ground. Next he set off from the palace for the Old Mosque in Fustat. Each time he passed one of the gates of the palace, he dismounted from his mule and kissed that door. When he reached the mosque, he remained standing at the side of the pulpit until the reading of the decree was completed, all the while kissing the ground each time there was a mention of the Commander of the Believers. Then he returned to his house in Cairo and received the books that were read in the palace to the faithful Ismailis.

On Friday 17 April,[103] the notables of the realm gathered at the palace after being summoned to do so and ordered not to leave anyone behind. A servant went out and spoke confidentially to the master of the curtain. He shouted, 'Salih b. ʿAli'. Salih b. ʿAli al-Ruzbari stood up. The man took his hand but no one knew what he was wanted for. He was taken into the treasury. Then, accompanied by Masʿud, the master of the curtain, he came out wearing a plain outer garment and a golden turban. He sat next to the Commander-in-Chief. A decree was produced, which Ibn ʿAbd al-Samiʿ read. Lo and behold, in it, all of the matters that had been under the supervision of the Commander-in-Chief Husayn b. Jawhar were transferred to Salih. As he was listening to the decree naming him, Salih stood and kissed the ground. When Ibn ʿAbd al-Samiʿ had finished the reading, the Commander-in-Chief stood up and kissed the cheeks of Salih, congratulated him, and then left. Salih went out preceded by a number of baskets and three mules with their saddles and bridles. Al-Musabbihi reports here: 'al-Hakim bi-Amr Allah asked me to summon Ibn Surin and have him swear on the Gospels that he would write the decree for Salih b. ʿAli and not reveal that fact to anyone including Ibn Jawhar and any others.' I said to him, 'Surely, you are aware of what manner punishment would be visited on someone who countermands my order. In regard to him rest assured. And, by God, no one learned of it except me and him until the event had taken place.'

Salih sat in the session for the Commander-in-Chief in the palace and began signing in the place of al-Hakim. In regard to the Ismailis and all others conducting the business of the government, their stories and concerns were passed up to him and he executed the commands of al-Hakim, apprising him about matters it was necessary for him to be aware of.

Honors went to Abu'l-Hasan ʿAli b. Ibrahim al-Rassi when he was appointed head of the corporation of descendants of ʿAli, and his gifts were carried with two horses. His decree was read in the palace and the mosque. Honors fell to Saqr the Jew and he was carried out on a mule preceded by three mules with saddles and bridles for baggage and 20 baskets of cloth went with him. Set up in a house that had been furnished and decorated, its doors locked and its rooms curtained, he was given everything he needed and told that that was his house. He thus acquired in one hour what was worth ten thousand dinars. He took up the position of physician to al-Hakim in place of Ibn Anastas.[104]

On 11 June, al-Hakim ordered the old Commander-in-Chief Husayn ibn Jawhar and the qadi ʿAbd al-ʿAziz b. al-Nuʿman confined to their houses. They and their children were forbidden to ride in processions. They were forced to wear wool; no one was to go to them and they were to sit on mats. On 26 July al-Hakim forgave the Commander-in-Chief and the judge ʿAbd al-ʿAziz and he permitted them to ride again. The two rode at once to the palace as they were, without cutting hair or changing clothes.

That year Christians went from Egypt to Jerusalem to be present at Easter in the Church of the Holy Sepulcre (al-Qumama), as was customary every year, bringing with them important adornments, much as the Muslims do in going out with the pilgrimage caravan. So al-Hakim asked Khatkin the Dayf al-'Adudi, one of his commanders, about that because of the latter's familiarity with the matter of this church. He responded, 'The Christians greatly revere this church and make pilgrimages to it from every country. Kings come to visit, carrying to it great wealth, vestments, curtains, furnishings, candle stands, crosses finely wrought in gold and silver, and vessels of the same. There are in it many things of that type. On the day of Easter, the Christians assemble at the church, setting up crosses and suspending candlesticks on the altar. They attempt to have fire transferred to it by means of elder oil mixed with mercury. It produces for the purpose a bright light that those who see this happen suppose has descended from the heavens.' Al-Hakim rejected that and directed Bishr ibn Surin, the clerk of the chancery, to write to Ahmad b. Yaʿqub, the *daʿi*, commanding him to proceed straight away to Jerusalem to destroy the church and have the people plunder it so thoroughly all traces of it were obliterated. He did exactly that. Subsequently, al-Hakim gave an order to raze the churches and synagogues located in the various districts of his kingdom. But, fearing that the Christians would destroy the mosques of the Muslims located in their countries, he refrained from having that done.

The Thirteenth Year[105]

Time for a new edict of religious tolerance.

The people in their entirety were given an order that none of them should publicly perform on the banks of the Nile any type of song, or listen to them in the houses there or drink in boats. A number of the houses were raided and a group arrested. A crier went round proclaiming that no one should enter the baths without a loincloth, and that Jews and Christians could walk about only if they wore the *ghiyar*. They were beaten for leaving it off. The baths were raided and a group seized. They were beaten and paraded because they were found in it without a loincloth. It was prohibited for anyone to enter the slave market other than those who were buyer or seller. Slave girls were to be kept separate from the boys, each was to have its own market day.[106] It was forbidden to set up the tents that women erected among the tombs on the days of visitation. Word spread among the people that the selling of wine would be forbidden. They rushed out to buy it and bought a great deal. It became so dear that ten jars of it sold for a dinar and then it could no longer be found. The whole population was also forbidden to leave their homes before the dawn prayer or after the evening prayer and that caused much distress. A group was thrown in jail for their having countermanded this order.

A decree was issued then prohibiting taking an interest in anything that is unnecessary; it ordered the people to be preoccupied with prayers at the proper time for them, and with commanding the good and forbidding the bad, and that no one should concern himself with the affairs of the sultan or his orders or the secrets of the state. In November a decree was read prohibiting the transporting of wine and *mizr*-beer along with a warning about any appearance of it or of *fuqqaʿ*, and *dalinis*, fish that have no scales, and moldy *tirmis*. Another decree was read in all of the mosques to reassure the hearts of the people, to put them at ease because of how much fear had spread. It had taken hold of them in response to the execution everywhere of the caliph's many orders.

On 11 January, ʿAbd al-ʿAziz b. al-Nuʿman was arrested. Husayn ibn Jawhar was sought but he fled with his two sons and a group of others. Much clamor in the household of ʿAbd al-ʿAziz ensued. The shops of Cairo were closed as well as its markets. Then ʿAbd al-ʿAziz was set free and the crier passed through Cairo saying that no one should close up. After three

> days, Husayn reappeared with his two sons. They went to al-Hakim and he ordered them to keep to their houses. A robe of honor was given him and ʿAbd al-ʿAziz and their children, and a letter of amnesty written for them.
>
> In March sickness increased among the people and death spread. The population grew more fearful of al-Hakim. A number of letters of amnesty were issued for various persons.

In May another decree was read out stating that: 'The fasters will fast and break fast according to their calculations. Those who use the sighting of the moon will not be in conflict in regard to how they fast and break fast.' Ending the fast of Ramadan constitutes a critical moment in the Islamic yearly calendar as it is also the beginning of the feast to follow. Ismailis alone allow the event to be determined by calculation whereas the rest insist on the actual sighting of the new moon. The difference can be a point of tension and possible conflict. In this edict the population has been offered a choice. Those who use one method may not oppose those who employ another.

The same edict commands a similar tolerance for several additional items of disagreement between the Shiʿa and the Sunnis and concludes:

> The *muʾadhdhins* can call to prayer by saying 'Come to the best of works' and those who do not call to prayer using it may not do so. No one is to curse the Companions, or object to any person's attributing to them what he attributes or swears about them what he swears. Every Muslim who makes an effort to understand his religion is an authority in it.

Public policy on Islamic religious issues could hardly have become more tolerant. Other matters, however, remained tense. Openness in one area did not necessarily apply to the others. Thus al-Maqrizi's report for the year continues:

> Al-Hakim did not ride for the feast of fast-breaking prayer; instead Malik b. Saʿid prayed with the people at the festival square and gave the sermon. The table for the feast of sacrifice was set up on 4 June as usual except that the amusements, show and games normally played each year during it were abolished. The qadi said prayers with the people on the feast of sacrifice and delivered the sermon. On the day of the feast of Ghadir, the people were prohibited from celebrating it. Churches on the road to Maqs were demolished, as was a church in the Cairene quarter of the Greeks. What was in these

churches was also looted.[107] During that same night many of the Slavic eunuchs and the clerks were executed after their hands had been cut off in the middle of the forearm against a piece of wood with a butcher's knife.

That year Abu'l-Hasan ʿAli b. ʿAbd al-Rahman b. Ahmad b. Yunis, the astronomer, died in January. General Fadl b. Salih was killed; he was hung on 16 July. Abu Usama Janada b. Muhammad, the lexicographer, was killed on 8 August along with Hasan b. Sulayman al-Antaki, the grammarian. ʿAbd al-Ghani b. Saʿid went into hiding. That was because of their having met and held teaching sessions in the House of Knowledge. Raja' b. Abi'l-Husayn was killed because he prayed the *tarawih* prayer during Ramadan.[108] Those who specialized in relating historical reports were all killed for having harmed the people with the lies they passed on to them and accepting money for it.

The Fourteenth Year[109]

Salih b. ʿAli falls; the Holy Sepulchre is destroyed.

Instructions drafted by Ibn Surin ordered the destruction of the Church of the Holy Sepulcre in Jerusalem.

Al-Hakim started a bureau called the Bureau of Sequestration (*diwan al-mufrad*) that would be responsible for the funds of those who had been killed and others whose property had been confiscated.

The monastery of Qusayr was destroyed and plundered. The affairs of the Jews and Christians grew harsher in regard to their having to wear the *ghiyar*.

On 24 June, Husayn ibn Jawhar, his children and his brother-in-law ʿAbd al-ʿAziz and his children fled in a group with property and weapons. They departed at night. In the morning al-Hakim sent horsemen searching for them until dark but they did not catch them. Their homes were seized and the contents taken to the Bureau of Sequestration. Abu'l-Qasim al-Husayn b. al-Maghribi fled disguised as a porter to Hassan b. ʿAli b. Mufarrij b. Daghfal b. al-Jarrah.[110] A number of letters of amnesty were read out in favor of the Kutama, among the troops from North Africa, the Turks, the judges, the notary witnesses, and the rest of the Ismailis and trusted people, the commoners, the clerks, the physicians, the black eunuchs and the Slavic eunuchs, with a letter of amnesty for each group. The rest of what was in the houses of Husayn ibn Jawhar and ʿAbd al-ʿAziz was transported to the palace after having been inventoried and stamped by the qadi Malik b. Saʿid.

A new decree ended the Sessions of Wisdom (the *majlis al-hikma*) that used to be read to the Ismaili faithful on Thursday and Friday. Another, read in the Old Mosque, turned the attention of the people to their own situations and ordered them to refrain from taking an interest in what was unnecessary for them personally. Another decree restored many Sunni practices. Subsequently, the *mu'adhdhins* in all of the mosques were assembled and read a decree stipulating abandoning the call to prayer using 'Come to the best of works', and adding in the morning call to prayer 'Prayer is better than sleep' and that it was the usage of the *mu'adhdhins* of the palace when they said, 'Peace be upon the Commander of the Believers and the mercy of God.' The people adopted that and began to use it.[111]

A great number of eunuchs, household servants, clerks and others were executed during this year.

The Fifteenth Year[112]

An Iraqi ruler proclaims his allegiance to al-Hakim; the caliph executes the general Husayn ibn Jawhar along with ʿAbd al-ʿAziz, the former chief justice.

On 18 August Ibn ʿAbdun the Christian was removed from office. The reason for the removal of Ibn ʿAbdun from the office of *wasita* was due to letters by al-Hakim sent repeatedly to the Commander-in-Chief Husayn ibn Jawhar and to his brother-in-law ʿAbd al-ʿAziz offering amnesty and their safe return. Ibn Jawhar, however, refused to come back as long as Ibn ʿAbdun was the *wasita*. He said, 'I was good to him during the time I governed but he slandered me to the Commander of the Believers, even while he got from me only what is proper. I will never return if he is the wazir.' Ibn ʿAbdun was accordingly removed. Husayn, along with ʿAbd al-ʿAziz and those who left with them, then presented themselves. All the notables of the state went down to greet him and witness the honors accorded him, his children and his brother-in-law ʿAbd al-ʿAziz. Mounts carrying gifts were led in front of them. When they arrived at the gate of the palace, they dismounted and walked. The rest of the people walked with them into the palace. They appeared before al-Hakim; then went out having been forgiven by him. Husayn was allowed again to use in his correspondence 'Commander-in-Chief' with his personal name coming after his title, and to be addressed in that fashion. He then departed for his house. It was a magnificent day! All that had been seized from him, the property and the rest, were brought back to him. He was treated most graciously. He and ʿAbd al-ʿAziz continued to ride to the palace.

A letter of amnesty was written for Ibn ʿAbdun by al-Hakim in his own hand. It said in part, 'No one served me or achieved in his service what Ibn ʿAbdun achieved. He collected for me funds that were outside of the monies of the bureaus in the amount of three hundred thousand dinars.'

The Judge of Judges Malik received honors and he was assigned the court of grievances in addition to the judiciary. His decree was read in the mosque. A decree issued next restored the Sessions of Wisdom and the collection of the *najwa*. Stronger measures imposed on the Christians the wearing the *ghiyar* along with heavy black turbans in place of other colors. Husayn ibn Jawhar and ʿAbd al-ʿAziz were arrested once again, jailed for three days and then, when they swore not to absent themselves from the court and testified to that personally, they were set free. Al-Hakim swore as much in the letter of amnesty he wrote for them. Ibn ʿAbdun was jailed and ordered to make an accounting, but then hung and his funds confiscated.

A decree read out in all the mosques forbad opposing the Imam in anything he did, taking an interest in anything not necessary. It required giving the call to prayer with 'Come to the best of works,' thus abandoning saying, 'Prayer is better than sleep,'[113] prohibited Sunni rites and restored the *daʿwa* and the *majlis* in accord with normal practice. Between prohibiting and allowing that, there was only a five month period.

A group was beaten and paraded for selling *mulukhiyya* and fish without scales. Another group, arrested because of selling wine, was jailed. Places for that were raided. The Christians, precluded from observing Epiphany, were not to appear on the banks of the river as they usually did for it.

On 21 January Husayn ibn Jawhar and ʿAbd al-ʿAziz rode as was their practice to the palace. When the receiving agent went out to them, he said to Husayn, ʿAbd al-ʿAziz and Abu ʿAli, the brother of al-Fadl, 'Obey the command to do what the caliph wants of you.' The three sat and the other people departed. Thereupon the three of them were arrested and killed in a single moment.[114] Subsequently, their funds, estates and houses were seized once more. As possessions of Husayn ibn Jawhar there were in all seven thousand containers of silk of all kinds, brocade and undulated silk (*ʿuttabi*) and others, nine Chinese bowls filled with *Fansuri* camphor balls, the weight of a single ball being three *mithqals*.[115] The letters of amnesty and the other decrees that had been written for them were likewise confiscated. The children of Husayn and those of ʿAbd al-ʿAziz pleaded and were promised good treatment; they left carried away on mounts presented to them.

A ewe slaughtered the same month was found to be carrying a fetus the face of which resembled that of a human.

Measures to prevent drunkenness intensified. Places where it happened were watched. Several of the quarters in which the *mukus* tax and other dues were applied were exempted from it. Songs and amusements were prohibited and an order issued not to sell female singers, that the people not congregate in the desert, women not to go to the baths.

Malik b. Saʿid prayed with the people the prayer of the feast of sacrifice, gave the sermon and performed the sacrifice at both the festival square and at the playing field during the days of sacrifice. Al-Hakim did not ride nor did he perform the sacrifice.

A very great many clerks, supervisors, eunuchs and women were killed that year. Al-Hakim had them executed.

The Sixteenth Year[116]

A year of measures against wine and women.

In August Muhammad b. Nazzal was appointed over the two police forces and ordered to watch carefully for forbidden actions and prevent them, and that raisins were not to be sold in quantities of more than five pounds, nor were clay jugs to be sold, and the Christians were interdicted from gathering for the Feast of the Cross and not to display lights publicly on the churches.[117]

In January the selling of large and small quantities of raisins was forbidden and a circular letter prohibited transporting them. Many were thrown into the Nile.

A decree read out stated that no one was to solicit from the Commander of the Believers an increase in salary or gifts or fiefs or any other sort of benefit.

Women were prohibited from going out after the conclusion of the evening prayer.

Measures to abolish the selling of *fuqqaʿ*, *mulukhiyya*, fish without scales became harsher still. The people were not to gather at funeral ceremonies or following funeral processions. Great quantities of raisins were burned. Chess pieces gathered up from numerous places were burned.[118] The fishermen were assembled and made to swear that they would not fish for fish that have no scales. Whosoever did that would be hung. The burning of raisins continued for several days in the presence of witnesses. The supervisor of the bureau of expenditure continued the supply of funds spent on transporting and burning them. Burning 2,340 units of raisins cost, in the expenditure for that purpose alone, five thousand dinars over a period of ten days.

Ghabn the eunuch sickened. Al-Hakim rode to call upon him and sent him five thousand dinars, 25 saddled and bridled horses, and appointed him to the police and market inspection of Fustat, Cairo and Jiza and supervision of all funds and situations pertaining thereto. Ghabn [once recovered] went down to the Old Mosque accompanied by the army with his robes of honor. His decree specified that he was to deal harshly with drunkenness and prevent the sale of *fuqqa'*, *mulukhiyya*, and fish without scales, to prohibit amusements, the gathering of people at funerals and the following of funeral processions, and to prevent the selling of honey except in quantities of three pounds or less.

Women did not go out to the desert and no woman was seen at the tombs. Gathering on the banks of the Nile was forbidden, as well as women riding in the boats with men and their going to places where they might be closely confined with men. The selling of grapes was forbidden except in quantities not to exceed four pounds. They were not to be crushed for juice. Eight pounds sold for a dirham accordingly. Many were thrown out on the roads. An order said to trample them and then it was forbidden to sell them at all. Quantities of them that had been brought already were sunk in the Nile. Witnesses dispatched to Jiza seized all the grapes that were still on the vines, which were then scattered under the hoofs of cattle in order to crush them. A similar order went to several other regions. Those who sold grapes for a living were watched carefully. Conditions soon became hard because they were no longer able to sell grapes.

The Seventeenth Year[119]

A tough year for the Christians.

In July warehouses for honey were sealed and all of it that was in the hands of merchants or sellers confiscated. In a four-day period, 5,051 of the jars of the seized honey were sunk in the river. Prices were disturbed. There was a great rush to buy bread. Al-Hakim distributed money to the poor. The purchase of swords, knives and other weapons by the people increased, as did the carrying of them by those of the masses and artisans who had never carried them before. And there was much talk about it. A decree read from the pulpits of the mosques reassured the people and urged them to ignore what they might hear from those who spread false rumors.

Zurʿa b. ʿIsa b. Nasturas died of his illness on 1 October.[120] The period of his administration as *wasita* had been two years and a month. Al-Hakim regretted having lost him without having killed him. He said, 'The thing I regret most is that Ibn Nasturas escaped my sword. I would have liked to hang him because he ruined my kingdom, betrayed me and spoke falsely about me. This man wrote to Hassan b. al-Jarrah hypocritically, speaking against me and he sent men who had deserted with this very letter.' Nevertheless his three brothers received honors and they were confirmed in the bureaus of government they already ran.

The caliph ordered the Christians, with the exception of the religious authorities, to wear black turbans and black hoods and to attach around their necks crosses of wood, to ride on saddles of wood, none to ride horses but rather mules or donkeys, and not ride with adorned saddles or bridles, and that their saddles and bridles have black straps, that they [the Christians] should fasten the *zunnar* around their waists, that Muslims should not act as servants for them, nor should they buy slaves or bondmaids that are Muslim. The people were given permission to look into and to watch out for evidence of anything of that kind. A number of Christians, clerks and others, thereafter converted to Islam. This matter was hard on them. Those whose business was to hire out donkeys and mules were forbidden to let the Christians ride them.[121] And the Christians were to use saddles that are the equivalent of no more than the sole of a shoe. Additionally they were prohibited from riding on the Nile with Muslim boatmen.

The Christians were commanded next to make their saddles out of sycamore wood. A group of people, arrested for playing chess, was beaten and jailed. The crosses the Christians wore on their necks now had to be a cubit in length and width. Their humiliation increased, as did the oppression imposed on them. An order specified that the weight of the cross be five pounds and that it be visible on the outside of their robes. So they did that. But, when matters began to oppress them most heavily, many of them feigned Islam. The affair of destroying churches also happened then. Whatever was in them or the property belonging to them, such as tenements and lands, were allotted as fiefs to another group. Mosques were set up in their place; in some others the call to prayer was said and their lands sold. In the Suspended Church in Fustat and in the church of Bu Shanuda there was a great quantity of finely worked items of exceptional value, such as vestments and other things. The destruction of churches continued without interruption. A letter composed and sent to the other governorates ordered their destruction and they were destroyed accordingly.[122]

In December denunciations for the selling of *fuqqa'*, *zabib* and fish intensified. A group was arrested and jailed and the order to hang them issued, but later they were freed.

In January an edict prohibited the people from kissing the ground before al-Hakim, and from kissing his stirrup and his hand when greeting him in a procession, thus ending the custom of using as a model the habit of the polytheists of bowing to the ground, which was the practice of the Greeks. The populace was commanded to extend greetings to the caliph by saying simply: 'Salutations to the Commander of the Believers, and the mercy of God and His blessings.' Expressing a prayer for him in correspondence and communications was forbidden. All correspondence, in letters and missives, should end in that way, that is, to be limited to a prayer for the peace of God and His greetings, followed by His blessing on the Commander of the Believers, requesting of him what was previously asked and nothing more. On Fridays the preacher would say only: 'O God, bless Muhammad, the chosen; give peace to the Commander of the Believers, 'Ali, the approved; O God, and keep safe the commanders of the believers, the forefathers of the Commander of the Believers; O God, extend the most excellent of Your peace to Your servant and caliph.'

On the feast of fast-breaking al-Hakim rode to the festival square without any of the adornments and accoutrements and the like that he usually appeared in on that day. The ten horses led in front of him with saddles and bridles were decorated with light white silver; the parasol was white but without gold; and he wore white without tiraz or gold and there was no gem in his turban. The pulpit was not furnished.

A new edict prohibited people from cursing the Companions and a man was beaten for doing just that. He was paraded, with the crier calling out 'This is the recompense of he who curses Abu Bakr and 'Umar.' People sought to be absolved; but it was difficult for many of them. They gathered to plead for help at the gates of the palace, exclaiming, 'We have no ability for opposing anyone or ability to endure all that has happened.' They were sent away with an interdiction. So they marched through the streets while pleading for help. Another decree read in the palace invoked the mercy of God on ancestors among the Companions and forbad taking an interest in matters like that kind. But al-Hakim saw in his path, while he was out riding, a signboard on which there was a curse on the Companions. He immediately disavowed it and stopped there until it was torn down. Other signboards followed in succession that had a similar message. All of them were torn down and what had been written like that on walls was erased until there was no longer any trace of it. Harsh measures were taken with a promise of punishment to rebuke anyone who opposed that order.

Al-Hakim proceeded to ride into the desert with leather boots on his feet and a scarf on his head. He used to ride each night after sundown. A man from Khurasan stopped him saying that goods had been taken from him by the arrangement of the government storehouse but he had not been paid their price. Al-Hakim paid him everything that was due him, which was almost five thousand dinars. He then passed through town in his company. Pleas to al-Hakim increased. Ten thousand dinars were carried to ʿAbd al-Rahim in bags on which was written, 'For the son of our uncle and the pride of creation, ʿAbd al-Rahim ibn Ilyas ibn Ahmad ibn al-Mahdi bi-llah, may God keep him and cause us to achieve through him that which we hope for.'

The Eighteenth Year[123]

An unusual choice of an heir apparent; the caliph cuts off the hands of al-Jarjaraʾi and the tongue of Ghabn.

In July an order stipulated that neither Jews nor Christians enter the baths unless they are wearing, in the case of the Jews, a bell and, for the Christians, a cross. Discoursing about the stars was forbidden. A number of astrologers absented themselves; a group of those that remained were banished and the people were warned not to hide any of them. One group publicly expressed repentance and they were forgiven. They swore that they would not investigate the stars.

Al-Hakim increased in this month his charity, giving away in fact a great deal of money and manumitting the remainder of his *mamluks* and slave girls.[124]

The Jews and the Christians received permission to travel to wherever they wanted; many set off for the territory of the Byzantines.

All the people of the various classes assembled at the palace where a decree read to them announced that Abu'l-Qasim ʿAbd al-Rahim ibn Ilyas had been made by al-Hakim bi-Amr Allah the heir to the covenant of the Muslims during his lifetime and the caliph after his death. Honors were bestowed on him and the people commanded to salute him and say in saluting him: 'Peace be upon the son of the uncle of the Commander of the Believers, the heir to the covenant of the Muslims.' A section of the palace was set aside for him to live in. Then another decree saying the same proclaimed it from the pulpits of the city and in Alexandria. Al-Hakim dispatched additional decrees with that information to North Africa. They were read in the mosque of Qayrawan and in other places there. Ibn Ilyas's name was fixed, along with that of al-Hakim, on banners, the coins and the tiraz.

Al-Hakim's riding increased, him wearing a white woolen outer garment and a *futa* turban, on his feet Arab slippers with two straps. The people approached him with petitions regarding either grievances or requests for charity and he gave out liberally presents and gifts among which were houses, dirhams, and clothes. No one went away disappointed. He also returned to its owner what was in the *diwan* of the estates and funds that had been seized and he allotted as fiefs a number of properties. In September al-Hakim spread his hand liberally with more giving.

On 27 October al-Hakim commanded the cutting off of the two hands of Abu'l-Qasim Ahmad b. ʿAli al-Jarjaraʾi and both were cut off completely. This man was at the time the clerk of the Commander-in-Chief Ghabn. The cause was that he had been in the service of Sitt al-Mulk, the sister of al-Hakim, and he left her. She was not pleased with him accordingly. He then served Ghabn. Subsequently, he sent her a note seeking to propitiate her. But she had doubts about him and she sent the note concealed inside the folded envelope to al-Hakim. As a result the caliph, furious about what had transpired, ordered that his hands be cut off. It is also reported that it was 'Aqil, the master of intelligence, who brought the note with its information to the general Ghabn to be conveyed to al-Hakim while still sealed. It reached him during the day reserved for letters as usual. Ghabn passed it to his clerk Abu'l-Qasim al-Jarjaraʾi, who was to see that it was intact and then bring it to al-Hakim. However, al-Jarjaraʾi broke the seal and read it, whereupon he realized that there was in a portion of it a criticism of Ghabn, speaking of him badly. He took out that part of the note by rubbing it out and then fixing the rest. Next he reaffixed the seal. What he had done reached 'Aqil who relayed it to al-Hakim, and the caliph then ordered his hands cut off.[125]

On 10 November, the hand of Ghabn was cut off 15 days after the cutting off of the hands of his clerk al-Jarjara'i. His other hand had been cut off three years and one month earlier. He thus became a person lacking both hands. Subsequently, al-Hakim sent him thousands of gold objects and several baskets of clothes and ordered treatment for him.

When 20 November arrived an order came down for the cutting out of Ghabn's tongue, which was done.

In January an edict restored what had been seized by the police, but also for the killing of the dogs. Accordingly, all of the dogs were killed. A great sum of money was released for charity. Riding at night increased. Al-Hakim went out on the night of the middle of February to the Qarafa cemetery and walked about in it, giving out many things as alms. The prohibition against women going out into the streets either by night or day now applied to all of them with the exception of the very young or very old. Women were thus imprisoned in their homes and none were to be seen on the streets. Their baths were closed and shoemakers were forbidden to make shoes for women. Shops for them were put out of commission.[126]

On 20 February, a great fear gripped the people alarmed by horrid talk that was then being widely spread that the sword was about to fall on them. People fled with the shops shuttered. Nothing remained but the spirit. A group who had violated the prohibition against selling *mulukhiyya* and fish without scales was beaten and paraded. Many women received a beating for having gone out of their homes and they were jailed. In Ramadan al-Hakim prayed with the people in the four mosques: the mosque of Cairo, the mosque outside the Bab al-Futuh, the mosque of 'Amr, and the mosque of Rashida. He gave a great deal of money in charity and he made the appeal himself from the top of the pulpit on behalf of ʿAbd al-Rahim ibn Ilyas. He said, 'O God, respond to me in the matter of the son of my uncle and the keeper of the covenant of the Muslims and the caliph after me, ʿAbd al-Rahim b. Ilyas b. Ahmad b. al-Mahdi bi-llah the Commander of the Believers, as You answered Moses in regard to his brother Aaron.'

Al-Hakim rode for Friday prayer in the mosque of Cairo. The people thronged about him on his return ride from the mosque to the palace. He stopped for them and accepted their petitions, speaking and laughing with them. Because of the frequency of his stopping and conversing with the commoners, he did not reach the palace until sundown. He also gave out many presents. For the festival prayer, he rode without the accoutrements of the caliphate. His parasol was white. ʿAbd al-Rahim accompanied him carrying the lance that the caliph normally carried. The caliph mounted the pulpit with him and made the appeal in his name. No feast table was set up in the palace. Women were not to be seen and none of the games and dolls ordinarily sold during the festivals were sold. The situation caused by the prohibition on women going out grew more serious. A number of elderly women and the weak, caught out in the streets, were detained. Riding at night persisted.

A decree declared that everyone in need or with a grievance should take it to the heir apparent. ʿAbd al-Rahim thereafter held sessions, petitions were presented to him, and he took the action required. In mid-May the land pilgrimage caravan set off. On the feast of sacrifice ʿAbd al-Rahim rode with the army to the festival square where he prayed with the people and delivered the sermon. He made the sacrifice at the square and at the playing ground. No feast table was set up in the palace. Al-Hakim continued riding in the evenings. He took under his patronage a black eunuch as groom whom he gave the patronymic Abu'l-Rida Saʿd, giving him gems and money of indescribable quality and allotting him many fiefs. People came to call upon this man for their needs and to congregate at this door for an answer to important exigencies. He would speak on their behalf to al-Hakim; the caliph never opposed his requests in any thing.

The Nineteenth Year[127]

Al-Hakim executes the chief justice Malik b. Saʿid and appoints a new one.

In July the incidence of fire increased as the setting of blazes in various places grew more numerous. The people were commanded to use candles in jars inside shops.[128] Roofs and skylights were torn off. Another order specified the killing of dogs and many were killed. The fires grew bigger. About all this many disgusting words were heard. A decree read in the mosques rebuked the foolish in an attempt to stop the commotion being created by them. It stated that the people were to enter their homes at the evening prayer. Following the sundown prayer houses were then bolted shut and also shops and alleys. But there was much agitation and pleas for mercy during the night.

That year al-Hakim rode twice during which petitions were presented to him and he issued an order to arrest those who did. The caliph himself set aside as a trust a number of markets and properties along with seven estates in Itfih and Tukh to benefit the Qur'an reciters and *mu'adhdhins* in the mosques and for the filling of the cisterns, the hospitals, and the cost of shrouds.[129]

In September his riding continued, and the taking of petitions and stopping for lengthy sessions with the people. Then he cancelled again his taking of petitions and issued an order to bring them to ʿAbd al-Rahim, to the qadi Malik, or to the *Amin al-Umana'*. These men were to receive petitions. Even so the number of his gifts, donations, fiefs and the granting of honors increased.

On Sunday 24 October, he rode in the night as was his practice to al-Jubb. People followed him, among them the chief judge Malik b. Saʿid. When the judge greeted al-Hakim, the caliph turned away and he fell back in surprise. Whereupon a Slav called Ghadi, the man in charge of the curtain and veil, took him and set off in the direction of the palaces. Shortly thereafter, however, he killed Malik and threw him down on the ground. Later al-Hakim passed and gave an order for his burial.[130] Accordingly, they buried him in his clothes and shoes at that spot where he had fallen. The period of his supervision of the judiciary was 20 years, of which six years and nine months were as chief judge, the rest as deputy to various of the al-Nuʿman clan. He had supervised the judges, the courts of grievances, charitable trusts, the *daʿwa*, the mint, the bureau of weight and measures, and command of the *adyaf*. His status had risen high and the people went to him with their needs because of his close intimacy with al-Hakim. His fief holdings consisting of houses with their furnishings and a number of estates that only increased. He continually rode with al-Hakim both at night and by day and advised him in matters of state and the supervision of the affairs of all the bureaus of the government. Malik was generous and openhanded, eloquent and articulate. Clamoring and irascibility never took control of him; there was never heard in his speeches any obscenity or slander or ugliness.

The reason behind his execution was that he was charged with being a supporter of Sitt al-Mulk and of deferring to her. Al-Hakim had become concerned about her.

Al-Hakim's riding increased to the point that he used to ride in only one day six times. His gifts and donations increased also. Then he gave an order to purchase a donkey and he began to ride it out from a subterranean chamber to the gate of the garden onward to al-Maqs. The gate from which he emerged going to al-Maqs would be locked for the time of his ride and the people were prohibited from going out of the city to places in that direction.

Al-Hakim took sick for some days, and so he rode wearing an uncovered cap. Trips during the evenings to al-Maqs became more frequent, including crossing over to Jiza, all the while on a donkey. Riding at night also became more frequent.

On Friday 26 February the heir apparent rode and led prayer in the new al-Anwar Mosque at the Bab al-Futuh in the procession of a caliph. Then he led prayer another Friday at the mosque of Cairo and subsequently on two more Fridays at the New Mosque. That year the donations by al-Hakim and his allocating of land grants to the people increased until he exceeded the limit. The heir apparent rode on the feast of fast-breaking in the procession of a caliph and prayed with the people at the festival square and delivered the sermon. Al-Hakim exceeded in the plethora of his giving and land granting anything previously known to the point that he allocated a land grant to the boatmen who rowed him in the 'Ushra, his river craft. He also gave a land grant to the torch-bearers[131] and many of the elite and the royal family, and even the Banu Qurra who were among those allocated portions of Alexandria, al-Buhayra and their districts.

The riding continued on each new morning, with him always on a donkey. Al-Hakim rode more frequently; in one day he rode six times, once on a horse, another time on a donkey, one more in a litter carried on necks, another in an 'Ushra on the Nile wearing a cap without a turban over it. The giving out of land grants to the army and the purchased slaves increased. The continuation of the riding lasted until the night of the sacrifice at the approach of nightfall. He passed through the city with a driver parting the people away from him. The heir apparent prayed the prayer for the feast of sacrifice, but offered no sacrifice and prohibited the people from slaughtering cattle.

The Last Years

From the 20th year (beginning in June 1015), except for a few small bits of information, we lose our most reliable source, al-Maqrizi's history. Its loss will leave us scrabbling for additional sources. And yet so critical are the events of this period, we must return to them at a later stage in a separate chapter.

The Twentieth Year[132]

The first of the lost years.

> In this year a registry was submitted to al-Hakim with the names of the legal scholars, the Qur'an readers, and the *mu'adhdhins* in Cairo and Fustat. The total for them each year came to 71,733 dinars plus two thirds and a quarter dinar.[133] The waters of the Nile rose so high estates became submerged and prices rose as well. Gardens were destroyed. Every place in the city was full of water. The Nilometer was submerged and the increase finally ended at three fingers away from 21 cubits. The water reached half way up the date palms that were around the Birkat al-Habash. Al-Ma'tuq was submerged. There remained no way into Cairo except the street and the desert.

That is all al-Maqrizi had to report for this year and he says nothing at all about the one to follow.

A simple comparison of the amount of information al-Maqrizi reports for the Islamic year 405, which is the 19th year, and 406, which is the 20th year of the reign, (or for that matter, most of the subsequent years) suggests that he could no longer find in his sources what he needed for a more complete record. In fact his account, which is fairly exemplary up to this point, from here on fails us miserably. He offers nothing at all for 407, the 21st year. The next year 408 has a brief description of the first stirrings of the earliest Druze, a subject better covered elsewhere, even by al-Maqrizi in his other writings. From 409, the 22nd year, we are told, again briefly, about the assassination, on 17 February, of 'Ali b. Ja'far b. Falah, the *wasita*, as he 'rode to the ponds that were before the canal on the outside of Cairo. Two horsemen assaulted him, one of whom stabbed him, with the blade running through him. They fled and nothing was learned about them. He was carried to his house where he died the next morning.'[134]

The entry continues:

> In that year al-Hakim removed Sadid al-Dawla from Damascus and appointed over it 'Abd al-Rahim ibn Ilyas, who set off for it on 3 November. While he was in his palace, a group of veiled men attacked him and they killed a group of his pages. Then they seized him, put him in a box and had him transported to Egypt. He had not been there more than two months.

> Later he was returned to Damascus and stayed there the night of the feast. A man called Abu'l-Da'ud al-Maghribi arrived from Egypt with a group. They threw ʿAbd al-Rahim out and beat him on the face. The morning of the feast dawned and the people had no one to lead them in the prayers. The people were astonished at the idea. In that year as well, the tax farmer for Upper Egypt was forgiven what he owed, which amounted to 64,765 dinars.

For 410, the 24th year, there are two pieces of information. In it the crisis in goods in the land of Egypt grew more intense to the point that flour sold for a dirham per pound and meat four *awaq* per dirham. Many of the people died from hunger. For the three months, January, February, and March, the number of dead reached 270 thousand without counting foreigners and they were more than that.

At this point al-Maqrizi's year-by-year story of the reign of al-Hakim comes to its natural end. He here interrupts the story to add, in a cluster, several versions of what actually happened to the caliph in 1021 and why. In truth the chronology of his account had already become unreliable, suggesting that for the years after 1015, he could find little or no information even though what transpired then is vital to the conclusion of the reign. If al-Maqrizi's best source was the writings of al-Musabbihi, which appear to have provided precise detail for much of the period prior to 1016, most especially for events in Cairo and Fustat, where this author was stationed, evidently what he recorded for the years 1016 through 1021 was no longer based on that same source. The pertinent volumes of al-Musabbihi's *History* had either gone missing (perhaps al-Maqrizi or his sources could not find those volumes) or had never existed.

Therefore, although al-Maqrizi's version of the reign of al-Hakim is surely the most detailed, fair and chronologically precise available, it is obviously flawed, especially in failing to cover the period 1016 to 1021, that is, the 21st to 25th years of his rule. Using him alone leaves us in the dark about this critically important phase. It is thus essential to find additional sources – a general requirement in any case – to fill in the blanks. Yet few of the others are as rich in information, or as trustworthy for impartiality. Nevertheless we draw on them, though cautiously. The best is Yahya of Antioch and it is he who provides much of what we are missing for the period al-Maqrizi did not cover. To him we will return later in a chapter devoted to the events of the final seven years of al-Hakim's life.

But what then do we make of the story thus far? Was al-Hakim a madman, an unstable lunatic, a tyrant out of control, as many observers both then and now insist? Is anything of the kind evident in the record at this point? Does al-Maqrizi even tell us enough for such a judgment? There is a lot of information in great variety. Does it add up one way or another, the big and little events, the dramatic moments and the banal, and does it ever reveal the true character of the caliph himself? Note that the evidence marshaled so far indicates clearly some of his positive traits: proverbial generosity, support of scholars and scholarship, maintenance of Islam and Islamic institutions such as mosques, concern for justice and equity, fearless accessibility to ordinary folk and the common citizens of his domain. Nothing in al-Maqrizi's account detracts from or diminishes this fact. Nor do honest observers, who otherwise might have detested him, deny it. His loyal followers rightly boasted of it. Yet the overly large number of executions and their continued regularity remains a disturbing feature of his rule, as does the ongoing restriction of women and the protected peoples. Obviously we need to know more. And we must find a way to fill in the last phase of the story, those final years leading to his disappearance. In the following chapters we will therefore investigate separate aspects of what happened, grouping them according to major themes – attempts at social reform, institutions of government, the fate of those who rebelled against him and those who remained his supporters and advocates, his relations with foreign entities – prior to a close look at the seven years at the end. And, in this next section, we no longer rely so exclusively on al-Maqrizi but add to his reports the information relayed by the other medieval authors, although he continues to be quite often our best source even so.

PART THREE

4

The Institutions of His Rule

The administration of al-Hakim's government depended on a series of subordinate ranks, a true bureaucracy, ranging from offices at the top – one that functioned like a wazir, two others for the chief qadi, and the chief *da'i*, the three leading positions – down through the heads or supervisors of various bureaus, commanders of units in the army, the police, market inspectors, thousands of clerks and more. The whole system was vast. The caliph stood at its head, but even a ruler as directly involved as al-Hakim was could not hope to control more than a small portion of it. Nevertheless what the government did, what actions it carried out successfully or failed to perform properly, affected how the imam at the top was judged. Was he to blame for its inaction or malfunction? Do we credit him for its accomplishments?

Information about the details and how the system worked is available but is severely limited. Documents from the Fatimid period, although once plentiful, are all but non-existent now. It is likely that they disappeared long ago when the rulers of Egypt ceased to care about what had happened under their predecessors. Later dynasties detested the Fatimids. In an extremely rare instance a copy remains but that is truly exceptional. For certain elements of Fatimid government, however, there are individual treatises, which cover, for example, the wazirate, the qadis, the *da'wa*, and the chancery, separately. Specialists who worked in the other bureaus at the very end of Fatimid rule later composed accounts to cover them as well. All these, however, provide, a general picture of the whole era, all 200 years of it, from 969 to 1171, but most particularly its final phase and not necessarily al-Hakim's reign. And, given that the empire in his time stretched over vast territories, only part of which was Egypt, a description of government operations in the capital does not reliably indicate the situation elsewhere. Naturally, also, those reports tend to deal in more detail with the highest ranks – wazir and qadi, for example – and pay less and less attention to the lower. For the reign of al-Hakim, who had no wazir, even that office, which, in many Islamic governments (including the Fatimids later on), was normally second only to the caliph or a sultan, is hard to define. Who or what took its place?

The Wasita (Lesser Wazirate)

The Fatimids were slow to accept the inevitability of the wazir's office, although by their time it had become widely used by Islamic regimes elsewhere. The term itself, moreover, might have applied to any aide or advisor, and not necessarily to a single person, let alone to an individual holding enormous state authority, which is often implied in the classical notion of such a position. But the very delegation of major responsibility by the all-powerful and infallible imam to a subordinate – a wazir or anyone else for that matter – implied that the ruler needed help and that carried the concomitant suggestion of weakness. A failure in the subordinate could likewise be read as a fault in the imam who had appointed him. Among the early Fatimid caliphs, whose direct involvement and participation in the details of governing was palpable, the idea of relying on a wazir did not come up. The choosing of the men appointed to high office was, in general, carefully managed; and those chosen were constantly supervised afterward by the imam.

The primary exception to such a policy occurred when al-ʿAziz raised one of his aides, Yaʿqub Ibn Killis, to the position of wazir in 978.[135] For the first time the dynasty had, by that act, allowed an individual to assume, with respect to the administration of the state, a power almost equal to that of the caliph. And Ibn Killis did in fact thereafter perform the functions of that office in the grand manner of the most famous and important wazirs elsewhere in the medieval Islamic world. With one brief interruption when the caliph had him arrested and imprisoned – al-ʿAziz was not entirely pleased with everything Ibn Killis did – the wazir remained wazir until his death in 991. But thereafter the imam avoided elevating anyone so high, preferring instead various lesser ranks for those who ran his government. Al-Hakim continued this latter policy of his father; he himself appointed no wazirs.

It was not until the reign of al-Hakim's son and successor al-Zahir that the Fatimids again returned to the use of a wazir. In the year 1028, the caliph raised al-Jarjaraʾi – by then a man without the use of either of his hands – to the same high rank as that held earlier by Ibn Killis. The wazirate had been out of favor for 38 years. From this much later event, we possess a copy of the formal decree composed for the occasion.[136] This case is especially interesting and important since it offers a clear example of the problem of how, when and why the imam might choose to delegate his august authority – even a portion of it – to another person. The act of delegation – the very problem of why it might be necessary – was in part the subject of the document itself. The decree insists on justifying the office of wazir by explaining the Qur'anic precedent for it. Another similar decree from slightly later carefully explains that it is God, and God alone, who requires no wazir. But humans do. If anyone, these decrees say, could have not needed a wazir, it would have been the prophet Moses. Nonetheless, it was he who asked God to appoint him a wazir, who was Aaron, his own brother. In Qur'an 20: 29–32 Moses speaks to God: 'Grant me a wazir from my family; Aaron my brother; add to my strength through him; and make him share my task.' This passage (and another with the same information) contains the single Qur'anic instance of the term 'wazir'.

According to the Shi'a, 'Ali b. Abi Talib, the ancestor of the caliph himself, was the wazir of the Prophet, and the brotherly connection between Aaron and Moses is parallel to that of Muhammad and 'Ali: the Prophet had said, "Ali is to me as Aaron was to Moses.' Thus two of the greatest prophets, men of the highest capacities and each exempt from even the possibility of error, both infallible, found it useful to have a wazir.

Even so, although Aaron and 'Ali were ideal wazirs, the decree goes on to cite Joseph as the true model for the present purposes, i.e. the appointment of al-Jarjara'i. Joseph's shepherding of the public welfare on behalf of pharaoh, especially of financial matters, is what the caliph now expects of his new wazir. Thus a better Qur'anic precedent – one also prominent in the same text – is that of Joseph, who said to Pharaoh (Qur'an 12: 55), 'Put me in charge of the storehouses of the land, for I am a guardian with great knowledge.' Clearly, for the Fatimid rulers, Joseph represented the ideal wazir, the management of money and resources being uppermost in their minds.

However, al-Hakim had available no Joseph, nor for that matter an Ibn Killis, whose combined talents had been broad and quite unusual. Although born and raised a Jew, Ibn Killis eventually converted to Islam and, in so doing, became not merely a Muslim but an Ismaili, that is, a believer in the imamate of the Fatimids. In the latter capacity, he took an active part in the propagation of religious law and doctrine, himself writing an important compendium of Ismaili legal materials. And his skill with financial matters and his knowledge of the affairs of state were even more impressive.

Absent an Ibn Killis, al-Hakim preferred not to appoint a wazir. As his father had done over the final six years of his rule, instead of a wazir, he used a lesser office, a kind of quasi-wazir, called in Arabic *wasita* (sometimes also *safira*), the holder being a go-between, a mediator, in the sense of mediating between the ruler, on the one hand, and the army and public, on the other. Where wazirs, especially in later times, were accorded full authority to run the government, the *wasita* merely conveyed the commands of the caliph to his subjects and made certain that such orders were promptly and efficiently carried out. His rank was high but never as elevated as that of a true wazir.[137]

The first to hold this office under al-Hakim was the regent Ibn ʿAmmar, who was one of two men al-ʿAziz had chosen to shepherd the government of his young son. The other man was the chief judge, Muhammad b. al-Nuʿman. Barjawan seemed to have been given, initially, no formal role, except direct responsibility for the person of the new imam. The coincident demand by the Kutama Berbers troops that no one other than Ibn ʿAmmar should exercise control over their affairs, confirmed his rise to power, and, perhaps, forced his recognition as the *wasita*. Thereafter, for the duration of his hold on that position, he was the de facto head of government, in part signified by the title 'The State's Trustee' granted him on the occasion of his formal appointment. His was the very first such title of honor accorded any Fatimid office holder.

The old Maghribi military commander carried with him an obvious prestige earned from distinguished prior service to the dynasty, but he lacked the political acumen essential for the task at hand. His initial acts overtly favored the Kutama and undercut or eliminated support for most of the Easterners, especially the Turks, the cultivation of whom had been a special project of al-ʿAziz. It was a dangerous game, played with little regard for the long-term consequences. The arrest and execution of ʿIsa b. Nasturas, who had been initially confirmed in his position as supervisor of financial matters, along with the removal of Manjutakin from command of the army in Syria, were popular with the Westerners, but were also symptoms of trouble to come. The demands of the Kutama increased, becoming, in part, uncontrollable, particularly among the younger soldiers. Eventually, the conflict between Westerners and Easterners erupted in a public battle. Unable to re-establish his authority over the parties, Ibn ʿAmmar fell from grace and retreated from the capital, thus relinquishing his position.

The fate of Ibn ʿAmmar was, even so, better than most of his successors. Where they were nearly all to face execution, he survived his downfall, and the extensive perquisites formerly granted to him by al-ʿAziz were later restored. His murder, three years afterward, at the hands of Turks, who continued to regard him as their enemy, was a consequence of his earlier actions, and did not happen as a result of the caliph's order.

Meanwhile, Barjawan had been waiting, all the while plotting his own rise. As *wasita* he brought to the office the political skill Ibn ʿAmmar did not have. His selection of Fahd b. Ibrahim as his clerk meant that the daily business of running the government fell to an experienced bureaucrat. Like the majority of those who conducted the mundane affairs of the various departments of the state, most especially those connected with revenue and expenditures, Fahd was Christian and that both provided him a mediating status within the bureaucracy of clerks and yet limited his ambition. He was not a threat to the new *wasita*. The combination of Barjawan, who, as a eunuch member of the inner circle of the palace, had access to the royal court in a way outsiders – non-family members – could not, and the Christian Fahd, who had risen to the top from within the bureaucracy itself, proved particularly apt. Barjawan was a wily intriguer but he brought a needed harmony to the administration, finally achieving a reconciliation between the Easterners and Westerners.

Nonetheless, he was not without his own faults and failings. At first quite attentive to the requirements of his new office, as time wore on his diligence waned and he spent more and more time in the pursuit of pleasures among the company of singers. More serious was his disregard for the caliph, who was, all the while, maturing and growing more accustomed to the idea of his own rights as imam, exclusive of what he came to see as the presumptuous insolence of his childhood tutor and caretaker.

The killing of Barjawan in 1000, after two years and seven months in office, was an execution ordered by the ruler, a fate shared ironically by all but two or three of the dozen *wasita*s yet to come. Nevertheless, if such an end were a normal feature of holding that position, no one refused to serve. Fahd must have reacted initially to the news of Barjawan's death with dread for himself. Al-Hakim quickly reassured him that he was safe and he continued to function as he had done. Two years earlier he had been granted the title 'The Executive' and that remained. But the new *wasita* was to be Husayn, the son of Jawhar, the general who conquered Egypt for the Fatimids more than three decades earlier. Husayn held the title Commander-in-Chief, as had his father, and his own status among the elite in Egypt was considerable. Related by marriage to the al-Nuʿman clan, he was intimately connected to the Fatimid establishment, among which he had many friends. Fahd was not so fortunate.

Three years later in 1003, he too fell from grace and was executed. Still, by then, he had managed to hold on to his position altogether for five years, nine months and nine days, which, as it would turn out, was a fairly impressive record of survival in so high an office.[138]

In truth Fahd's rank, as high as it was, never quite reached that of *wasita*. That might have been because he was Christian but more likely because, during the earliest phase of al-Hakim's rule, the imam preferred to rely on men he himself knew well and who, like Ibn ʿAmmar, Barjawan, and Husayn ibn Jawhar, were closely allied to the dynasty and had deep roots in it. Later al-Hakim did appoint Christians to the office of *wasita*; in fact three of the 11 (or 12, depending on exactly whom to include) who were to hold that position following the removal and replacement of Husayn ibn Jawhar were Christian.

After the execution of Fahd, Husayn managed to continue as *wasita* for five more years. In place of Fahd as his chief clerk, that honor went to ʿAli b. ʿUmar al-'Addas, a man who had himself once served as *wasita* under al-ʿAziz in the period after Ibn Killis. On this later occasion and in a lesser role, he was to survive only briefly before being himself killed.[139] Husayn, however, survived and remained in office until quite unexpectedly replaced in April 1008. Without warning, a formal court ceremony was convened and Salih b. ʿAli al-Ruzbari was called out and made the new *wasita*. Salih was then the director of the bureau for Syrian affairs with which he was familiar from an earlier career there. In the next year Salih received the title 'Trusted of the Trustees of Both Sword and Pen', but in either October 1009 or more likely April 1010, he was demoted, confined to his house and then executed in May 1010.[140]

His replacement as *wasita* was the Christian clerk Ibn ʿAbdun, who was given the title 'The Efficient'. This Ibn ʿAbdun was strongly disliked by Husayn ibn Jawhar, however, and, when al-Hakim sought to entice the latter to return to Cairo after he had fled from it, the price demanded by the old Commander-in-Chief was the demotion of this *wasita*, who even so was the recipient of a letter of amnesty and high praise composed and written by the imam in person.[141] After less than four months in office, he was succeeded by Ahmad b. Muhammad, who was known as al-Qashuri, yet another clerk. Although formally appointed *wasita*, a mere ten days later this man was arrested in the midst of performing his job and hung for displaying far too much deference to Husayn ibn Jawhar. It was a quick end, but not the quickest. Al-Fadl b. Jaʿfar b. al-Fadl ibn al-Furat, the son of a wazir from much, much earlier, occupied the *wasata* for only five days in 1015, prior to removal and execution. His tenure was so short there was no time for formal recognition of it.

After al-Qashuri, al-Hakim appointed another Christian, Zur'a, the son of the former *wasita*, 'Isa b. Nasturas. He had the title 'The Satisfier' and he survived two years and a month before dying of natural causes in 1012. About him al-Hakim is reported to have remarked that he regretted having missed the chance to execute him, so poorly had he run his office. He was also suspected of treason.[142]

Next al-Hakim brought in Husayn Ibn Tahir al-Wazzan, a member of the elite who was mentioned among those of rank in the royal court a decade earlier. Now he was to be found in the retinue of the powerful eunuch Ghabn. Al-Maqrizi comments:

> Al-Hakim summoned Husayn ibn Tahir al-Wazzan, who had been devoted to Ghabn the black eunuch, and offered him the post of *wasita*. He accepted on the condition that there be, for each of the tribal groups in the regiments of the army, a leader on whom they would rely and that he would administer them through their leaders. For each group he set aside a day for the supervision of matters pertaining to them exclusively via its leader. That was done and honors were bestowed on him. The office of *wasita* and the executive were handed over to him. His decree was read in the palace on 8 October 1012. Al-Hakim gave the order and in accord with it there was written on his seal: 'By the support of God the Magnificent, the deputy who aids the Imam Abu 'Ali'. ... In November Husayn ibn Tahir al-Wazzan was given the title *Amin al-Umana'* and a decree was written to announce that.[143]

However this man had the audacity to question the caliph's acts of largess. Al-Maqrizi reports that Ibn Tahir's hesitation in the matter prompted the following stern letter from al-Hakim:

> Praise be to God as He deserves. I associate, I hope not, or rely on any other than my God, and He is the most excellent. My grandfather was my prophet and my imam is my father; my faith is the most sincere and just. Money is the money of God, the glorious and most great; creatures are the servants of God; we are His trustees on the earth; release the sustenance of the people, and do not stop it. Peace.

It was clearly a rebuke and quite possibly a warning. Shortly thereafter we read:

> In December 1014, al-Hakim rode accompanied by *Amin al-Umana'* al-Husayn ibn Tahir al-Wazzan as usual. When they came to the quarter of the Kutama outside the gate of Cairo, the caliph ordered Ibn al-Wazzan to be hung and burned in his house. The period of his administration as *wasita* was two years, two months and 20 days.[144]

Two brothers were to succeed Ibn Tahir: al-Husayn and ʿAbd al-Rahman (or al-Rahim) who were the sons of Abu'l-Sayyid.[145] ʿAbd al-Rahim had been supervisor of the bureau of expenditures. Now both, jointly, became the *wasita*. Their tenure lasted, however, a mere 62 days before they were deposed and killed.[146]

At this point in chronological order comes the rise and swift fall after only five days of al-Fadl, the son of the pre-Fatimid wazir Ibn al-Furat.[147]

During the next two months – the exact date is vague – al-Hakim turned for the office of *wasita* to a trusted military figure, a former commander of armies in Syria, and a ranking member of the Kutama hierarchy from one of its most esteemed families. That was Abu'l-Hasan ʿAli b. Jaʿfar ibn Falah, who held the titles 'Wazir of Wazirs, He of Two Directorships, The Victorious Commander, Pole of the State'. According to Ibn al-Sayrafi[148], the author of a history of the Fatimid wazirate, a decree from December 1017 specified that this man's position gave him control over all the men of the state and added the governorates of Alexandria, Tinnis and Damyetta as well as the two police forces, market inspection, the chancery, the bureau of review and affirmation, and supervision of stipends. Without precise information about the scope of his earlier duties, it is hard to know what of these items might have been added in 1017. Whatever they were, a little more than a year later, we hear that 'On 27 February 1018 the wazir ʿAli b. Jaʿfar ibn Falah rode to the ponds that were before the canal on the outside of Cairo. Two horsemen assaulted him, one of which stabbed him, running the blade through him. The two fled and nothing was learned about them. Ibn Falah was carried to his house where he died the next morning.' The death of this *wasita*, in contrast with most, was apparently mourned in truth; the heir apparent rode out to say prayers over him along with the chief qadi.

Al-Maqrizi adds here somewhat cryptically, 'al-Zahir Saʿid b. ʿIsa b. Nasturas was appointed wazir after him. It is said also that after him, Shams al-Mulk Masʿud ibn Tahir al-Wazzan was the person appointed.' The first of these two was the brother of the ill-fated Zurʿa, known by the title 'The Satisfier'. This latter brother had more impressive titles: 'The Supporting

Trustee, Honor of the Kingdom, Crown of the August, He of Two good fortunes.' But even with the addition of 'Partner of the Caliphate', a new title granted in the decree appointing him[149], he was dead just as quickly. His replacement at the end of that month – April 1019 – was Abu'l-Fath al-Masʿud, the brother of Ibn Tahir al-Wazzan. He was the one who had assumed charge of treasury after his brother was elevated to wasita. He held the titles 'Commander, Sun of the Kingdom, the Trusted Master'.[150] At the end of April this al-Masʿud took over the office with the difference that he moved the seat of administration – that is, of the bureaus of government – to his own house, thereafter setting aside a day on which he rode to the palace to handle matters that needed to be taken up there. That order remained in effect until al-Masʿud was removed from the post, although exactly when that occurred is not known. The same person, however, was again made *wasita* in 1023, during the reign of al-Zahir. Clearly therefore he survived his removal from office in the earlier case.

His successor, still under al-Hakim, was the grandly titled 'Important Commander, Director of Directors, The Importance of the Kingdom (*Khatir al-Mulk*)', Abu'l-Husayn ʿAmmar b. Muhammad, who had been previously the supervisor of the chancery.[151] To that responsibility was added the office of *wasita*, specifically in respect to the Easterners and Turks. It is unclear if that meant more. Did he have responsibility for the Westerners in addition? The record does not say. In October 1021, barely four months prior to al-Hakim's disappearance, he began to sign the caliph's signature on documents in place of the caliph. He continued to have these same responsibilities through to the end of the reign.

Although there are gaps and uncertainties in the dates, the 14 or 15 individuals (counting separately the two brothers who held the office jointly) just named appear to complete the list of the *wasita*s under al-Hakim. Several other men held a rank almost as high, and they perhaps ought to be added. Among them are Fahd b. Ibrahim and Ibn al-'Addas, the former surely since he, in effect, functioned at that level for over five years. Still Fahd was never formally accorded that title, especially not by decree. Saʿid b. Saʿid al-Fariqi, the royal tutor, whom al-Hakim executed in 1001, also performed similar functions. Maqrizi says[152] that he introduced the affairs of state to the young caliph *as if he were a wazir*. One more case deserves consideration, if only as a means to establish, as much as possible, exactly what the term *wasita* meant, a task best undertaken by an inductive review of all instances of its actual use.

Ghabn was a black eunuch who rose to such heights in al-Hakim's regard that in November of the year 1011, he was honored and granted the title Commander-in-Chief.[153] A decree issued at the time stated formally that he was to be addressed by that title in letters and correspondence. One report claims, moreover, that his status had risen by then above all others of the realm. Al-Hakim was certainly much taken with him. When a bit later Ghabn became ill, the caliph rode to call upon him personally, with quite generous gifts and an appointment 'to the police and market inspection of Fustat, Cairo and Jiza and supervision of all funds and matters.' The report continues: 'Ghabn went down to the Old Mosque accompanied by the army with his robes of honor. His decree was read out. In it he was to deal harshly with drunkenness and prevent the sale of fuqqaʿ, *mulukhiyya*, and fish without scales, and prohibit amusements, the gathering of people at funerals and the following of funeral processions, and forbid the selling of honey except in quantities of three pounds or less.' But two years later, in 1013, on 12 August, he was removed from the two police forces and the market inspection. Three months after that, on 10 November, 15 days after the cutting off of both hands of Ghabn's clerk al-Jarjaraʾi, the remaining hand of Ghabn was ordered cut off. Ghabn's other hand had been cut off three years and one month earlier. Like al-Jarjaraʾi, he thus became a person lacking both hands.

The cause of both actions – the punishment of Ghabn and al-Jarjaraʾi – was likely a consequence of the same incident. Al-Jarjaraʾi had once worked for Sitt al-Mulk but later switched to Ghabn. She objected and that led to this punishment of first one and then the other. Subsequent to his punishment, however, al-Hakim sent him thousands in gold and several baskets of clothes and ordered medical treatment for him, thus seeming to honor him yet once again. When the 20th arrived, however, an order was issued for the cutting out of Ghabn's tongue, which was done. Needless to say, he died not long afterward.

Clearly Ghabn achieved a status like that of the *wasita* even if there is no record of his having the position itself. Still his responsibilities seem to have been connected primarily with the military and the police, not with the regular bureaucracy as was true of Fahd and a number of the others. One question about the *wasita*, which means in itself 'mediator', is what precisely the holder of the office mediates between. On one side there is the imam-caliph. That is not in doubt. But who or what is on the other side? The judiciary, for example, was, from the beginning of Fatimid rule until the advent of the all-powerful wazirs of the type of Badr al-Jamali in 1074, an independent office. The functions controlled by the chief qadi were outside the domain of the *wasita*. The same is true of the *da'wa*. Moreover, employment of the lesser *wasita* in place of a wazir, indicates, and likely is a consequence of, al-Hakim's wish to have a direct role in as many government operations as he could physically manage. That he, in any case, might decide to intervene at any moment had to be expected. In a few situations, lines from a decree of appointment suggest that the office-holder was to mediate between al-Hakim and various divisions of the army, or, in others, with a broader range of affairs to include the bureaus and the bureaucrats in them. In some instances the report merely states that the new person is to take charge of the same matters as his predecessor without further detail.

One duty mentioned involves the authority to apply the caliphal signature to documents issued by the government. Several individuals of those listed above are said specifically to have possessed that power. A written decision or rule at the highest level required the signature of the imam. He normally affixed the Fatimid motto *al-Hamd li-lah Rabb al-'alamin* ('Thanks be to God, Lord of the Universe') on the document itself. That made the document fully legal and binding.

Review of the individual cases of *wasita*s suggests that most came to the position backed by important family connections. Ibn 'Ammar, Ibn Jawhar, two called Ibn 'Isa b. Nasturas, two Ibn Tahir al-Wazzans, 'Ali b. Ja'far ibn Falah, and an Ibn al-Furat were all sons of the Fatimid establishment. Of those, at least two had previous experience as field commanders in the military. Another, Husayn ibn Jawhar, was Commander-in-Chief but his was more of an inherited rank; he had not led an army in the field. All those in this shorter list belonged to the elite of the time. Several others may not have been, among them the Christian clerk Ibn 'Abdun and possibly al-Qashuri. Salih b. 'Ali was also a ranking member of the court but his family background is not explained and there appears to be no information about it. Significantly, despite his execution by the government, his son al-Hasan b. Salih was to rise to the post of *wasita* under al-Hakim's son al-Zahir. The disgrace of one member of a family did not carry over to the others.

A key question about these men would reveal their religious affiliation. Which of them were Ismaili? Obviously not the Christians. And, if Christians could hold the office of *wasita*, surely also non-Ismaili Muslims, Sunnis and others. Unfortunately, there is little or no discussion of this issue in the surviving sources.

The Chief Qadi and the Judiciary

In contrast with the *wasita*, where the historical record is difficult to follow and where the concept of the office and its exact responsibilities is defined vaguely at best, the judiciary is clearer.[154] The position of the chief judge, the *qadi al-qudat*, is reasonably well known from other Islamic regions, although perhaps not under precisely the same conditions, and the various subordinate functionaries – clerks and specialists in separate legal departments (such as the complex matter of divisions for inheritance) – were common elements of the work of judges from both earlier periods and in other places. One area of difference might have been Fatimid insistence on allocating control of the minting of coins and the bureau of weights and measures to the qadi, but even that was not entirely new at the time. Much later it became a great rarity; Mamluk-era historians in fact marveled at the practice, obviously envious of the good order it had provided the currency when it had been the rule rather than the exception in a later age of constant debasing of the coinage.

An important aspect of the Fatimid chief justice's role was its territorial scope. He was to control and supervise all judges throughout the empire including those areas, such as the Maghrib and Sicily, ruled by vassal states that were otherwise not directly under the command of the caliph. How this responsibility, which presumably required him to appoint subordinate judges and other judicial officials, functioned is obscure to say the least. Surely the chief qadi in Cairo did not actually choose the judges for the cities of Sicily or North Africa. The information available provides examples of his authority to appoint subordinates only for Egypt. Nonetheless, the decrees that invested these men with this highest judicial office cite his authority over specifically named regions and they consistently include North Africa, the Holy Cities of the Hijaz and the military districts of Syria-Palestine.

In addition, where the chronology of the *wasita*s is often vague, that of the chief judges under al-Hakim is not in doubt. The holders of the highest office were in order: Muhammad b. al-Nuʿman until his death on 25 January 999; Husayn b. ʿAli b. al-Nuʿman, nephew of the previous qadi, from 999 until he was demoted on 7 July 1004 and executed on 23 October 1004; ʿAbd al-ʿAziz b. Muhammad b. al-Nuʿman, cousin of the former and his long time rival, until the elevation of Malik b. Saʿid al-Fariqi on 27 March 1008; al-Fariqi lasted until his execution on 11 September 1017; and finally Ahmad b. Muhammad b. ʿAbdallah b. Abi al-ʿAwwam, who outlasted al-Hakim himself.

The first four of these justices also held the post of chief *daʿi*, the head of the *daʿwa*, which nonetheless was not a part of the judiciary. Still the exact relationship of the two positions was not always completely separate and distinct. In his outline of Fatimid administration, al-Maqrizi comments curiously that, if one man held both, he had the right to drums and bugles when he rode in formal processions, otherwise he did not.

The first major event in this succession occurred upon the death of the chief justice Muhammad b. al-Nuʿman in 999, in January, just a month before al-Hakim turned 14.[155] This Muhammad was the same person who had accepted the responsibility for arranging the transition from al-ʿAziz, under whom he had risen to his own post in 984, long before.[156] He was highly respected, well known for his legal knowledge and for his careful administration. By the time of his death, he had occupied the post of chief justice for more than fourteen years. For much of that period he suffered from chronic bouts of gout and colic often so serious that he had to delegate his court duties to his son ʿAbd al-ʿAziz. Though ill and confined to his home over the last year, Barjawan would himself come, in spite of the demands of his exalted position as *wasita*, to visit every Thursday. That he did so was a clear indication of Muhammad's lofty status.

Nevertheless, after an audit of the man's estate, a sum of either 20,000 or 36,000 dinars—both figures are reported—was found missing from it. That amount should have been available to repay the funds deposited with the judge over the years for orphans.[157] Such monies should have been restored to the heir of the deceased when the child reached maturity. Once notified that they were gone, al-Hakim promptly ordered Barjawan to investigate. The latter sent his secretary Fahd to do a detailed inventory of what was left. Subsequently it became necessary to seize and sell the judge's processions in order to settle the claims that arose over the missing funds. Portions of the debt in this case had been deposited with the judge by notaries. They now insisted that the qadi had taken it from them improperly. Some could prove the allegation by producing a document written by the qadi himself. They were absolved. Those who could not were fined. Despite such efforts on the part of the authorities, they managed to raise from either the estate of the judge or from these fines only half of the lost amount. As a result they paid the claimants much less than due. It was a public scandal, and clearly an embarrassment for the government, even for the caliph himself.[158]

Funds belonging to orphans and those whose heirs happened to be absent ultimately fell to the responsibility of the qadi. That was the normal practice, but it created a situation in which the possibility of corruption was always present. However, incompetent or incomplete record keeping, rather than deliberate fraud, produced a similar result. While a qadi lived, his own funds and those he held in trust came and went. The latter were always a temptation; many judges borrowed from these funds, intending eventually to repay what they had taken. If, before he could, death intervened, the original intention might be lost. Subsequently the debt turned into a charge against his estate. Following the scandal created by a judge appointed by him, al-Hakim attempted to correct the system itself. He issued an order that no judge or notary should thereafter hold funds belonging to orphans or those who were absent. The government leased a storehouse in the Lamp Maker's Alley as a repository where all such monies were to be kept in the future. Four notaries were assigned the duty of locking and sealing it each time funds went in or out, and all four had to be present on any such occasion.[159]

Following Muhammad, the country then waited seventeen days for the appointment of a new chief judge. Eventually Barjawan called in Husayn b. 'Ali b. al-Nu'man[160], nephew of the deceased judge, for an audience with the caliph. Along with his appointment this man was granted a generous salary, in addition to bonuses and fiefs, all of which were double those of his uncle. They came, however, with the stern warning that he should not be tempted in any manner by the funds of another person even when held merely in trust. Following the bestowal of a white robe, a cloak with gold thread, a turban likewise with gold, a mule to ride and two to carry many other gifts, the decree of his appointment was read out in public. A copy of it survives. It states clearly that he was, among other specific provisions mentioned, to assume responsibility for the administration of justice in all portions of the empire. He was thus to supervise subordinate judges in all the territories under Fatimid rule, including North Africa, Sicily, Syria and the Hijaz. His responsibilities also gave him control of mosques, the mint, weights and measures, and matters of inheritance. From citations recorded in our histories we learn the names of a few of the subordinates he appointed, even for duties in and around Cairo. His authority was to be extensive and his status extremely high. Moreover, in addition, a separate commission granted him direction of the Ismaili *da'wa*, its appeal, and the agents who taught and propagated its doctrine. As his grandfather, father, and uncle had done before him, Husayn, not only functioned as chief qadi, but thereafter composed and read weekly lesson to the Ismailis as part of the Sessions of Wisdom, the *Majlis al-hikma*.[161]

The Decree of Investiture for al-Husayn b. 'Ali b. al-Nu'man

Lacking any other examples from the period of al-Hakim – in fact we have none for the many other offices in his administration – the decree in favor of Husayn offers a unique opportunity to read the exact language used by his government to express the imam's policy in making this appointment (or any appointment for that matter): what did the caliph expect of his chief justice and precisely what duties does the document specify for this office. Though drafted in the chancery, it states the policy of the ruler. Moreover, it is the sole example we possess from al-Hakim's time. Here are the main points of the text.[162]

> This is what the servant of God and His agent al-Mansur Abu 'Ali al-Hakim bi-Amr Allah, Commander of the Believers, entrusts to the qadi Husayn b. 'Ali b. al-Nu'man in appointing him to act as presiding judge over Cairo the Victorious, and Fustat, Alexandria and its dependencies, the Holy Cities [Mecca and Madina], may God the exalted protect them both, the military districts of Syria, and the governorates of the Maghrib, along with [responsibility for] those mounting the pulpits, the leaders of the congregational mosques and those assigned to look after them, and those who call to prayer, the rest of those who operate in these and others of the mosques. He is to supervise all matters pertaining to their welfare and he is to oversee the mint and the weighing of gold and silver. This is in addition to what the Commander of the Believers may employ him to do or not do, have in mind for him or propose to him, in following his examples or his being brought to a certain choice based on what is widely accepted and current among all the people of distinction in the state ... . There is no success except through God, the Patron of the Commander of the Believers, He on whom both he and the rest of the Muslims rely for the good things in what matters of theirs that God appoints and assigns to him. ....
>
> [The caliph] orders him to arrange his sitting for judgment in places near the vicinities of the litigants, to remove barriers and open his doors to them, to make his court session agreeable to all, to divide between them his phrases proportionately, not to favor in that a powerful man because of his power nor to ruin in that a weak man because of his weakness, but rather lean to the truth and incline in its direction, upholding thus the truth always and maintain the balanced scale. ...
>
> [The caliph] commands him to take great care in supervising the notary witnesses who fall under him and who affect deeply the implementing of judgments and extracting of decisions. Try to see into their conditions with

appropriate perception, apprehending their private affairs with sufficient realization. He should ask about their religious schools, investigating their private and public lives, affairs that are open and those keep secret. Those of them he finds are just and of good faith, upright and self-respecting, intent on the truth, bearing witness to what is right, of good character, a manner near to perfection, he will retain ... .

[The caliph] orders him to act in accord with the standard set for him by the Commander of the Believers in regard to those in charge of the funds of orphans and of bequests, those persons who are defective in the mind, those unable to handle their own funds. He is to proceed in a way that these matters will be in conformity with what pleases God and His agent, protecting them and preserving through those trustworthy persons assigned over them ... .

[The caliph] orders him to supervise the imams of the congregational mosques and the administrators of them, the preachers in them, those who give the call to prayer, and the rest of those involved in serving it. His supervision will not permit faults to enter any thing pertaining thereto: from the cleaning of its courtyard and open spaces, replacing its mats that are used at appropriate times, furnishing them with lamps at times that need them, announcing prayers at the hour for them, and the *iqama* at the times for it, having them fulfill the duty of *rak'a*s and prostrations, along with observing the stipulations and measures for them without innovation or any thing in them left out. 'Most certainly prayers are for the believers at times fixed' [Q 4: 103].

[The caliph] commands him to watch over the mint and the weighing of gold and silver by means of trustworthy persons who guard both from every sort of adulteration. Those who work in either will not have the means to introduce into the operation any manner of debasement; because it is through cash and coin that tenements, estates and goods are obtained, slaves purchased, marriages contracted, claims paid. The introduction of deception and the entry of any thing like it is injurious to the religion and causes harm to the Muslims. The Commander of the Believers declares to God that he is innocent of both. ...

This is what the Commander of the Believers has commissioned. Fulfill his commission, being led by his guidance, directed by his direction....

Written on Sunday seven nights remaining in Safar 389 [12 February 999].

One notable aspect of the chief qadi's responsibilities is supervision of the mosques and all those who work in them, for example, the prayer leaders and the *mu'adhdhins*. The proper order of a congregational mosque and its observance of ritual performances was thus a part of his commission. He likewise had to hire and regulate the preachers (men who delivered the Friday sermon), which included the politically and religiously charged naming of the ruler by asking for God to bless him. Curiously the only preachers mentioned specifically for the years of al-Hakim were either of two brothers, Ahmad and 'Ali, the sons of 'Abd al-Sami', who had been the leading preacher of Egypt when the Fatimids first took over. Ironically, he and his sons carried the kinship name *al-'Abbasi*, the Abbasid, indicating that they were members of the rival caliph's own family.

Husayn had once been stabbed in the mosque while performing his duties and so al-Hakim allocated him a detachment of leading members of the paramilitary *adyaf* corps to ride with him to each session of court and another group of them to walk before him every day with swords drawn. When he was present at the Old Mosque and began his prayers, these *adyaf* stood in a row behind him in order to shield him. None of them said prayers until he had finished his and had returned to his court session. When he sat in court, they would stand to his left and right. He was the very first judge for whom that was done.[163] As well he was, according to reports, the first to have written into his decree of appointment the title Judge of Judges (*qadi al-qudat*).[164]

We have a short list of his subordinates: al-Husayn b. Muhammad b. Tahir was his judge in Fustat, Malik b. Sa'id al-Fariqi, in Cairo, his brother al-Nu'man was to oversee weights and measures and to be qadi of Alexandria, and Ibn Abi'l-'Awwam was given responsibility for the division of inheritances.

His status with al-Hakim rose quite high and the caliph relied on him privately as well as publicly. A group around al-Hakim would speak his praises and go to lengths in extolling him. One among them was Rayhan al-Lihyani, another Zaydan, and yet another Muflih al-Lihyani. His influence spread and his importance became great. He did not apply coercion in a dispute between a man and his wife, or treat the people harshly. But, if a notary witness was slow to arrive at his house to ride with him on a day when he sat in the mosque, he would note it and fine the man an amount as a reproach. He forced his clerks into a constant attendance at his house.

From the first there was trouble between the two cousins Husayn b. 'Ali and 'Abd al-'Aziz b. Muhammad and the matter grew ever more serious. Al-Maqrizi reports that the people fell into harm and misfortune in the struggle between ʿAbd al-ʿAziz and the chief qadi Husayn.[165] ʿAbd al-ʿAziz accepted the testimony of a group of notary witnesses that he had chosen personally. A litigant whose opponent had gone before Husayn might then decide to take the case to ʿAbd al-ʿAziz, or vice versa. When ʿAbd al-ʿAziz sat to hear a case of grievance, his witnesses would be there and he would hear their testimony by having them testify concerning what was happening and what had transpired. None of them attended Husayn or came near his house. Testimony there was confined to the old witnesses who testified for him but who were not present at the court of ʿAbd al-ʿAziz in that connection and who had not ridden with him.

Al-Hakim had tried to resolve the dispute amicably; recall his personal note to the chief judge that read in part:

> O Husayn, may God be good to you. I have been apprised of the nasty rumors running about among the people and those up to no good, and their spreading lies. We renounce anything of the kind in regard to one who occupies the position you hold in our service, for you are our qadi, our *daʿi* and our trusted friend. We propose to put an end to that. .... The fine opinion we have of you will provide you felicity in this world and in the next. ....[166]

However, on 7 July 1004, ʿAbd al-ʿAziz was appointed judge, in addition to the duties he already held in regard to the court of grievances. A robe of honor was given him; he was girt with a sword embossed with gold, carried away on a mule with a basket of fine clothes in front. He went out in a great procession to the Old Mosque, where he sat beneath the pulpit as Abu ʿAli Ahmad ibn ʿAbd al-Samiʿ mounted it and read out his decree of appointment. Then he departed for his house, settled into it and commenced judging. He delegated to Abu'l-Hasan Malik b. Saʿid al-Fariqi the judgeship for Cairo in addition to the similar position he already held as deputy. Abu Yusuf Bayan was given the job of court clerk and recorder. Shortly thereafter another decree had ʿAbd al-ʿAziz receive the two fees, the *fitra* and *najwa*, paid by those Ismailis who attend the Sessions of Wisdom at the palace. He was also to administer the appeal to the people and read what was read to those who entered the *daʿwa*.[167] His decree mentioned, we are told, his authority over Cairo, Fustat, Alexandria, the Holy Cities, the military districts of Syria, of al-Rahba, of al-Raqqa, and of the Maghrib and its dependencies. One additional note in the sources indicates that, as chief judge, he was to supervise the caliph's new House of Knowledge, the Dar al-'ilm, created in 1005.

On Thursday 16 July, he was present and read what was normally read in the palace and he collected the *fitra* and *najwa*. He suspended all of the notary witnesses that Husayn in his day had accepted and he removed some of those deputized to act in outlying districts. He made Abu Talib the son of al-Sanadi, clerk who stood next to him. Abu'l-Qasim ʿAli b. ʿUmar al-Warraq was also made clerk. This man wrote out the decrees, records of cases and judgments. Husayn b. ʿAli was confined to his house and his fear intensified. The records of the judiciary were moved from his house to that of ʿAbd al-ʿAziz.[168]

The total length of Husayn's supervision of the judiciary had been five years, six months and 23 days. He was born in 969 in the Maghrib. He was, al-Maqrizi adds, coincidently the first judge to be burned after being executed. Al-Hakim had him burned after killing him on 23 October 1004.[169] According to the account of al-Nuwayri, the caliph rode on that day in procession with the elite. They passed by a place selling firewood that was stacked on the spot in great quantities. Al-Hakim stopped, ordered a fire to be ignited in a portion of the stack. He commanded Husayn to dismount whereupon he was thrown into the fire and died. There was apparently no advance warning; the rest of the party then proceeded on as if nothing had happened.

Ultimately, ʿAbd al-ʿAziz, who, like Husayn, was born in the Maghrib in 965, fared no better than his predecessor, eventually himself falling from grace, leading finally to his death. His fate, however, was closely bound up with that of Husayn ibn Jawhar. The two, who were related by marriage, suffered having to flee Cairo on two separate occasions only to return each time and, in the end, face execution in the palace. The exact cause of al-Hakim's anger is uncertain.[170] Given that Husayn was involved along with ʿAbd al-ʿAziz, the latter's performance as a judge may not have contributed directly to his demise as much as his association with his in-law.

ʿAbd al-ʿAziz had been the fifth member of his family to hold what was basically an analogous degree of responsibility. He was also the third of them to have such a position during the reign of al-Hakim. But, when the caliph decided to remove him in 1008, the imam declined to continue what may have by then seemed a tradition. Instead of yet another descendant of al-Nuʿman, he selected for the combined office of judge and *daʿi* al-Fariqi, who had been previously qadi of Cairo. In fact Malik had been a major figure in the judiciary for the past 13 years and was the senior judge within the system. His elevation to the supreme rank of *qadi al-qudat* was therefore natural, except in that such a move ended the dominance of the al-Nuʿman family. Malik was also appointed *daʿi al-duʿat* and that suggests that he had strong ties to the

Ismaili community and was viewed as one of them. Or, at the least, he was considered religiously devoted to al-Hakim, the imam for whom the *daʿwa* made its appeal. Unfortunately, there is no information about Malik's background beyond the name of his father, Saʿid, and grandfather, Malik, and the other members of his immediate family and the *nisba* of origin *al-fariqi*, which means someone from Mayyafariqin, a town in the Diyarbakr region of north Mesopotamia. This *nisba* obviously became the equivalent of a family name for the many al-Fariqis, although alone it says little about why.

The investiture of Malik and the accompanying ceremony is, accordingly, described more fully than for most other instances of the kind. Al-Musabbihi had copied Malik's decree of appointment into his account verbatim and must have observed personally the event as a whole. The new supreme judge received his gold threaded robes and turban, and sword in the palace. He was also given one richly caparisoned mule and two others loaded with luxurious goods. As his decree was being read out to those assembled in the palace, Malik stood and, at each mention of al-Hakim's name, he knelt down and kissed the floor. After completion of this ceremony, the entire court with all its notables proceeded *en masse* from Cairo to Fustat and to a repetition of the same formalities in the Old Mosque.

Malik was himself noted for his eloquence, for his clemency, above all for his generosity. The latter trait seems to have left a distinct impression and he was later remembered for having never turned away those who sought his help. There are several examples of his judicial acts in which, to solve a hotly disputed matter between contesting parties, he provided funds for a settlement out of his own pocket. A woman claimed that she had been married to a man who denied it. The judge gave the man money with which he could then arrange a divorce for the woman by their paying an agreed compensation out of these same funds. In another instance, a dispute about whether a woman owned a house or whether it was *waqf* trust property was solved when the judge donated his own money to settle the matter. Yet one more case involved a man accused of stealing silver candlesticks from the mosque in Fustat. The man's excuse was that the candlesticks were God's property and his daughters were destitute and hungry. The qadi again used his own funds to provide for these same daughters and the candlesticks were promptly restored to the mosque.

Not all such stories were as simple or could be resolved as happily. In one more instance of the judge's penchant for generosity, it caused him considerable risk and eventual peril. It occurred during the period when al-Hakim had ordered that no woman should appear on the street and, to make sure that it did not happen, had actually forbidden shoemakers from fashioning shoes for women so that they would be physically unable to go out at all. Malik happened to pass by a house from which he heard a woman pleading for help and calling out to him. She said that her brother was in a terrible way and that she wanted to go to see him before he died. The judge, at great risk to himself, took pity on her and, in direct violation of the law, had her escorted by his men to the brother's house and once there locked securely inside. A short time later, he began to realize his mistake and suspect the worst. The woman's husband soon appeared before him asking the whereabouts of his wife, who, he swore up and down, had no brother. The judge then knew he had aided and abetted the commission of a horrendous evil and not the least of his misdeeds had been to countermand the explicit order of al-Hakim. Understanding that the imam would soon know everything, he went immediately to explain his error and beg forgiveness, which was, apparently, granted. The police were dispatched at once to the house where, upon entering, they discovered the woman and her lover quite intoxicated and sound asleep, wrapped in each other's arms. Both, needless to say, suffered the severest punishment.

Despite this last episode and in all likelihood because of the other instances of his unfailing generosity, al-Hakim clearly favored Malik in ways that he had not any of Qadi al-Nu'man's descendants. In fact there is a fair amount of evidence that al-Hakim distrusted all of the latter's family. On Malik, by contrast, he showered gifts of material goods and properties of land. On one occasion al-Hakim gave him outright a grand house that formerly belonged to the amir Muflih, who was known as the 'Bearded (eunuch),' including with it all of the sumptuous contents that were to be found inside. Al-Hakim kept raising Malik's status, bringing him into an ever more intimate relationship with the imam. He, for example, ate constantly at al-Hakim's table, where he was seated in a more lofty position than any judge who preceded him. On public occasions Malik ascended the *minbar* with the caliph and, for the years 1009 and 1012, al-Hakim delegated him to lead prayers, give the *khutba*-sermon, and make the sacrifice on the feast days in the imam's own place.

The range of Malik's duties included all those of his predecessors and one list of them specifies the following: the judiciary, the court of appeals against injustices, supervision of pious endowments, the religious appeal, the mint, the bureau of weights and measures, and command of the *adyaf* corps (*amr al-adyaf*). To oversee all of these institutions personally would have been impossible; Malik obviously had to delegate many matters and some of his deputies are named in the sources. But the demands on his time were even more extreme than indicated by this list. Al-Hakim required his presence constantly and yet Malik also enthusiastically performed, not merely his duties as a judge, but those of chief *daʿi* in addition.

Nevertheless, despite ample evidence of the high regard al-Hakim had for al-Fariqi, in the year 1017, after he had held office for six years, nine months and 21 days, the imam ordered his execution. The cause is reported to have been Malik's visits to the house of Sitt al-Mulk, complicity with whom the imam regarded as treason in some manner. Nothing in this affair is quite clear; but it is the only information available to explain al-Fariqi's sudden fall from favor. Even after putting Malik to death, al-Hakim honored his two sons, the older, Abu'l-Faraj, by having him ride in public processions and the younger by allowing both to inherit their father's land holdings completely even though much, if not most, of the estate had been a gift from the imam. The net income from it is reported to have been 15 thousand dinars per annum; the sons of Malik were thus very rich indeed.[171]

The death of the highly respected al-Fariqi added to the general turmoil and unease throughout an already unstable government. The anomalous appointment at that time of Ibn Ilyas as heir rather than al-Hakim's own son created doubt in the most loyal of followers. In this situation the caliph did away with his *wasita* and made yet one more surprising move. He took the general administration on himself. However, he also soon realized that he could not do without a chief judge for long. Among those few individuals he himself held in respect one was the blind lexicographer and grammarian Abu'l-Fadl Jaʿfar, whom al-Hakim had dubbed 'The Scholar of Scholars' (*ʿAlim al-ʿulamaʾ*) and assigned a post in the Dar al-ʿilm. Al-Hakim tried out on him the names of various candidates for the judgeship until they came to that of the Hanafi jurist Ibn Abi'l-ʿAwwam, one of al-Fariqi's deputies. Jaʿfar replied that, although the man was 'a supremely competent Egyptian and was fully conversant with the judiciary and the people of the country – there being no Egyptian better suited for the job than he – he does not belong to your religious school nor that of your forefathers.' In other words the man was not an Ismaili. Nonetheless, al-Hakim accepted this advice and made the appointment[172], requiring only that four Ismaili jurists were to sit in his court in case a matter arose in which the Ismaili legal view should prevail. Naturally, the decree of appointment, which gave Ibn Abi'l-ʿAwwam control of the judiciary for the whole of the empire – except Palestine[173] – did not include the *da'wa*, which remained, therefore, for the moment without direction.

Honors were then given to Ibn Abi'l-'Awwam along with the decree appointing him the judge of judges. He was born in Egypt in 958 and had been a witness for Muhammad b. al-Nu'man, later assuming charge of the divisions of inheritances. There may be some special importance in Ja'far's comment about the judge's Egyptian background. Al-Hakim himself was born in Egypt. Significantly the two members of al-Nu'man's family he demoted and executed were both born in North Africa.

The new chief justice was carried away on a mule with a saddle and bridle plated with gold. Another mule was led before him. He went down to the mosque where his decree was read from the pulpit. It said, in part, 'The Commander of the Believers appoints you to the judiciary, prayer, sermons in his presences and to issue binding rulings in situations beyond his curtain in Cairo, Fustat, and their districts, Alexandria, the Holy Cities, Barqa, the Maghrib and Sicily, along with supervision of the mint in these governorates, control of the trusts of the congregational and other mosques, ... and grants you the power to appoint deputy judges.' The office of the judiciary was transported from the house of Malik b. Sa'id to the treasury of the Old Mosque. Ibn Abi'l-'Awwam was the first of the judges to do that. The office of the judges had been in their homes. He moved it to the mosque and held his court sessions in the Old Mosque on two days, Monday and Thursday, and in Cairo on Wednesday and for attendance at the palace he reserved Sundays.

The Da'wa

In 1010, Qirwash b. al-Muqallad, the 'Uqaylid ruler of north Mesopotamia, a supporter of the Abbasids, switched his allegiance to al-Hakim. In doing so he in fact set up a *da'wa*, an appeal, in the latter's name. A *da'wa* is a call for allegiance, a summons to a specific cause. In this case it involved not merely proclaiming loyalty to al-Hakim in the political sense but religiously as well. It seems that, by accepting the caliphate of the Fatimids, Qirwash had declared himself to be a Shiite instead of a Sunni Muslim.

In typical fashion the formal public declaration of the change occurred in the next Friday *khutba*-sermon. The 'Uqaylid ruler handed the preacher (*khatib*) the text of his new sermon and the man dutifully read it to the assembled worshippers. In his invocation of the name of al-Hakim as caliph, he, too, had overnight become Shiite. Two months later, the same or a similar announcement greeted the Muslim community in the congregational mosque of al-Anbar and one week after that also in al-Mada'in and Qasr ibn Hubayra.[174] The cities that had unexpectedly gone over to the Fatimids formed what amounted to a noose around Baghdad. The Abbasid caliph could not but be alarmed; his position had, seemingly overnight, become perilous.[175] All around him the countryside was turning Shiite.

Ibn al-Jawzi, a Sunni historian writing in Baghdad at a much later date, reports that agents for al-Hakim worked persistently to win over the 'Uqaylids and eventually succeeded. Those very agents would have been Fatimid *daʿis*, members of the Ismaili *daʿwa*, a hierarchically organized network whose head was the imam and whose chief executive officer was the *daʿi al-duʿat*. Their conversion of the 'Uqaylids so close to Baghdad was a spectacular, if momentary, success, a clear indication that al-Hakim's *daʿwa*, though largely operating in secrecy outside of his domain, retained a potency powerful enough to threaten his most distant enemies.

The conversion of Qirwash, as it turned out, lapsed within a few months. He quickly reverted to the Abbasids. But other examples exist in which an important prince came to acknowledge the rights of al-Hakim due to the efforts of his world-wide *daʿwa*. Agents like those who had won over the 'Uqaylid ruler operated in all Muslim lands. Occasionally we know their names but mostly we do not. Obviously, outside the protection of the Fatimid state, the *daʿwa* necessarily acted underground clandestinely.

It would be useful to know more about it, particularly the details of how foreign operations related to the office of chief *daʿi* in Cairo. But for that we have only hints, little items of information, which, however, may add up and might provide, when all totaled, a more complete picture of the *daʿwa* in action. For example, al-Fariqi, says one report, received all the correspondence coming in from the *daʿis* abroad and then apprised the imam of what messages it contained and what was happening in the vast network elsewhere. A Syrian *daʿi*, Abu'l-Fawaris Ahmad b. Yaʿqub by name, was the agent ordered to arrange for the destruction of the Church of the Holy Sepulchre. The father of al-Mu'ayyad fi'l-din al-Shirazi, much later head of the *daʿwa* under the caliph al-Mustansir, was a *daʿi* in the Iranian province of Fars. He wrote to the imam to ask that his sons succeed him there. Hamid al-Din al-Kirmani, the most famous member of the *daʿwa* in al-Hakim's era, was active somewhere in Iraq until he came to Egypt in 1015. Once there he worked directly under the new chief *daʿi*, Khatkin al-Dayf, for several years before returning to the east.

Al-Maqrizi claims that Husayn b. ʿAli, the chief qadi, was the first to hold the title *daʿi al-duʿat* and that by formal decree. If, however, by this title, he refers to the preparing and reading of weekly homilies to the Ismaili community, that had been done as well by Husayn's predecessors back to Qadi al-Nuʿman himself. What appears to be different in the time of al-Hakim is the added responsibility of directing the *daʿwa* in general, both within the empire and abroad. For periods earlier our information is sketchy. One title mentioned is the *Bab al-Abwab* (Gate of Gates), apparently a person at the head of the *daʿwa* who controlled access to the imam. The earliest example was a man named Abu ʿAli, who had once much earlier also gone by the name Hamdan Qarmat. Upon his death in 934, his son Hasan assumed the same position which he continued to hold into the reign of al-ʿAziz.[176] Surely Hasan, this son of Abu ʿAli, had died long before the time of al-Hakim; and it appears quite reasonable to assume that one of the chief qadis who were also said to be chief *daʿi*s succeeded him. The problem remains, however, of how, or even whether, the *Bab al-Abwab* became the *Daʿi al-duʿat*. From Husayn onward, however, the matter of who ran the *daʿwa* is a bit clearer; the *daʿwa* was one of two offices that were held by the same person for the next 16 years.[177]

With the fall of Husayn in 1004 (he was executed in 1005), ʿAbd al-ʿAziz b. Muhammad rose to the position, only to lose it himself in 1008 (he was put to death three years later). Al-Maqrizi describes his initial elevation to the position of chief justice and then adds that,

> another decree had ʿAbd al-ʿAziz receive the two fees, the *fitra* and *najwa*, paid by those Ismailis who attend the sessions of wisdom at the palace. He was also to administer the appeal to the people and read what was read to those who entered the *daʿwa*. On Thursday 22 July[178], he was present and read what was normally read in the palace and he collected the *fitra* and *najwa*.[179]

The latter two items were, as al-Maqrizi says, the standard dues each faithful Ismaili paid to attend these sessions.

Here then is one account of the *daʿwa* in action. Unfortunately, reading these lessons and collecting dues must have been only the most obvious of its tasks. In that era it was the public face of an operation far more complex and sophisticated featuring a network of hundreds of agents spread throughout the Islamic world and even beyond.

Fortunately, several treatises by *daʿi*s of that period have come down to us. Two authors in particular supply important data and observations: al-

Kirmani and al-Naysaburi. From the latter we possess three works. One, the *Concealment of the Imam* (*Istitar al-imam*), concerns events in the early history of the Ismaili *daʿwa* that were long past by the author's time.[180] The other two are his treatise *Proof of the Imamate* (*Ithbat al-imama*), and another on the *daʿwa*, the *Concise Summary* (*Mujaza*). Near the beginning of former,[181] in the traditional section of benedictions for the prophet and the imams – and al-Hakim in particular as the living imam – he adds a note calling for such blessing to apply as well to 'the heir apparent, the successor to the Commander of the Believers' (*wali ʿahd al-muslimin wa khalifat amir al-muʾminin*). That phrase can only refer to the cousin of al-Hakim, ʿAbd al-Rahim ibn Ilyas, who was proclaimed heir apparent in 1013, and the titles for which office this man continued to hold until his death in 1021, shortly after the end of the reign. This formula became a standard phrase added to all public documents including coins over the whole of this same period. Al-Naysaburi's *Proof of the Imamate* was therefore a treatise written while that declaration was in effect.[182] It falls, moreover, in the years between 1017 and 1021. Despite all his fine and glorious traits, al-Hakim was, the author confesses, so unusual in his manner of rule no other Muslim leader was or had been like him. To judge him and his actions by the standard of human beings, al-Naysaburi claims, can only lead to confusion and possible rejection of his authority. Those who view what he does in its true light will see that his commands and prohibitions, his giving and his taking away, are to be compared with the acts of God, not with those of mere humans. Yet, many fail this test; they are thus perplexed by what they see or hear reported about the imam. The measure for human actions is simply not appropriate for him. But, also, some regard him with a tendency toward exaggeration and then, moving in the opposite direction, claim that he is, in fact, divine. It is necessary to avoid both these extremes, al-Naysaburi insists.

For him to confess so openly that some followers of al-Hakim regarded his unusual behavior as a sign of his divinity matches what we know about various groups that eventually coalesced into the Druze. They first went public with their claim about his divinity in the year 1017. Al-Naysaburi was evidently cautioning against them and what he considers their heresy. But, for him even to mention that possibility, if only to reject it, means that it was already happening at the time he wrote and is thus testimony about what was happening in this period. Evidently al-Naysaburi's status within the *daʿwa* was especially high during the last years of al-Hakim and that allowed him the authority to compose an extravagant defense of this imam and his rule against the exaggerators of his divinity.

The other treatise by him, the *Mujaza*, in the form it has come down to us, unfortunately, contains no precise information as to its date.[183] The work itself, however, is replete with advice, counsel and commands directed toward the proper comportment of the agents of the *da'wa*, its *da'is*. About this we have in all surprisingly little in other Ismaili works. Al-Naysaburi tells us what were the qualifications of the ideal agent and how he was to perform his duties. Portions of it follow:

> With respect to the ranking of religious matters, the *da'wa* is at the highest level and has the most exalted and sublime position. It is what the exalted God ascribed to His own self when He said: 'His [God's] is the *da'wa* of truth' [13:14].
>
> He who summons to God, to the imams, must himself perform good deeds, maintain prayers, both outwardly and inwardly, pay the alms tax, outwardly and inwardly, in compliance with the command of his superior. He will be a worshipper and one who commands good deeds and does them. He who is not knowledgeable nor does good deeds, does not maintain the appeal nor emanate knowledge upon those who deserve it among those novices he is supposed to educate, he is not fit to be a *da'i*.
>
> In the matter of false *da'is*, God has said: 'Truly, those who appeal other than to God will never create so much as a fly even if they join together for that purpose; and if the fly should rob anything from them, they could not rescue it from the fly so feeble are the seeker and the sought' [22:73]. This means that those who appeal to the false or to the imams of error are not able to create religious beings alive with knowledge even if they should all join together, and if a fly should steal anything they could not retrieve it from him.
>
> The *da'wa* is a difficult matter and its qualifications are many, including all that God has stipulated in the Qur'an to describe a believer as well as what the imams have specified in their books concerning the faithful. These things are required also of the *da'i*. He should have even more of these excellences and they should be more evident in him.
>
> The qualifications for the *da'wa* are based on three things: on knowledge, on God-fearing piety, and on governance. ....
>
> The *da'i* firstly requires governance of the individual, which means to govern his own self. Thus he provides for the welfare of his own soul, governing and controlling it, preventing it from having any of the vices and any bad habits of character, keeping it from reprehensible desire for things

that are illicit, bearing itself in conformity with the virtuous, and fulfilling required duties and established regulations. He will censure himself sincerely if he behaves badly, accompanying that with condemnation, regret, reproach and repentance, and he will reward himself if he is good with delight, praise and the urging of more fine actions and drawing on knowledge in order to direct the novice to it so as to have him adopt his own fine character, follow his words, actions and wise lead.

Governance of the household is the governing by a man of his own family and retainers, controlling them, teaching and educating them, instilling the virtues in them and preventing vices, rewarding those who are good, punishing those who are bad. ... He who succeeds in governing himself and his family is fit to have charge of governing the rest of the people in matters of faith and he who cannot govern himself and his family is not fit to be a *da'i.*

Governance of the community involves supporting the administration of the person who is their leader in matters of the welfare of this life and of their salvation, who teaches them the discipline of communal laws, keeps them from reprehensible and illicit actions, promotes the virtues, rewards those who do good and punishes those who do evil. It is he who is responsible for the well-being of their religion. A person who is not good at the governance of the individual, the family, and the community is not fit for the *da'wa.*

The *da'i* must educate the *da'i* below him in knowledge, test and try him and arrange his affairs, punishing and rewarding him, each according to his rank ... A person lacking these three forms of governance cannot be a *da'i.*

If the qualifications we have mentioned are not truly in the *da'i* and yet he is called a *da'i*, it is a name devoid of meaning and is of no avail and no benefit. Rather it is a curse on him, an offense and crime that counts against him.

We hold that the *da'i* must be firmly grounded in the principles of the religion to which he summons with a sincerity and certainty untainted or mixed with another purpose, loyal to the imam for whom he appeals and to the messenger who is the foundation of the religion on whom, to whom, and by whom the *da'wa* is based.

He must be sound of opinion and skilled in administration. The affairs of the *da'wa* cannot be carried out by bad administration of them. If an error occurs in his administration of the *da'wa*, it will corrupt it, destroy those who believe in it, and there will be no way or any means to correct it.

He must keep secret what is secret. Religion is based on the preservation of secrets that need to be kept from those who are not worthy of them.

He will be able to take the measure of everyone by observing them and listening to their words. He thus learns about those best suited to religion and those not so, or whose purpose is religious and whose is not religious, who is able to acquire knowledge and who is unable.

He should be well acquainted with the lives of the imams, the arrangement of their *da'was* so that he can follow them, and their example and their traditions.

A *da'i* should dispatch to the various regions *da'is* who speak the language there.

A *da'i* must be acquainted with the religious proclivities of the inhabitants of each region, their knowledge and natures, and what they might be inclined to accept and their aptitude for knowledge so that he can overcome them in debate and disputation with them and have them come to accept knowledge from him.

He must not take a risk with anybody who has not been tested and has not proven himself and for whom there is no evidence of his integrity. A *da'i* should not invest a person with authority in the *da'wa* unless he has served previously and shown that he can guide and has been found acceptable to all. Only at that point should he be relied upon. ... If he is not suitable for the *da'wa*, the *da'i* is not permitted to employ him in the *da'wa* and thereby put at risk the souls and property of the believers. If he errs in that, it is not like treachery in monies because, in something like this, there is the destruction of the inhabitants of the provinces due to the corruption of the *da'is*, the wickedness of their administration, the magnitude of their greed, and their lack of piety and knowledge. On the measure of the risks and their difficulty it requires investigation and special effort in choosing the *da'i*, most especially in provinces that are under the control of iniquitous sultans.

At all times he should exhort those who attend his session by urging them to be thankful for what they have and by recalling for them the hardships that occurred in other moments. When an emissary from one of the other regions or an immigrant or a visitor comes, he should look into his situation with respect to his position, make him feel at ease, and encourage and reward him. Indeed God will not lose his reward or block it. He should not ask, 'What have you come for?' and 'Who invited you?' 'Coming is not up to you!' 'Times are hard and corrupt and the government has no money to give you. In fact the imam is averse to a group such as this.' 'The Commander of the Believers will be angry with you and fed up with you, and he turns his face toward others than you.' That would merely break their hearts and weaken their resolve, crushing their hope of any good. His duty is instead to gladden their hearts, give them hope, and have them anticipate the kindness of the Commander of the Believers and his good will.

When necessary, the *da'i* should spend of the personal funds that have been granted him by the Commander of the Believers on matters connected to the benefit of the *daʿwa* which are not in doubt and are of such a kind that it is not possible to take the matter to the government and make a request for it, since not to do so at the moment, would bring harm upon the *daʿwa*. In this respect, the *da'i* in the religious affairs of the members of the *daʿwa* is like a mother the man casts his sperm into but she preserves it, puts up with it, forms it, and prepares it until the completion of its gestation. Next she raises the child, preserving it from water and fire. Then she arranges for its nourishment, its care, and its education. The father is responsible only to provide for her maintenance.

In a similar way, the *da'i* should promote unity and amicability in the hearts of the believers, bringing them into harmony with each other, prompting them to mutual aid and love, and to the cooperation of some with the others, and warn them against envy, malice, slander, and hostility toward one another.

The *da'i* must constantly entreat the believers to obey the imam and love him, appeal for him, dedicating their wealth and souls to his cause, and in pleasing him and obeying him, and undertaking holy war with him if he so orders them. The *da'i* should make clear to them that God is pleased by his being pleased and obeying Him means obeying him; their salvation lies in obeying and in pleasing him. Also he will make clear that there is no obligation of any kind on the imam. What is bestowed on the people by the imam in the way of worldly goods and knowledge, he does as a favor and a kindness and what he holds back he does so justly.

Assuming that, in part, al-Naysaburi's stipulations, which combine in any case rules covering both theoretical and practical aspects of the work of the *daʿwa*, were to apply broadly during that time, he may have provided us the most detailed outline of its form and function available. Yet other hints in it also point to the troubles and uncertainty of the period. For that we need to return to the record of successive chief *da'is* and their apparent failures.

'Abd al-'Aziz's successor was Malik b. Sa'id al-Fariqi. The first from outside the clan of al-Nu'man, Malik was extremely active in pursuit of his duties as head of the *da'wa*. As *da'i al-du'at*, it was al-Fariqi who regularly prepared and read the various weekly *majlis al-hikma*, which during his tenure increased in frequency to as many as five a week, each given in a different place and for a different audience. Number 42 of the Druze *Epistles*, by Baha' al-Din, mentions, for example, a 144th *majlis* that was read to the faithful by Malik. It is unclear, however, if this citation implies that this was Malik's own *majlis* number 144, which would mean that he had already himself given well over 100 prior to it. There are additional citations of *majlis* by 'Abd al-'Aziz and al-Fariqi in the Druze epistles indicating how active either one had been and how much of what they produced once existed. In that sense the *da'wa* under al-Hakim was a flourishing institution.[184]

But Malik, too, like his three predecessors, eventually ran afoul of the imam and was himself put to death in 1014 for reasons that are nowhere clearly explained. With this event, this series of joint appointments to the judiciary and the *da'wa* ended. As natural as it had been for the same person to function in both capacities, it is not certain that there ever was a policy of combining them.

After a brief hiatus in 1015, al-Hakim soon decided to appoint Ibn Abi'l-'Awwam to the position of chief qadi. Ibn Abi'l-'Awwam was not an Ismaili, a fact that did not preclude assuming the supreme judicial office. He had already served in subordinate legal positions for many years and his general qualifications as a judge were never in doubt. But, as a Hanafi, he obviously could not direct the Ismaili *da'wa*.

What then would happen to the *da'wa*? Al-Maqrizi reports that 'on 23 March 1014, those who had gathered at the palace to listen to the *majlis* had found that they were prevented from doing so.' How long did this particular closing last? What relationship did this have to the subsequent death of al-Fariqi and the decision to appoint a non-Ismaili to the position of *qadi al-qudat*?

This function of the *da'i*'s office had been shut down by al-Hakim before. We know of three occasions during the reign when such an event took place. From the year 1006, prior to canceling his insistence on cursing the Companions, which this caliph first ordered in 1004 and then rescinded in 1007, al-Hakim sharply rebuked his own Ismaili followers. Al-Maqrizi, the principal source for this information, does not say much but he does report that some four months prior to the edict commanding tolerance, when the

Ismailis gathered for the *majlis* at the palace, they were beaten instead and nothing was read on that occasion.[185] Although during the course of the following year, 1008, the imam removed the head of his judiciary who also was the chief *daʿi* – the *daʿi al-duʿat* – from office, there appears to be no connection with that later event and the closing of the *majlis* a year or more before. Nevertheless, two years afterward, in the midst of a policy shift away from strict Shiism, another closing occurred. Numerous edicts about religious policy were issued at the time, generally, but not consistently, in favor of Sunni practices, and among them was one in 1010, 'canceling the collection by the *qadi/daʿi* of the *khums*, the *fitra*, and the *najwa*' – dues customarily paid by loyal Ismailis. Another, at the same time, ordered the 'cessation of the *majlis al-hikma*, which were ordinarily read to the Faithful each Thursday and Friday.'[186] But some five months later, perhaps slightly less, yet another decree 'restored the *majlis al-hikma* and the collection of the *najwa*.'[187] Shortly thereafter a new edict again stressed that no one is to object to whatever the imam does, nor to delve into matters beyond understanding. Elements of the Shiite cult were returned and 'the *daʿwa* and *majlis* were reinstated according to the usual pattern for them.'[188] Again the role of the chief *daʿi*, who would have been Malik b. Saʿid al-Fariqi, is not indicated. On the contrary this man who directed both the judiciary and the *daʿwa* retained the favor of al-Hakim for another three years.[189] Even so did the closing of the *majlis al-hikma* indicate the imam's displeasure with the chief *daʿi*, or was it a sign of dissatisfaction with something else in the *daʿwa*?

As he closes the *Concise Summary*, al-Naysaburi declares that,

> The heart of the imam is preoccupied with what ... happens to his community. He becomes impatient with them ..., he turns away and becomes angry ... Yet each day they increase their corruption and thus add to the chastisement in store. That becomes like *the corruption that we are seeing at the present moment*. We ask God for mercy and compassion ... and that He grant us repentance, ... and bring an end to actions like these and remorse on our part for what we did earlier. Perhaps God will incline the heart of the imam to feel compassion for his servants, restore them and show mercy ... and that he forgive us for what we did before which required this punishment by locking the door to repentance.

Obviously the imam is angry with his own followers who have done something '... which required this punishment by locking the door to repentance.'

The author's tone is quite specific; he surely speaks of events that either are happening as he writes or have occurred recently.

That the imam might express anger and displeasure with his *da'wa* and its *da'is* could have transpired on many occasions but, given the date already determined for al-Naysaburi's *Proof of the Imamate*, which indicates when its author was most active, the condition of the *da'wa* and its history during the same period is most likely the time of the 'corruption of ... the present moment,' when 'the door to repentance' was locked and the adherents of the *da'wa* excluded from the imam's mercy. A condition of that kind would explain the reasons for the author's forlorn wish for forgiveness.

There are, moreover, additional details in the final paragraphs of the *Mujaza* that appear to allude to serious issues that have arisen at the highest levels of the administration of the *da'wa*, particularly in relation to the governance of the Fatimid state as a whole. That concluding section begins to focus more narrowly on those few of such a lofty rank as to be directly in contact with the imam, that is, the leading *da'is* who hold offices close to him, most certainly to include the head of the *da'wa* the *da'i al-du'at*. Note that here the imam is alternately referred as to the imam and as the 'Commander of the Believers', a title normally reserved solely for the caliph.

For the present purpose the essential passages are the following:

> The *da'i* must see to the affairs of the *da'wa* and its proper administration, thereby relieving the imam of that obligation.... ... The *da'i* is responsible for the management of all the business of the *da'wa*, its administration and that of the various provinces.... It is the responsibility of the imam to provide him with knowledge and funds, but the *da'i* is responsible for the repair and amelioration of all corruption, trouble, the perversion of doctrine, doubt about religion, going astray, insurrection, and rebellion that happens in the *da'wa*. If he fails out of willfulness, or lack of effort on his part, carelessness, inattentiveness, or incapacity, he is the one who is accountable for the consequences. ... He is the one answerable for it and it was up to him to arrange matters. If he was unable, it was up to him to make his inability known to the Imam. ...
>
> The *da'i* ought to educate the believers properly so that they do not become, due to their neediness, a burden on the Commander of the Believers. If great harm does befall them, they may, at the proper time, in the correct manner and through the right channels, and on the measure of what they require, seek help from him. But they should not take advantage

of the imam's funds or seek more than that. ... The *da'i* will urge them to be pleased and content with the actions of the imam, and with his orders, prohibitions and rulings. They will not object to any part of it but rather know that all of it is in conformity with a vast wisdom. If they do not comprehend it at the time, they will come to understand the wisdom in it later. Because they understand that the imam is the wisest man in his time, it is essential that they know that all he does is done wisely, even though they may not perceive exactly how it is wise. It is like that with the actions of the imam.

The *da'i* should prepare and exhort the believers for service in an office or as an emissary if one of them is called upon to do so, either in a religious matter or one of the state, and urge them to carry out such duties in good faith, offer sound advice and sympathy, cautioning them against disloyalty, neglect, indolence, and cowardliness.

A *da'i* should know that the kingdom is the protector of the faith; the kingdom of the imam is built on religion. If the affairs of both the religion and the *da'wa* are in proper order and well maintained, the kingdom will run properly and without disorder. All of the populace will be servants of the imam, whether in his presence or in other regions; they become like his army, supporters and well-wishers, none able to betray or rebel against him. But should all the people become his adversaries, his enemies, and opponents and, if there are defects in the religion and the *da'i* is unable or is remiss in dealing with the governing of the religion and managing it, perhaps because he is himself ignorant or impious, or incompetent and unsound and untrustworthy, he will ruin the beliefs of the believers. They will apostatize and chaos will reign. ... They will become skeptical of religion and sick at heart, falling into antagonism, quarreling, fighting and treating each other treacherously, lying to one another in disloyalty and greed and usurping the rights of others, some of them against the rest. Thus harm comes to both the religion and the kingdom, the provinces fall into ruin, the people become enemies of one another. Security, decency, piety, life and honor cease. The people revert to their animal natures becoming like savage beasts, some attacking others.

The conditions that have alarmed al-Naysaburi so profoundly possess at least two features both causing the imam to express outwardly his anger: one seems to imply the failure of the *da'i* – here surely he mean the chief *da'i* – to perform his duties successfully, and second the closing of the *majlis al-hikma*, the regular weekly sessions of instruction for the faithful. In regard to the latter condition, we have seen already that, 'On 23 March 1014, those who had gathered at the palace to listen to the *majlis* had found that they were prevented from doing so.'[190] Not long after that, al-Hakim did away with al-Fariqi.

At this juncture we can turn to information supplied by our Melkite historian. Yahya says that:

> Al-Hakim had locked the door of the *majlis*, which was where he had himself received the oath of loyalty (*bay'a*) from his own *shi'a* and where their special wisdom (*'ulum*) was read to them. It remained locked for a period until Khatkin the *Dayf* was given the title *da'i al-du'at*. Al-Hakim returned control of the *majlis* to him and henceforth it functioned in the same manner as it had previously. Subsequent to that, al-Hakim added *al-Sadiq al-Amin* to Khatkin's title.[191]

Yahya does not say how long the *majlis* was closed this time but it cannot have been brief. Khatkin was not selected until well after the elevation of Ibn Abi'l-'Awwam, probably not until the summer of 1015.[192]

Having taken care of the judiciary, al-Hakim eventually turned to the *da'wa*, the direction of which he had recently let lapse. His choice for the new chief *da'i* was a prominent agent of his, Khatkin al-Dayf, a member, it seems, of a corps of *adyaf* who served possibly as a kind of paramilitary. Khatkin's previous career – he was twice Fatimid governor of Damascus, for example – did not fit that of most *da'is*. He was neither a preacher nor a teacher. His two predecessors had composed a great number of their own weekly lectures and collections of their writings were in circulation. Not so Khatkin. From the period of Khatkin's supervision of the *da'wa*, we have a number of important works by al-Kirmani, who spent time in Egypt at this juncture, quite likely at the invitation of Khatkin, the support of whom al-Kirmani explicitly credits. But nothing by Khatkin. Nonetheless, despite not composing or perhaps not even reading his own writings in the weekly sessions, Khatkin was clearly the *da'i al-du'at*. It was he who ran the affairs of the *da'wa*.

And Khatkin was even so evidently quite effective. Beginning in 1017 or slightly before, the *da'wa* had to confront a series of challenges to its authority raised by the leaders of various groups that later became the Druze. For a while the threat was serious but the *da'wa* survived this rebellion against its control eventually. Khatkin must have played a major part. Two of the five arch-villains in the Druze hierarchy are Khatkin, as the *da'i al-du'at*, and Ibn

Abi'l-ʿAwwam, as the *qadi al-qudat*, both of whom were responsible in part for the suppression of the earliest Druze and their prophet and messiah Hamza b. ʿAli. Druze doctrine thus confirms Khatkin's role. At the moment of al-Hakim's disappearance in 1021 both men, judge and *daʿi*, continued to hold their respective offices.

Additional evidence of a disturbance in the *daʿwa* just prior to the appointment of Khatkin comes from the testimony of al-Kirmani, who wrote his treatise *Glad Tidings of the Good News* (*Mabasim al-bisharat*) in the summer of 1015. The work of reconstituting the *daʿwa* had recently begun under Khatkin, although as yet al-Kirmani does not mention him. Surely al-Kirmani witnessed something of the unhappiness that previously prevailed amongst the faithful. From the other sources we have learned that al-Hakim had only recently shut down the *majlis al-hikma* and temporarily interrupted the system by which the *daʿwa* in Egypt provided contact and instruction to ordinary members of the Ismaili community. Further inside eyewitness testimony, obviously trustworthy, occurs in the following highly important passage of the *Happy Tidings* in which al-Kirmani speaks rather bluntly about the situation that awaited him when he arrived in Cairo in that very period.

> When as an immigrant (*muhajir*) I reached the Prophetic Presence, a pilgrim having come to the Aliid Seat, I beheld there a sky that had become dark with pervasive clouds, the people under the weight of a great tribulation, the observance of previous practices had been cancelled, and the faithful saints were kept from what they had earned. The practice of holding the Sessions of Wisdom (*majlis al-hikma*), which had provided them such a dividend of benefits, had been abandoned. The high among them were humbled; the low were on the rise. I observed that the saints of the Rightly Guiding *daʿwa* – may God spread far and wide their lights – and those most steeped in the defense of the imamate and most loyal to it had become confused by what had befallen them of such matters as to put premature gray in the temples and they were overwhelmed by the repetition of such conditions which rightly ought to destroy none but the perpetrators of hypocrisy and rebellion. They were then in the throes of causing agitation one upon the other, each person accusing his associate of deviation and violations. Evil thoughts were playing tricks on them and malicious insinuations circulated among them. Thus they could not perceive what plain smoke had covered them nor what obvious trials afflicted them. As a result some entered upon a course of extremism and ascended even to its uppermost limit.

> Some turned away from religion and abandoned the preservation of the faith and its bonds. A few even overturned the very pillars of their belief and what they had once accepted freely and willingly, having come to the brink of dissolution and disorder with necks outstretched to the misappropriation of the two horned devils, their ardor in searching for true belief frustrated. Only individuals among them approve by themselves of themselves since their spirits escaped by being reconciled in the words of God, 'He who is astray cannot harm you if you are properly guided.' [5: 105]
>
> A superabundance of concern for the faith prompted in me a desire to save these suffering brethren – except for those who had so corrupted their being with a transformed doctrine that their very elements were inverted because their own hearts had imbibed the water of change and they had become like burnt silver which no art can restore to its silverness or to its original state – by a regimen of effort and obedience that might fortify their hearts and put resolve back in their steps. [To accomplish this purpose I offer the following] clear affidavit of the imamate of the Imam al-Hakim bi-amr Allah, Commander of the Believers, and of its true reality ...

From this opening declaration, al-Kirmani proceeds to outline a complete endorsement for and defense of the imam and the imamate. Unlike much of his own previous writing, however, it is evident that here he is speaking directly to members of the Ismaili community, especially to those who have wavered and strayed from the accepted doctrine. He is attempting to bring order and calm back into the *da'wa*. Surely he wrote this treatise with official blessing, although it does not explicitly credit anyone but the imam. A note at the end states that he dictated it to the *mu'adhdhin* of the al-Azhar mosque. The next work by him, which must have been composed at about the same time, clearly identifies Khatkin as the chief *da'i* with an explicit recognition of his new role. By now Khatkin was, this treatise confirms, the 'door (*bab*) to the imam's mercy, entitled *al-Sadiq al-Ma'mun, da'i al-du'at*.' Khatkin's job was to order and protect 'the sons of the rightly guiding *da'wa*.'[193] This same title, *al-Sadiq al-Ma'mun*, is also mentioned by Yahya, thus confirming it and the event in question.

The Lesser Bureaucracy

Aside from the three offices just discussed in detail, there were many more at a lower rank. Information about them is, however, scarce. From much later – a full century and a half and near the end of Fatimid rule – we possess considerably more, including separate treatises on the practice of a specific bureau of government, as, for example, the chancery. Al-Maqrizi also compiled a series of notes on Fatimid administration, providing there a description of positions and responsibilities.[194] He recorded as well a scale of monthly salaries and that allows us to judge on that basis which were regarded as most important and which least. But does that help to indicate reliably what existed in the time of al-Hakim? It is hard to be sure.

Based strictly on reports from his era, we are limited to an occasional mention of this or that bureau or department, often with little more than the name. Typically, we hear of a bureau because the man selected to become the *wasita* had been previously the head of that department. The bureau of finance and the treasury are relatively commonly cited. Others include the office for salary payments, an office charged with supervising the other bureaus, the bureau of the army, the department responsible for Syrian affairs, and one newly created by al-Hakim, the office that was to audit and control properties and moneys seized from the estates of persons executed by the government. Another bureau regulated land grants that were allocated to army officers, government officials and members of the caliph's family. In addition there were various chamberlains, deputies, in all a substantial bureaucracy requiring a considerable monthly outlay in salaries. The governors and staff of each of the major cities and districts under direct rule should also be included here. Governors, for example, of 'Asqalon, Damascus, Aleppo, and other cities of Syria–Palestine; Alexandria, Qus, the Sharqiyya and Gharbiyya, two cities and two provinces of Egypt, to name a few. The corporation of descendants of the Prophet, the *Ashraf*, had its own leaders and it is possible to find the names of the Naqib, its head, who likewise benefited from government support.

The chancery is a good example, which perhaps can stand in for the rest. The great medieval expert on Islamic chancery practice, al-Qalqashandi, commented, moreover, that the Fatimids were the first dynasty to develop a full-blown office dedicated to the production and circulation of official documents and correspondence. Much of the earlier work of this kind was done individually by clerks attached directly to the ruler and thus not necessarily by a separate department of government. Still, as with many other aspects of administration, this judgment may apply more to later practice under the Fatimids. Significantly, from that later time we have a work that describes in careful and exemplary detail how to run a chancery. It was composed by Ibn al-Sayrafi, the head of that very bureau.[195] A person of that rank, incidentally, drew a salary of 120 dinars a month.

Several sources stress the necessary closeness of the head of the chancery to the caliph, an intimacy required if the former was to compose letters and decrees to express the policies of the latter. Obviously the clerks who wrote official pronouncements needed a good feel for what to say and how to say it. The argument of a given decree had to conform to the doctrine and policy of the dynasty; and the words and phrases used in it necessitated at the same time a knowledge of the traditional eloquence employed in chancery Arabic. Still, in general, many of these chancery clerks were not Muslims. One of those under al-Hakim whose names are known was Christian; another was a Jew. Interestingly, the sources mentioned on more than one occasion that al-Hakim wrote out in his own hand a decree or an order. The person who recorded that event commented that the edict in question was not of the type produced in the chancery, as if it was important to distinguish it from the rest. That the caliph would take the time to write his own was noteworthy.

At least two supervisors of the chancery were elevated from it to *wasita*, which may be another indication of its importance. But perhaps the most famous head of the chancery was Abu'l-Mansur Ibn Surin, a Nestorian Christian. His name appears more than once in the historical record as having composed this or that decree, one among which was the order sent to Palestine for the destruction of the Church of the Holy Sepulchre, a deed long remembered by Christendom with horror. That the decree was actually written by a Christian added a strange twist not easily accepted.

The Army, Navy and Police

Parallel to the bureaucracy of civil servants, who were the men of the pen, were the soldiers and police, the men of the sword. A description of al-Hakim's army would be difficult to draw with precision. Most of the available information derives from accounts of various military campaigns that provide a limited picture of the armed forces in action. Few of them are extensive in any case. The two possible exceptions are some operations in Syria and Palestine and the revolt of Abu Rakwa where reports are more detailed. Typically, however, the names of the commanders are known but little about the make-up of the forces, except in terms of gross divisions: the Westerners, the Easterners, and the Bedouin Arabs.

From the period of Nasir b. Khusraw, three decades after the close of al-Hakim's reign, we have slightly better information in this writer's travel book.[196] Allowing that Nasir's figures are likely both exaggerated and from a later time, what he says about the composition of the army may nevertheless approximate what it was earlier.

He mentions in first place the Kutama, Berber troops who had long been the mainstay of the Fatimid military. They numbered 20 thousand according to what Nasir heard. Next he cites a group of Batilis, another battalion of mounted Berbers, ethnically distinct from the Kutama. They were 15 thousand. An additional large force – some 20 thousand – of foot soldiers came from the lands of the Masmudis, also in the Maghrib. Those three groups formed the Westerners. The Easterners consisted of Turks, Persians, mainly Daylamis, most of whom were acquired as mercenaries, some recruited in whole regiments, others individually. By the era of Nasir, he could report that most of those he saw were actually born in Egypt, a second generation of those who had served previously under al-ʿAziz and al-Hakim. This group numbered ten thousand. The Arab Bedouin belonged principally to the southern Palestine region and to the Tayy tribe, under the leadership of the Jarrahids. Seldom to be trusted explicitly, but when necessary as many as 50 thousand strong, they nonetheless contributed an important portion of the army in critical situations, as most notably the rebellion of Abu Rakwa. They could also form the opposition as in the revolt engineered by Ibn Jarrah in the name of the amir of Mecca who declared himself counter-caliph. Another group on Nasir's list were the Purchased Slaves, the *'Abid al-Shura'*, most likely all Sudanese, who formed a unit of as many as 30 thousand but were probably substantially fewer in the time of al-Hakim. Nasir continues his review of the military with 30 thousand eunuch horsemen, both black and white, ten thousand foot soldiers of a palace guard, and 30 thousand Zanjibaris.

How many of these existed under al-Hakim is hard to determine. It is likely that all these numbers are too large. Even so the military was of considerable size, and difficult to fund, supply and control. Each division has its own commanders, who were for the most part from the same ethnic background. Eunuchs may have been an exception. The Slavs were another. White slaves from the north flowed into Fatimid territory, many captured during military operations. A large number of them were ethnically Slavic. Jawhar, the conqueror of Egypt, was one. His son Husayn, who was the *wasita* from 1000 to 1008, was therefore considered a Slav. For a while he toyed with the idea of creating a regiment that would consist entirely of Slavs.

The composition of the navy in al-Hakim's time, although notably present and active, is even more difficult to determine than the army. Likewise the police force. In the latter case, however, the names of those appointed to command it are often mentioned. For example, a certain Ibn Nazal, with the title Commander of Armies, was given responsibility for the two police forces, that of Fustat and that of Cairo, in 1011. Later he was sent to Damascus. One appointment to the same police command specifies carefully that the person in charge should implement the laws that regulate foods, drink and the movements of women, a matter of serious concern to al-Hakim. Control of the police often accompanied appointment to the *hisba*, the office for market inspections and regulations.

Al-Hakim also made considerable use of a kind of secret police, or at least a network of informers. There are several references to their work and to the information they supplied to the caliph. One description says that he employed women, particularly old women who had access to the inner workings of a household that men could not have. Still it might be wrong to regard these agents as a police in the normal sense of that word. It is also unclear who organized them or to whom they reported.

The Palace

Almost immediately after crossing the Nile to complete the Fatimid occupation of Egypt, Jawhar commenced construction of Cairo, which was to become the seat of the new government and eventually the administrative capital of the empire. The city itself was a walled and fortified cantonment housing the army and most major officials of the regime. Rectangular in shape, it ran south to north between a canal, on the river side, and the Muqattam foothills on the other. There were two gates in the northern wall, the Bab al-Futuh and the Bab al-Nasr, and one in the south, the Bab al-Zuwayla, following the precedent of Fatimid cities in the Maghrib and a specific plan provided to Jawhar by the caliph al-Muʿizz. As with al-Mahdiyya in Tunisia, at the heart of the urban configuration lay the massive palaces of the imam, two set facing each other, an eastern and a western palace with a grand open esplanade between one and the other, called appropriately 'Between the Two Palaces' (*Bayna'l-Qasrayn*). In addition Jawhar began building a congregational mosque, al-Azhar, which was to serve as the principal site of Friday prayer for the army and those Ismailis who flocked to Egypt once al-Muʿizz had moved the court there. But, in contrast with many other Muslim centers in other lands, al-Azhar did not retain its status as the most important mosque, nor did it ever function as the central focal point of the state. That distinction belonged to the palace.[197]

As significant as they once were, all remnants of these Fatimid palaces disappeared so long ago it is difficult now to describe them with any assurance as to accuracy. Yet their general shape and size is clear enough. Medieval authors from later times, most importantly al-Maqrizi, who could still find traces of them in his day, tried to reconstruct on paper what they must have been like. The eastern palace was larger by about double and was both the residence of the imam and the main seat of government. It contained a vast collection of connected buildings interspersed with open courtyards, which altogether occupied as much as 28 hectares (69 acres) of land. Inside that complex was space – living quarters and offices – for most bureaus of government and the huge staff needed to maintain the whole as well as the private retinue of the caliph. When the Persian traveler Nasir b. Khusraw saw it some 30 years after the era of al-Hakim, he commented that looked it like a mountain, so high were the various buildings in it. It housed, according to him, a staff of 30 thousand individuals, including 12 thousand ordinary servants, plus women and slave girls, and others.[198]

Nasir, who was a devout Ismaili and thus a loyal advocate of the Fatimid imams, was perhaps given to some exaggeration. It is also hard to gauge how much change might have intervened between his visit and the years of al-Hakim much earlier. Still, descriptions of the legacy of al-ʿAziz, who, benefiting from substantial prosperity and a seemingly endless flow of revenue into his treasury, and a taste for the royal life of ceremony, pomp and luxury, greatly enhanced and embellished his palace with both furnishings and servants. His stables, for example, contained thousands of animals. It was he, moreover, who is reported to have ordered the construction of the western palace, eventually granting it to his daughter Sitt al-Mulk, al-Hakim's half-sister. She was living there when he died and al-Hakim succeeded.

Al-Hakim's world was in the main circumscribed by the palace he inherited. The furthest he ever traveled away from it was to the Nile Delta city of Bilbays, only one day's journey north-east of Cairo. He was there when his father died. There is no record of any other trip of greater length and, despite his well-known penchant for riding out of the palace and the city, the accounts of these activities all revolve around the capital. He seldom went farther than Fustat and areas just south of it, to the Rashida mosque and the cemeteries south-east of it. Moreover, he was, in contrast to all of his ancestors, born in that very palace. He grew up there and, though from the age of

11 held, in theory, absolute authority over it and everything it contained, both people and goods, he revealed no overriding desire to move away from it, even briefly, or to modify or alter substantially what was bequeathed to him and which had always been his home.

Upon al-Hakim's accession, the eunuch Yanis ran the palace. A core staff of eunuchs constituted the key to the efficient administration of this semi-private domain of the caliph and his family. Barjawan was one of that number; many other names appear in the sources, both personal servants of the imam and functionaries at one level or another. Another large bloc of servants were the grooms charged with handling the animals of the stables. One master of these grooms had the odd name Mulukhiya, a fact known because al-Hakim at one point ordered his execution.[199] Concubines formed another group. About them there is almost no information except that in one period the caliph tried to set them all free, either by manumission or by being sold for those who preferred the latter. Al-Hakim's wives remain nameless and the concubines likewise. The mother of his other son al-Harith Abu'l-Ashbal was one of the latter but she has no further identity.[200]

From the end of Fatimid rule, there are historical accounts that provide fascinating and tantalizing details of palace life and how those living in it functioned, often in connection with the preparations for a major event, such as a review of the troops or the caliph's riding to deliver the sermon on the festivals. Not only were the horses and other riding animals arrayed for these occasions, but they and the members of the military who rode them and walked in the procession were outfitted with the finest attire brought out for that purpose from the various storehouses and treasuries which were themselves a part of the palace. There was a depot especially for flags and banners; another for arms. Not everything that was true of the late Fatimid period can be traced back to the time of al-Hakim but it is nevertheless certain that most changes after him were ones of scope and not of kind. The principal elements appear to have been in place already by his time.

One early custom was the ritual of the night guards. The palace complex, reports Nasir, was open on the outside all around, no other buildings abutted it. Each night a special contingent of watchmen, 500 mounted and 500 on foot, marched about it in regular succession throughout the night to the sound of drums and bugles. These numbers are those provided by Nasir for a later time but we can be certain of the same or a similar practice during the reign of al-Hakim because, in 1012, he gave an order to silence the drums and bugles, a fact duly recorded by the historians.

There were nine gateways into the palace complex, which are known by name and general location. In the middle of the western façade facing out onto the Bayna'l-Qasrayn was the Golden Gate, so named in part because it was the grandest entrance and led into the Gold Room, the most important area for reception of dignitaries. South around the corner was the entryway to the kitchens and further along on the south the gate into the Royal Mausoleum (the *Turbat al-Zaʿfaran*), which was the burial place for members of the dynasty. When al-Muʿizz moved from the Maghrib to Cairo, he brought with him the bodies of his immediate predecessors and theirs, along with his and al-ʿAziz's, with some other family members, were kept in that section of the palace. In the north-eastern corner a gateway, called appropriately the Festival Gate, served as the assembling point for processions from the palace out to the festival square, which itself was outside the walls of the city to the north.

One unusual feature of the palace was its underground passageway – of such a size that a person could ride through it on a horse – that led directly from the larger complex out to the west. The caliph could ride without attracting unwanted attention through this tunnel beyond the small palace, giving him easy access to the belvedere overlooking the canal on that side, or to the gardens on its western side from which it was possible to reach the port of al-Maqs at the edge of the river Nile.

Information about the smaller western palace is scant, although ironically traces of it survived beneath newer buildings until modern times. But, otherwise, except for its use by Sitt al-Mulk during the reign of her father al-ʿAziz, little is known. How long did she remain there after her brother took over? Unfortunately, we do not know.

Ceremonies in the Yearly Cycle of Rituals

Riding from the palace was often a major event for the caliph, but no more so than the yearly procession out northward from the city to the open festival square, the *musalla*, for either the festival of fast-breaking to close the month of Ramadan, or for the ritual slaughter on the feast of sacrifice during the season of the pilgrimage.[201] Both were nearly always treated as the most elaborate of affairs. The Fatimid caliphs regarded both as a duty not to be missed if at all possible. On each, they rode with great ceremony to the festival square and there led public prayers before mounting the *minbar*-pulpit and delivering the sermon appropriate to the occasion. The latter included Qur'anic passages and pointed advice as to either the payment of alms for the first or the basic requirements concerning what animals to sacrifice and how. Protocol for these rituals was precise and fully developed, including most particularly the order of march for the procession and for placement during prayers and the sermon. Those nearest the imam were obviously of the highest ranks. The few individuals who were asked to follow the caliph up the *minbar* and remain there during his delivery of the sermon constituted the elite of the elite.

A most extravagant example of such an event occurred in 1005, when al-Hakim rode in procession for the feast of fast-breaking. A surviving account takes care to note that he was wearing a plain yellow robe with a head kerchief of an indeterminate style and a turban with a hanging tail. Between his eyes he wore a jewel. Before him grooms led six horses, bearing saddles studded with gems, six elephants and five giraffes. He prayed the festival prayer with the people and then gave the sermon. The same report goes on to add that, for that occasion, the commander of the armies and chief judge climbed the *minbar* with him.[202]

In general, information in our sources about such events provides more detail than for many other occasions, describing for example who walked behind the caliph and in what order, family members, notables and others. The historian al-Musabbihi, who would have been present for them during the era of al-Hakim, comments in the section of his work that we still have, that he himself accompanied the procession. It was obviously an important event for him. Unfortunately, we possess his account solely for a single year under al-Zahir, son and successor of al-Hakim. It is, however, almost certain that the earlier parts of his history contained a similar description, including of his own participation.[203]

Even prior to his elevation to the imamate, al-Hakim had, although less than 11 years old, performed this duty, either accompanying his father or, during the latter's illness, on his own. As caliph he delivered his first sermon on the feast of sacrifice two months after the death of al-ʿAziz. For that occasion he rode to the festival square, led prayers and preached. The men on the pulpit on the steps just below included most significantly the chief qadi Muhammad b. al-Nuʿman, Barjawan and Ibn ʿAmmar, the three most powerful officials of the new administration.

From the next year onward for a dozen years to 1008, we have a fairly complete set of reports year by year all noting that al-Hakim rode for the festival and delivered the sermon. In 1009 he delegated the task, for reasons unknown, to his chief judge Malik al-Fariqi. But the following two years appear to have reverted to the normal pattern. Our reports often state simply that these events happened as they usually did, that is, according to normal protocol. For the year 1012, however, the responsibility again fell to Malik, at least for the festival of sacrifice, which is the only one of the two covered in our record. For the following year, 1013, both events saw a change. On each al-Hakim rode but without the elaborate adornments and accoutrements that had been typical of his regalia. Ten horses were led in front of him with saddles and bridles decorated only with light white silver. The royal parasol was white without gold. He wore white without embroidery and there was no gemstone in his turban. The pulpit, which was normally elaborately furnished, was kept plain. For the ceremony of sacrifice, although al-Hakim led prayer and delivered the sermon, the imam's cousin ʿAbd al-Rahim performed the actual slaughter in his stead. What exactly these alterations meant began to become clear the following year, 1014, when the caliph announced that ʿAbd al-Rahim would succeed him. The two festivals were different in that, for the first, the imam rode without the normal attire of the caliphate. ʿAbd al-Rahim accompanied him carrying the royal lance, which the caliph usually carried. The cousin climbed the *minbar* with the caliph and he was named in the benediction along with al-Hakim. For the feast of sacrifice, ʿAbd al-Rahim went out alone to lead prayers and give the sermon. On neither occasion was the customary feast offered at the palace. The following year, 1015, saw ʿAbd al-Rahim perform prayer duties and the sermon by himself for both festivals. In the latter no sacrifice was offered and the public was forbidden for that occasion to slaughter cattle.

With this report for 1015, our information dries up. These details of the annual ritual observances likely depended initially on the records kept by al-Musabbihi and then, second, on al-Maqrizi's chronological notes taken from them. Unhappily, from 1016 to the end of the reign, we have no such reports. Yet, for the changes just noted to mean something, we would require material from the subsequent years to confirm a lasting trend. Was, for example, al-Hakim seriously engaged over the course of these years in a process of withdrawing from public life by turning over to his cousin more and more of the ceremonies incumbent on him as caliph and imam?

There were two other rituals in the yearly calendar almost as important as the festivals. One, quite similar to them, involved giving the sermon and leading prayer on the Fridays of Ramadan, and the other, more secular, of riding to the head of the canal and opening the temporary dam that blocked the water of the Nile from entering until the period of flood.

Riding to one of the congregational mosques for Friday service during Ramadan was first done by al-ʿAziz who appears to have thus established an enduring precedent which lasted until the end of the era of the Fatimids. As a boy al-Hakim had already participated in this ceremony, which was much like that of the festivals except in taking place not at the *musalla* but in the mosque. Again, as with the festivals, the reports of this event are not complete. For several years 1002, 1004, 1007, and 1008, we know simply that al-Hakim rode to the mosque on at least one Friday of the month. For 998, 999, and 1000, he did it on two Fridays and in 1006 and 1013 he visited three mosques on different Fridays. For the latter year he rode to the mosque of Rashida, to the mosque outside the Bab al-Futuh, which would later take his name, and to the Old Mosque of Fustat. The first two were mosques that he had built himself; the last was the mosque associated with the name of ʿAmr b. al-ʾAs – an old enemy of the Shiʿa – and it had not had, until that moment, the honor of having the Fatimid imam lead prayers in it. Al-Hakim was the first to do so.

For the year 1014, the caliph added to these three a visit to the mosque of Cairo, the Azhar, just south-east of the palace. As he rode to these four mosques on successive Fridays, he gave a great deal of money in charity. In his sermon he made the customary appeal for himself from the top of the pulpit and similarly another on behalf of ʿAbd al-Rahim b. Ilyas, his cousin and heir. He said, 'O God, respond to me in the matter of the son of my uncle and the keeper of the covenant of the Muslims and the caliph after me, ʿAbd al-Rahim b. Ilyas b. Ahmad b. al-Mahdi bi-llah the Commander of the Believers, as You answered Moses in regard to his brother Aaron.' On the Friday he rode for prayer in the mosque of Cairo, our report says that the people thronged about him on his return from the mosque to the palace, that he stopped for them and accepted their petitions, and that he spoke and laughed with them. Because of the frequency of his stopping and conversing with the commoners, he did not reach the palace until sundown. The distance from the mosque of al-Azhar to the nearest palace gate was several hundred meters only although, perhaps, he went out and came back in through the more northerly Festival Gate. Still the total distance would hardly occupy him for the whole afternoon unless he proceeded at great leisure indeed.

In 1015 the heir apparent ʿAbd al-Rahim rode out for the same Friday ceremonies, in a procession fit for the caliph but absent the caliph, first to the new al-Anwar Mosque just outside the northern gate, next at al-Azhar, and finally twice more at the New Mosque.

The record of riding to open the canal is more spotty than for the festivals and the Fridays of Ramadan, indicating, possibly, that it was of less importance or of less interest to the historians who observed it. As a summer event that depends on the annual flooding of the Nile it takes place in accord with the solar calendar, not the Islamic year. It is thus not tied to Islamic ritual. Still, al-Maqrizi, who normally records the date using the Coptic calendar, states that al-Musabbihi noted the riding for this purpose by al-ʿAziz, al-Hakim and al-Zahir, year by year,[204] thereby suggesting that it occurred with great regularity. In his chronological *Itti'az*, al-Maqrizi mentions it specifically for the years 1000, 1001, 1005, and 1007, but also comments that in 1006 al-Hakim did not participate.

There were several other feasts and observances during the year that did not involve the caliph riding from the palace. One had him sit for salutations on the Islamic new year, which event is, however, mentioned only once. There are two reports concerning the celebration of the Persian new year, Nawruz, a holiday widely accepted in Egypt. The specifically Shiite feast of Ghadir Khumm, which commemorates the day on which the Prophet had formally designated (according the the Shiʿa) his cousin ʿAli b. Abi Talib as his successor, remained, under the Fatimids, limited to loyal Ismailis. Accordingly, the ceremonies connected to its observance, including the procession, were held within the palace complex, not outside. A report from the year 999 states explicitly that this festival was celebrated as it usually was with a procession of the faithful through the palace compound. The same event is cited again in 1008, but for some reason was forbidden in 1009. It was permitted once more, however, in 1012. The mourning ritual of 'Ashura' was another part of Shiite practice but did not directly involve the caliph. When they could, the Shiʿa of Egypt observed it under al-Hakim. Even so, in 1013 it was forbidden, though why and for how long is not known.

One more major event of the year was the departure of the pilgrimage caravan. Although the caliph did not necessarily have a direct personal role, nevertheless his prestige was involved. The holy cites of Mecca and Madina were loyal to him, a fact recognized most notably by the benediction said in his name and honor there in the Friday sermon. The local rulers of the two cities were members of the Ashraf, the descendants of the Prophet and of ʿAli. Their acknowledgement of al-Hakim's imamate carried substantial weight. Soon after the Fatimid conquest of Egypt, Mecca and Madina accepted the new imam in Cairo, in part because of a fairly long-standing connection with and dependence on support emanating from Egypt which consisted of donated funds and supplies that were critical for the well-being of that part of Arabia. Al-ʿAziz at first asserted his authority by dispatching troops to the Hijaz but thereafter relied on less aggressive means. By the time of al-Hakim relations with the holy cities were reasonably good, with the exception of the revolt of the Meccan ruler who claimed himself to be the imam-caliph for a short period. To insure the maintenance of good will and the expected allegiance of the Hijazi *ashraf*, each year Cairo prepared and sent with the caravan gifts, charitable and otherwise, plus needed supplies. The arrival of these donations was expected and anticipated. The Egyptian pilgrimages also brought every year the ritual covering for the Kaʿba, the *kiswa*, which was produced under government supervision in Egyptian textile factories.

Both the departure of the caravan and the pilgrims' return were carefully noted, along with a record of events and problems encountered on the way there and back. The pilgrims returning to Egypt in 997, for example, reported that the Friday sermon had been said in Mecca in the name of al-Hakim. It was the first time for him.

The Egyptian caravan would have included Muslims traveling from farther west and from Spain and Sicily. From the staging area outside Cairo, the assembled group moved east to Qulzum, from which some might sail south through the Red Sea, but most others went overland joining up with the Syrian pilgrims in southern Palestine. Additional caravans similarly set off from Iraq and from the Yemen. All the land routes involved the danger of predatory desert tribesmen, who typically extracted large fees from the travelers. To counter these threats the caravans, which could be quite large, were carefully organized and led by a person with great authority. The Islamic pilgrimage is time sensitive and is not valid unless it allows the pilgrim to observe a precise ritual on a fixed day of the year. Missing that moment invalidates the whole pilgrimage, which then became what is known simply as the 'visit' (*ʿumra*). Ideally, a successful pilgrimage would permit each participant to complete the required stages in Mecca and the surrounding area as ritually defined and then also to move on to visit Madina, the city of the Prophet's burial. However, the risks in the whole venture were acute. For two years during the period of al-Hakim, 1012 and 1013, it failed altogether; no pilgrims from Egypt reached Mecca. The likely cause was governmental policy in reaction to the revolt of the amir of Mecca. In 999, 1010, and 1015, the caravan returned to report that they had not managed to add a visit to Madina. In this last year the rites occurred during the most intense phase of the early summer sun and the account specifically noted the difficulty of doing so due to fear, hunger and thirst. More than once the government tried to start the process in a way to allow extra time by ordering its departure at an earlier date. In 1011 the pilgrims were commanded to visit Madina on the way to Mecca, rather than on the return.

The Baghdad historian Ibn al-Jawzi adds a curious note for 1006[205] in which he claims that returning Iraqi pilgrims that year reported that the *khutba*-sermon in Mecca was said in the name of al-Hakim as had become usual but that, at each mention of him, the people stood up, a rather unusual practice.

Institutions of Learning and Worship

Under al-Hakim, government-sponsored institutions of learning received unusually close scrutiny and supervision. The caliph took a remarkably personal interest in several of them, most notably the Ismaili Sessions of Wisdom (*majlis al-hikma*), the congregational mosques, the House of Knowledge (Dar al-'Ilm), and the royal libraries.[206] All of these were funded and controlled by the state over which he had absolute power in theory. Nevertheless, evidence of his own commitment to them is not hard to find, both in regard to the maintenance of those that already existed and in the inauguration of new ones. On a number of specific occasions the sign of his personal involvement came with an order to close or desist. Al-Hakim could be both happily supportive and angrily disapproving with corresponding good and bad consequences for the people connected. Still the institutions themselves survived and in the end prospered.

By the era of al-Hakim, the Ismaili *da'wa* – as previously described – along with its teaching institution the Sessions of Wisdom had been in operation in one form or another for at least a century and a half. Both pre-dated the Fatimid rise to power in the Maghrib. After the creation of the state, the teaching role changed only in that a portion of its activities were carried out within the safety of Fatimid hegemony. According to several accounts the instruction provided by the *da'wa* operated through a strict hierarchy of authority. Here is how al-Kirmani described it in the sixth passageway of the fourth rampart from his masterwork *The Comfort of Reason*.

> there are ten ranks, three of which are universal, and seven subordinate. The three that are universal are the prophetic message, which consists of the emanation of blessings by establishing laws of worship. By means of it, the soul comes to exist and obtains its first perfection. Next is the office of

> the legatee [heir of the prophet], which consists in receiving the blessing in its entirety and acting in concert with it, thereby instituting worship by inner knowledge, [that is] by interpretation through which the soul takes on an everlasting form and obtains a second perfection. Finally, there is the imamate, which is command over the governance of the community as a whole acting in accord with the legal tradition of the faith. ... The seven that follow are ...

At this point al-Kirmani runs through the seven ranks of *da'is* from the Gate (*Bab*) at the top down to the lowest level within the whole system of the *da'wa* (with the exception of its novice members). Then he concludes:

> Each one of these ten ranks controls the one below it and not vice versa. The speaking-prophet controls all below it and the legatee the same but he does not have control over what is above. The higher are to the lower like universals; the lower are particulars of the higher.

Ordinary Ismailis, those at the bottom of this exalted hierarchy, regularly attended a weekly meeting where and when they could, even if such session had to be convened in secret. The principal job of the *da'is*, whatever their rank, was to provide instruction for the faithful, a lesson in doctrine, and to collect a fee, the payment for confidential discourse (*najwa*). The latter was in part a donation to the *da'wa* and to the imam. These Sessions of Wisdom – also sometimes called explicitly Session of the *Da'wa* (*majlis al-da'wa*) – had grown more organized and formal, especially at the seat of the imamate in Cairo. They were also popular and well attended; crowds coming to them grew to the point that we have reports on a couple of occasions, when the assembled mass was so large individuals were crushed to death in the throng. The *da'i* was the officer in charge and in the capital that meant the chief *da'i*, the *Da'i al-Du'at*. His personal popularity – perhaps also the eloquence and quality of his lectures – contributed to the size of his audience. Such sessions were obviously held outside of Cairo, there by *da'is* appointed and supervised by Cairo.

According to a late Fatimid account the process of preparing the weekly lecture included presenting the final draft of the handwritten text to the imam who, if he approved, added to it his motto-signature. After the *da'i* read it at the *majlis*, the audience would approach one by one to be touched on the forehead by the caliph's signature. It is not clear if that practice existed at the time of al-Hakim but it likely did. Faithful Ismailis regarded the words of the homily, or at least the sentiment expressed in it, as those of the imam himself.

Unfortunately, no copies of the readings given in these earlier sessions now exist as far as we can determine. Yet it is clear from references in Druze writings from that time or slightly later that numbered lectures by both ʿAbd al-ʿAziz and al-Fariqi once circulated. The Druze authority Bahaʾ al-Din al-Muqtana, who had himself witnessed the era of al-Hakim, could quote passages from numbers 110, 117, 125, 126, and 127 by the former and 7, 140, and 144 by the latter. He may also have been present at the very sessions where they were originally delivered. If a *daʿi* composed and presented one lesson a week throughout the year, such high numbers are perfectly plausible. The famous chief *daʿi* of much later under the caliph al-Mustansir (he died in 1077) left a corpus that includes 800 *majlis*.

Moreover, when al-Fariqi took over from ʿAbd al-ʿAziz, he increased the number of sessions during the week to as many as five. Al-Musabbihi reports that he convened separate *majlis* for the most loyal of the Ismaili elite, one for the leaders of the state, one for palace servants, another for commoners and casual visitors, and two more for the women (in the palace and in al-Azhar). In each he collected the *najwa*, and on the feast, the *fitra*. The main venue for the Sessions of Wisdom was a special hall in the palace that had been set aside for that purpose. Note that the great mosque of al-Azhar was used in this instance only for women and solely for one of two sessions dedicated to them.

Despite al-Fariqi's vigorous schedule and his closeness to al-Hakim, he, as with his predecessors, failed to please the imam in several respects, who ordered the Sessions stopped more than once. Al-Fariqi's eventual replacement, Khatkin, resumed the *majlis* but its exact form under him is unknown. He summoned from Iraq the most gifted *daʿi* of the time, al-Kirmani, and put him to work in the local *daʿwa*, possibly giving the lectures in the *majlis*. Druze accounts do not help since the leading members of al-Hakim's government, including specifically Khatkin, became, in the eyes of the Druze, a hierarchy of satans. Still we have many of the books and treatises al-Kirmani wrote during his years in Egypt but none of them appear to have been used for the Sessions of Wisdom, being as they are much too abstract and erudite in tone and content. They would have constituted a real test for any beginning student let alone a casual visitor. But that does not preclude either his involvement in some capacity or the study of what he wrote by those more directly responsible for the weekly lessons.

Ultimately, what we learn about the instruction provided by the *daʿwa* is confined to two aspects of this work: these Sessions of Wisdom at a more popular level, and a series of doctrinal treatises, some of major size and importance, authored by either al-Kirmani or al-Naysaburi. There were obviously other figures in the *daʿwa* and its program of teaching comprised much more than the Sessions of Wisdom that were open to all Ismailis. But about the advanced training of the *daʿis* we know little beyond a list of books, those by contemporaries and those by their predecessors in the mission, the latter to include the famous expert in Ismaili law Qadi al-Nuʿman, the exoteric exegete Jaʿfar b. Mansur al-Yaman, the Neoplatonist philosopher Abu Yaʿqub al-Sijistani, as well as Abu Hatim al-Razi, Muhammad al-Nasafi and others. Having the names of these earlier Ismaili works and in a number of cases the actual text of them does not reliably indicate how they may have been taught at the time of al-Hakim. Were they all in favor then? Al-Kirmani offers positive comments about these authors but is, in part, highly critical of certain doctrines advocated by some of them. His own metaphysics is often sharply at odds with that of al-Sijistani and al-Nasafi, for example.[207] It is likely that, at its more exalted ranks, the *daʿwa* operated in secret and its teaching was largely done in private highly restricted meetings of two or three individuals. There are no records of such gatherings and even to assume that Cairo functioned as a center of such instruction is merely an assumption lacking concrete evidence.

If any of the mosques had given rise to a *madrasa*, a type of residential college, the situation might be different. Normally, the concept of an Islamic madrasa is limited to a school of advanced study in Sunni law. However, an institution close to that ideal, except in that it probably taught Shiite law, existed for a time under al-ʿAziz at al-Azhar. The wazir Yaʿqub Ibn Killis created in and near Cairo's principal mosque a college for that purpose. That much is not in doubt. But as the wazir's own personal fortune paid for its upkeep, it seems to have withered and died soon after his death. By the era of al-Hakim the sources no longer mention it or its cadre of teachers and students. Al-Azhar was not a university and there exists, moreover, almost no evidence that it functioned as a center for the Ismaili *daʿwa*.

Its role in this period was further diminished by the building of other congregational mosques that received comparable – and often greater – attention from the caliph. Later, when al-Hakim came to endow several favorite institutions in the year 1009, he selected as beneficiaries of his largess the mosques of Rashida and Maqs, in addition to al-Azhar, and as well the newer Dar al-ʿilm, an educational establishment of a radically different type. A copy of the endowment deed is preserved.[208] Significantly, in the case of al-Azhar, it does not provide for scholars or students. Moreover, in the list of venues for the *majlis al-hikma*, al-Azhar has the distinction of hosting the public sessions for women and that may have been its only teaching function.

The two other mosques to receive endowments in al-Hakim's trust of 1009 were one in the district of Rashida, to the south of Fustat, and Maqs, the port on the Nile to the west of Cairo. In 1003 the caliph ordered the construction of the mosque of Rashida on a site that formerly held a church.[209] That area had nearby many churches along with the graves of Jews and Christians. The new mosque was first constructed of brick. Later the churches adjoining it were also demolished and in the following year in Ramadan the mosque was at last finished. From at least 1008, al-Hakim rode to it for a Friday sermon and prayer during Ramadan. But, in 1011 it was torn down and rebuilt in stone. Another report comments that its *mihrab* was oriented incorrectly and had to be rebuilt as well. It is mentioned specifically for Ramadan services of the years 1013 and 1014. In contrast to the mosques of Rashida and al-Azhar, the mosque of al-Maqs, which he had built in 1003 and which benefited like them from al-Hakim's endowment of the year 1009, was apparently never included in his observance of this Ramadan ritual. It is reported, however, that the caliph used to ride there and observe the fleet in review from a belvedere at its side.[210]

Most important of them all was the mosque just north of the Bab al-Futuh, which would eventually bear this caliph's name.[211] At first it was called simply the New Mosque, and somewhat later al-Anwar. It took the name al-Hakim after the Fatimid period was over. His father had begun building it in the time of the wazir Ibn Killis but, although it had been used for Friday services by al-ʿAziz, it remained in part incomplete until 1003, when the son allotted the substantial sum of 40 thousand dinars for the work, along with the order to finish it. It appears that at that time he added its monumental entryway and the two towering minarets that can still be seen. Later, in 1010, he ordered both minarets encased at the base with a rectangular column measuring 100 cubits per side and rising up to the height of the mosque walls. Finally in Ramadan of 1013 it was fitted out with sumptuous furnishings worth, it is said, five thousand dinars, and officially inaugurated. The year after al-Hakim established a trust for its support by dedicating to that purpose several markets and other properties. Inscriptions that testified to his regard for this mosque once existed. The early Mamluk era historian and government official, Ibn ʿAbd al-Zahir, recorded in his notes the inscription on the entryway which stated that it was built by al-Hakim in May 1003 and another on its *minbar*-pulpit that credited him also for having had it constructed for the mosque in 1012.[212]

It is clear that al-Hakim preserved an active interest in the support of mosques for most of his reign. The Mosque of al-Lu'lu'a, which still sits hauntingly isolated up along the base of the Muqattam, was put up by his order, possibly in 1015 (the exact date is highly uncertain).[213] In addition to building and furnishing new ones, he contributed to the maintenance of many already in existence. A report from 1013, for example, notes that seven boxes containing 1,298 Qur'ans of different sizes, some entirely written in gold, were sent from the palace to the Old Mosque in Fustat to be used there by the people. He also contributed precious silver objects to it. Another says that two thousand dinars were allocated to refurbish the Old Mosque and to build a minaret there.[214] In 1013 he had a census taken of the number of mosques without revenue to provide upkeep. More than 300 were found and he allocated for them a monthly total of 9,220 dirhams, equal to 12 dirhams for each mosque.[215] Yet another report from that year says that he supplied the Mosque of Ibn Tulun with 814 Qur'ans.[216] Nor was his largess confined to the capital. In 1013 he issued an order for the rebuilding of the mosque of Alexandria, which he had ordered torn down in 1004.[217] The following year he set aside as a trust a number of markets and other properties and estates for the benefit of Qur'an reciters and *mu'adhdhin*s in the mosques along with other charities.

But perhaps his most interesting, and certainly most novel, institution of learning was the House of Knowledge, the Dar al-'ilm, which was also called the House of Wisdom, the Dar al-hikma; the two names apparently were interchangeable.[218] As a 'House of Wisdom', it could easily be confused with the Session(s) of Wisdom, the *majlis al-hikma*, by those who were not close enough to either institution to see the difference. Accordingly, several historians, most especially those from distant lands, report facts about one as if it were the other, some even claiming that al-Hakim had two Houses of Knowledge, an Ismaili and a non-Ismaili.[219]

That same endowment by al-Hakim in the year 1009, which provided support to the three mosques, also granted generous benefits to the Dar al-'ilm and these provisions were more in line with the requirements of a true academic establishment. Begun in 1005, five years prior to the creation of this *waqf*, the Dar al-'ilm was obviously a favorite project of al-Hakim. Unlike the three mosques, the Dar al-'ilm was an institute for the advancement, preservation, and propagation of knowledge and with no other purpose. Moreover, it did not have a direct relationship with the Ismaili *da'wa* or with propaganda and conversion. In many respects it was unprecedented, although the Bayt al-

Hikma, frequently cited as a foundation of the Abbasids some two centuries earlier in Baghdad, was a possible model or at the least an idea to imitate. Al-Hakim seemed to want an open and genuinely public academy, one available to scholars and commoners of all intellectual persuasions.

The information about the creation of the Dar al-ʿilm comes from a report by the historian al-Musabbihi, who was a contemporary observer and therefore certainly reliable and accurate. Several slightly different versions of this one account now exist in the reports of various historians.[220] All agree that al-Hakim set up the Dar al-ʿilm in Cairo, that he supplied it with books from his own palace treasury on a wide variety of subjects, that he paid stipends to a number of scholars who were to teach there, and that he also provided support staff and furnishings. Whoever wanted to could go there and read the books in its new library, could also copy them using the ink, paper and pens that were provided, or they could study with the masters who taught the various disciplines in its curriculum. The authors who recorded this information expressed what must have been contemporary amazement; nothing like this new institution existed anywhere else at that time.

Yahya of Antioch, who, in any case, had a dim view of al-Hakim, in part because of his own exile from Fatimid Egypt in the middle of that reign, adds a further curious footnote to his entry about the founding of the Dar al-ʿilm. After only a short time, he says, al-Hakim executed several of the scholars who worked there and the remainder hid from him.[221] The cause of this incident is unknown but it serves here a useful purpose in revealing the names of at least three of the professors at the Dar al-ʿilm in its earliest phase. The person in charge was ʿAbd al-Ghani b. Saʿid al-Misri; the other two were Abu Usama Junada b. Muhammad, the lexicographer, and Abu'l-Hasan ʿAli b. Sulayman al-Antaki, the grammarian. In August 1009, al-Hakim ordered the arrest and execution of all three (and perhaps others unnamed in our sources). Abu Usama and Abu'l-Hasan were caught and done away with, but ʿAbd al-Ghani went into hiding and survived as a result.[222] Most importantly, he soon resumed his post at the Dar al-ʿilm; his presence was, for example, explicitly noted at an assembly held there in 1013.[223] Yet one more name can be added to these three. Some time prior to 1015, a blind scholar, Abu'l-Fadl Jaʿfar, arrived in Cairo and attracted the favorable attentions of al-Hakim, who conferred on him the honorific title *ʿAlim al-ʿulama'* and gave him a post in the Dar al-ʿilm as a professor of lexicography and grammar.[224] What is most remarkable about all four of the named teachers is that none were Ismaili or even Shi'i. The new academy was simply not oriented to the requirements of the *daʿwa*. Some distant observers went so far as to insist that, because of the presence of these Sunnis, al-Hakim himself must have thought of renouncing his Ismaili heritage.

That al-Hakim's disapproval of the three professors who suffered his wrath in 1009 did not extend to the institution itself is proven by his generosity not too long afterward when he created the endowment mentioned previously. That act was a true trust, a *waqf*: the dedication of personal property in perpetual support of the institutions named as its beneficiaries. But, in contrast to the expenditures for the upkeep of a mosque and its staff, the Dar al-ʿilm was granted 257 dinars annually to be spent for the following: ten for reed mats, 90 for the paper used by copyists, 48 for the keeper's (*al-khazin*) salary, 12 for water, 15 for the *farrash*, 12 for the paper, pen, and ink of the *fuqaha'* who taught there, one dinar for the repair of the curtains on the doorways and windows, 12 for repairing books or replacing pages that might fall out of books, five for felt given to the *farrash* in the winter, and another four for carpets (*tanafis*) in the winter. This list covers only 209 out of the 257 allotted annually for the support of the Dar and it conspicuously leaves out salaries for professorships. The relatively small balance certainly would not go far in that direction, however. Still, the academic nature of al-Hakim's plan for the Dar al-ʿilm is obvious and it should be noted that, by this endowment, he made it a free-standing institution protected legally from the vagaries of future governmental intrusions. The Dar al-ʿilm was, from the year 1009 onward, a *waqf* according to the stipulations of Islamic law and not, therefore, an instrument of the state nor technically under its direct control.

A major institution that is difficult to classify is the royal library.[225] The Fatimid caliphs collected books avidly and by the time of al-Hakim the treasury devoted to them was already substantial, if not larger than any that might have existed elsewhere in the Islamic world, or possibly anywhere at all. From the beginning of their rule in Egypt, as with many other topics and subjects, the caliphal libraries merited an entry in al-Maqrizi's *Khitat*. And, as is also typical, his information covers hit and miss several different periods. The first report pertains to al-ʿAziz who, in the year 993, happened to have someone mention to him the famous *Kitab al-'ayn* by al-Khalil b. Ahmad, a masterpiece of lexicography. For his part the caliph produced from his library some 30 copies of it, one in the hand of the author himself. Another person presented to al-ʿAziz a copy of al-Tabari's *Ta'rikh* which he had purchased for 100 dinars. Al-ʿAziz thereupon ordered the keeper of his library to bring out the 20 copies he owned, including, again, one in the hand of the author. Similarly, when the *Jamhara* of Ibn Durayd was brought up, al-ʿAziz was able to produce 100 copies it. If one assumes that these are but examples that illustrate the immense holdings in the Fatimid collections, the palace library was by then already enormous. And also comprehensive – the three books cited in this case do not belong to the category of 'knowledge of the imams,' and they are not Shiite or pro-Shiite in respect to religious orthodoxy. Unfortunately, al-Maqrizi provides no information about the library that is specific to al-Hakim, nor does he indicate how it was used and by whom. Still, that the caliph could create a library within his new House of Knowledge and send various mosques many copies of the Qur'an suggests that what remained in the palace collection was vastly greater.

Beyond the institutions of learning just discussed, there were others, some less formal. Enduring Fatimid interest in the sciences is undeniable and easily confirmed on the basis of the surviving books and treatises produced in the *daʿwa* by the most outstanding of the *daʿis*, notably those by al-Sijistani and al-Kirmani, to name only two leading figures from al-Hakim's period and the one before it. None of these writers, however, was primarily concerned with the physical sciences. But in Cairo, under al-Hakim, the Fatimids assembled a small group of experts that included among them two giants of medieval Arabic science: Abu ʿAli al-Hasan b. al-Haytham, a mathematician and physicist, and ʿAli b. ʿAbd al-Rahman ibn Yunus, an astronomer. Both rose to prominence under the Fatimids in the time of al-Hakim.

Al-Hakim was himself deeply interested in astronomy and his government employed its own chief astronomer, Abu'l-Hasan ʿAli b. Ismaʿil al-Munajjim al-Tabarani, a friend and colleague of Ibn Yunus. Al-Musabbihi relates the following story about the two: 'I was told by Abu'l-Hasan al-Tabarani, the astronomer, that he once went up with Ibn Yunus to the Muqattam mountain and set up there hoping to record an observation of the planet Venus. On arriving Ibn Yunus took off his cloak and turban and replaced them with a woman's gown and hood, both of a red color. He then produced a guitar, which he began to play all the while burning incense in front of him. It was, says al-Tabarani, an astounding sight.'[226] The famous astronomer was already known about town for being careless in his appearance and absent-minded. He was tall and would normally dress quite shabbily. Even al-Hakim noted that his manners lacked grace.[227] Nonetheless, he maintained his standing, eventually dying of old age in 1009.

Although there is a suggestion that a regular observatory was planned and started not long after Ibn Yunus's death, nothing came of it and no formal observatory existed in Egypt at that time. Ibn Yunus, with the others, actively followed a program of observations, many made from the top of the

Muqattam which is just east of Cairo. The results of these observations were assembled by Ibn Yunus, in conjunction with others known from older sources and collected by him, into a major resource for all subsequent calculations by professional astronomers. He called it the *Zij al-Hakimi al-kabir*, in honor of its patron, the caliph al-Hakim.[228]

The caliph's relationship with the great scholars of his era involved patronage and support of their work but also on occasion his anger and rejection. The order to execute the professors attached to the House of Wisdom is but one example. In that case two died but one, ʿAbd al-Ghani b. Saʿid, escaped later to regain al-Hakim's favor and resume his post.

ʿAbd al-Ghani was famous then and long afterward for his knowledge of Sunni hadith, a subject in which he is considered a major figure. It is doubtful, however, that al-Hakim hired him for anything of the kind. The cultivators of Sunni traditions were not favored and may have been at times persecuted. Although the record is by no means clear, one report mentions the killing of proponents of traditions in 1008.[229] Matters are more certain in regard to another group: the astrologers. The Arabic term for astronomer and astrologer often does not distinguish between them. Professionals in that field may have earned a living casting horoscopes regardless of what they personally believe about their validity. In about 1003 or 1004 – the date is uncertain – al-'Ukbari, an astrologer, who is described as quite close to al-Hakim but even so as not too bright, suffered the wrath of the caliph and was killed.[230] Subsequently, word was broadcast that the blood of astrologers was henceforth licit, that they were heretical unbelievers, and they all fled the country. No astrologer remained in the land of Egypt.[231] But at least one other astrologer was caught and executed before that.[232] The case of al-'Ukbari is more complex in that he had been successful with his predictions twice, once in setting the time for the departure of the fleet against the rebel al-'Allaqa and another in the discovery of treasure beneath a mosque. Success went to his head, which was already weak, and he began to exceed and exaggerate his authority in making predictions inciting unrealistically thereby the expectations of the people who started depending on him for them.

The fate of astrology and its practitioners did not carry over to the astronomers, as far as we can tell. Ibn Yunus was not affected, nor was the chief court astronomer al-Tabarani. Many scholars likewise retained the support of al-Hakim. The blind lexicographer Jaʿfar, the Scholar of Scholars, was one.[233] Others would include his personal physicians, several of whom are prominent in the sources. Ibn Maʿshar treated al-Hakim during an illness and for his effort received ten thousand dinars, a staggeringly large sum. He became the caliph's personal doctor, a rank of high standing as is clear from the order of seating at an audience in the year 1000.[234] He died four years later in the winter of 1003–04 and was replaced by Abu Yaʿqub ibn Anastas, about whom more needs to be said later in connection with his death in 1007 as a result of an accident during a drinking party. But he died needless to say a wealthy man. His successor was Saqr the Jew. Al-Maqrizi writes of this man's appointment as follows: 'Honors went to Saqr the Jew [in 1008] and he was carried out on a mule preceded by three mules with saddles and bridles for baggage and there was transported with him 20 baskets of cloth. He was set up in a house that had been furnished and decorated, its doors locked and its rooms curtained. He was given everything he needed and told that that was his house. He thus acquired in one hour what was worth ten thousand dinars. He took up the position of physician to al-Hakim in place of Ibn Anastas.'[235] Saqr died in November or December 1010.[236] Who took over is not known.

No biography of al-Hakim can exist without including his government and its handling of the affairs of state. Information about him derives most often from a report concerning his actions as they affected those who served him in official positions: the promotion or demotion of a prominent official, an order to implement this or that policy, commandment, edict or decree. He seldom appears separate from the administration he directed. Much of the record, however, simply comments passively on events as if an unnamed power were responsible for them. But it would be hard not to notice how the shadow of al-Hakim himself hangs over everything. At no time was he absent, and more frequently than not our history indicates his direct involvement. If an officer of the state was executed, surely in every instance it happened by the explicit order of the caliph. Were it otherwise there would be some note to that effect. Whatever the final judgment of al-Hakim, facts of this kind establish without doubt his abiding interest in his own rule. To the end, as far as we can tell, he never once, even in the final period when he adopted an ascetic habit, relinquished his personal control. The association of ruler and government was and remained, in his case, as intimate as almost any of the kind and perhaps as it could possibly ever be.

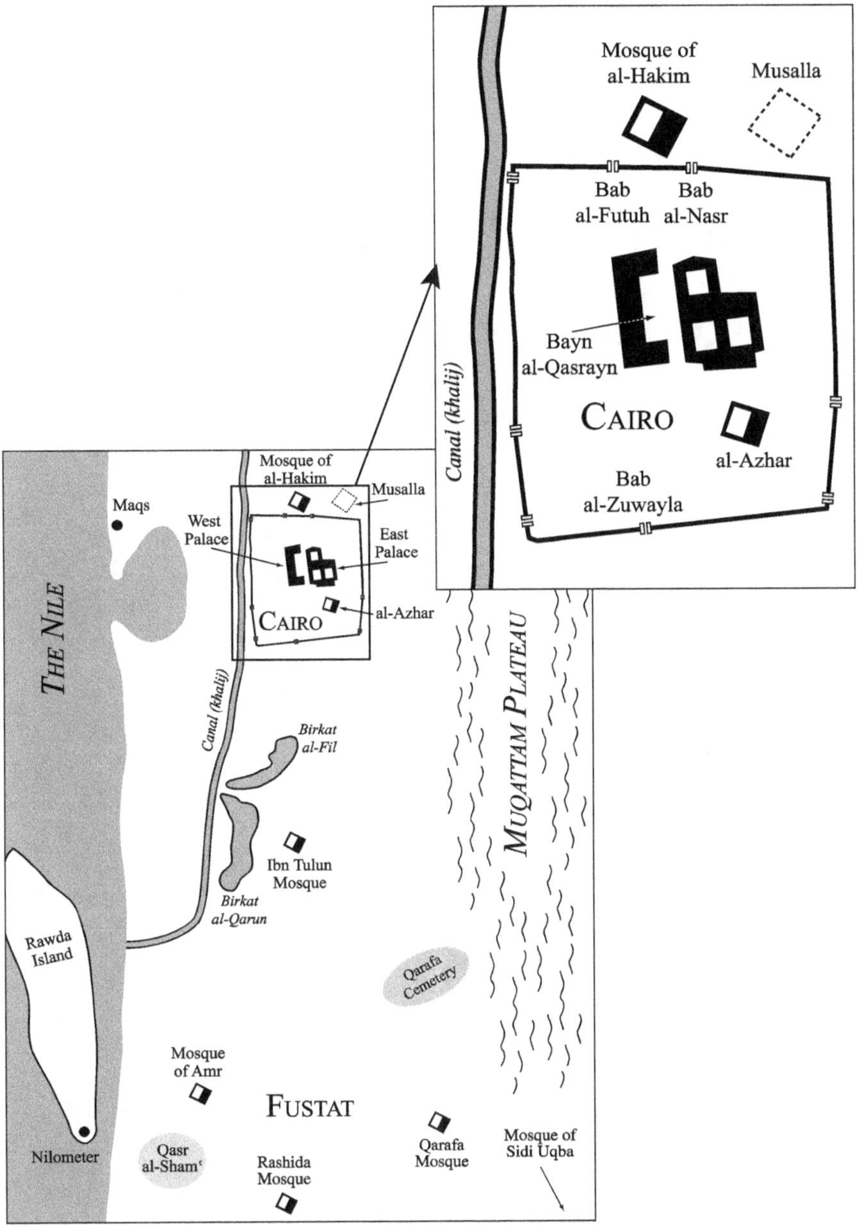
Mosque of
al-Hakim
Musalla
Bab
al-Futuh
Bab
al-Nasr
Bayn
al-Qasrayn
CAIRO
al-Azhar
Bab
al-Zuwayla
Canal (khalij)
Mosque of
al-Hakim
Musalla
Maqs
West
Palace
East
Palace
CAIRO
al-Azhar
THE NILE
Canal (khalij)
MUQATTAM PLATEAU
Birkat
al-Fil
Ibn Tulun
Mosque
Birkat
al-Qarun
Rawda
Island
Qarafa
Cemetery
Mosque
of Amr
FUSTAT
Nilometer
Qasr
al-Sham'
Rashida
Mosque
Qarafa
Mosque
Mosque of
Sidi Uqba

5

Friends and Rebels

It must be obvious by now that the era of al-Hakim, quite in contrast to that of his father, was bloody and violent, most particularly for the stream of executions and other killings carried out by his orders. The number of those put to death became a matter of note and later historians took pains to record as many names of the victims as they could, a task that appealed to some more than others perhaps depending on a personal view of either him or of the dynasty as a whole. But a list of names in and of itself reveals little about why the caliph did what he did. What crimes had these men committed? Why inflict such a final and ultimate judgment? One answer, propagated and possibly embellished by enemies of the state, was that al-Hakim was himself unstable and prone to fits of pique, sudden outbursts of ill-temper and deadly anger. Yet there is also evidence of his good will and clemency in some matters that created consistent policy and that would seem to deny that his actions were simply the result of variations in mood. Is there reason to view the killings as in some manner justified? Was it, as certain loyal supporters of the regime argued, a time of unusual perfidy, of corruption, duplicity and deceit among the elite – a privileged class more interested in their own wealth and status than that of the policies of the imam? Here it is useful to examine closely individual cases, first some that involve the execution of men quite close to al-Hakim, then second several where the rebellion against him is clearest, and finally treatises by members of his *da'wa* that display the quite ardent defense of his God-given right to absolute rule that is typical of those who maintained their unqualified devotion to him through to the end.

The Plot of the Uncle

The first case to note occurred in the year 1004. It normally comes up in the middle of a small list of men al-Hakim killed at the time. Ibn Saʿid, one of the historians[237] who relates the story, having himself likely taken it from a writer contemporary to the event, possibly the North African Ibn al-Raqiq, comments at this point that, in this year, the son of prince Hashim sought permission from al-Hakim to go out to visit one of his estates and the caliph granted his request. Al-Maqrizi, as we have already seen, adds this man's full name: he was ʿAbd al-A'la, son of Hashim, who was himself the son of the caliph al-Mansur, and thus a brother of al-Muʿizz, al-Hakim's grandfather. That a prince of the royal family would have to seek a permit to leave Cairo is curious, suggesting, for want of better information, that a policy existed to watch and control relatives of the imam and that they could not move about without explicit permission to do so. We know otherwise that few if any members of the caliph's family – with the exception of the heir apparent – were ever permitted to hold a position of authority in the state. In this instance, however, the man was allowed to do as he had requested and he departed along with a party of his boon companions and friends, among whom were, according to our source, the sons of al-Mughazili, Ibn Kharita, Ibn Abi'l-Fadl b. Hinzaba, and some of the younger Kutama. The caliph secretly dispatched with the group a spy to note what they did and record every word they said and report back to him. The group proceeded to the estate in question, intent on enjoying themselves and there they began eating and drinking. In the midst of their merrymaking, one of the sons of al-Mughazili, who happened himself to be an astronomer-astrologer, commented to the son of prince Hashim: 'Surely you ought to be caliph; you are the imam of this age.'

A statement of that kind could have been uttered as hyperbole, an over-the-top compliment from a friend or admirer, but the literal implication is obviously treasonous, an interpretation, once it had come back to him, the caliph no doubt accepted with alarm.

After the party had returned to town, Hashim's son went to the palace, which he evidently entered without permission to do so. Once he had offered his salutations and taken a seat, al-Hakim pulled from under his cloak a sword and struck him with it. Wounded, he was carried to his house and there he wrote a letter hoping to excuse himself from any crime that might have been reported about him. He swore that he had been struck without just cause.

Furthermore he asked that a doctor might be admitted to him to treat his wound. That was granted him. When he had recovered, he also sought permission to go to the baths and that was allowed as well. However, al-Hakim sent to the bath someone to kill him and bring back his head. Subsequently, all those who had been present at this same party – those named above and presumably others not mentioned – were executed and their bodies burned.

The incident just related is unusual for the amount of information we possess about it. Yet it is certainly not enough. What is reported raises more questions than it answers. Was, for example, the threat of sedition or treachery by members of the royal family real, or perceived to be real? Note in addition the explanation provided by al-Maqrizi[238] that it was reported that ʿAbd al-Aʿla sought the caliphate and that he had met with a number of persons to whom he promised the position of governor of a province. That indicates evidence of sedition more seriously than idle flattery. In this case the anger of al-Hakim is palpable; he himself took revenge on his cousin by personally striking him with a sword. There are few if any other situations of this kind among the many, many official executions over the long course of his reign. The direct involvement of al-Hakim, as is evident in this case, is exceedingly rare. More typically, as here, the killing of persons who had been involved in an earlier incident occurs later, possibly much later, making it difficult to determine the exact cause or the caliph's personal attitude. Ibn Kharita, a member of the original party above, was put to death in 1004, a year after the event, as apparently were the rest. This man had also been an associate of Barjawan. Did that also figure in the eventual outcome?[239]

One or two isolated pieces of information appear to confirm the need for the young caliph to be wary of his male relatives. A report indicates that, at the commencement of the reign, the authorities seized the house of a grandson of al-Mahdi because he had been accused of having *daʿis* working on his behalf, implying therefore that he had thoughts of his own succession.[240] Another account mentions the arrest and killing, late in the reign, of a grandson of al-Muʿizz.[241] But are either of these accounts reliable? As with much of the information about specific events during the rule of al-Hakim, we have only the notes copied by a much later historian from an older source, which far too often cannot be identified. And the possibility of misinformation, either inadvertent or deliberate, is always present.

Even so the death of ʿAbd al-Aʿla, which is partially understandable as a matter of dynastic politics, does not explain countless others. Nor is the information about these other executions to be discounted. What we know of the elite members of medieval Islamic societies often derives from obituary lists and, for the era of al-Hakim, many names entered those lists not as a result of natural death but of execution by the state. The roll includes a considerable number of scholars, poets, bureaucrats, the highest government officials, and ranking officers in the military.[242] So many died in certain periods, uncontrollable apprehension and unease spread unchecked throughout most of the social classes, particularly those connected closely to the state. We have reports of groups of them assembling at the palace gate to beg for a declaration of amnesty. One incident of this type is reported by al-Maqrizi from the year 1005. Fear of al-Hakim, he says, caused the people to gather and beseech him for a guarantee of personal safety. The groups involved included members of the private Turkish guards and their commanders and those who served them, household retainers, slaves, and pages; the holders of fiefs and those receiving stipends. Others making a similar request at that time were servants of the palace and of the caliph himself. In al-Maqrizi's account there follows a lengthy list of groups: palace cadres, nobility and notables, various regiments of the military by name, *mu'adhdhins* of the palace gates, tradesmen and practitioners of the professions, and more.[243] Two months after that the merchants attached to various markets came also, group by group, each seeking a decree of amnesty. A hundred were issued all on the same model, one for each. Al-Maqrizi preserves a copy of the master text.[244]

For the study of the social order of the time, these lists are remarkable in providing detailed information about the units that form it. They attest equally to the apparent seriousness of the matter at hand; what happened was unusual. The fear that prompted such a reaction by the populace must have been quite real. Still exactly what set it in motion and how is not clear. Who was responsible for it?

Despite such evidence of the dread al-Hakim inspired amongst his people, most continued to serve him willingly. In fact, in several prominent cases, where a leading member of a family or clan was executed by his order, others in the same family, a son or brother, later rose to a similar position as if the blame for the death in question affected neither the caliph or the relatives of the deceased, the latter having accepted what had transpired rather than harboring a motive for revenge.

The Drinking Party

There is a second incident that is worth recounting in this context, in part because it involves yet another drinking party and the consequences of disappointing the caliph. In that al-Hakim, from 1004 onward, determinedly promulgated laws that forbad the consumption of intoxicating beverages, this latter case, which again saw the participation of members from the highest ranks of the elite, takes on an even more curious, even sinister, aspect.

In the late summer of 1007 at the time of a Christian fast, several friends gathered at the house of the *wasita*, Husayn b. Jawhar, who was by title the Commander-in-Chief. One of those who had come to visit was the chief justice ʿAbd al-ʿAziz, who was, moreover, the head of the Ismaili *daʿwa*. He was also Husayn's brother-in-law. Abu'l-Hasan ʿAli b. Ibrahim al-Rassi, who was then head of the Ashraf nobility, was already there. This al-Rassi officiated, for example, at the birth rituals for al-Hakim's sons along with Husayn. One more person present was Abu'l-Hasan ʿAli b. Ismaʿil al-Tabarani, a member of Husayn's inner circle but also the official court astronomer.

The report of the event and what follows comes from the amir al-Musabbihi who claims that al-Tabarani told him about it.[245] However, one account states that Musabbihi was himself present at the party. Perhaps, given the poor outcome, he preferred to leave himself out and credit his information to al-Tabarani, as if he had it only second-hand.

As the festivities commenced in the early evening, a servant entered to say that a noted gentleman was at the door seeking permission to join them. He was none other than Abu Yaʿqub Ishaq b. Ibrahim Ibn Anastas, the caliph's personal physician, someone as close to al-Hakim as humanly possible.[246] Though the group was already seated at the table, they were quite pleased to add him and they quickly ordered up another place setting. Evidently he was well known to them, already one of this circle of friends.

Following the repast the table was taken away and drinking materials were brought in. We could remember here that the prohibition against all manner of intoxicants was in effect, even for the lately arrived Melkite Christian doctor. Surely the elite would have been loath to countermand the caliph's explicit commandments. However, it is amply clear from the account that these pillars of the state set to drinking beverages that shortly deprived them of their sobriety. They were in fact soon drunk. The judge then departed but the rest passed out, falling asleep one by one on the spot. However, the good doctor, evidently more used to such affairs than the others, continued to enjoy himself. He was a gifted musician with a prodigious memory for hundreds of songs.[247] As his companions abandoned him, he played on, becoming ever more intoxicated. Finally realizing that he alone remained awake, he decided to depart himself. He went out to order up his riding mule, but the sleepy servant he encountered brought the one that belonged to al-Rassi instead. He refused it. The servant then begged him to return inside and wait until his own could be located. Back inside, he lay down beside al-Rassi and fell asleep. Later one of the servants went over to check on the two. Raising the curtain that secluded them, he spotted al-Rassi but not the doctor, who had meanwhile, some time in the night, awakened and, though still in a drunken state, decided to go for a dip in the pool at the river's edge. Confused in the dark and inebriated, he attempted to remove his *jalabiyya* by pulling it up over his head, only for it to become tangled about his face, whereupon he lost his balance and tumbled head first into the water. And there, unable to extricate himself, he drowned.

It was dawn when the servants spotted his clothes. They had to locate someone who knew how to swim to go out, and find and drag his body into shore. Alarm of the sort only imaginable ran quickly through the house. The servants at once notified Husayn who immediately sent for the judge. He then told al-Rassi. They all knew of the doctor's intimacy and favor with al-Hakim. The three men next asked al-Tabarani to go break the news to the caliph, which he did forthwith, telling the caliph that Ibn Anastas had become confused in the night and had fallen into the river, where the servants found him tangled in his own clothes and drowned. Al-Hakim was obviously upset and openly revealed his displeasure, expressing his desire to determine exactly what had happened. They had to tell him more. At that moment the three others arrived on foot wearing the lightest of turbans. Asked to come in, they swore oaths that they had had no hand in the tragic outcome; all three insisted up and down that they were innocent in the matter. The body of the poor doctor – although by the time of his death he was not poor at all, leaving as he did a sizable estate – was carried to a church in a coffin, passing in mourning through the whole city. It was then brought to his house where he was buried.

And so might this affair have ended. Still we are entitled to suspect that al-Hakim did not forget or forgive. Surely he understood quite well that drunkenness, if not more serious forms of debauchery, was to blame, and that the highest officials of his government had participated, notably his chief executive Husayn, in whose dwelling the party was held, as well as the head of the judiciary 'Abd al-'Aziz, the very man responsible for enforcing the law of the land. For the modern observer, however, this event reveals a good deal more. Notice, for example, that the participants represented a cross section of the elite, with a Christian, Sunnis and Ismailis together in what amounted to a men's drinking club, the powerful class at play. There is another, much odder, but nonetheless strangely valid, interpretation. The doctor who died is reported by Yahya of Antioch, himself a Melkite who lived at the time in Egypt, to have diagnosed the caliph as suffering from a kind of melancholia, a form of depression. His treatment for this condition was a regimen that had the patient sit in a tub of oil of violet while listening to singing girls.[248] That sounds like medicine specifically designed to fit the preferred lifestyle of this particular physician, but according to our information this treatment worked well and seemed to alleviate al-Hakim's symptoms. Unfortunately the demise of the doctor brought an end to the treatment and consequently a resumption of the caliph's melancholia. It continued to plague him for the rest of his reign. For those who believe that many of his uncommon or unfamiliar actions were due to insanity, this event has special importance, as does the doctor's diagnosis of mental illness. The physician's death had many consequences.

But for the present purpose the further story of Husayn and 'Abd al-'Aziz is of the most interest.[249] Approximately six months after the fateful drinking party, a rumor began to circulate that the judge was about to be removed from office. Shortly thereafter he was in fact replaced by Malik al-Fariqi. Less than three weeks later Husayn suddenly found himself also fired, replaced without warning by Salih b. 'Ali. Both of the recently demoted men feared and even anticipated execution, yet each rode to the palace regularly, hoping for a better outcome. During the feast of fast-breaking, as if they were still in good standing, both sat at the caliph's table. But on 11 June 1008, they were confined to their homes; they and their children were no longer to ride in processions. Weeks later they were pardoned. Nearly a year passed like that. One day in January 1009, however, after entering the palace and extending salutation, the authorities seized 'Abd al-'Aziz. Husayn and others hid fearing the worst, but, on this occasion, al-Hakim relented. As the news of 'Abd al-'Aziz's arrest spread, merchants in the market closed shop. To calm the situation, the caliph released 'Abd al-'Aziz and granted an amnesty decree to Husayn, who then re-emerged. Al-Hakim also bestowed on each a robe of high honor and many costly gifts. The judge was given back jurisdiction over the court of complaints which he had supervised by then, on and off, for 13 years in all. Honors and gifts likewise came with this reappointment. Near the end of 1009, previously seized land grants were likewise restored. That same year two sons of ʿAbd al-ʿAziz were married to two daughters of Husayn, apparently a sign that the two families had become less apprehensive. Five months later, however, they decided otherwise and commenced to flee as a group, traveling by night into the Delta, possibly to seek cover and protection among the Banu Qurra.[250] Soldiers dispatched by al-Hakim failed to locate them. Meanwhile all their properties were confiscated, inventoried by the new chief judge, and moved to the government's *Diwan al-Mufrad*.

Nevertheless, the caliph soon decided again to seek a reconciliation with the fugitives; he sent them several letters expressing his desire to have them back. The text of one survives; it was composed and written personally by the caliph himself, a fact that elicited special notice from the man dispatched to deliver it. He asked for a copy precisely because it had not come from the chancery but from the imam.[251] Apparently a sticking point in this negotiation was the new *wasita*, Ibn ʿAbdun. Husayn thought this man had wronged him and he refused to return as long as Ibn ʿAbdun remained in office. Once the latter was removed, Husayn accepted, and, in the words of al-Maqrizi:

> Husayn, ʿAbd al-ʿAziz and those who had left with them presented themselves. All the notables of the state went down to greet him and to witness the honors accorded him or poured out on him, his children and his brother-in-law ʿAbd al-ʿAziz. Mounts carrying gifts were led in front of them. When they arrived at the gate of the palace, they dismounted and walked. The rest of the people walked with them into the palace. They appeared before al-Hakim; then went out having been forgiven by him. Husayn was allowed again to use in his correspondence 'Commander-in-Chief' with his personal name coming after his title, and to be addressed in that fashion. He then departed for his house. It was a magnificent day! All that had been seized from him, the property and the rest, were brought back to him. He was treated most graciously. He and ʿAbd al-ʿAziz continued to ride to the palace.[252]

Al-Maqrizi's source, who is, in all likelihood, al-Musabbihi, betrays in this account his personal feelings. The day of their return was, he comments, 'magnificent.' Even so, soon afterward, both were arrested again, though yet once more forgiven and granted another decree of amnesty.[253] The final act loomed, however. On 21 January 1011, Husayn b. Jawhar and ʿAbd al-ʿAziz b.

al-Nuʿman rode as was their practice to the palace. When the agent in charge of reception went out Husayn, ʿAbd al-ʿAziz and a third man, Abu ʿAli, the brother of al-Fadl, were told by him: 'Obey the command to do what the caliph wants of you.' The three sat and the people departed. The three of them were then seized and killed in a single moment.[254]

Here also we are given a list of what was found in the estate of Husayn. These men were obviously wealthy; government service had been generous to them. The children of both asked for and were promised good treatment. We are told, however, that the agents of the government who went through their estates were careful to gather up and confiscate all copies of the many decrees of amnesty that had been written for the two men in the past. Fearing the good will of al-Hakim would not last, Husayn's older sons Jaʿfar and Abu Jaʿfar soon fled along with a minor son named Jawhar to the Banu Jarrah. There they were granted protection. With the two out of his easy reach, the caliph, however, employed the stratagem of feigning punishment and confiscation on one of his eunuch servants Muflih and then to arrange his escape. He too fled to the Jarrahids and once there advised Husayn's sons not to rely for long on the hospitality of the Bedouin who had betrayed others before for money. They decided to head for Baghdad. Muflih secretly notified Jaysh b. Samsama, the Fatimid governor of Damascus of their intention to pass through his territory. Alerted he apprehended them both and killed them, sending their heads back to Cairo in October 1012. For Muflih's service all that had been taken from him was restored and then some.[255]

That same year, reports al-Maqrizi, the caliph arranged the marriage of Husayn's two wives to his cousin ʿAbd al-Rahim Ibn Ilyas.[256]

The Rebellion of al-ʿAllaqa

Although eventually executed, none of the figures involved in either of these drinking parties, or of any number of other persons who were put to death by order of al-Hakim, had actually rebelled against him. In most cases we do not know what caused the caliph's anger, or what crime might have brought about this punishment. Most of the men cited persisted in a display of loyalty, real or feigned, until the end. Active opposition to al-Hakim was rare, outright rebellion even rarer. Nonetheless, there were serious threats against him, in particular the revolt of Abu Rakwa and the counter-caliphate of the amir of Mecca, both of which involved Bedouin tribes – the Banu Qurra in the first, and the Tayy under the Jarrahids in the second – whose loyalty to the Fatimids, or lack of it, was always based on opportunity. In addition events in Syria often brought this or that faction into what amounted to a rebellion against the caliph's governor there. One such incident, a revolt at the coastal city of Tyre early in the reign, is noteworthy.

The inhabitants of this port rose against the Berber force that occupied it on behalf of the Fatimid authority and killed most of them in 998. The leader of the rebels was a sailor known by the name of al-ʿAllaqa.[257] Once news that Tyre was no longer in Fatimid hands reached Damascus, the governor ordered various contingents to proceed there. A large naval squadron was dispatched from Egypt as well. Faced with the prospect of a siege by both land and sea, al-'Allaqa appealed to the Byzantines for help, promising to turn over to them the city afterward. Meanwhile al-'Allaqa issued his own coins with the curious legend *ʿizza baʿda faqa, shatara bi-labaqa li-amir al-ʿAllaqa* ('Power after poverty, cunning with quick wit, has the commander al-ʿAllaqa'). This clever slogan, however, did him no real good. Byzantine ships were essentially powerless against a large force and soon suffered a defeat. Al-'Allaqa along with the gang members and other rabble who supported him retreated inside towers at the walls of Tyre. At that, realizing that the town was about to be captured, many of the citizens sought a guarantee of safety. Soon Fatimid troops began to loot the city, taking away incalculable riches. They hauled al-ʿAllaqa away in chains. He, and many of those with him, were taken to Cairo and there paraded. Al-ʿAllaqa was made to wear a lead dunce cap so heavy it threaten to fall down upon his neck. He was then flayed alive, his skin stuffed with straw and what remained of him was crucified. His associates were all executed.

The Revolt of Abu Rakwa

The fate of al-ʿAllaqa was shared by other rebels, but none so dangerous as the famous Abu Rakwa, whose campaign against the Fatimids came exceedingly close to success. So momentous was this rebellion a notice of its occurrence entered nearly all histories of that time and later medieval writers all have something to report about it, often details not included elsewhere.[258] We have already seen al-Maqrizi's version which he placed under the Islamic year 396 (1005–06), as had done his own source, al-Musabbihi.

The origin of this Abu Rakwa – whose nickname means the 'carrier of the water bottle', an attribute associated with wandering Sufi mystics who were typically accompanied in their travels by a water bottle – was commonly said to have been the royal family of Umayyad Spain. Accordingly his name was al-Walid b. Hisham b. ʿAbd al-Malk b. ʿAbd al-Rahman and his story began with a dynastic dispute in al-Andalus that saw him forcefully driven out, leaving no choice but to seek his fortune elsewhere. From Qayrawan he is reported to have taught hadith and Qurʾan in various territories, Upper Egypt, Mecca, the Yemen, until finally connecting with the Banu Qurra, an Arab Bedouin tribe whose lands stretched from the Nile Delta to Barqa in what is modern Libya. Abu Rakwa claimed that, because of his Umayyad heritage, he knew things that no one else knew and that he could predict events. The Banu Qurra, already quite disposed to support a rebellion against al-Hakim, signed on to his cause.

An important factor in the success of Abu Rakwa was the willingness of this tribe to adopt him. The Banu Qurra had five years earlier been ordered to accompany Fatimid troops, under the command of Yahya b. ʿAli, to the relief of Tripoli against the Sinhaja. In the end they returned without having accomplished the task; al-Hakim blamed them in part for Yahya's failure. He demanded that they send him hostages and he ordered others, as a delegation, to come to Alexandria, and there he had them all killed, including the hostages.

Abu Rakwa therefore found a willing force in these Arabs. In the western region of their territory, moreover, their lands abutted those of the Berber tribes of Zanata, Lawata and others, who also rallied to the standard of the Umayyad pretender. Eventually Abu Rakwa announced that, whereas he had been preaching the cause of the one who would rise, the Qa'im, a messianic expectation, he was actually appealing for himself. He was this Umayyad messiah. The tribes swore allegiance to him as the imam-caliph, the Commander of the Believers, al-Nasir li-Din Allah. The Arabs among them insisted on cementing their relationship by a ceremony in which the parties both drank sheep's milk.[259] Claiming that he had no desire for worldly possession, Abu Rakwa promised his followers extravagant riches and lands in the Nile valley once they had supplanted the Fatimids. The great *bayʿa* took place on 31 March 1005 at ʿUyun al-Nasr.

As Abu Rakwa's force increased, al-Hakim's governor in Barqa warned of the coming trouble. Cairo sent a fairly large army, composed mainly of Kutama Berbers, commanded by Yanal al-Tawil, a Turk. Given the former animosity between the Kutama and the Turks and Yanal's role in suppressing the Westerners, the choice of leader was unwise. Moreover, Abu Rakwa was on the home ground of the Banu Qurra. He easily put the wells along the route from Alexandria to Barqa out of commission. Yanal arrived there in August 1005 to face Abu Rakwa in disarray. Fighting on the same ground where Abu Rakwa had received the oath of allegiance, he suffered a total defeat, was captured and killed. The booty seized from his camp strengthened the rebels considerably. They were now in a position to undertake a full siege of Barqa. Seeing that he could not resist for long, Sandal, its Fatimid governor, fled by sea along with its elite. First he wrote to al-Hakim to explain the gravity of the situation, which, in fact, became only worse once Abu Rakwa captured and looted Barqa in April 1006.

Information from non-Egyptian sources, particularly as reported in the North African history of Ibn ʿIdhari, indicates that climatic conditions were unusually harsh with widespread drought in the region of Tripolitania. The growing force behind Abu Rakwa could not hope to sustain itself there. It became essential that he move toward Alexandria. Armies formed there under various commanders tried to prevent him reaching it, among them the local commander at al-Hammam, Ibn al-Armaniyya, but all suffered defeat not far from the city. Victorious again, Abu Rakwa, in anticipation of additional conquests to come, began to divide Egypt into lands he granted to his followers, including the homes and estates of the Fatimid elite in Cairo.

At this point, according to al-Maqrizi and Ibn ʿIdhari, al-Hakim attempted to trick Abu Rakwa. He ordered his senior officials to write to the rebel to suggest that they were disaffected with the caliph, with the constant stream of executions, with the resultant insecurity, and that they preferred the religious doctrine of the Sunni Abu Rakwa. Once he approached Cairo, they claimed, they would go over to his side. Al-Maqrizi's account of this ruse is, as we have seen, fairly fully described as such. He insists that, even though it was a ploy invented by al-Hakim, it worked because Abu Rakwa received so many separate individually composed and sent letters more or less to the same effect, he began to trust them. Other historians, however, regard the letters as an authentic expression of what the senders actually felt. They discount the involvement of al-Hakim and refuse to believe that it was a trick to lure Abu Rakwa to Cairo.

Whatever the truth, the rebel and his supporters marched south along the western side of the Nile aiming for Jiza opposite Cairo and Fustat. To counter that move, the caliph granted honors to the general ʿAli b. Falah, ordered him to assemble an army at the Birkat al-Habash south of Cairo, and then to take the troops over the river to Jiza, portions of it coming later, unit by unit. That was early summer. On 17 July al-Hakim wrote to ask the Jarrahids to send aid, which they did, the three sons of Mufarrij in the lead.[260] All three were given special honors and these Bedouin auxiliaries crossed over as well. Maqrizi mentions here only Safuh b. Daghfal b. al-Jarrah but other sources include the sons of Mufarrij. The supreme commander of the Fatimid armies was still Fadl, who now, with great show, received even greater honors and rewards. He too crossed over accompanied by yet more soldiers, each of whom drew a bonus of 50 dinars. Word arrived in Cairo that Abu Rakwa's men were raiding the Fayum. A detachment sent after them caught and defeated them. Many heads of the enemy from this encounter later reached Cairo. On 2 August Fadl arrived in Jiza. ʿAli b. Falah was already encamped there with the bulk of the army, weapons and supplies. Anticipation of failure created a general panic in Cairo and Fustat. Troop after troop went through the city at night down to the river. On 16 August, Abu Rakwa attacked the center of Ibn Falah's camp, plundering his stores. The fighting was intense with a great many deaths on both sides. With troops and weapons still arriving, and the heightened anxiety among the population, Ibn Falah ordered the dead burned where they fell rather than allowing the families to claim the bodies. But many of the deceased were never found or acknowledged. People spent Friday night weeping for those they knew had died. That was Sunday 20 August. Shortly thereafter news came in that Abu Rakwa was moving what remained of his army into the Fayum. Fadl set off to confront him there. On 31 August 1006, the following Saturday, the battle commenced at Raʾs al-Birka (a half stage from Madinat al-Fayyum). There was great slaughter and Abu Rakwa was finally defeated. His Arab allies abandoned him and he fled south toward Nubia, with Fadl on his trail. Six thousand heads of the dead enemy reached Cairo along with 100 prisoners, both to be paraded. Prior to execution the captives suffered a brutal scourging at the hands of the populace, so merciless, reports al-Musabbihi, the beatings exposed the bone of their shoulder blades. 'It was,' he says, 'a dreadful event.' But soon more heads began to arrive.

Ibn Falah and ʿAli b. al-Jarrah came back over to receive honors, while Fadl continued to pursue Abu Rakwa, all the while capturing more of the rebels which he sent back along with the heads of those killed. Finally on 23 February word spread that Fadl had at last apprehended Abu Rakwa. He was actually taken two months earlier. The rebel had managed to enter Nubia and there receive shelter in a monastery for a couple of weeks, only then to be turned over to the Fatimids, or according to another version, seized by soldiers under Fadl's orders.

Fearing that his new captive might attempt suicide, Fadl treated him with special regard, even honor, while transporting him carefully from Aswan to the outskirts of Fustat where he stopped at the beginning of March. During the period Abu Rakwa was held at this last encampment, many of the notables went to observe the rebel first hand, among them Husayn b. Jawhar the Commander-in-Chief, Khatkin al-Dayf, an intimate of al-Hakim and later the head of the *daʿwa*, and, some say, the caliph himself, though that seems unlikely. A conversation between Abu Rakwa and Khatkin is recorded in which the latter offers to convey a message to al-Hakim for the condemned man. On 10 March Fadl took away his troops. Abu Rakwa was strapped on a raised platform on a camel wearing the standard lead dunce cap, a monkey held behind him to beat the back of his head, and the procession commenced, led by elephants to keep the populace at bay and followed by the general who had captured him.[261] Here it is worth repeating the description provided by al-Maqrizi, which is surely that of al-Musabbihi himself.

> People had gathered on all sides, a crowd so large its like had never before been seen. The houses and shops became empty caves as a result. The people spent the night along the roadways that took him eventually to the palace. He was held at the gate of the palace, stopped there for an hour, with him motioning with his finger and imploring forgiveness, while being slapped on the nape of his neck. He was told to kiss the ground and he did that. Then he was marched to the mosque of Tibr. As he went out of the gate of Cairo, he motioned to the people, who pelted him with stones and bricks, slapping him and pulling his beard, until he was on the point of death several times, before finally reaching the mosque of Tibr. There he was hung and his body crucified. His head was taken to al-Hakim. Honors were accorded General Fadl and others of the commanders and authorities who had been with him. Honors went also to the commander-in-chief. It was a magnificent and amazing day because of the multitude of people gathered for the occasion who remained for two nights in the shops and street and at the doorways of the house expressing delight and happiness.[262]

Al-Maqrizi's source adds that Abu Rakwa '...was brown-skinned mixed with red on top with sharp features and a long brow and with black eyes tinged with blue. He was curved, a small beard, varying from reddish brown to blond, revealing, when frowning a seriousness in him. He had barely passed the age of 30 on the day he died.'[263] That sounds like the observation of someone who had actually seen the man at close range: surely al-Musabbihi.

Several historians note additional details, also likely taken from al-Musabbihi, such as the fact that some people paid as much as a quarter dinar to secure the best seats for the final procession of Abu Rakwa. Others dwell on the career of the man who trained and controlled the monkey, a person named al-Abzari, and how much he was paid.[264] Al-Maqrizi inserted into his account, again most likely from al-Musabbihi, that the threat of Abu Rakwa, in particular his rising power and march from Alexandria toward the capital, the battles in Jiza and the Fayum, occurred coincident with the appearance of an incredibly bright tufted star or planet that rose in the night sky shining as brilliantly as the moon. It intensified over that summer and then faded and disappeared, much, says our source, as did Abu Rakwa.[265]

This celestial event left its own record. Long afterward the Egyptian physician and polymath Ibn Ridwan wrote out carefully a precise description, including the exact location of the star in the heavens, of what he had himself witnessed as a young boy during that troubled summer. Many others as far away as China and Switzerland saw it too. We now know that it was a supernova, the brightest ever recorded.[266]

The head of Abu Rakwa was put initially in a special storehouse for the heads of deceased enemies. Eventually 30 thousand from this rebellion were assembled there and finally loaded on 100 camels for a tour of Syria and ultimately to be thrown into the Euphrates.[267]

From the wide record this one rebellion left in Islamic historiography, it is obvious that it was extremely serious, clearly threatening the most catastrophic result, if Abu Rakwa had succeeded in defeating the army of Fadl, for the reign of al-Hakim, if not for the dynasty as a whole. The caliph threw into the battle and the effort to apprehend the rebel huge sums, said to amount to more than one million dinars. Contemporaries observed what happened with fear and dread. Some further afield who opposed the Ismaili caliphate may have rooted for the rebellion, though it is hard to imagine most welcoming an Umayyad caliphate in its place. Later Sunni historians, however, may have preserved information about it because they saw it as a sign of Sunni opposition. Some are quick to claim that al-Hakim rescinded in this time of crisis many of his new pro-Shiite orders in order to win back popular support.

The Rebellion of the Jarrahids and Counter-caliphate of the Amir of Mecca

Once Abu Rakwa was finally dead and the threat he posed gone for good, letters were dispatched to all outlying districts with the news of this triumph. In April the elders of every region and its judges, and also the judges of Syria and its notables, came to Cairo to offer congratulations to al-Hakim for this victory. Abu'l-Futuh Hasan b. Ja'far, the Hasanid amir of Mecca, arrived that month as well, likewise to offer congratulations. He was presented with a robe of honor, treated generously and put up in the house formerly belonging to Barjawan.[268] Two of the oddities in all this are, first, the active participation on the Fatimid side of the Tayy Bedouin and their Jarrahid chieftains and, second, this offer of felicitations delivered personally by Abu'l-Futuh, who had come all the way from Mecca. Both would not long after themselves commence a revolt against the authority of al-Hakim, a rebellion less threatening to Cairo itself but nonetheless quite serious.

The story of this latter rebellion[269], however, begins atypically with a rivalry in the governing bureaucracy in Egypt. Even so, the participation in it of the Jarrahid chieftains and their Tayy Bedouin henchmen was not unusual at all.[270] Mufarrij b. Daghfal b. al-Jarrah, the father of the three sons who had come to the aid of al-Hakim against Abu Rakwa, and the supreme leader of the clan, had by this time engaged in a long string of actions contrary to the interests of the Fatimids stretching back to their earliest days in Syria. On one occasion or another he had formed alliances with the Qarmatians, the Byzantines, and several rebels among them Alptakin, all against the Fatimids. Still he was not above accepting cash payments from Cairo in exchange for a promise now and then of his loyalty and good will. Clearly his policy followed closely temporary expediency and his own self-interest. That he or his sons might rebel yet once more was to be expected.

The case of Abu'l-Futuh, the amir of Mecca, was different but most likely also driven by a personal motive, perhaps residual resentment of Fatimid claims to a more exalted genealogical descent than that of himself. He was after all, although through the line of Hasan rather than Husayn, the offspring of Fatima and 'Ali, which is what the Fatimids also claimed. Still, previous to this rebellion, he appears to have promoted good relations with Cairo. As far back as 992, even before he took over from his brother as commander in Mecca, an incident there reveals his attitude. The Abbasid caliph had sent to Mecca a letter recognizing formally the amirate of his family.

Acting for them he dispatched the letter instead to al-ʿAziz in Cairo, who responded by issuing his own decree of appointment in their favor, which he returned along with money and robes of honor for distribution among them. Assembling at the Kaʿba, they divided the money and accepted the honors. Abu'l-Futuh then said as they dressed the Kaʿba in its ceremonial covering (*kiswa*), which was now, in keeping with Fatimid suzerainty, white in place of Abbasid black, 'Thanks be to God, O descendants of the Radiant Fatima, you partisans of the noble law, that His house is adorned with a dressing of happiness after previously having been dressed in sadness. He grants dominion over the holy cities to the Husaynid and Hasanid members of the family of the apostle's daughter, approving thereby both.' As Abu'l-Futuh's visit to Cairo in 1007 to extend his felicitations on the victory over Abu Rakwa demonstrates, if he harbored plans to proclaim his own independence, it was not obvious.

The source of the trouble to come was a feud between the powerful Christian bureaucrat Mansur (or Abu Nasr) Ibn ʿAbdun, a man with considerable experience in the financial management of various government departments, and Abu'l-Qasim Ibn al-Maghribi, the most prominent member of a family of clerks and officials.[271] The name al-Maghribi, which was common to them all, derived from a recent ancestor's service in the Abbasid bureau of tax affairs for western lands (hence *maghribi*), which was located in Baghdad, not the Maghrib. This meaning for the name, however, was not necessarily widely accepted or recognized; many medieval sources doubt it, some suspecting that it meant instead 'adherent of western doctrine', a euphemism of the time for Ismaili Shiism.

This same Ibn ʿAbdun had equally offended Husayn b. Jawhar, who at a key moment forced al-Hakim to remove him from the chief executive position. There is thus, as suggested in some sources, possibly a Christian–Muslim conflict involved. Ibn ʿAbdun would then have been the protector of Christians in the government against Muslims who wanted them excluded. In any case, whatever the exact cause of their dispute, Ibn ʿAbdun eventually prevailed on the caliph to order the arrest and execution of the whole al-Maghribi clan. Abu'l-Qasim managed to hide but his two brothers, his father and father's brother, plus two or three additional members of the family were all put to death. The date was 18 June 1010.[272]

Having escaped, Abu'l-Qasim fled under cover toward the territory of the Jarrahids. There he encountered Hassan, the eldest son of Mufarrij. Admitted to his presence al-Maghribi then recited a long poem in praise of the Jarrahids and the Tayy. The whole text of this poem survives.[273] Abu'l-Qasim was a master of language and expression.[274] Hassan was delighted with it and he at once extended his protection to the poet against the attempts of al-Hakim to apprehend him.

Once safe among the Tayy, Ibn al-Maghribi urged them to renounce al-Hakim, counseling them to attack Ramla, the headquarters of the Fatimid occupation in southern Palestine. Alarmed, the Fatimids appointed a new general for Palestine, Yarukhtakin, who set off toward Syria intending to assemble forces there to oppose the Jarrahids. He departed Egypt with little protection, however, except a party of merchants, though he took along his wife, the daughter of Yaʿqub Ibn Killis, and his family and belongings. Abu'l-Qasim advised Hassan to ambush Yarukh, which he did. Al-Hakim attempted in vain to rescue his commander by ransom but before matters reached that stage Hassan had killed him.

Ibn al-Maghribi also argued for recognition of the amir of Mecca as caliph. It is unclear how much of this move was already communicated to Abu'l-Futuh, but Ibn al-Maghribi soon departed for Mecca to explain it and convince him to accept. That he did apparently without much hesitation. He announced himself from the *minbar* now as the Commander of the Believers al-Rashid bi-llah. Advised by Abu'l-Qasim, the new caliph confiscated estates of several wealthy men and added to the fund he realized gold and silver deposited in the Kaʿba. With all that he commenced to mint coins, called locally *kaʿbiyya*, bearing his title, which he then distributed to those who joined him, among them several of the Arab tribes of the region. As a party they left Mecca headed for Ramla, there to meet up with the Jarrahids. Mufarrij, his sons Hassan, Mahmud and ʿAli, with their retinue, went out to greet Abu'l-Futuh. Upon his arrival they kissed the ground before him, saluted him as caliph, and set him up in the government house in Ramla.

On the following Friday he rode for the *khutba*, with Mufarrij, his sons and the commanders of the Tayy behind on foot. In the mosque he mounted the *minbar* and began the sermon by quoting Qurʾan 28: 1–6: '*Ta, mim, sin*; these are the clear verses of the Qurʾan; we recite to you the story of Moses and Pharaoh in truth for people who believe. Truly Pharaoh exalted himself in the land and divided the people into parties (*shiyaʿ*, plural of *Shiʿa*), denigrating a group of them, killing their sons but keeping their women alive because he was one of those who do evil. We wish to be gracious to those who were denigrated in the land and make them leaders, making them those who inherit. We make for them a firm place in the land, to show Pharaoh and

Haman and their armies that which they previously took precautions against.' Al-Hakim had now become Pharaoh.

The Jarrahids then held all of Palestine from al-Farama to Tiberias and their revolt threatened that area and adjacent territories, which they ravaged at will. Their control over it also precluded travel through their territory for the pilgrimage. In 1011, the caravan set off but returned soon after departure. No one from Egypt, Syria, or, say other reports, from Iraq (and Khurasan) made the pilgrimage that year, only the Yemenis and those few who were already resident in the Hijaz. In the following year a decree was issued forbidding all travel from Fatimid domains to Mecca. Anyone who had begun preparations for a pilgrimage cancelled them; those en route returned. Commerce from Egypt with the Hijaz ended, as did the annual flow of donations normally carried by the pilgrimage caravan.

Sufficiently agitated by these events, al-Hakim now commenced an alternate plan, one that had proven itself many times before. Slowly and patiently he began sending funds, gifts and sumptuous goods to the various Jarrahids to draw them away from Abu'l-Futuh. Each of the brothers is reported to have received a payment of 50 thousand dinars. Gradually they abandoned Abu'l-Futuh, who eventually realized his loss of authority and growing peril. Finally he asked for an escort to deliver him safely once again to Mecca. There he resumed the amirate and reverted to the situation prior to the rebellion. Once again al-Hakim was named in the Friday sermon and on the coinage. A letter from the amir seeking forgiveness and absolution was accepted in Cairo. One report mentions a substantial sum sent to him by al-Hakim and an order from the Fatimids for the people traveling to Mecca to carry there food and other goods. There were, it seems, no repercussions in his case; 27 years later when he died, Abu'l-Futuh was still the amir of Mecca, his brief caliphate long forgotten.

Abu'l-Qasim, who had instigated much of what happened, soon sensed, like Abu'l-Futuh, that he had worn out his welcome. He requested and was granted an escort to Iraq. There he was to serve various governments, the Abbasid caliphate among them, as wazir. He died in 1027 then living in Mayyafariqin and was, by his own request, taken to Kufa and buried there. The Jarrahids remained in rebellion into 1013 but thereafter ceased their opposition. Mufarrij himself died just as al-Hakim was sending a large force against him from Egypt under 'Ali b. Falah. His sons vanished into the desert.[275]

Defenders of the Caliph

Along with reports of these rebellions and of a long record of persons put to death by his regime, al-Hakim had no lack of supporters and well-wishers. The *daʿwa*, though perhaps troubled by actions of his not readily explained and by occasional signs of his displeasure with it, nevertheless loyally followed his lead. The more difficult the situation, it seems, the more concentrated the effort to propagate and defend its doctrine, above all that of the absolute necessity of the imamate. Curiously, among the fairly numerous writings by members of the *daʿwa* prior to the time of al-Hakim, almost none focus on this topic. The many treatises of the highly important *daʿi* al-Sijistani (d. about 975), for example, hardly mention the imamate, let alone argue for it. As a result it is possible to conclude that the specific institutional role of the imam was not under threat from outside or doubt from within, and that therefore no authority felt required to explain it explicitly or to defend it in writing. That the imamate was a basic and essential component of Islamic government must have appeared obvious, and so it does in Qadi al-Nuʿman's *Pillars of Islam*, the entire content of which depends on the words of previous imams and their overarching authority in all matters.

The era of al-Hakim was different. The progress of his rule did not accord with earlier notions of kingship – that is, of political government – or of the imamate – religious and civil authority in combination. Under the circumstances engendered by the atypical methods of his administration, the *daʿwa* suffered severe stresses, partially the result of internal uncertainty and misgiving, partially of the desire to shield the institution of the imamate from its detractors, especially as many of those same detractors based their own propaganda against it on the oddities they saw in this caliph's policies, which were widely reported and thus well known.

From this period, quite in contrast to any before, we possess three Ismaili works on the imamate, and two of them seek to provide a convincing proof of its undeniable necessity in general and that of al-Hakim specifically. All explicitly cite him by name and title as the imam of the time.

The shortest is actually a series of answers to questions about the imamate. Its author was Abu'l-Fawaris Ahmad b. Yaʿqub, a *daʿi* responsible for Palestine. When the order for the destruction of the church of the Holy Sepulcre was issued, it went to him and he, with others, arranged to carry it out. In his 'Treatise on the Imamate' (*al-Risala fi'l-imama*)[276] he provided the standard doctrine about its necessity, refuting the notion that the Qur'an, the

Hadith or the sacred law can substitute for it. The imam must be raised to office by divine appointment. Abu'l-Fawaris then reviews the imamate of ʿAli, of his descendants, including most particularly Muhammad b. Isma'il b. Jaʿfar (rather than Musa b. Jaʿfar). The imam, he says, must produce an heir, but he might, nevertheless, come to his office as a youth and he might, during certain periods of strife, remain in concealment. Near the end he offers a brief list of the virtues to be found in the imam: sacred descent, knowledge, courage and generosity. All these, he notes finally, are present in the most complete form possible in 'our lord and master, the imam of our epoch and time, al-Hakim bi-Amr Allah, God's blessings be upon him and his selected and chosen predecessors.'

One of the other two is by an obscure *daʿi* named Ahmad b. Ibrahim al-Naysaburi. It has the title 'Proof of the Imamate' (*Ithbat al-imama*)[277], which again suggests that its primary purpose is to establish the necessity of this institution as an inevitable requirement of Islamic governance. Yet, despite the significance of this subject and this particular treatise, we know almost nothing about its author. Two additional works of his exist and one of them – on the rules for the comportment of *daʿis* and the *daʿwa* – is just as important. Nevertheless the rank of the author or even his country of residence remains in doubt, though, because of the tone of authority that is evident in his writings and lack of circumspection, it appears he composed them, with the imam's approval, within the safety and protection of the Fatimid state. But no detail in either indicates precisely who he was. Even so his treatise proving the imamate contains a crucial reference to the 'heir apparent'. Near the beginning, in a section for benedictions on the prophet and the imams, particularly for al-Hakim as the current imam, al-Naysaburi appends a wish for such blessing to apply as well to, as he puts it, "the heir apparent, the successor to the Commander of the Believers" (in Arabic *wali 'ahd al-muslimin wa khalifat amir al-mu'minin*). In this context this phrase refers to none other than al-Hakim's cousin, 'Abd al-Rahim b. Ilyas, who had been declared heir apparent in 1013. He retained this title until his own death in 1021, not long after the caliph disappeared. Throughout this same period this formula was a standard phrase added to all public documents including coins. Al-Naysaburi's *Proof of the Imamate* was surely composed while that declaration was in effect and the treatise therefore must itself date to that time, which would have also been when its author held perhaps his highest rank.

Another detail in it points to the years between 1017 and 1021. At the end of al-Naysaburi's laudatory account of the Imam's achievements, which concludes this treatise, he hints at another, secondary motive that may have caused him to write. He notes there that with all his fine and glorious traits, al-Hakim was, as several contemporary witnesses also admit, unusual in ways no other Muslim leader was or had ever been. His rule was simply not that of ordinary kings or caliphs. Therefore to judge him and his actions by the standard of other human beings, even the most exalted among them, is bound, he says, to lead to confusion. One possible reaction would be to reject his authority. But those who see what he does in its true light will come to understand, he continues, that al-Hakim's commands and prohibitions, his giving and his taking away, ought to be compared with the acts of God. He is thus not human in any ordinary sense. However, even so, many, even of his most loyal followers, fail to grasp this fact and take it to heart. As a result they become perplexed by what they see or hear reported about the Imam. The standard measure for human actions is simply not appropriate in this case. But, also, some regard al-Hakim with a tendency toward exaggeration. Moving in the opposite direction, these people then claim that he is, in fact, divine. Al-Naysaburi remains adamantly opposed to both extremes. However, it is especially significant that he confesses openly that some followers of al-Hakim already regard his unusual behavior as a sign of divinity. That matches what we know about various groups from the same period who eventually became the Druze. They first went public with their claim about al-Hakim's divinity in the year 1017. Al-Naysaburi was evidently cautioning against them and their heresy. For him even to mention that possibility, if only to reject it, means that it was already happening when he undertook to write his defense of the imamate. Perhaps that also explains in part why he considered it important to do so.

The major portion of the work, however, consists of al-Naysaburi's proof for the imamate, not necessarily that of al-Hakim. Yet even there his language depends on a kind of hyperbole and exaggeration hardly common to works on Islamic leadership, even among the Shiʿa. The imam is the best of mankind, the end for which the world exists; he is the sun that shines in the hearts of God's friends. He holds the place of the universal intellect in his own realm; he is God's shadow on the earth; he is the ultimate sage in each age. In his own era he is the speaking-prophet. Several of these claims, and others like them in the treatise, exceed the normal bounds of Ismaili doctrine. The central question involved is the relationship between a prophet-messenger, e.g. Muhammad, and the imams who come after him. Clearly, as exalted as they are, none of the latter receive revelation. But what then does al-Naysaburi's assertion about the imam being the speaking-prophet (the term in Arabic is *natiq* and it is ordinarily reserved strictly for the prophets who compose a sacred law: Adam, Noah,

Abraham, Moses, Jesus and Muhammad, that is, who have the benefit of revelation) mean? That the imam has dominance over all men and the world is not at issue but that he is the universal intellect is questionable. In a display of unbridled enthusiasm for the imamate, quite possibly enhanced by what he had witnessed of al-Hakim, al-Naysaburi observed few doctrinal cautions; surely he had reason to expect that his work would be read only by those who shared his devotion to the caliph in Cairo.

The rhetorical exaggeration employed by al-Naysaburi should have been fairly obvious and it likely also appealed to many Ismailis. The imam has become, in his words, the be-all and end-all, the ultimate ruler of a divinely conceived kingdom on earth. That all of this was true of al-Hakim strains the bounds of Islamic doctrine to the furthest limit, perhaps even exceeding, or at the least testing, the normal boundaries of Ismaili doctrine as it had existed previously. But, though mindful of the Druze heresy and its excess, al-Naysaburi withholds little, even going so far as to claim that al-Hakim is the messiah, as in the following passage.

> ...He [al-Hakim] completes all who have gone before. Possibly someone will say, but this is the attribute of the messiah (*qa'im*) of the last days and the Commander of the Believers is not the last. We reply: the Commander of the Believers is the messiah of his time and period, and the messiah of those in the past, and their completer (*mutimm*) (p. 85).

Al-Naysaburi claimed for al-Hakim the following: man is the best of creatures and end of the world; the imam is the best of men and the best is naturally perforce the ruler and leader of them. As the holder of power the imam is God's shadow on the earth, the complete and ultimate sage, the brain of the world in its entirety, its head. Many Ismailis may have believed as much about their imam but few would have said it publicly, let alone written it down in a treatise to be read by others.

Missing here is a confirmation that al-Hakim will not be the last, that the imamate will continue in his progeny, and that many more imams will come. Al-Naysaburi's failure to indicate that the imamate will proceed beyond the current imam is, however, most likely a rhetorical device that serves merely to enhance the meaning of the moment, as he confidently predicts a surpassing ultimate victory for al-Hakim in the near future, one in which all or most of his enemies will fall and he will rise to a position of dominion over the whole of the Islamic community.

The third author is the famous Hamid al-Din al-Kirmani, undeniably the outstanding scholar in the *daʿwa* of the time, all of whose works are dedicated to al-Hakim.[278] As with al-Naysaburi and many other *daʿis*, there is no mention of him in the chronicles of that period or later. Nonetheless facets of his career are clear from clues in his writings: a citation of the name of a contemporary, a place or event. Enough treatises by him survive to allow a reasonable reconstruction of his activities including his visit to Cairo for the years 1015 to 1020 approximately, where he taught and wrote under the leadership of Khatkin al-Dayf who was over that period the head of the *daʿwa*. Several of his treatises contain material essential for the defense of the Ismaili imamate but one constitutes purely and simply a proof for it. Given al-Kirmani's mastery of the philosophical tradition, and inclination for using its technical methods alongside that of religious theology, that he would employ it to demonstrate the absolute necessity of the imamate is to be expected. In addition, however, in his 'Lights to Illuminate the Proof of the Imamate'[279], he provides a series of interconnected proofs –105 in all – leading logically from primary and general premises not merely to the requirement of the Islamic imamate but to that of al-Hakim specifically (as the sole imam of the time in which he lives). Obviously philosophical logic, which might apply to the general argument, had to give way to historical facts in the particular case of named imams. This work offers, nevertheless, a major statement of Ismaili doctrine combined with a careful, knowledgeable defense of al-Hakim's reign.

Interestingly, however, he did not write it in Egypt but rather about 1014 in Iraq, where he lived prior to coming to Cairo. His expressed purpose in the treatise was to convince the Buyid wazir in Baghdad, Fakhr al-Mulk, to drop his allegiance to the Abbasid caliph and accept the Fatimids. Al-Kirmani knew that this man was Shiite and he hoped to appeal to him as a devoted partisan of the descendants of ʿAli. Most of al-Kirmani's arguments, many quite generically Shiite, might well have raised no alarms among the non-Ismaili Shiʿa. The claims he makes specifically about al-Hakim, however, were provocative enough to invite condemnation by them. Nor does al-Kirmani downplay certain of the most troubling features of the reign. Instead he regards them as a sign of the validity of this very imamate. That the Fatimid caliph was known to ride about by night or day, all but alone, although many had sworn to kill him, for example, is turned by al-Kirmani into a virtue: 'His riding about alone in spite of the great position God gave him is no secret and, despite the knowledge among his troops and his men, both small and great, that his riding has as its only purpose to kill them for their disobedience and previous error from other times, they are unable to act [against him], as would not be the case with anyone other than him in a similar situation.'

Note the use of facts specific to al-Hakim and not true of any imam previous to him. Clearly al-Kirmani defended in this treatise a situation unlike any other, even if in its broader methods it depended on philosophical reasoning that would apply generally. Several additional passages from the same work may help elucidate both that method as it concerned this caliphate and the admission, albeit using quite laudatory language, of the unusual characteristics of it.

> The characteristic of what might be claimed, but for which there exists no evidence or proof, is that it is not true, and the characteristic of what might be claimed and for which there exists evidence and proof is that it is true. What al-Hakim bi-amr Allah, Commander of the Believers, claims about his being an 'Aliid, Husaynid, the one designated, knowledgeable, just, pious, commander of the good and prohibiter of the bad, brave, ascetic, the sum of virtuous qualities, chosen by God, is established on the basis of evidence and proofs. Testimony as to the validity of his claim comes from Hasanid and Husaynid descendants of 'Ali in the Holy Cities publicly and, from those who are not in his kingdom, it comes from Hasanid and Husaynid descendants of 'Ali whose testimony is otherwise prevented by a continuous stream of statements from those who disapproved of it whether out of some desire or some fear. But those whose testimony approves are not less than the testimony of the others. By contrast, resisting they commit themselves in fealty to him and his imamate in private. The existence of evidence of his justice, which unites the elite and the masses and which has caused his repute to emanate far and wide, and evidence of his piety, which none deny, is his refraining from taking the property of people by force and his abstaining from expropriating what is not his out of mercy, so that strangers who die and others who have no heir present and who leave what they leave, he does not brandish the lance of his piety seeking their money, nor does he employ it to further the sin of greed through the oppressing of women and men. He commands that it be deposited in the Warehouse of Deposits, the policy for the erecting of which was a consequence of the goodness of his justice in safeguarding the property of Muslims and in searching for the heirs and giving to them what was due them. There is ample evidence of his commanding the good and prohibiting the bad, which none can deny, in the way he lives, devoting his nights and days to strengthening the word of truth, aiding the

oppressed, building mosques, tearing down churches, preserving the communal prayer, applying the regulations of the law and confirming them and the corporal punishments, extending justice to the masses, and acting with respect to them with clemency and charity to the extent that the countries whom the protection of his orders include are in the cradle of security at home, neither evil nor sadness touches them. There is evidence for his prohibiting the bad, reports of which have spread far and wide, from his closing down sources of depravity and dissolution, which are permitted quite openly in their cities by those who claim the imamate among the family of Umayya and the family of ʿAbbas. There is much evidence of his *jihad* in the service of God and his preservation of the borders, and his familiarity with the commoners and his discouraging the word of the false and what pertains to shortchanging the law that his ancestor Muhammad brought. There is also considerable evidence of his knowledge of the Book and the law and religious affairs and the unequivocal interpretations of it in matters concerning which mankind has no ability nor were those in the nations that preceded who were the specialists in the explanation of it, of those some have been spread by his trusted followers and his friends in the various districts [of the Islamic world]. He has explained symbols with answers that put spirits at ease and cause doubting to cease. As evidence of his asceticism, the report of which has spread in the cities, there is his riding a donkey and wearing rough clothing, eating grits, all despite the great position that God conferred on him. There is also good evidence of his bravery, which cannot be hidden and mention of which has spread throughout the world. His riding about alone in spite of the great position God gave him is no secret and, despite the knowledge among his troops and his men, both small and great, that his riding has as its only purpose to kill them for their disobedience and previous error from other times, they are unable to act, as would not be the case with anyone other than him in a similar case. Even with the great concern caused by his riding without many men or a force of his own, fear does not prevent him from doing that, nor is he held back by imagining what might befall him from his enemies should he be by himself and he does not lose courage. Finding himself in the middle of them without men, knowing that individuals among his soldiers and staff have sworn more than once to kill him and that they had distributed among them a large sum to encourage capturing him, the army was incapable of finding him. How much more so would cowardice have hobbled a man alone other than him, but weakness did not overcome him because of them. Instead dread was cast into their hearts and

> these men scattered on different paths, all of this showing that God is supporting and safeguarding him. The evidence of his generosity is that no day passes by nor week nor month but he disperses huge sums of dinars in relief of those in need and to support those seeking help. From this we determine that he is the guarantor of what is true and, if it is true, he is the truthful, and the truthful by the words of God: 'be with those who are the truthful' [Qur'an 9: 119] requires being in his company and following him. Therefore al-Hakim bi-amr Allah, Commander of the Faithful, is the truthful imam and following him and obeying him is obligatory.[280]

Or, as in two summary statements, also by al-Kirmani:

> Al-Hakim bi-amr Allah, the Commander of the Faithful is a lineal descendant of al-Husayn; he is pure in body and soul, spends his funds for religiously commendable purposes and its benefit, knows what is permitted and what is forbidden and legal affairs and decisions, commands the good and prohibits the bad, and was designated by his pure forefathers who were offspring of the apostle.

> Al-Hakim bi-amr Allah, who descends from the offspring of al-Husayn, is from the offspring of prophecy and is a descendant of al-Husayn; he is not infertile owing to the existence of his progeny, and he knows the Book of God and the law of the Apostle, both literally and by interpretation; he performs what the Prophet established, combining all the traits we have explained above; he has been designated by pure forefathers back through 'Ali b. Abi Talib to Muhammad, the Chosen; he maintains the commanding of good and forbidding of the bad, the effect of which is the good and not the bad; he maintains the appeal to God and to His absolute oneness by supporting agents (*da'is*) in all the lands of Islam.[281]

Thus, alongside a host of detractors, al-Hakim had his many friends and supporters, and they were moved to compose a vigorous defense of his imamate, whatever its peculiarities. Ultimately both views of him, the mad and despotic tyrant irrationally given to killing those around him on a whim, and the ideal supreme ruler, divinely ordained and chosen, whose every action was just and righteous, were to persist, the one among his enemies and those who rebelled against him, and the other in the hearts of the true believers, who, while perhaps perplexed by events, nonetheless remained avidly loyal to him to the end.

6

Social Reform and Legislation

Commanding the good and prohibiting the reprehensible is a fundamental principle of Islam. Although most ethical codes, religious and otherwise, include a prescription to do what is right and forbid the bad, not all make this commandment a cornerstone of public responsibility. The prescriptions and proscriptions inherent in this order are social and comprise the duties each member of the Islamic community owes to its collective observance of the law and the religion. Muslims, however, understand that, in so far as they are personally able, they should follow this rule and act in accord with it. It constitutes a key feature of their faith.[282]

Naturally, what a powerless individual might hope to accomplish pales in comparison with a person endowed with authority and backed by armed force. It is commonly acknowledged that no one should attempt corrective measures, either in favor of good or against the bad, if such actions will put oneself in danger. Challenging a corrupt government official could be life threatening to the challenger; the injunction to act does not extend that far. A fairly normal standard allows the individual to proceed physically only if possible; if not to resort to verbal admonishing; and if that also is fraught with unacceptable risk, to take a stand mentally, that is, in the heart.

These restrictions and conditions obviously apply more to the weak than to the powerful. Accordingly the stipulation to command the good and prevent evil assumes greater weight with rising authority and position. It is possible therefore to imagine readily how at the very highest rank, that of imam, there are no longer any restrictions and conditions; the obligation to insure what is right and prevent what is wrong becomes absolute, or nearly so.

It is essential to approach the complex topic of al-Hakim's social legislation from this angle. Few Islamic rulers have ever attempted to impose such a broad range of reforms on a society quite unused to them. Islam had reached a stable accord with Egyptian custom and sensibilities. He threatened all that.

Moreover, he decreed measures that in aggregate amounted to an imposition of Shiism on its Muslims, who were then and remained afterward predominately Sunni. That they had accepted him as caliph did not automatically mean that they had adopted a Shiite doctrine. For them his authority was not as august and unassailable as his Ismaili followers would have it.

The list of his reforms regulated many areas of life: religious rituals and venerations, the consumption of food and drink, the movements of women, games and amusements, animals, identifying clothing and symbols for Jews and Christians, the destruction of Jewish and Christian houses of worship, and more. Each measure, taken separately, might have had a parallel elsewhere within Islam. Certainly medieval writers would comment favorably often enough when describing his acts. But few would approve them all, most especially those measures he decreed to deprecate and curse those Companions of the Prophet who had rejected the right of ʿAli to succeed Muhammad at the latter's death. These same Companions are highly revered in Sunni Islam as the founding fathers of the Islamic social order, a position Shiism considers an anathema. Significantly, among all his social reforms, the cursing of the Companions came to an end most quickly. He rescinded his earlier order in this regard and adopted a tolerant policy, one that insisted those same Companions be mentioned henceforth solely with respect and appreciation.

Observers, even those who otherwise hated him and what he stood for, noted al-Hakim's commanding of the good and forbidding of evil, as if his upholding of this injunction were a model of its kind. One aspect included the dispensation of justice. On that score critics fault him for the long list of individuals he had executed but, regardless, they also commend him for his constant attention to the fair and impartial administration of justice in his realm. An important component was the redress of grievances, rectifying the claims made by some plaintiff against a miscarriage or misdeed of the government or its agencies. A special court, the *mazalim*, existed for this purpose in all Islamic lands. Rulers who otherwise were not especially attentive to the actions of judges they had appointed or to the officers of their governments gave lip service support to this institution. Many sat themselves to receive the complaints at least often enough to earn credit for having done it. During the reign of al-Hakim these courts were normally within the jurisdiction of the chief qadi. For a period, however, ʿAbd al-ʿAziz controlled the *mazalim* instead of his cousin Husayn who was the *qadi al-qudat*. But that seems to have been an exception. And all along petitions of complaint might go directly to the caliph, if the plaintiff could manage to deliver it to him. That is why his riding in public proved so important and why, when on the occasions the crush of people attempting to reach him threatened his well-being, he sought to stop the practice and have the petitions go to others, to the chief qadi, for example, or to his heir apparent ʿAbd al-Rahim ibn Ilyas. Still he never managed to escape this responsibility entirely; to the end he was the target of a constant stream of persons seeking help, redress or compensation of one kind or another.

Critics of his rule cite evidence of what they consider al-Hakim's disregard for Islamic tradition and its legal principles. Persecution of Jews and Christians and the destruction of their houses of worship is an example of a set of orders issued by him that run contrary to Islamic law and precedent. But to judge him against any notion of what that law might have been, to argue that he was bound by a law he did not set or had not personally approved, is to mistake the loftiness of his position as imam. In Shiite doctrine, the imam determines what the law is and governs accordingly. The only sense in which the law exists without him, and without his confirmation of what it is, applies solely to the law set by those who preceded him in the imamate. If he perceives that the law has changed for any reason, his will must be followed. His authority is absolute.

In Sunni Islam the situation is fundamentally different; the law is what the community has agreed it is, here meaning the community of those members of the Islamic polity most knowledgeable about its religion and its legal principles. The law exists in the abstract and the role of the jurisprudent is to determine exactly what it is. For the Fatimids, by contrast, the efforts of an expert in the law serve to explain what the law has been under earlier imams, which, despite having been affirmed by that method, remains provisional pending a ruling on the matter by the current imam. However, his determination of the law does not supersede that of his predecessors as much as reinterpret the issue at hand in the light of present conditions.

A second tendency of critics and detractors is to question al-Hakim's authority by attacking his lineage. If, they argue, his claim to descent from the Prophet and ʿAli is dubious, if not spurious, for him to undertake the wholesale remaking of society because he stands in the present for the Prophet and holds the same degree of command as had ʿAli, is a sign of absurdly preposterous presumption. It denotes someone deluded by insane megalomania. The Abbasids, who observed the rising power of al-Hakim with great trepidation, cultivated this approach by urging anti-Fatimid writers to refute the Fatimid assertion of genealogical descent from the eighth-century

Shiite imam Ja'far al-Sadiq. A famous manifesto issued by the leading men of Baghdad in 1011 at the request of the Abbasid caliph is one example of such attacks.

On the other side, the Fatimids both proclaimed their rights by virtue of a prophetic lineage and denounced that of their opponents. The Abbasids were ignorant usurpers, falsely passing as heirs to an authority they did not merit. Any notion that the Fatimids were hesitant as to their status is belied by a record of official pronouncements and decrees, of doctrinal writings issued under their control, and of actions of theirs to assert their 'Aliid descent. In one case al-Hakim ordered his agent Khatkin al-Dayf to journey to Madina and open the long sealed house of Ja'far al-Sadiq, there to retrieve items belonging to the caliph's ancestor. Al-Hakim, so this story goes, knew exactly what would be found because of information he had inherited from his forefathers.

Medieval writers and modern scholars have, nonetheless, puzzled over precisely why al-Hakim chose the measures he decreed and what they imply. Did his attempts to rid society of the foods, drink and other practices he prohibited depend on Shiite doctrine, for example? Were some based on mere personal whims or wishes? He ordered the killing of all dogs except those used in hunting. One reason may have a connection to his proclivity for riding around the city at night, a time when the menace of prowling dogs would have been most threatening. But, although the new rules and stipulations were issued by decrees read in public or by town criers going through the streets, explanations, if any were in fact offered, are rare or non-existent, leaving later historians to insert their own.

One key to al-Hakim's program of reform as a whole may emerge from a careful investigation of the chronology of the new regulations. But the record is neither exact nor precise, and may be less than dependable. Another method involves separating them into categories: Shiite-Sunni disputes, food and drink, control of women in public spaces, games and amusements, animals, the identification of Christians and Jews in mixed assemblies, the destruction of their houses of worship. Hereafter we will look at each of these areas separately. Still it is important to see the possibility that the caliph's prohibitions are linked, a religious motive, perhaps one that eludes us, underlying all.

The Imposition of Shiite Doctrines

1004 was the first year of many of the new regulations. The month of November saw the most controversial of them, the order for the cursing of the Companions. What made the situation particularly difficult was a further command to write out 'in the other mosques as well of the Old Mosque, inside and outside, on all walls, and on the doors of shops, cornerstones, tombstones and cenotaphs curses and insults directed against the Companions of the Prophet. They were written and painted with a variety of colors and gold; that was done on the doorways of the bazaars and the doors of houses, having been forced to do so. ... When the pilgrimage caravan returned, those in it were assaulted and cursed by the masses, who asked them to insult and curse the Companions even while they refused.'[283] There was simply no easy way to avoid being confronted with a religious doctrine so anathema to the Sunnis that their position under the Fatimids would have likely become, by dint of this act, untenable in the extreme.

Sunni-Shi'i conflict in a state that contained many more of the former than the latter would have arisen almost inevitably. In the earliest period of Fatimid rule in the Maghrib, Shiism assumed a pervasive dominance over public religious observance, excluding thereby Sunnism. The leading authorities of the formerly dominant Sunni school lost employment and support; they ceased having a standing recognized by the government. However, that uncompromising imposition of Shiism soon gave way to a more moderate policy of accommodation. Eventually, the caliphs accepted the Sunnis and allowed them their own sphere of operations. The chief qadiship of Qayrawan, a largely Sunni city, was once again allocated to the Malikis even while the cities of the Maghrib with substantial Ismaili population had a separate judge who was Shiʿi.[284]

The major items of difference between the two sects comprise several that readily created tension and possible violent opposition, though none as serious as the cursing of the Companions. One concerns the commencement of the new month, a critical moment in Islamic ritual observance, as, for example, in the beginning of the fast of Ramadan or its end. Ismailis, alone of the Islamic sects, allow the astronomical determination of the new moon, rather than the visual sighting required by all the rest. If mathematical reckoning should produce the same result there is no problem, but if one method delays the fast or the feast over against the other, the two communities will observe the fast or the feast on the same day. Three other points of conflict deal with prayers. The Shiʿa regard the forenoon prayer, the *salat al-duha*, as an unacceptable addition.[285] Likewise they reject the extra nighttime prayers, the *tarawih*,[286] said with an imam-leader, as an innovation of the second Sunni caliph ʿUmar, a figure they see as the great satan for his role in promoting Abu Bakr (and thus himself) over ʿAli. In the call to prayer said by the *muʾadhdhin* in the morning, the Shiʿa insert the formula 'Come to the best of works' whereas the Sunnis recite 'Prayer is better than sleep.'[287]

There were other matters at issue, some of much less importance but potentially irksome nonetheless. Which of all these were in contention prior to 1004 is hard to determine. In 1001 a Syrian man was arrested for maintaining that he would not acknowledge the position of ʿAli b. Abi Talib. 'I hold,' he said, 'that the Prophet, may God bless him and keep him, is the one that was sent, but I do not acknowledge ʿAli b. Abi Talib.' He was imprisoned, then checked again, but he persisted in maintaining that he did not recognize ʿAli. The general Husayn treated him gently but he still would not admit to the acknowledgement of ʿAli. The matter ended with an order for his execution; he was hung and crucified.[288]

The Fatimids certainly insisted generally on the Shiite call to prayer and the calculation of the advent of the new moon. A report from the year earlier says that 13 men were arrested, beaten and publicly paraded on camels prior to confinement for three days for having prayed the forenoon *duha* prayer.[289] Moreover the vilification of Abu Bakr and ʿUmar may have been relatively common. Commemoration of ʿAshuraʾ in mourning for the death of the imam Husayn involved a forced closing of shops and the cessation of commerce. Those practices may have been in place already. In 1005, the year after the edict on cursing, a report says, '...observing ʿAshuraʾ in the customary fashion involved closing the markets and singers and mourners gathering at the mosque of Cairo. They manifested during it the cursing of the Companions openly.' But then, 'one man was arrested and the call against him said, 'This is the punishment for he who curses ʿAʾisha and her husband." He was hung. An order was then passed to the police that no one should publicly exhibit the cursing of the Companions. Should someone do that he should be arrested. The rabble thereupon desisted from the cursing and interfering with the pilgrimage caravan.[290]

Were these measures a sign of a policy reversal in the making? Or was it an attempt to dampen the uncontrolled exuberance of Shiite mobs? If so perhaps disorder was more to be feared under the circumstances than religious orthodoxy. Significantly, on 2 January 1007, al-Hakim issued a new order that the curses that had been written on the mosques and doorways and other places condemning the Companions be thoroughly effaced. Accordingly, all were carefully erased. The superintendent of police even went around to make sure that nothing remained. A second decree was read out aimed to prevent any one becoming involved in matters that did not directly concern that person, and that it was henceforth incumbent on every one to occupy themselves solely with matters of their own livelihood and not be distracted by the actions of the Commander of the Believers or be unusually concerned with his orders.[291]

It appears that the policy of promoting cursing ended quickly, possibly in 1006, certainly by 1007. From 1009 we have an even more comprehensive declaration against cursing the Companions and, more broadly, in favor of a wide latitude for the accommodation of both Shiʿi and Sunni practice. In May of that year yet another decree was read out about it. It stated in part that, 'The fasters will fast and break fast according to their calculations. Those who use the sighting of the moon will not be considered in conflict in regard to how they fast and break fast. The prayer of those who include fifty *rakʿas* in the performance of their daily prayers [i.e. the Shiʿa] and those who pray the *duha* and the *tarawih* prayers [i.e. the Sunnis] are not precluded from or denied them. Those who say five *takbir*s during the funeral may say five; those who say four are permitted to say four. The *muʾadhdhin*s can call to prayer by saying "Come to the best of works" and those who do not call to prayer using it are allowed not to do so. No one is to curse the Companions, or object to any person's attributing to them what he attributes or swears about them what he swears. Every Muslim who makes an effort to understand his religion is an authority in it.'[292]

With this edict endorsing a remarkably tolerant policy in regard to Sunni-Shiʿi issues of contention, most of these matters appear to have been settled[293], and that has been noted by several scholars. The situation is, however, not so clear. Certainly there was no return to the open cursing of the Companions. A decree of 1013 reiterated the prohibition on cursing; it specifically urges the invocation of God's mercy on them.[294] Al-Kirmani composed a major work entitled in part *The Validation of the Superiority of ʿAli Over the Companions*. In it he comments that he will not fault the Companions for their mistreatment of ʿAli and the imams because the imam – here meaning al-Hakim – has decreed that we should remember them for the good they did before that transgression.[295] In respect to this aspect of the policy put in place in 1004, it had come to an end and was not resumed.

Other issues, however, reappeared more than once. In fact some medieval writers claim that al-Hakim's reversal of policy was a ploy used to see which of his followers would remain faithful to their professed loyalty and Ismaili devotion to him. If allowed free choice, would they revert to some form of Sunnism or not? Once the edict that permitted everyone to adhere to whichever school they wanted was read, a man named Raja' b. Abi'l-Husayn, relying on its saying what it said, prayed the *tarawih* in Ramadan of that same year and was executed for having done so.[296] Another man known as Ibn al-Riqaq was also killed for the same offense.[297]

In 1010 a decree restored the *tathwib* – reiteration of the phrase 'Prayer is better than sleep' – to the call to prayer, and allowing the people the *duha* prayer and the prayer with the standing *qunut* – silent prayer.[298] Subsequently, the *mu'adhdhins* in all of the mosques were assembled and read a decree stipulating the abandonment of the call to prayer using 'Come to the best of works', and adding in the morning call to prayer 'Prayer is better than sleep'. They were told that was the usage of the *mu'adhdhins* of the palace when they said, 'Peace be upon the Commander of the Believers and the mercy of God.' The people then adopted that practice and used it.[299] But only months later in 1011 reports al-Maqrizi, 'A decree was read out in all the mosques in which it was forbidden to oppose the imam in anything he did, and not to take an interest in anything not necessary, and to give the call to prayer with 'Come to the best of works,' and to abandon in the morning call to prayer saying, 'Prayer is better than sleep,' prohibiting the *duha* prayer and the prayer of *tarawih*, and restoring the *da'wa* and the *majlis* in accord with normal practice.' Between prohibiting that and allowing it, there was a five month period.[300]

The second of these two reports hints that, between the imposition of Shiite practice and relaxing or rescinding it, there was a connection to simultaneous closing or opening of the Ismaili Sessions of Wisdom and the public programs of the *da'wa*, which had been shut for five months as well. There is certainly no doubt that many citizens were confused. Ismailis had begun to wonder about their imam. At a minimum they were unsure of his intentions toward them. Sunnis by contrast apparently took the actions and decrees that favored them as a sign of al-Hakim's possible conversion. Later writers would insist that he had started to lean in the direction of Sunni orthodoxy.

For example, in 1013, the people, i.e. the Shiites, were prevented from performing the mourning of 'Ashura'. Later that same year, reports al-Maqrizi, the government prohibited cursing the Companions and a man was beaten for doing just that. The crier who walked in front of him as he was paraded through the streets called out 'This is the reward of anyone who curses Abu Bakr and 'Umar.' The citizens, anxious and confused, sought to be absolved; but it was difficult for many of them. Many gathered at the gates of the palace to plead for help, saying, 'We have no ability for opposing anyone or patience for all that has happened.' They were sent away. Thereupon they marched through the streets pleading continuously for relief. Instead, another decree was issue invoking the mercy of God on the ancestors among the Companions and forbidding taking an interest in matters connected with the old Shiite antagonism to these early figures who had once opposed 'Ali. Nevertheless, while he was out riding, al-Hakim encountered a signboard that contained a curse on the Companions. Although he immediately disavowed it and stopped at the spot waiting until it was torn down, additional signboards followed in succession all bearing a similar message. All were torn down and what had been written on walls of a similar type was erased until there was no longer any trace of the original words. To rebuke anyone who opposed this policy harsh measures followed along with a promise of severe punishment.[301]

But from the year after that we have the following item which seems to reverse the earlier command. The government now ordered the closing of all offices and all of the places in which produce and fruit and other items were sold for three days in observance of the mourning of 'Ashura'. Accordingly, on the day of 'Ashura', all remaining shops in Fustat and Cairo were closed with the exception of bakeries. The reciters and others whose custom was to perform in public on the day of 'Ashura' went out to Cairo, although individually, not as a group and without speaking to each other. No two gathered in one spot.[302]

Yet again the policy of the government remained inconsistent, alternating from one position to another year on year. Even so the rule against cursing, once cancelled, persisted throughout. The other issues are hard to pin down. Unlike the celebration of Ghadir Khumm, which was held within the palace complex and thus not open to the public, 'Ashura', as the reports indicate, involved the closing of shops and the procession of mourners through the streets of the cities.

Measures against Alcoholic Beverages

Most of the reform decrees were issued for the first time in 1004. The list of new rules promulgated then is fairly long and includes nearly all the items al-Hakim wished to forbid or interdict, two of which concern intoxicating beverages and the public movements of women. The policy instigated then for both remained in effect to the end of the reign with various attempts to apply the prohibition more intensively and in many ways to make it far more comprehensive with the aim of a total ban. A connection between the stipulations restricting women's access to public spaces and the suppression of alcoholic drinks is not obvious. It also may not have provided the motivation for these laws. Still an incident reported from four years earlier suggests otherwise. By the end of 1000—our report says explicitly, in the month of December—the previous occasional nightly riding by the caliph had increased, reaching once each night. He would ride to one place after another, one street after another, and from alley to alley and, apparently to facilitate his wanderings, he ordered the people to light lights and then to add to them in the streets and alleys. As a result the markets and bazaars were festooned with various decorations. People sold and bought, lit candles throughout the night and expended a considerable sum of money on food and drink, music and games. As al-Hakim proceeded men walked in front to prevent any of the people from approaching too closely, thus driving them back. But he told his guards not to prevent them. As a result he was surrounded by the people, frequently pleading to him.

Obviously the situation was ripe for abuse. Al-Maqrizi indicates what happened next.

> The arsenal was decorated and the people went out at night to observe. Of those going out at night women outnumbered the men. Crowds in the street and roads increased. The large number of them who were intoxicated became evident. The matter was especially acute from the night of 19th until 24th. When the people had exceeded the proper bounds, al-Hakim ordered that women not go out from evening time onward. If they did, they were given an exemplary punishment. He also forbad the people from sitting in the shops.[303]

From the following year we have a briefer report that might also be pertinent. In January a decree was issued specially concerned with the abolition of reprehensible acts and ending them with the imposition of legal steps against its various forms. A number of pleasure palaces, drinking establishment, and perhaps brothels, in which such things happened were shut down and sealed closed. Without additional information it would be hard to state what these 'reprehensible acts' were except that clearly they took place in houses or perhaps taverns set up for that purpose. Was it prostitution? Or drinking? Or both together?

From this point on, it become difficult to notice the connection between women and alcohol. In the later legislation regulations against intoxicating beverages and drinking tend to appear alongside the prohibition of various foods in situations where, at least initially, our information associates these measures with Shiism. Among the decrees of 1004 one outlaws the selling of *fuqqa*ʿ beer and proscribes the making of it thereafter, because of 'evidence that ʿAli [b. Abi Talib], may God be pleased with him, detested the drinking of *fuqqa*ʿ.' This type of beer is made, usually from barley, in a gourd-shaped ceramic vessel tightly sealed around the protruding opening. Puncturing that seal releases the beer, which comes out as fizz, hence the name which means to burst or bubble.[304] According to many Islamic authorities, this kind of drink, which is only mildly alcoholic at best, is, however, not an intoxicant; obviously ʿAli disagreed. *The Pillars of Islam*, Qadi al-Nuʿman's authoritative digest of Ismaili law, notes Imam Jaʿfar al-Sadiq's prohibition of it as well.[305]

That al-Hakim likely meant his prohibition to apply to all drinks that produce any degree of inebriation becomes clearer in subsequent legislation. Already from late 1004, a report notes that homes were searched to find out who was making intoxicating beverages and that a great quantity of containers for it were smashed in the process.[306] In 1006 a group of those making *fuqqa*ʿ were arrested.[307] The first specific reference to wine occurs in 1008. 'Word spread among the people that the selling of wine would be forbidden. They rushed out to buy it and bought a great deal. It became so dear that ten jars of it sold for a dinar and then it could no longer be found.'[308] In the same year another decree forbad the transporting of wine and also a second type of beer, called in Arabic *mizr*.[309] There was to be no appearance of it or of *fuqqa*ʿ.

Egypt then as now has a substantial population of Christians who use wine as part of the sacrament. Traditionally, wine is allowed and the Muslim authorities did not attempt to rid the country of it, even though, obviously, non-observant Muslims could obtain it without too great a difficulty. Al-Hakim's new rules, however, aimed to stop all trade in wine, or any other intoxicating drink. In the year 1009, for example, a group found to possess *fuqqa*ʿ were beaten and paraded.[310] The drinking of wine was subject to ever more harsh a punishment.[311] In 1010 a group that sold wine was arrested and jailed. Places for selling wine were raided. Measures against it and drunkenness intensified; places where that happened were watched closely.[312]

Obviously, however, it continued because at the onset of the following year the chief of police for Cairo and Fustat was ordered to watch extra carefully for forbidden acts and to prevent them.[313] Most significantly, a command was issued that raisins were not to be sold in quantities of more than five pounds and clay jugs were removed from the market so that they could not be used as containers for making wine or beer.[314] Raisins were the prime ingredient in yet another alcoholic drink, *zabib*, which is the Arabic word for raisin as well as the beverage made from it. This campaign against intoxicants was to be relentless. At mid year, '...the selling of large and small quantities of raisins was forbidden and a letter issued prohibiting the transporting of them. Many of them were thrown into the Nile.'[315] Three months later, 'Measures to abolish the selling of *fuqqa*ʿ, ... were made more harsh. ... Great quantities of raisins were burned. ... The burning of raisins continued for several days in the presence of witnesses. The supervisor of the bureau of expenditure continued the supply of funds spent on transporting it and burning it. Burning 2,340 units of it cost, in the expenditure for that purpose, five thousand *dinar*s over a period of ten days.'

The eunuch Ghabn was appointed to command of the police about then and ordered to 'deal harshly with drunkenness and prevent the sale of *fuqqa*ʿ, ... and forbid the selling of honey except in quantities of three pounds or less.' Honey, which can be used to make mead-wine, had now joined the list of controlled and suppressed commodities. Additional rules added other substances. The selling of grapes was declared illegal except for small quantities not to exceed four pounds. None were to be crushed for juice. Many were thrown out on the roads with an order to trample them and then it was forbidden to sell them at all. Those that had been brought were thrown into the Nile. Official witnesses from the government were dispatched to Jiza to seize all the grapes that were still on the vines. They were to be scattered under the hoofs of cattle to crush them and thus prevent their use. A similar order was sent at the same time to several other regions. Anyone who sold grapes for a living was watched and the situation for them became especially difficult because they were no longer able to sell their produce.[316]

The severity of these restrictions affected many whose livelihood depended on selling the commodity in question, grapes, for example, quite apart from dealing in a beverage made out of it. But, obviously, those whose trade was making wine were hurt most. Possessing even a small quantity of wine for whatever reason was now a cause for panic and fear of imminent punishment. Al-Maqrizi reports the following incident to illustrate the point.

> It happened about then that an elderly man was transporting his wine on a donkey over a bridge when it fled suddenly, dumping its load there and then. Al-Hakim happened on to the poor fellow in the middle of the day on that narrow bridge. The caliph said to him, 'From where do you approach?' He replied, 'From the land of God, the very narrow and confined.' Al-Hakim exclaimed, 'O Shaykh, is the land of God highly narrow and restricted?' The old man responded, 'If it weren't so narrow, it would never have had me run into you on the same bridge.' Al-Hakim laughed and let him be.[317]

The caliph's leniency in that case did not carry over to others or signal a change in policy. In July of 1012, 'the warehouses for honey were sealed, and all that was in the hands of merchants or sellers of it was seized. ... In a four-day period 5,051 of the jars of honey were [thrown in the river] and sunk.'[318] 'In December denunciations connected with *fuqqa*ʿ, *zabib* ... intensified. A group were arrested and jailed and then the order to hang them was issued, but later they were freed.'[319]

With this data the story disappears from view, though it is unlikely the regulations changed. Rather it is the information about them that comes to an end. Possibly the campaign against intoxicants slowly abated in its severity over the final years of the reign but that is an assumption not based on evidence but the lack of it one way or the other. Still, from what we do know, al-Hakim's efforts were noteworthy for his sustained attempt to rid his kingdom of drunkenness, and that surely did not end until his disappearance and beyond. That he was not entirely successful has to be assumed; in the case of alcohol consumption extreme prohibition rarely has worked. One more story from then needs to be related, if only to complete the record.

According to this tale, in the year 1010, al-Hakim gave the order that every open door should not be locked shut, every locked door must not be opened, and every thing that is covered up should not be uncovered. In connection with the order of al-Hakim that every thing that is covered should not be uncovered, it is said that a drunken man set out one of the nights at the time aiming to make his way from the place he was to his home. He did not quite get there but instead passed out en route. A passer-by happened upon him and took off his turban, unrolled it and draped it over him. The man thus fell asleep while covered over with the cloth of the turban. A policeman came along and poked him, asking, 'What are you?' The man replied, 'I am something covered, and the Commander of the Believers al-Hakim has ordered that covered things should not be uncovered.' Thereupon, according to this account, the policeman was so taken aback by the man's words, he let him be.[320]

A story of this kind, even while it confirms the existence and the seriousness of al-Hakim's policy, shows also that not only was compliance with the new regulations intermittent – a reprobate is not easily reformed or kept from his vices by a few laws – but that it became the context for amusing anecdotes like these that subtly attempt to subvert it with humor.

Additional Prohibitions of Food

The series of edicts enacted in 1004 established a prohibition also on several kinds of food, which, like those against alcoholic beverages, appear to have arisen initially from a religious motive. Al-Maqrizi's record of the original decrees says as much. It forbad *mulukhiyya*, jew's mallow (*Corchorus olitorious*), a green herb used in soup and stews and a great favorite of Egyptians and others in that region, because 'it was much loved by Muʿawiya b. Abi Sifyan', the first of the Umayyad caliphs and the arch enemy of ʿAli and the Shiʿa. *Jirjir*, a variety of water-cress, known elsewhere as rocket or arugula, was outlawed due to its association with the Prophet's wife ʿAʾisha, who had been another major opponent of ʿAli. The same decree added to these something called *mutawakkiliyya*, the exact nature of which is hard to determine but the name connects it to the Abbasid caliph al-Mutawakkil. One more item cited is a small fish that has no scales called *dalinis*. It was no longer to be eaten or even fished.[321]

There were additional provisions among these early stipulations concerning food. Bread dough was not to be kneaded with the feet; cows that had not produced offspring were not to be slaughtered except for the festival of sacrifice and otherwise only if they were not suitable for plowing.[322] Thus aspects of al-Hakim's new policy may have been purely practical, based on a concern for hygiene or economic production. But parts of his program have a less clear explanation. One more prohibited food, cited explicitly in later reports, is *tirmis*, lupine beans.[323] Did it also belong to a list of the favorites of the enemies of the Shiites? The interdiction against eating fish without scales, which is certainly what the proscription of *dalinis* actually entails, is familiar from Jewish law; it is likewise forbidden in Ismaili law.[324] *Jirjir* is strongly disapproved on account of its effects, among which, according to some authorities, is a tendency to function as an aphrodisiac. Qadi al-Nuʿman quotes a hadith from the Prophet against it.[325] But to ban *mulukhiyya* simply because a well-known enemy had a marked liking for it is strange, especially in Egypt, where it is highly popular.

Evidently the common citizen responded to these prohibitions with little or no enthusiasm and even less compliance. Reports subsequent to the initial decree continue to reiterate the illegality of harvesting, selling and eating the proscribed foods. Later in 1004, another edict specified that no part of a fish without scales could be eaten and fishermen were not to fish for them.[326] In 1006 fishermen were arrested for doing that.[327] In 1008 there was another decree against *dalinis* and moldy *tirmis*.[328] In 1009 a group found to possess *mulukhiyya*, *tirmis* and *dalinis* was beaten and paraded.[329] The following year yet another group received the same punishment for the same crime.[330] In 1011 the measures to abolish the selling of *mulukhiyya* and fish without scales were made harsher.[331] On his appointment to command of the police, Ghabn was ordered, along with other items, specifically to prevent the sale of *mulukhiyya* and fish without scales.[332] The fishermen were assembled and made to swear that they would not fish for scaleless fish. If they did they were told they would be hung.[333] In the next year some were nonetheless arrested for having done it. They were jailed and the order for hanging issued, though luckily for them they were later freed instead.[334] Finally in 1014 yet another group of those who had violated the prohibition against selling *mulukhiyya* and fish without scales was apprehended, beaten and paraded.[335]

There is a monotonous repetition in these reports that reveals a constant need to reinforce them, either by a repetition of the edict or by exemplary punishments, and it shows the difficulty of removing these foods from the Egyptian diet and taste. That our information ends with the year 1014 is, moreover, most likely an accident in the survival of the historical record. These prohibitions surely continued in effect without pause until the end of the reign seven years later.

Restrictions on Women

The most famous, or infamous, of al-Hakim's social reformations was his severe restriction of women's freedom to move about in public, which became eventually as harsh and total a ban as any of its kind, when he forbad shoemakers from crafting and selling footwear for them. But, in contrast to his proscriptions concerning food and drink, which are linked more readily to religious dogmas, the record in regard to women is not so clear. To be sure Islamic societies have often imposed confinement on their female members, or at the least complete covering for those women who go out of their houses. The situation under al-Hakim, however, became even more serious, resulting in great hardships of a kind not that common.

The record in this case requires, however, a careful review of all the measures taken by him in the exact order chronologically, commencing with the events of 1000 associated with the incident that appears to forecast his interdiction of intoxicants. Back then he had begun to ride about at night and he ordered the populace to light the streets and markets suggesting a kind of festival in the offing. Crowds of people responded by buying and selling and by spending their gains on food and drink, music and games, until the streets were clogged with people, many of them drunk, the women outnumbering the men. Although the affair lasted only about a week in all, the caliph took the matter seriously. He issued an order that women not go out during the evening; those who did were threatened with exemplary punishment.[336]

In 1004, among the long list of edicts, bells were rung in the streets to announce that no woman should show her face in the street, or follow behind a funeral, or adorn herself. A cry also went round Cairo that no one was to go out into the street after sundown, nor was there to be any buying or selling, and the people obeyed that order.[337] Are these measures connected with what happened in 1000? If so, the matter does not reappear in our sources, until some vague hints four years later, and even then the regulations issued were more general and less specific to women. In 1008 all people were told not to perform songs publicly on the banks of the Nile or listen to them in houses there or to drink in boats on the river. Public houses were raided and many arrested.[338] More specific was a command not to erect tents among the tombs on the days of visitation of the dead as women had evidently commonly done in the past.[339] Another edict ordered all, women and men, to remain at home following the evening prayer and not to leave until the dawn.[340] In 1010 taverns were watched; songs and amusements were prohibited; and there was an order not to sell female singers. People were not to congregate in the desert outside the city and women were not to go to the baths.[341] The effect of these rules may be indicated in a report from 1012: women did not go out to the desert and no woman was to be seen at the tombs there. Gathering on the banks of the Nile was no longer allowed; women were not to ride in boats with men, nor frequent places in which they might become closely confined with men.[342] The next year the edict against female singers was upgraded; women were not to sing or chant.[343] Finally in 1014 women were prohibited altogether from going out into the streets either at night or in the day with the exception of the very young or old. Women were from that point onward imprisoned in effect in their own homes; none were to be seen in public. Baths formerly reserved for them were closed and shoemakers ceased to produce footwear for women. Shops devoted to that purpose were put out of commission.[344]

Women who for one reason or another went out of their houses were beaten and jailed. They could not be seen at all; none of the games and dolls ordinarily sold to them during festivals were sold. The situation this blanket prohibition caused only grew more serious, even elderly women and the weak who were caught in the streets were detained.[345] Over the following year the matter created more and more of a hardship.[346]

Again, as with the other measures of al-Hakim, the chronology ends with 1015, although there exists plenty of evidence that the restriction persisted until 1021. Other medieval sources tend to bundle the information they have into a single report, making an exact dating impossible. Nonetheless they both confirm the seriousness of the situation and add, fortunately, a few more details. One of them inserts here the story of the chief qadi and the married woman he inadvertently helped to arrange a tryst with her lover.[347] Another mentions the possibility in extreme need or in pursuit of the professions, either of washing the dead – women were required to wash a deceased woman – or midwife, of seeking a permit for that via a petition to the caliph. If granted, the same petitioner would then carry al-Hakim's personal note to the supervisor of the police who would thereafter assign a trusted officer to escort the woman to the place she needed to reach. This same report says that this regime remained in effect until 1019, but does not indicate what happened to change it in that year.[348] Yet another writer provides a longer list of exceptions: women presenting appeals to a court of law; those leaving for the pilgrimage or other travels; girls for sale in the slave market; the very old and weak who had to obtain water from the cisterns; women going to meet relatives in the absence of strangers within the same alleyway as theirs where leaving and returning could happen under cover of night; women newly arrived in Egypt coming there by land or sea; women who sell yarn and cloth; and a few more.[349] One last account describes how merchants were to deal with women when they could not meet them any longer face to face. The seller would pass through the streets listening for women who desired his wares. He carried with him a long pole with a basket attached to the end, which he pushed into the interior of the house. The lady could examine the goods, deposit the price in the basket, and the merchant would retract the pole without ever seeing his client.

Not all the stories related in this connection report facts so believable as these. A sharp bias against the Fatimids more generally is often evident. Occasionally some reveal great hostility and a tendency to exaggeration for negative effect, especially when the subject is al-Hakim and his excesses. Thus we hear of his passing by the golden bath and hearing from within the clamor of bathing women. Offended he orders its exits blocked and the fires heating the water stoked higher and higher until, unable to leave, all the women inside die without, says this author, their having committed any crime at all.[350]

Baths and Funerals

Lurid stories of this type are common enough in many medieval histories but their historical value is dubious except as evidence of the bias of the author. However, the connection here with the bath may have arisen from al-Hakim's concern for them and proper behavior and modesty in them. In 1004 he had bells rung in the streets to proclaim that no one should thereafter enter the baths without wearing a loincloth (a *mi'zar*); the baths were then watched and persons caught in them without loincloths were beaten and paraded.[351] There are similar reports from 1006[352] and 1008.[353]

Another set of regulations dealt with funerals, the public aspect of which often invited unruly displays of grief and mourning. The lists of 1004 mention women following the funeral procession.[354] Those of 1012 stipulate that the people were not to gather at funerals or follow them. In his appointment to command of the police Ghabn is told to prevent these gatherings and the following of funerals.[355]

The same instruction to Ghabn has him also prohibit amusements, although without stating exactly which kinds are forbidden.[356] In 1009, at the celebration of the feast of sacrifice, the amusements, shows and games normally played each year on the occasion were abolished.[357] In 1011 a report notes that songs and amusements were prohibited[358], but another from later in 1011 comments that the people gathered in the Qarafa cemetery, as was their custom, for games and jesting.[359] Perhaps Ghabn was to put a stop to those. The one popular game al-Hakim outlawed was chess. The evidence of his proscription in this case is a report from 1012 of having chess pieces collected from wherever they could be found and burned.[360] The following year a group of people caught playing chess was beaten and jailed.[361] Medieval forms of chess were not identical to the modern game; some involved gambling, and the Ismaili attitude, as stated in Qadi al-Nuʿman's *Pillars of Islam*, disapproves. The imam Jaʿfar al-Sadiq regarded it as a form of the senseless play (*laghw*) mentioned negatively in the Qurʾan (25:72). Significantly, another, according to this same hadith, is singing.[362]

Animals

Among the edicts of al-Hakim hardest to understand is his order to slaughter dogs. It is true that dogs are not considered clean by Islam and unrestrained they pose a clear menace especially in large numbers. A person riding through the city at night could hardly avoid confronting the canine presence either by rousing their bark or, if roaming freely, the actual threat of their attack. The first command to kill the dogs was issued in early 1005. It thus fell in with the many other measures taken in that seminal year. Al-Maqrizi relates about it that an uncountable number were put down, so many in fact that none were left in the alleyways and streets. The bodies were dumped in the desert and along the banks of the Nile.[363] This slaughter was repeated twice in 1014.[364] Another source claims, without specifying when, that upward of 30 thousand dogs were killed by the caliph's command. Dogs in this instance did not include those used in hunting, particularly the saluqi.[365]

The Protected Peoples

Yet one more law from that fateful year 1004 ordered the Jews and Christians to fasten on the *zunnar* and wear the *ghiyar*. The first item is a type of waistband or alternately a cord tied around the waist and the latter a badge, a kind of insignia, perhaps only a strip of colored cloth. Both were used to provide a way to distinguish publicly these 'protected peoples' from Muslims and they were a well-known aspect of Islamic regulation of the peoples of the book, although the application of the rule requiring Jews and Christians to wear either came and went, often not enforced at all. Thus al-Hakim's new requirement was not actually new except in that it had not been the policy of the government to insist on its use. In this instance, however, in addition, the caliph stipulated that these items should be black as a symbol of the seditious Abbasids whose color it was. Or, at least that is what we are told in al-Maqrizi's report of this incident.[366]

That same year al-Hakim moved against the slave dealers, specifically to prevent them selling slaves and bondmaids to the Christians and Jews.[367] There were likely other measures initiated at the time, or possibly merely some signs of the caliph's intent to impose still harsher conditions. Unexplained actions of his generated great fear for many, particularly those in government service, among whom there were large numbers of Christian and Jewish clerks. As a group the latter staged an elaborate show of their loyalty and beseeched al-Hakim to forgive them. It is, however, quite unclear for what they thought they needed to be forgiven. Nonetheless, they were received at the palace with appropriate formality, then forgiven and granted an amnesty in a decree composed for the occasion with copies to each of the various parties. One group that joined in this matter was comprised of Muslims. Subsequently, they along with the Jews and Christians obtained a copy of this decree, a separate one for each group.[368]

It is difficult to make sense of this event. What exactly caused the fear and panic on display that year? How much was it due to the cumulative effect of all the newly imposed regulations, coupled, perhaps, with the growing list of those executed? Christians and Jews, however, could not have avoided the feeling that their privileged positions in the bureaucracy were under threat. The execution only two years earlier in 1002 of Fahd b. Ibrahim, who had once been the most prominent Christian in the government and was a leading figure for other Christians in the bureaucracy, added to the general tension and uncertainty.

One explanation for Fahd's downfall was a charge of corruption, possibly false, but effective in removing him nonetheless. The man's brother had tried to make amends by delivery of a huge sum to the caliph and that suggests that he believed he had to buy back his family's good standing. Al-Hakim refused to accept the money and that may indicate that missing funds were not involved.[369] Coincidently, days after the death of Fahd, the caliph ordered the arrest and jailing of the Christian clerks in the government, only to release them all a week later at the personal request of Sahl b. Muqashshar, his private physician, himself a Christian.[370]

Another factor that may have influenced al-Hakim's attitude toward Christians was his own father's highly tolerant acceptance of them.[371] Al-'Aziz's favorite woman was a Melkite Christian and her brothers occupied, partly due to his intervention, major positions in the Christian community. There are indications that the brothers preserved a family connection with the woman's daughter even after her death. Sitt al-Mulk may thus have had an interest in maintaining her father's policies. The caliph, her half-brother, apparently did not. There is no suggestion in any event that either brother had influence with him. Arsenius, who was earlier the metropolitan of Fustat-Cairo, rose to the rank of patriarch of Alexandria on the death in 1000 in Fustat of the previous holder of that position, but that was not necessarily a sign of al-Hakim's own approval rather than the interests of the Melkites themselves.[372]

A report from 1008 reveals that, on the night of Palm Sunday, Christians were forbidden to decorate their churches as they were used to doing. A group of them was arrested in March and ordered to gather what was held in trust in the churches and to deliver it to the offices of the Sultan. Letters to the same effect went to all other districts. The same report adds that many crosses, presumably take from churches, were burned at the doorways of mosques and at the police stations.[373] This measure appears aimed as much against Christian practice as against churches and church properties. Significantly, that same year the caliph issued an order to destroy the Church of the Holy Sepulcre in Jerusalem.[374] This measure was directed as much against Christian practice as against churches and church properties.

In 1008 the requirement of the *ghiyar* was repeated and those caught without it were beaten.[375] Two years later Christians were precluded from observing Epiphany. In fact they were not to gather on the banks of the river as they were accustomed to do as part of the ceremony associated with it.[376] A Christian source from 1010 reports that the protected peoples were to use only black *zunnar*s – evidently there was some variation in its color at the time – and also wear black turbans.[377] In 1011 they were forbidden to assemble for the feast of the cross and to display lights on the outside of their churches.[378] Much of the information supplied by al-Maqrizi appears to come from Egyptian sources that may give more weight to the Copts than to other Christian denominations. Fortunately, the Melkites are well represented through one of their own, Yahya of Antioch, who witnessed himself what happened in Egypt. He was able to contribute additional details, particularly those that affected his community.

For the festival of baptism, it had been the custom, most notably for the Melkites, to conduct a celebratory procession of lights led by the prefect of the Fustat police through the streets of that city from the Church of Michael down to the river bank and back. It was a grand event, the police chief mounted on his horse preceded by hundreds of torches, and hordes of people chanting pleasantly and melodically, carrying before them the cross. Muslims often joined the throng, mixing freely with the Christians. Al-Hakim himself in earlier years came to observe. But, having already announced by town crier that Muslims were not to get involved, in the year 1010 he forbad the ritual procession altogether.[379] Not long afterward he ordered the monastery of Dayr al-Qusayr destroyed.[380] Until then it had been the residence of Arsenius, Melkite patriarch of Alexandria and uncle of Sitt al-Mulk. Other Melkite shrines were also torn down and, according to Yahya, Arsenius himself was secretly put to death.[381]

The culmination of this series of measures against the protected people, however, came in 1012 with a far more comprehensive act, described for us by al-Maqrizi. His account, which is especially important for its specific details, is worth repeating here:

> He ordered the Christians, with the exception of the religious authorities, to wear black turbans and black hoods and to attach around their necks crosses of wood, to ride on saddles of wood and none of them to ride horses but rather they should ride mules or donkeys, and not ride with adorned saddles or bridles, and that their saddles and bridles should have black straps, that they should fasten the *zunnar* around their waists, that Muslims should not act as servants for them, nor should they buy slaves or bondmaids that are Muslim. The people were given permission to look into and to watch out for evidence of that. A number of Christians, clerks and others, converted to Islam. This matter was hard on them. Those whose business was to hire out donkeys and mules were forbidden to let them ride. And they were to use saddles that are the equivalent of the sole of a shoe. They were prohibited from riding on the Nile with Muslim boatmen.[382]

A second report from the same year contains additions to the previous order. The Christians were now commanded to make the saddles on which they rode out of sycamore wood. They were thereafter compelled to have the crosses they wore around their necks measure a cubit by a cubit. Al-Maqrizi himself comments, 'Their humiliation increased, as did the oppression imposed on them.' As if the policy was not oppressive enough, another order followed specifying the weight of the cross be five pounds and that it be visible on the outside of their robes. They did as ordered, but, 'when matters began to oppress them most heavily, many of them feigned Islam.' Here our source adds, 'The affair of destroying churches happened then also.'[383]

This last item concerning what amounted to a new broadly applied policy of destroying houses of worship needs to be considered separately although clearly it was connected to the other measures against Christians and Jews. Note here that the information provided by the two accounts al-Maqrizi related from the year 1012 mentions solely the Christians, as if they alone bore the brunt of the caliph's restrictions. That is, however, highly unlikely. In 1013 in July another edict said that neither Jews nor Christians were to enter the baths unless they wore a bell, in the case of the Jews, and a cross for the Christians.[384] A full account of the rules for these years would thus have them apply to Jews as well as Christians even if the former are not specifically cited in the report we have.

That it was a cross Christians were required to wear needs no explanation but a bell for Jews is odd. Another source says it was the figure of a bull, or, better, the head of a calf, a symbol for the golden calf the Jews came to worship when they deviated from the true religion of Moses.[385]

The Destruction of Churches and Synagogues

The destruction of churches and synagogues is a topic that requires careful distinctions. Ordinarily the peoples of the book under Muslim protection are not allowed to construct new houses of worship, and major projects to refurbish older ones can provoke violent opposition if not handled with care. Still, by the time of al-Hakim, Cairo, which had been in existence only since 969, contained churches and a synagogue or two. They had to have been built under Muslim rule. In any event the situation on the ground was often volatile, and popular reactions were easily inflamed.

Al-Hakim's measures fed into that sentiment, but not all cases were the same. His earliest order brought down churches either on the site of or adjoining the new mosque at Rashida. That was 1004.[386] In 1009 churches on the road to Maqs were demolished, as were those in the Greek quarter of Cairo; the latter area was needed to enlarge the mosque complex of al-Azhar.[387] In these cases the Christians were compensated by being allowed to construct churches, that is, new churches, in another district, al-Hamra', between Cairo and Fustat.[388] Thus the policy itself did not envision the wholesale destruction of churches rather than select buildings required for another purpose, a mosque or the expansion of one. A more disturbing aspect of what happened was the involvement of Muslim mobs in the work of demolition and the concomitant looting of the churches and any adjoining non-Muslim cemetery.[389]

The destruction of the church of the Holy Sepulchre in 1009 appears to represent a new policy and an attack against Christian and Jewish houses of worship for a different reason.[390] According to the main account provided by several Muslim historians[391], including al-Maqrizi, the motive in the latter case arose when al-Hakim first learned from his agent Khatkin al-Dayf of tricks employed in the church at Easter to produce fire in its lamps at a key moment as if that fire had descended miraculously from heaven. The explanation offered involved the use of filament coated with oil that allowed a flame to travel a distance from one lamp to another seemingly without human agency. The date when the caliph initially heard this story and ordered the destruction was 1007 or 1008. The chief of his chancery Ibn Surin then composed the official decree, which was next sent to Yarukh, Fatimid governor of Ramla and to Abu'l-Fawaris al-Dayf, the Ismaili *da'i* responsible for southern Syria and Palestine. Together they and others next arranged to carry out the order in Jerusalem by inciting a mob to raze the church.[392]

A secondary motive might have involved stories of the purported wealth in the church itself. Known to the Christians as the Church of the Resurrection, al-Qiyama, it was widely regarded by them as a major, if not the major, goal of Christian pilgrimage. Rumors circulated that Byzantine emperors came to it in disguise.[393] Certainly they donated to it substantial gifts.[394] When these agents of the Fatimid caliph arrived, did they first loot it for the benefit of al-Hakim? Or alternately, did they, as in some other cases of church destruction, allow the locals to run free to grab whatever they could? In any event the building ceased to exist when they were done with the exception of base walls too thick to break up. The rabble next turned on other churches and shrines in Jerusalem, including a convent for women, and many Christian cemeteries there, which were uprooted and looted of grave goods.

For European Christians, Byzantines and more particularly the Latins, this one event reverberated with special resonance as with none of the others, leaving a lasting impression of the perfidy of the Muslims and of al-Hakim in particular. Two centuries afterward, well into the era of the crusades, its great historian, William of Tyre, would comment quite pointedly in the introduction to his *History of Deeds Done Beyond the Sea*: 'Conspicuous among the many other impious acts for which [al-Hakim] was responsible was the total demolition of the church of the Lord's Resurrection ... originally built ... at the command of the Emperor Constantine... .'[395]

In al-Maqrizi's report about this episode, which he places in 398/1007–08, evidently intending only the initial steps in the process and not the actual destruction, he adds the information that once the demolition had taken place al-Hakim thought to destroy the churches and synagogues elsewhere in his kingdom but, fearing that such actions would provoke the Christians to tear down all the mosques in countries they controlled, he cancelled or revoked this order.[396]

By late 1012 he was not so reticent. Most accounts say he commenced that year a widely applied policy of destroying churches and other houses of worship, seizing their contents and the land along with tenements and other properties, the income from which was used to support them. Much of the land was allotted as fiefs and land grants; some of the churches were converted to mosques. One report claims that thereafter churches and monasteries in the various districts of Egypt were allotted as land grants to anyone who asked for them.[397] Of those either torn down or stripped of their goods, the list includes the Suspended Church, Bu Shanuda, Church of Mary al-Qantara, along with the Yaʿqubi church Mar Qosma in Fustat, al-Aqraniyun, Church of Mary Constantine, and Church of Marat Maryam elsewhere, and the Church of Our Catholic Lady in Damascus.[398] A complete list would be impossible to compile and the date of destruction is not always clear. Some losses belong to earlier actions by al-Hakim; others to the period 1012–1014. Nonetheless all reports imply that many more were demolished than are named anywhere in our sources, most in fact suggesting that the destruction was quite widespread and thorough. Letters were dispatched to outlying districts with an order to destroy churches and synagogues or, perhaps more precisely in many cases, to allow the Muslims there to loot and then tear them down.[399] One figure of the total from the period 1012 to 1015 claims that upwards of 30 thousand churches, synagogues and monasteries were destroyed.[400] It would be extremely difficult to confirm that. If a given church disappeared, it might have left no record at all. Those later rebuilt possibly preserve a record that might indicate their having been rebuilt in the decade after this period. One prime example of the latter is the Ben Ezra synagogue in Fustat, which was reconstructed and reopened about ten years after having been destroyed by al-Hakim. A lumber-room attached to the new building from then on served as a storeroom for discarded papers that were deposited there for later burial as a geniza. Because, in contrast to nearly every other geniza, they were never buried, what had been thrown away so long before was still in that room when, in the latter decades of the nineteenth century, scholars removed them for preservation in various European libraries.

In the year 1013 al-Hakim suddenly announced that any of the protected people – here for obvious reasons most likely meaning the Christians – were now free to leave his realm and take with them all their possessions, that is, those they could transport.[401] For Melkites the offer allowed them to depart from Fatimid territory and move to the Byzantine empire, particularly to the city of Antioch in northern Syria. Some of the Copts and others may have gone south to Nubia or Ethiopia, both countries that were predominately Coptic Christian. One of those who left at that time was the historian Yahya, who was later to become Melkite bishop of Antioch. Certainly many others abandoned Egypt for more hospitable countries. At a later period, possibly near to the end of his reign, al-Hakim also began to moderate his restriction of Jews and Christians, seemingly reversing himself to the point that he started to show marked favor for them. Great numbers of Christians and Jews had by then converted to Islam. He now permitted those who had converted to revert to their original religion if they so wanted. Destroyed houses of worship were rebuilt with his permission, and trusts that had previously supported them were restored or recreated.[402]

Unfortunately, the data about these changes, which occurred over the final years of al-Hakim's rule, is largely missing (along with that concerning so much else). The Coptic *History of the Patriarchs* tells here a curious story of the caliph's affection for a monk named Poemen (Bimin) who, once allowed to reclaim his Christianity, sought permission to rebuild churches and to construct a new monastery at Shahran. Eventually both were granted, the monastery first and the churches later. According to this tale al-Hakim himself frequently visited Poemen in his monastery and it was there that the caliph met and finally accepted the release of the Coptic Patriarch whom it is said he jailed years earlier in connection with the purported selling of church offices, an internal dispute that had been brought before the Muslim ruler by a disgruntled priest. Al-Hakim was evidently quite impressed with the Patriarch and with the spiritual stability of his form of Christianity.[403]

Curiously the Melkite Yahya offers his own version of a story remarkably similar to that of the Copts. His hero is Anba Salmun, the champion of first the monks of Mount Sinai and then various other Melkite establishments, most notably the monastery of Qusayr, which, until its destruction, had been the residence of their patriarch. Again al-Hakim came to visit, to encourage the restoration and to hold private conversations with Anba Salmun. However, in contrast to the Coptic history, which is vague on dates, Yahya is fairly precise. Moreover, he includes in his account the full texts of three dated imperial decrees issued by al-Hakim in favor of the Melkites specifically and the Christians in general. They appear to be quite authentic, attesting thus to actions of the caliph to restore relations with his Christian subjects. These events took place over the last six months of 1020. Al-Hakim would himself disappear the following February. More needs to be said later in chapter eight concerning the details of the affair of Poemen and of Anba Salmun and of what they might suggest about al-Hakim and his policies and behavior during the final seven years of his rule, a period in many ways unlike the rest. Here it is enough to note that the persecution, if that is what it was, of the Christians eventually came to an end and that it was the caliph himself who ended it.

Cursing the Prophet's Companions, destroying churches, forbidding beer and wine, killing dogs, outlawing *mulukhiyya* and the making of women's footwear all caused a sensation at the time, both in Egypt and abroad. The caliph's attempt at these kinds of reform and social change left a permanent record if only as a sign of an aberration, a ruling authority gone mad. None of these measures outlasted al-Hakim; even many of the Christian and Jewish houses of worship were eventually rebuilt. Still what had happened was remembered and the fame or infamy attached to it persisted in the later histories and other accounts of his reign. Memories of these acts are alive today.

Not so several other elements of his program of reform that were, and are, less dramatic and not at all shocking, among them his alterations in the protocol of titles, address, and royal ceremonies, attempts to cancel or repeal non-canonical taxation, and efforts to stabilize the common currency of market transactions. For his actions in these areas he does not stand out; many other Islamic rulers did likewise. But they are nonetheless parts of what he tried to accomplish. To obtain a complete picture of his reforms and attempts at social change, it is necessary to include these more ordinary acts along with those that were the most unusual and outlandish and for which he is best known.

Matters of Protocol

A decree from the year 1000, following the execution of Barjawan, runs as follows:

> O people who hear this appeal, truly God, who is most great and powerful, requires that the imams have singular obligations that no one else in the community shares. Those who, after the reading of this public decree, have the audacity to address in correspondence or communications to anyone other than the hallowed presence by the term 'our lord' or 'our master,' the Commander of the Believers has declared his blood lawful. So let those present inform those absent, God willing.[404]

The 'hallowed presence' is of course the imam-caliph and this edict states clearly that none but he is to be addressed as our lord or our master, a matter of protocol evidently until then in doubt.

In the next year an ambassador from the Byzantine emperor arrived. The elaborate ceremony devised for the occasion indicates another aspect of protocol. Soldiers were brought in from outlying districts to stand in rows between which the ambassador would ride until he reached the Bab al-Futuh. There he dismounted and walked to the palace kissing the ground along the whole distance until he came into the presence of al-Hakim. The great hall of the palace was furnished especially for this event, with rarely seen drapes of brocaded silk and gold thread. The walls of the hall and its floors were thus covered with gold. It gleamed with majesty and luxury. At the center a golden shield was suspended encrusted with gems; as the sun hit it its radiance was so bright that no one could look directly at it. Into this ambience the ambassador entered, kissed the ground and presented the letters and gifts he carried with him.[405]

These two items begin to reveal the immense importance of the protocol attached to the ceremony of an audience with the caliph or of how to address him, matters unique to him, not to be used by any of his subjects. More details of this kind can be culled from reports here and there about court ceremony and the occasions of public processions and audiences. There is, for example, a brief but interesting delineation of the order of sitting for nightly sessions of the court in 1000.[406] Who sat where and in exactly what order? At that period those who attended were for the most part the same men or men of the same ranks as had attended al-ʿAziz. Until then al-Hakim had maintained the basic elements of royal protocol as practiced under his father. Later that began to change.

One sign of a new policy was his constant riding with less and less of a formal escort, or riding at night often absent any purpose involving public display. More and more he shed the trappings of lavish pomp in favor of a simpler ascetic style. These changes affected the protocol of both ceremony and of address. Already in 1004 he issued a decree to disavow anyone who tried to address him in correspondence as 'lord of all creation.'[407] But the most revealing declaration is contained in one from 1013 prohibiting the people from kissing the ground in front of him or, during a procession, from kissing his stirrup or his hand. That was, according to the edict, to imitate the practice of the polytheistic Greeks. Those extending greetings to him should say simply: 'Salutations be upon the Commander of the Believers and the mercy of God and His blessings.'[408] Additional details are mentioned. In riding for prayers at Ramadan or the festivals, he avoided clothing and emblems with gold[409], later in fact adopting black in place of white, now a sign of asceticism rather than the Abbasids.

From the very commencement of his reign al-Hakim bestowed titles fairly generously. Thus Ibn ʿAmmar became the 'Trustee of the State' and most of the *wasitas* were given a title, as were many commanders in the army and the rulers of the vassal states in North Africa and Sicily. Yahya comments that he granted such titles to the elite amirs, the commanders and most of the clerks in the government. We have many examples. But oddly, though perhaps in keeping with his desire for simplicity during the last phase, he announced at one point that all titles of the kind were to be annulled, except in the case of nine individuals, among them the Zirid ruler of the Maghrib, the Kalbite amir of Sicily and his son, and closer to home the chief qadi and the chief daʿi. Yahya, who supplies this information although it is confirmed elsewhere, connects this action with the onset of the Druze troubles. He adds that it ended soon enough and most titles were restored.[410]

Reform of the Currency and Taxation

Reports from various years indicate a problem with wild price fluctuation and the hardship it implied, especially for the urban poor. Hoarding and the resulting scarcity of bread and some other commodities were common enough. One year – 1009 – an epidemic of sickness set off a scramble for sugar, pomegranate seeds, oil of violet, grapes, pears, watermelon and other goods thought to have medicinal properties. The price of such items rose dramatically, making the search for medicine that much harder.[411] Any government, that of al-Hakim included, had to monitor the situation closely and, if possible, act to control both price and supply. Measures undertaken by him in this regard were those often used, among them attempts to set a fair price and strict regulations against hoarding or withholding commodities by merchants.

Fatimid coinage depended on the gold dinar and that maintained a reputation for purity and fineness that wavered little or not at all. However, ordinary market transactions, the buying and selling of bread and other common goods, required a currency of much less value: the silver dirham. In general the supply of gold held up well but silver was not as plentiful. The great demand for dirhams caused pressures on the latter particularly for coins adequate for the smaller amounts employed in the daily give and take of the market. To put more silver coins into circulation they were broken into smaller pieces with less silver in each. That in turn created doubts about their value especially in the critically important rate of exchange between dirhams and dinars. At least two reports from the reign of al-Hakim speak of problems caused in part by the inflation of dirhams. One from 1005 notes that following a period of crisis, the dirham settled at 26 to the dinar.[412] But by the end of 1006 the matter became worse, reaching 34 dirhams per dinar. Under the circumstances prices ranged out of control throwing the markets into disarray. At that point, the government acted. The old dirham was withdrawn and 20 boxes of a new issue were sent from the treasury to the money changers for them to put these dirhams into circulation. A decree then explained that the old dirhams were invalid. The populace had three days to turn them in. A new dirham was worth four of the old. Previously a dirham bought three pounds of bread, now the rate was 12 per dirham. The prices of many commodities were fixed by the government. When, also, the vendors of key goods were beaten with the lash and paraded publicly for disobeying these new regulations, the public took heart. The concern and agitation of the people subsided.[413]

One additional reform needs some consideration as the evidence suggests that it involved an issue that al-Hakim returned to often. In an Islamic state certain taxes are to be levied in accord with Qur'anic injunctions and religious tradition. Land taxes, the poll tax on the protected peoples, dues for charity and others are regarded as canonical. Most taxation of commerce, however, falls outside of religious law and many authorities disapprove of it. The main tax is what was called the *mukus* (singular *maks*), either an excise tax or a kind of custom dues. It applied principally to goods entering the country and was most often collected at the port of entry.[414] Like other Islamic rulers intent on a reputation for piety, al-Hakim, to judge from the number of attempts he made either to forgive taxes due or to cancel them, obviously hoped to avoid the use of this kind of taxation. Al-Maqrizi's records show him trying to discontinue the *mukus* in at least one instance for 997, 1008, 1011, 1012, 1013, and 1014.[415] Yet in 1009 another mentioned that it was restored.[416] Clearly, as in other Islamic lands, this tax provided needed revenue and was therefore hard to do without. That al-Hakim's government had to lift it as frequently as this record indicates suggests that it was just as often re-imposed. The desire for reform was constantly trumped by the reality of fiscal necessity.

Ultimately, does the record of al-Hakim's attempts to change society indicate anything but a desire for reform, even those measures that appear now inexplicably harsh and repressive? Which if any were simply capricious, or signs of an unbalanced mind? Certain of them seem odd and extraordinary, but the irregularity lies more in the vanity of supposing it might have been possible, for example, to outlaw *mulukhiyya*, or *fuqqa*ʿ beer, or any of the other items he tried to prohibit. Al-Hakim may have thought himself more powerful than he really was, but was that the delusion of a madman? Or the dream of an imam bent on using his position for the good of all? His loyal Ismaili followers would have surely obeyed his commandments; if they had consumed *mulukhiyya* previously, after his decree against it they most certainly no longer did. Others who had never liked the stuff (a view shared in modern times by many a visitor to Egypt) would have been happy to see it gone. Reactions to the caliph's broader program, if that is what it was, were mixed, while to individual particulars – the campaign against this or that item – which normally garnered some support or favorable comment even from his detractors, are difficult to judge fairly. Often, moreover, we do not possess sufficient information about it. And in most cases we have no idea what he expected or what prompted him to do it.

7

Foreign Affairs

Seemingly without warning, in 1010, the ʿUqaylid ruler of north Mesopotamia, Qirwash b. al-Muqallad, abruptly announced that he had switched his allegiance from the Abbasid caliph to al-Hakim. He was in fact setting up a *daʿwa*, an appeal, in the latter's name. He and those he ruled had become overnight part of the Fatimid empire. This development constituted stunning and dramatic proof of the efficacy of its agents' secret efforts. No foreign territory could feel safe from the underground penetration of the Ismaili mission. Most importantly it gave clear evidence of how the fame of al-Hakim had spread far and wide. For many quite distant from his domain, what he appeared to stand for, what he claimed to be and represent, resonated with positive effect. The caliph in Cairo had for these Muslims become a hero.

In typical fashion Qirwash's formal public declaration of the change occurred in the next subsequent Friday *khutba*-sermon delivered in Mawsil, the capital city of the 'Uqaylids. The ruler simply handed the *khatib* (the preacher) the text of his new sermon and the man dutifully read it to the assembled worshippers. That was 18 August. Two months later, on 13 October, a similar announcement greeted the Muslim community in the congregational mosque of al-Anbar and one week after also in al-Mada'in and Qasr ibn Hubayra, possibly in Kufa as well. A glance at a map of Iraq indicates that the cities that had gone over to the Fatimids form what amounted to a noose around Baghdad, which lies at the center of the territory included. The Abbasid caliph could not but be alarmed; his position had, seemingly overnight, become perilous.[417]

Later Sunni historians, principally Ibn al-Jawzi and Ibn Taghri Birdi, both of whom hated the Fatimids, provide far more details about the event than any other sources, perhaps because they had a hard time making satisfactory sense of what happened. Ibn al-Jawzi claims that agents for al-Hakim worked persistently to win over the ʿUqaylids and eventually succeeded. Both historians insist that the inhabitants of Mawsil agreed to the change with the 'positive response of an enslaved flock, while concealing their true aversion and disgust' and both marvel at how easily the preacher, who had previously pronounced the sermon in the name of the Abbasid caliph, al-Qadir, would acquiesce in the change, which amounted almost to converting from Sunni to Shiʿi Islam. They offer a list of rather sumptuous new accoutrements – by implication a bribe – bestowed on him for the occasion.[418] But one explanation for Qirwash's having bestowed what amounts to a formal robe of honor on his *khatib* is that the Fatimid colors were white whereas those of the Abbasids were black. Accordingly, the tunic of *dabiqi* linen he received would have been white to symbolize the change officially. His older black robes were no longer appropriate.

For the Abbasid al-Qadir the matter had become urgent, even critical, and yet he himself possessed no real army. His throne depended on the good will of Buyid overlords who were themselves Shiite. To make a case to them, he sought the help of the famous Maliki jurist and Ashʿarite theologian, Abu Bakr al-Baqillani, whose anti-Ismaili sentiments were well known. Al-Baqillani went to Bahaʾ al-Dawla, the supreme Buyid amir, who was himself also bothered by Qirwash's act, seeing it as a challenge to his own authority. The Buyid ruler then ordered a hundred thousand dinars to be spent either on a military force or a bribe to convince the ʿUqaylid to reverse course and return to the Abbasids. Our historians claim that al-Hakim had offered no more than 30 thousand. In any case, Qirwash quickly realized where his best interest lay; the *khutba* in his lands soon once again called for God's blessings on al-Qadir. Within a couple of months at most – some say a month only – the matter had been resolved in favor of the Abbasids.[419]

In typical fashion our Sunni writer comments at this point: 'Subsequently, Qirwash learned of the unstable rule of al-Hakim and his having killed the leading notables of his government and that he had been overcome by melancholia. Thereupon he reverted to the Abbasid *khutba*.' But al-Nuwayri, another Sunni, reports, in addition, that the *daʿwa* to al-Hakim, with its attendant *khutba*, commenced about this time in Hilla under ʿAli b. Mazyad, ruler of another portion of Abbasid Iraq. He neglects to mention that the ʿUqaylids announced their support of the Fatimid caliph on other occasions, among which is one many years later.

While Qirwash's declaration of 1010 was not itself a lasting stage in this competition, an odd and unexpected benefit of it is that a verbatim copy[420] of the actual text of the *khutba* he issued for the occasion survived. And, most curiously, it was carefully preserved by the same Ibn al-Jawzi. For a vehemently anti-Fatimid writer to include this sermon, which is clearly pro-Fatimid, in its entirety, is at the least a curious oddity, but is nevertheless most fortunate for it allows us to see the other more positive side to these exchanges.

Of the thousands and thousands of *khutba*-sermons delivered in the name of the Fatimid imams – one each Friday in every mosque of the realm – virtually none survive. That our prime example comes from outside the empire is thus remarkable. It must therefore stand for the others. Here is what was said in Mawsil in 1010; we will imagine its like everywhere else, all as evidence of the public appeal on behalf of al-Hakim.

Qirwash's sermon

God is great, God is great; there is no god but God.

For Him is the praise of those who are, by His light, above the floods of fury, who, by His power, burst asunder the pillars supporting idols, who, by His light, cause the rising of the sun of truth from the west, who, by His justice, blot out the tyranny of injustice and break, by His might, the back of inequity so that matters revert to their original state and truth returns to its owners. Distinct in His essence, alone in His attributes, manifest in His signs, solitary in His indications, time passes by Him not so that the seasons preceded Him and forms do not resemble Him so that places contain Him. Eyes do not see Him so that tongues can describe Him. His existence is prior to all existences; His goodness surpasses all goodness. His oneness is fixed in every intellect; His presence exists in every vision. I praise Him with what is required of His grateful friends, the highest of praise for Him. I implore Him to do as He wills and wants. I acknowledge about Him what His most sincere friends and His witnesses acknowledge. I bear witness that there is no god but God, alone, no partner does He have; this is testimony unadulterated with the filth of idolatry or afflicted with delusions of doubt. It is free of deceit; it consists solely of obedience and submission.

I bear witness that Muhammad is His servant and His messenger, may God bless him. He chose him and selected him for the guidance of the people and for the upholding of the truth so that the message and guidance away from error arrives. The populace was at that time heedless and astray from the path of truth because of following personal whims. He saved them from the worship of idols and commanded them to obey the most Merciful so that the proofs of God and His signs were upheld. He brought to perfection his words by the delivery of them, may God bless him, and bless the first to respond to him, ʿAli, the Commander of the Believers and Lord of the Legatees, the establisher of excellence and mercy, the pillar of knowledge and wisdom, the root of the noble and righteous tree generated from the sacred and pure trunk. And [blessings be] on his successors, the lofty branches of that same tree, and on what comes from it: the fruit that grows there. O people, fear God with the piety He is due; seek His reward: beware of His punishment. You have seen what was recited to you in His book. God the exalted said: 'the day We summon all the people by their imam' [17: 71] and He said: 'O you who believe, obey God and obey the messenger and obey those with command among you' [4: 59]. So beware, beware, O people, it is as if the present world were leading you to the next. Its conditions have become clear, the pathway looms up, interrogation is its reckoning and entry is according to its book: 'thus whosoever does an atom's weight of good he will see it; whosoever does an atom's weight of bad he will see it' [99: 7–8]. Climb aboard the ship of your salvation before you founder; 'hold fast to the rope of God altogether, do not scatter' [3: 103]. Know that He knows what is in your souls, so beware of Him. Return to God with the best of returns, respond to the summoner who is the gateway of compliance, before 'you yourself should say, Ah, woe is me, I neglected my duty to God and am now among those who scoffed; or should say, alas, if God had guided me I would have been among the God-fearing; or should say, upon seeing the punishment, O that I could have another chance that I might be among those who do good' [39: 56–58]. Be on your guard against heedlessness and indifference before that remorse, and the sorrow, the hoping for another chance, the begging for redemption, and it is too late to escape. Obey your imam and you will be well guided; cling to the holder of the covenant and you will be led on the right way. He has shown you knowledge by which you are led rightly and the path by which you are guided. May God make us and you those who follow His wish; He makes faith his provision. He inspires him with his piety and good sense. May God the most magnificent grant us and you forgiveness, and for all Muslims the same.

[Then the preacher sat briefly and rose again and said:]

Praise be to God who is the most glorious and who is the creator of mankind, who determines the divisions though He is [Himself] matchless in eternity and perpetuity, who causes the dawns to break, who creates phantoms and makes spirits. I praise Him as the first and the last. I testify that He is the outward and the inner. I seek His aid as the divine power. I request His support as the victorious guardian. And I testify that there is no god but God, alone, who has no associate, and that Muhammad is His servant and His messenger, this testimony from one who affirms His absolute oneness in true faith and who confesses to His divinity willingly, knowing the demonstration of what He summons to and understanding the truth of the proofs for Him. O God, bless your radiant guardian and your greatest friend, ʿAli b. Abi Talib, the father of the rightly guided imams. O God, bless the two pure grandsons al-Hasan and al-Husayn and the righteous imams, the best and most excellent, those of them that stood forth and appeared and those of them that were concealed and hidden.[421] O God, bless the imam who is 'The One rightly guided by You' [*al-Mahdi bi-llah*], and who conveyed Your commandments and made manifest Your proofs and who took up the cause of justice in Your lands as the guide for Your servants. O God, bless 'The one who takes charge by Your order' [*al-Qaʾim bi-amr Allah*] and 'The one who is victorious through Your support' [*al-Mansur bi-nasr Allah*], these two who expended themselves for Your satisfaction and waged holy war on Your enemies. O God, bless 'The one who makes strong Your religion' [*al-Muʿizz li-din Allah*], a warrior in Your cause who revealed Your authentic signs and prominent proofs. O God, bless 'The one who is mighty because of You' [*al-ʿAziz bi-llah*] by whom the land is cleared and by whom the servants are guided. O God, extend all of Your blessings and the most perfect of Your favors to our lord and master, the imam of the age, fortress of the faith, head of the Aliid *daʿwa* and prophetic religion, Your servant and guardian on Your behalf, al-Mansur Abu ʿAli al-Hakim bi-amr Allah, Commander of the Believers, just as You blessed his rightly guided forefathers and as You ennobled Your saints who were rightly guided. O God, bear in mind what You have appointed him to do and safeguard him in what You observe of him. Favor him in what You bring to him; support his armies; raise high his banners in the east of the land and its west, for indeed You are capable of all things.

Though short-lived, recognition by a major ruler in the Islamic east, as was the case with Qirwash, offers clear evidence of al-Hakim's appeal deep in the realm of his sworn enemies and, as here, occasionally produces a dramatic triumph, a valid reminder that, as with the inhabitants of the Fatimid state, others farther away included both friends and foes, among them loyal upholders of his right to the supreme imamate, as well as detractors of many varieties.

The rivalry between the two caliphates was old by then. The Abbasid al-Qadir required little to provoke him at any time into the strongest reaction and take what countermeasures he could. The famous Baghdad Manifesto of 1011, one year later, which declared false the validity of the Fatimid claim of descent from ʿAli b. Abi Talib, is an example. Again it is Ibn al-Jawzi who reports the event.

> In November of 1011 there was written in the caliph's bureau a circular concerning matters relating to those who rule in Egypt, comprising a denunciation of their lineage and their doctrine. A copy of it was read out in Baghdad and the Aliid nobility, the judges and jurisprudents, the devout and the upright, the trustworthy and the exemplary, affixed their signatures to verify that they knew and admitted to a Daysani descent and that they [the Fatimid caliphs] were related to Daysan b. Saʿid al-Khurrami, a partisan of unbelief and the vice of satans, an attestation from those wishing to draw near to God, great is His glory, expressing the anger of religion and Islam, and a conviction that God requires the scholars to expose this truth and explain it to the people and not hide it. They all affirmed the person who appeared in Egypt, who is Mansur b. Nizar, known by the name al-Hakim, may God impose on him perdition, ruination, disgrace, exemplary punishment and extermination, is the son of Maʿadd b. Ismaʿil b. ʿAbd al-Rahman b. Saʿid, may God never favor him. When he went to the west, he called himself 'Ubaydallah with the throne name al-Mahdi, and those of his filthy and dirty forbears who preceded him, upon whom may the curses of God and the curses of those on whom curses fall, were imposters and rebels having no relationship to the son of ʿAli b. Abi Talib, nor were they connected to him in any way. He is free of their falsehoods and what they claim about being related to him is false and untrue. They do not know of anyone belonging to the family of the Talibid who is unwilling to state, in regard to these rebels, that they are imposters. This renunciation of their falsehoods and their claims has been spread to the holy cities [of Arabia] and, at the very commencement of their affair in the west, it was published in such a way as to preclude their lies having deceived anyone or inclined them to believe them. This person who appeared in Egypt he and his ancestors are unbelieving, iniquitous, shameless heretics, atheists and agnostics who reject Islam and uphold the doctrines of the Dualists and Manicheans, who do not observe the law, who permit fornication, consider licit wine and the shedding of blood, who revile the prophets, curse the Companions, and assert a claim of their own divinity.[422]

Ibn al-Jawzi continues:

> A great many of the Aliids added their signatures, among them al-Murtada and al-Radi, as well as Ibn al-Azraq al-Musawi, Abu Tahir b. Abi'l-Tayyib, Muhammad b. Muhammad b. 'Umar and Ibn Abi Yaʿla. Among the judges there was Abu Muhammad Ibn al-Akfa'i, Abu'l-Qasim al-Kharazi and Abu'l-ʿAbbas al-Suri. Of the jurisprudents Abu Hamid al-Isfara'ini, Abu Muhammad al-Kashfali, Abu'l-Husayn al-Quduri, Abu ʿAbdallah al-Saymari, Abu ʿAbdallah al-Baydawi and Abu ʿAli b. Hamakan; and of the notary witnesses Abu'l-Qasim al-Tanukhi. This declaration was also read out in Basra and many signed it there as well.

Although not the first rejection of Fatimid genealogy, nor by any means the last, this one was odd in its blunt use of the scattershot rhetoric of all inclusive denunciation often employed against suspected heresies, such as a claim that the heretics permit unlawful fornication and the drinking of wine. Neither makes obvious sense in this instance. As but one example, al-Hakim's campaign against alcoholic beverages was certainly already widely recognized. Better was the assertion that he advocated the cursing of the Companions, except that, again, by 1011, he had annulled that edict and no longer allowed the practice. On balance, most particularly in its attempt to trace Fatimid lineage to Daysan, a connection quite far-fetched, this Baghdad Manifesto likely fooled few. Those who signed it, as later historians admit, probably felt compelled to do so.

Still, there are many other examples of Sunni and even Shiite hostility to al-Hakim and the Ismailis. Al-Baqillani, whose role in restoring Qirwash to the Abbasid cause, composed, about this time, a treatise he called 'Exposing the Secrets and Tearing Away the Veil' as his refutation of the Fatimid position. A major Zaydi Shiite theologian Abu'l-Qasim al-Busti wrote another with a similar title: 'Exposing the Secrets and Critiquing the Thinking', again to rebut the Ismailis. Yet another repudiation came from the pen of the Zaydi imam Abu'l-Hasan al-Mu'ayyad bi-llah. And finally the Abbasid caliph al-Qadir, not content with his manifesto, commissioned the leading Mu'tazilite authority in Baghdad to produce one more. Since al-Baqillani died in 1013 and al-Istakhri in 1014, and since the Ismaili *daʿi* al-Kirmani wrote a response to the Zaydi imam, this outpouring of anti-Ismaili tracts was surely associated, perhaps a direct response to, the growing fame or infamy of al-Hakim during this period.

One more incident of a slightly different type illustrates the vehemence of al-Hakim's opponents, in this case of Mahmud, the Ghaznavid sultan from much farther to the east. In the year 1013 al-Hakim sent this ruler a letter inviting him to accept allegiance to the Fatimids. Why he would go to the effort is hard to see. Mahmud was already known to be an implacable enemy. Nonetheless the letter was sent. Yet again it is the Baghdadi historian Ibn al-Jawzi who provides the best account of how it was received. He reports that in the summer of 1013, Mahmud forwarded to the Abbasid caliph a letter that had come to him from the ruler of Egypt, requesting that he accept obedience to the Fatimids and join those who followed them. The Ghaznavid sultan simply tore it apart, spat on it, and then dispatched it to Baghdad.[423]

Al-Hakim's world was circumscribed by territories and governing entities, partly under the control of those adamantly opposed to him, such as the Abbasids in Baghdad and the Ghaznavids in Khurasan, partly in the hands of Christian princes and emperors, such as Byzantium to the north and the Kingdom of Nubia to the south, and partly held by men who were ostensibly his vassals, such as the Kalbite amirate in Sicily, the Zirids in the Maghrib, and the two amirates of Mecca and Madina. Nearer were the cities of the Tripolitania on the Libyan-Egyptian border and of Syria, which comprised a range geographically from Ramla in the extreme south to Aleppo in the far north, with the most important, Damascus, in the middle. Syria never ceased to provide trouble for the reign; the revolt of the Jarrahids, just recounted, provides only one of several examples. Far away to the west, in Spain, there were the Umayyads, long detested by the Shiʿa. They had been bitter rivals of the Fatimids in North Africa and the western Mediterranean. By the era of al-Hakim, however, less is heard of them.

Ironically, Christian enemies proved, in general, more amenable to civil relations than the Muslims of the Sunni east. That was not always the case. The Byzantines regarded Fatimid attempts to bring northern Syria into its orbit as an encroachment on their own. Either directly or through surrogates, the Greeks believed strongly in preserving a presence in Syria – especially the northern sections – in part as a buffer for the defense of Byzantine territory proper, which included, by their reckoning, the city of Antioch. Still the major conflicts between the two empires were largely in the past by the time of al-Hakim, which saw, instead, the exchange of ambassadors and gifts, along with a treaty of peace, an option not sanctioned by Islamic rules except on condition that the cessation of hostilities never become permanent. The Fatimid caliph could conclude a truce with his Christian antagonist, but not with the Abbasids (except in the highly unlikely event the latter were to admit and accept his exclusive right to the imamate.)

Even so the reign did not begin so auspiciously. The Byzantine emperor Basil initially retained an ambition for conquests in Syria and events there into 1000 followed that policy. When appealed to, for example, he supplied aid to the rebel al-'Allaqa. Either himself or his field commanders conducted forays into the territory of the Muslims. Still, prior to his last venture in Syria, he sent two emissaries to Egypt to ask for a treaty. That was 999. One returned after delivering the message, but the other remained in Cairo to await a formal reply. Meanwhile the emperor moved from Antioch against the forces of Jaysh b. al-Samsama, governor of Damascus on behalf of the Fatimids. Battles at Antioch and Apamea were victories for the Muslims. Jaysh was able to send one of his lieutenants to Cairo with prisoners and the heads of the slain. After all were paraded, the Christian prisoners were released. But the poor Byzantine ambassador, caught in the middle, must have feared for his life. He asked to be allowed to leave, a request more than once denied. Early in 1000, the Byzantines seemed to have recovered and renewed their offensive, taking at that time the fortress of Shayzar and the city of Hims, and then threatening the port of Tripoli, before weakening once again and retreating. Basil was thereafter diverted toward Armenia, and later Bulgaria, thus relinquishing all thought of additional campaigns against the Muslims. Relieved to be sure by the news that the emperor had departed from Syria, the Byzantine ambassador was finally granted a favorable response to his request for a treaty.[424]

According to the Melkite historian Yahya, the word finally came down at a meeting arranged by Barjawan who had summoned Sitt al-Mulk's maternal uncle Orestes from Jerusalem for the purpose. The Patriarch was instructed to accompany the ambassador to Constantinople and there to conclude the treaty. Barjawan said at the time that whatever Orestes saw fit to arrange, his master – meaning al-Hakim – would sign and agree to. Both men were given splendid robes of honor and a liberal allowance. In the Byzantine capital, Orestes concluded an agreement for a truce of ten years' duration. Once there he also stayed; he died in Constantinople four years later.[425]

The exact date of the treaty cannot be precisely determined, but in mid-1001 another Byzantine embassy arrived in Egypt. The situation evidently demanded a great display of pomp, a sign both of how important cordial relations with the Byzantines were judged and how al-Hakim, in those early days of his reign, hoped to suggest the grandeur of his rule to his Christian adversary. Here again is al-Maqrizi's account:

On 13 May, an emissary from the Byzantine emperor arrived. Soldiers from various districts were mustered for the occasion. They stood in two rows, with al-Hakim positioned to be seen by them. The emissary approached between the soldiers to the Bab al-Futuh where he dismounted and walked to the palace kissing the ground along the whole distance until coming into the presence of al-Hakim at the palace. The great hall of the palace had been furnished, rare drapes hung in it that were said to have been ordered searched for in the storehouses of furnishings until there were found in it, 21 individual but similar pieces that the lady Rashida, daughter of al-Mu'izz, remembered had been in the train of furnishing transported from Qayrawan to Egypt with al-Mu'izz. The clerks of the furnishings' treasury found written on one of them the date 331 (942 or 943), the work of the servants, in brocaded silk and gold thread. The whole of the hall was furnished with it, hiding in the process all of its walls, so that its entire floor and walls were of gold, gleaming with majesty and luxury. In the center of the hall the golden shield was suspended crowned by a splendidly unique gem of each variety, radiating what surrounded it. When the sun hit it, eyes could not look at it out of feebleness. The emissary entered and kissed the ground, then presented letters and gifts.[426]

For the next 12 years there is little or no information about Byzantine relations with the Fatimids. Presumably the treaty held. Was it renewed, and if so when? It seems quite likely as it appears to have been still in effect more than ten years later. Al-Maqrizi reports that, in 1013, al-Hakim dispatched a load of gifts to the 'king of the Greeks' worth some seven thousand dinars.[427] One year later in 1014 the savant 'Abd al-Ghani b. Sa'id received special honors along with 1,500 dinars, 15 items of cloth and more, and then was sent off to accompany a returning emissary of the Byzantine emperor, who was also granted such honors and gifts. They departed together laden with gifts for the Byzantine ruler.[428] Yet one year after that, in December 1013, they returned. Again the army formed two rows from the door of the palace out to the spot where the ambassador would dismount. The caliph rode to the station where he received the man, accompanied this time by his cousin and heir apparent, both heavily robed and wearing jewels. The Byzantine emissary approached with 'Abd al-Ghani and with gifts. He was settled in a house in Cairo. Tragically, al-Hakim later learned that in the process three members of the honor guard had accepted presents from the man and they were executed for having done so, although apparently without repercussions for Byzantine-Fatimid relations.[429]

Relations with two southern entities, the Yemen and Nubia, might have been important, except that a paucity of information concerning either one suggests nothing out of the ordinary. The situation of both with respect to the Fatimids remained, it seems, as it had in the years prior to the reign of al-Hakim. Nubia, as a Christian sovereign nation, was, like Byzantium, subject to the rule of war except during periods of temporary truce. Exceptionally, however, it fell under a semi-mysterious pact, the *baqt*, concluded so long before that its exact provisions were vague, so vague that reports about its observance are fairly rare and seldom consistent. The Nubians were to send gifts, which when it happened featured exotic animals, particularly elephants, and commodities such as ivory and ebony. One proviso stipulated that either side would repatriate fleeing criminals caught in the territory of the other.[430] Might that rule have applied in the case of Abu Rakwa? It is not mentioned in our sources, though surely it did.

The Yemen had once been a scene of considerable activity by the *daʿwa*, leading eventually to the conquest of most of it and the establishment there of a fledgling Ismaili state just prior to the advent of the Fatimid caliphate in North Africa. Those early successes did not last, however, and by the era of al-Hakim not much was left. Even so the Fatimids had their agents in the region as is clearly proven by a letter from al-Hakim to one of them, the text of which survives. In it the imam counsels a *daʿi* of his named Harun b. Muhammad on several matters that this man had raised in a letter he had sent to Cairo 13 months earlier. Al-Hakim specifies in it that, on questions of what is licit and illicit, in addition to the Book of God and of His messenger 'our grandfather Muhammad, as these have been transmitted by the rightly guided imam and the Legatee', the agent in the field should rely on the *Pillars of Islam* by Qadi al-Nuʿman, and no other book than these. So important did the Yemeni *daʿwa* regard this instruction, its members both preserved the words of this very letter carefully and referred back to it for centuries afterward.[431]

The next closer circle of foreign governments consisted of those who were actually not technically outside the Fatimid empire but rather within it. These vassal states included Mecca and Madina, the various cities and governorates of Syria, Zirid North Africa and Kalbite Sicily. Throughout the reign of al-Hakim the latter two preserved a formal bond with Cairo even while displaying otherwise obvious signs of growing independence. With the exception of Abu'l-Futuh's brief revolt, the Holy Cities did likewise. Syria as always exhibited a mixture of adherence and of incipient disloyalty.

The case of Mecca has already been discussed. A critical matter here is the value of the gifts, stipends, good and supplies sent every year with the pilgrimage caravan and to what extent the Holy Cities depended on it. With Madina there is also one curious incident that needs to be recounted. In the year 1009 or 1010, al-Hakim dispatched his agents, under the *daʿi* Khatkin al-Dayf, to open the long sealed house of Jaʿfar al-Sadiq in Madina and bring its contents back to Cairo. Versions of the basic account appear in both Egyptian and Eastern sources, among others Ibn al-Jawzi[432] and Ibn ʿAbd al-Zahir.[433] Idris ʿImad al-Din, the Ismaili historian of the imams,[434] also records it as, most significantly, did Hamid al-Din al-Kirmani, who was a contemporary of the event itself.[435] Ibn al-Jawzi's note, recorded under the Islamic year 400, claims that al-Hakim obtained the consent of the Aliid *ashraf*-nobility in Madina to open the house with the promise that he only wanted to see what was in it and that the items would be returned to their original place once they had been brought to Cairo for his inspection. The house had reportedly not been entered since the death of Jaʿfar, over 250 years before. But now from it Fatimid agents retrieved a bed (*sarir*), carpets or mats, utensils, and a Qur'an (*mashaf*), which they carried to Cairo, accompanied by a delegation of Husaynid and Hasanid nobles. In the end al-Hakim gave back only the bed and kept the rest, arguing that they were more rightfully his. Idris, writing from the Ismaili side, adds that al-Hakim had already known what was in the house and exactly where. He was thus able to instruct his agents accordingly. His knowledge derived from inherited family memory; it was proof of his imamate and his true descent from Jaʿfar. But why had he decided to prove it in this manner only at this juncture? That he did so seems beyond question, however.

The preceding event was historical fact; not so the stories that would enter circulation less than a century later claiming that al-Hakim sent his men to Madina to tunnel secretly from a house a safe distance away under the tombs of the Prophet and of Abu Bakr and ʿUmar in order to steal the remains of all three for reburial in Egypt, which are hardly credible at all. But the charge was made nonetheless both in western sources, such as the writings of the Spanish geographer al-Bakri, and the Easterner Ibn Fahd al-Makki.[436] Why al-Hakim might even have entertained a notion of this kind is difficult to imagine. Abu Bakr and ʿUmar were to the Shiʿa hated villains and great satans. Of what use could their remains be in this situation? And, despite hints that the Fatimids hoped to create a cult center in Cairo, there is no evidence that they wanted to negate or in any way annul the pilgrimage to the holy cities of the Hijaz. The *hajj*-pilgrimage remained important to them and they went to great lengths to co-opt and thus control the Aliids who ruled both Mecca and Madina.

Sicily was especially closely connected to Cairo at the commencement of al-Hakim's rule since Ibn ʿAmmar, the new *wasita* and chief executive, was a ranking member of the Kalbid family of governors there.[437] A large share of his standing was based on his heroic service against the Byzantines on the island prior to coming to Egypt. When al-Hakim came to power, Ibn ʿAmmar's cousin Abu'l-Futuh Jusuf b. ʿAbdallah held the amirate. His title 'Trustee of the State' (*Thiqat al-Dawla*) had been conferred by the Fatimid imam. The first decade of his administration, roughly to 998, perhaps later, was a high point for Islam in Sicily, but the succeeding period witnessed the beginning of a long steady decline. A stroke paralyzed him and his son Jaʿfar assumed his duties, ruling from Palermo, more and more giving to inaction except in the pursuit of courtly pleasures. The caliph granted him the title 'Crown of the State and Sword of Religion' (*Taj al-Dawla wa Sayf al-Milla*).[438] Complaints of his tyranny, however, created tensions even within his own family. One brother rose in revolt and eventually in 1019 Jaʿfar himself was forced to flee, yielding power to yet another of his brothers. In keeping with their tradition of allegiance to the Fatimids, when he had to leave he went to Cairo; his father even sent after him a substantial sum to provide for his retirement in Egypt.[439]

Fatimid relations with the Zirids in the Maghrib, who were, like the Kalbids, technically vassals of the empire, preserved a formal decorum even while suffering a declining sense of loyalty. When al-Muʿizz moved his court to Egypt, he left behind this family of Sinhaja Berbers to rule over a hereditary, but nevertheless subservient, governorship in the territories he then vacated. As with Sicily, the Hijaz and Syria, the appointment of officials in such areas – judges, for example – remained theoretically the responsibility of Cairo. For the Maghrib one outstanding problem was systemic: the Sinhaja never converted to Ismailism and the vast majority of the local population was Maliki Sunni, with a history of grievances, both real and perceived, against the Fatimids. To a large extent Cairo's hold on North Africa depended on the willingness of the Zirid ruler to keep matters in check. Small events were to test that resolve.

In the year 986 the Fatimids in Cairo dispatched a missionary to the Kutama. His original purpose was to generate among them renewed enthusiasm for military service in the Fatimid armies of the east – a matter of no consequence to the Zirid governors of the Maghrib. This man was accorded their hospitality and provided money and the means to pass on to the region of the tribes he was sent to recruit. Once there, however, Abu'l-Fahm began to promote his own cause, forming an army of rebellion and minting coins. Belatedly alarmed by this growing insurrection, the Zirids angrily suppressed it as soon as they could.[440] Did they blame Cairo? It is possible but there is no evidence of long-term consequences.

A critical turning point arrived with the advent of Badis b. al-Mansur, who succeeded his father in 996, ironically the very year of al-Hakim's own accession. In the long run Badis was to remain loyal and observe cordial relations with his nominal overlord. But the first years were difficult. The cause was Libyan Tripoli and Barqa, the latter of which the Fatimids had retained as an independent governorate under the direct control of Egypt. It, for example, provided its own yearly offering of funds and gifts. Tripoli was passed to the Zirids as far back as 975 or 976.[441] The governor there was Tamusalt b. Bakkar until the accession of Badis when a dispute arose between this Tamusalt and his new overlord, leading to the former's defection. He gathered his possessions and extensive family and moved to Egypt, after first requesting to be relieved of his responsibilities, a request he addressed to Cairo and not to Qayrawan. Barjawan was then in charge. He had already forced his rival, the eunuch Yanis, to leave Cairo for Barqa. Now he drove him even further west, this time to Tripoli as a replacement for Tamusalt. Badis answered this challenge by sending his own force against Yanis, who was defeated and killed. Stranded a long way from Egypt, what remained of the Fatimid army tried to hold Tripoli until reinforcements reached it. A new army dispatched by al-Hakim, however, fell apart en route, a failure the caliph would blame on several factors, among them the Banu Qurra who were supposed to accompany this expedition.

As it happened neither the Zirids nor the Fatimids benefited. An enemy of both, the Zanata Berbers, under their chieftain Fulful (Falfal), seized Tripoli during the chaos and declared themselves adherents of the Umayyads of Spain. It took Badis many years to undo the damage. Long after in 1013 al-Hakim eventually recognized the difficulty of trying to hold on to these western cities; in that year he formally added Barqa to the domain of Badis.[442]

These few indications of minor friction – the first clearly not instigated or intended by the Fatimids and the misadventure at Tripoli, which might be charged to Barjawan and thus excused by his execution – do not fully explain the desire of the Zirids for independence, which grew slowly but steadily. Still at the announcement by al-Hakim in 1013 that his cousin ʿAbd al-Rahim Ibn Ilyas was to be his heir and the concomitant command to add this man's name to all coins and documents of the realm, Badis, though perplexed and troubled by this odd and irregular development, obeyed. The decree that had come from Cairo was dutifully read out in the mosques of Qayrawan and al-Mansuriyya. ʿAbd al-Rahim's name was added to that of al-Hakim on the coinage.[443] Badis himself is said to have remarked, 'Were it not that the imam cannot be gainsaid in matters of governance, I would write to advise him not to take this away from his son and give it to the son of his uncle.'[444]

The first major rupture might have occurred in summer 1016, the year after the accession of al-Muʿizz, the son of Badis, earlier that year at the age of a little over eight.[445] Sunni mobs, possibly secretly abetted by the old administration but led by ardently Sunni shaykhs, stormed into the Shiite sections of Qayrawan, al-Mahdiyya and other towns of the Maghrib, massacring all those they considered Shiʿa.[446] It was an ugly and horrendous development, one the Maliki authorities could not justify however much they tried. In short order the entire Shiite Ismaili population of the urban centers disappeared. Thereafter little or no evidence of religious support for the Fatimid imams remained, only the formal tie still professed by the ruler who nonetheless continued to recognize his allegiance, as he would for many more years before finally renouncing it over three decades later.

The record of gifts and exchanges between the two, which is reasonably complete, belies these unpleasant undercurrents. Already in 993 we have a report of a Zirid gift to the future caliph. That year the North Africans sent to Cairo many items of great value including prized horses and mules, some with the finest of trappings, along with hunting dogs, gold and servants. There were five horses with saddles especially designated for al-ʿAziz's son.[447] For 997 Ibn ʿIdhari notes the arrival in al-Mansuriyya, the Zirid capital, coming from Egypt of the qadi al-Sharif al-Bahiri who brought among other things two decrees, one granting the title 'Defender of the State' (*Nasir al-Dawla*) to Badis, and the other announcing the death of al-ʿAziz and the succession of al-Hakim. Yet a third decree asked that the pledge of allegiance (the *bay'a*) be taken by Badis and all the elite of the Sinhaja.[448] The following year the famous historian Ibn al-Raqiq al-Qayrawani came to Cairo bearing gifts from the Zirids.[449] For that same year the North African Ibn ʿIdhari notes gifts coming to the Maghrib from Egypt.[450] In July 1001, a caravan of gifts for the Maghrib set off with 300 of the best horses and ten more with baggage and 45 mules carrying arms and coverings, 20 more transporting boxes of gold and silver.[451] A long hiatus in the record follows but that is not unusual. The next report announces the arrival on 4 August 1012 at the port of al-Mahdiyya of al-Hakim's gifts for Badis and his son. ʿAbd al-ʿAziz b. Abi Kudayna was in charge of this embassy; he also carried with him al-Hakim's decree adding Barqa and its dependencies to the Zirid domain. Badis went out to meet him accompanied by the judges and notables. 'It was,' says one of our sources, 'a famous day!'[452] In 1014 Badis prepared and dispatched from al-Mansuriyya a magnificent gift destined for al-Hakim. Before leaving it was paraded and a North African historian could thus offer a description of what was in it. There was also a gift from Umm Mallal, Badis's sister, for Sitt al-Mulk, al-Hakim's sister.[453] Al-Maqrizi notes what happened next. The party bringing the gift reached the region of Barqa where they were intercepted by the Banu Qurra and all of it was taken by the tribesmen.[454] In fact the Banu Qurra, who, under their chieftain Mukhtar b. Qasim had departed from the Nile Delta aiming for Barqa, now attacked that city. Hamid, a son of Tamusalt, who was then its governor on behalf of the Zirids, fled to the Maghrib. Mukhtar captured Barqa, taking away from both the Fatimids and the Zirids.[455] That same year al-Hakim sent ʿAbd al-ʿAziz b. Abi Kudayna and another man, Abu'l-Qasim b. Hasan, to Badis with robes of honor, swords, and decrees especially for Mansur, Badis's son, appointing him to what his father had given him during his lifetime and after.[456] In 1019 the caliph sent Abu'l-Qasim b. al-Yazid to the Zirid ruler, who had now been granted the title 'Nobility of the State' (*Sharaf al-Dawla*). This emissary brought a sword adorned with a rare gem and a robe of honor. He reached al-Mansuriyya in June 1020 and was accorded hospitality. He read out the large decree he carried. Our historian comments, 'Those were days of happiness and amusement.' Later Muhammad, the son of ʿAbd al-ʿAziz b. Abi Kudayna, the former Fatimid ambassador, arrived with yet another decree along with 15 flags woven with gold. Al-Muʿizz b. Badis bestowed honors and gifts on both. In their company he marched around Qayrawan with the flags they had brought carried in front. From this record alone it would appear that all was well between Cairo and Qayrawan.[457]

In contrast to the Maghrib, the Fatimids attempted to rule Syria directly through military governors attached to Cairo by a short leash.[458] Al-ʿAziz, throughout his reign, preserved a hope of total conquest, a task that he pursued avidly up to the moment of his death. He was then in the midst of preparing a massive army for a final campaign. Al-Hakim inherited the same desire but not the intensity shown by his father. In the end he would hold his own in Syria; the Fatimids under him lost none of the territory they had mastered previously. In fact Aleppo in the north, a key entry point into Mesopotamia, eventually both acknowledged his caliphate and then acceded to Fatimid control with the arrival in 1017 of ʿAziz al-Dawla Abu Shujaʿ Fatik, the first governor appointed over it from Egypt.

Other parts of Syria were also ruled by appointees, notably the coastal cities, but most conspicuously Damascus, which proved unusually difficult to subdue and pacify. Over the more than two decades of al-Hakim's reign, he appointed as many as 20 governors, some more than once. They included Manjutakin, whose rebellion against Ibn ʿAmmar and the Westerners occurred at the beginning, and ʿAbd al-Rahim Ibn Ilyas, the cousin and heir apparent, who was in charge of it at the end. Tamusalt, the North African renegade, was one, as was Khatkin al-Dayf, who advised al-Hakim on the destruction of the Holy Sepulchre and later was to become head of the *daʿwa*, the *daʿi* of all *daʿi*s. Within Damascus various factions – local militias and gangs, scholars and merchants, along with the ever present rural Arab tribal groups – vied for control, in various combinations, but all commonly in opposition to the Fatimid army of occupation, especially when it was predominantly Maghribi and therefore Berber. Tension between the native inhabitants and the North Africans seldom failed to engender such friction that it resulted in armed clashes. An especially brutal repression of one such incident by Jaysh b. al-Samsama, the Fatimid governor, in 998 and thus early in the reign, helped quell the almost natural hostility of the city. However, the situation was never completely calm. Even so, when the caliph disappeared in 1021, Syria, and Damascus, remained securely within the empire.

In general, although, in the hindsight of later times, some signs of structural weaknesses in Fatimid dealings with foreign entities and its own satellites are evident for this period, there were remarkably few, if any, negative consequences of the policies pursued under al-Hakim in this regard. His father bequeathed him an empire and it persisted to the end quite nearly exactly as it was in the beginning, nothing gained but also nothing lost.

PART FOUR

8

The Final Seven Years

It might seem odd to include here a separate chapter devoted to the last seven years of al-Hakim's reign. That begs the question: why seven? Why single out a specific period, a set number of years, but not others. Presumably it must point to a dramatic change, an alteration in the character of his rule or of himself that is clearly notable seven years prior to his disappearance. The actual answer, however, is more complex, though hardly less interesting or compelling. Since the caliph disappeared in February 1021, 1013 would have witnessed the beginning of this ultimate phase. The major act of that earlier time, one so prominent as to elicit comment and discussion, was his naming of his cousin ʿAbd al-Rahim Ibn Ilyas as the heir apparent, thus ignoring his own son, the future al-Zahir. Ibn Ilyas's name was for the following seven years added to the coinage, all official documents and decrees, flags and banners, and the Friday sermon. No one in the realm could have missed it, or failed to wonder what this extraordinary action really meant. Did the caliph actually intend his cousin to succeed, or was it a ruse to distract attention from himself, possibly a stand-in, a kind of official alternate for ceremonial use? We have in our records the reaction of the Zirid ruler of North Africa who, although he accepted the change, expressed his bewilderment and incomprehension as to why. Nonetheless Maghribi and Sicilian coins, to mention only these two of the vassal states, have Ibn Ilyas's name on them for the period 1013 to 1021. But would this step by al-Hakim have suggested a moment so profound as to have shaped the next years into a block unlike those before it?

Other trends could be traced to 1013, but are less obvious, including the growing ascetic demeanor of the caliph, his increasing propensity to do away with royal pomp and ceremony, to avoid it when he could, even to refuse to carry out the functions of his office as it had been conducted traditionally, eventually to delegate the formalities to others (Ibn Ilyas, for example) while he withdrew, adopting in the process the habits of a simple monk or a threadbare sufi dervish. Toward the end he rode only his donkey, almost never a horse; he stopped cutting his hair and nails, and seldom washed or changed his clothes. His excursions away from the palace, both by day and by night, increased; no armed guard accompanied him, no one was sure what he was doing, why or where exactly he went.

The second aspect of his new behavior involved his charity. He gave away so much money, land, and other items that he was soon famous for it. One lasting judgment of him and his character singles him out for generosity, a trait often mentioned alongside his cruelty, a strange juxtaposition sometimes taken as evidence of his instability and possible madness. Few Islamic rulers were ever as openhanded, and that is the verdict both of contemporaries and of later medieval writers. It is also a finding based mainly on this caliph's actions over the last years of his reign, when his proclivity to give away everything evidently accelerated markedly, so much so that it is a valid question to ask whether it alarmed the keepers of the dynastic trust to the point that they – whoever they were (Sitt al-Mulk is often suggested) – conspired to have him killed.

Yet one more new policy that began in 1013 saw the Christians and Jews, who had been quite harshly treated up to then – 1012 was a particularly trying year for the Christians –suddenly granted permission to depart the kingdom and to take with them their moveable possessions. Moreover, commencing perhaps about then many of the protected peoples who had previously converted to Islam were allowed to revert to their old religion. Churches and synagogues that had been torn down and destroyed could be rebuilt; lands and trusts once dedicated for their maintenance were reclaimed where possible or reconstituted if not. Historians belonging to the two major Christian groups, the Copts and the Melkites, both insist that al-Hakim himself took a special interest during these final years in some of this rebuilding and that in each case became attached personally, perhaps spiritually, to a prominent monk belonging to their own group.

Ultimately the best testimony to the importance of these seven years comes from the writings of the Druze, some epistles of whom actually date to the period. They make a great deal out of the fact that the number is seven. The high point of human contact with God, when He had adopted the figure of a man, occurred precisely then, just prior to al-Hakim's reversion in 1021 to his divine form after he ceased to appear in earthly garb. The acts of al-Hakim (God) in that period all possessed a meaning; they were His way of communicating with human beings. The Druze appeal began at that time, peaking in 1019–1021; it lapsed thereafter for seven years, to be restarted in 1027 and continued for two more periods of seven, finally ceasing altogether in 1042. The first treatise from about 1027, moreover, is replete with lists of sevens, among them the following: 'Before his *ghayba* (disappearance) our Lord wore black seven years, let his hair grow seven years, imprisoned women seven years, and rode a donkey seven years.' And each of these items holds a meaning. Seven years of wearing black indicates the length of trial and oppression for the faithful.[459] Thus the importance of this seven-year period looms especially large in Druze doctrine.

Unfortunately, after stressing the necessity of providing an accurate and detailed account of the years from 1013 to the end, our sources, it must be admitted, frequently fail us. Most medieval histories on which we depend for much of the information available – at times the only information – tend to offer in a lump a series of comments and reports about al-Hakim and his reign without careful regard for chronology. It is thus difficult to compile a dated record from this material. What might have happened in 1017, for example, or 1019, is imprecisely distinguished, if at all, from other years. For that reason al-Maqrizi's history of the Fatimids holds a value not shared by most of the rest. He alone attempted in that book to assemble his data in strict chronological order, a commendable aim he could not, however, always achieve in practice. Despite his best efforts, parts of his narrative are vague as to order and date, and, most significantly, for the crucial final section covering the years in question, he simply could not locate the information he required. From 1015 to 1021 his account lacks the detail it had in the earlier years. It is often totally inadequate or even non-existent. Why we can only guess. If his main source had been the history of al-Musabbihi, we need to wonder what happened to it. Perhaps al-Maqrizi could not find the appropriate volumes, but it would appear that no on else could either.

Luckily, the Melkite historian Yahya, whose account also follows a reasonably clear chronological order, contributes information covering many aspects of what happened over those years and that, when it applies, appears sound. Would only that there was more to it. Yahya by that time had moved to Antioch in northern Syria and he was no longer a direct witness, nor was his interest centered as narrowly on Egypt.

Under these circumstances it becomes necessary to piece together a history from a scattered record: the writings of the Druze prophet Hamza and his associates, works composed by the Ismaili *da'is*, principally al-Kirmani and al-Naysaburi, what little al-Maqrizi and Yahya report, and information provided by other medieval writers, some parts of which are surely of dubious value, but must be taken into account nonetheless, especially given the impossibility of proving it faulty on the basis of conflicting evidence, which here does not exist, and thereby rejecting it outright.

Naturally to fix on seven in this instance in part reflects a judgment of hindsight, which blurs reality by creating artificial limitations. A good example of how it could be wrong involves al-Hakim's tendency toward asceticism. From early in the year 1013 we hear already that he issued a decree forbidding anyone kissing the ground in front of him or kissing his stirrup. On the feast of sacrifice he rode to the square in plain attire and his riding each night after sundown was well known. Such trends continued and accelerated thereafter; they did not commence in 1013.

One aspect of his policy that never seems to have changed and for which 1013 means nothing was his infliction of the harshest punishments on those who served him and several areas of his attempts at social reformation. A major event of 1013 was the amputation in October of al-Jarjaraʾi's hands[460] and the hands and tongue of Ghabn, followed in October 1014 by the execution of al-Fariqi and others (including the *wasita*). January 1014 is the date on which he gave the order to prohibit shoemakers from producing footwear for women, and other measures designed to insure their confinement continued unabated. It was also that year he had all the dogs killed. Ultimately, arguably the most heinous act of his, if the accounts that put the blame squarely on the caliph as presented by some sources are to be believed, was the deliberate ravaging of Fustat by the Sudanese guard near the end of the reign. That an event of the kind occurred is not in doubt, only the severity of what happened and the truth of the charge that al-Hakim was personally responsible for it.

Another area for caution is his turn from persecuting the protected people to leniency and then sympathy. We have a date for the decree allowing them to leave: August–September 1013, which is thus at the beginning of 404, the corresponding Islamic year. The best evidence for the permission to reclaim a pre-conversion religion and for the rebuilding of houses of worship dates to 1020, many years later.[461] Thus a finer view of his policy suggests first a willingness only to have the Christians and Jews depart, followed a full six years afterward by the latter step in which he appears to have reverted to the tolerant attitude of his father, perhaps even including an attempt to make amends and to restore conditions of a time before the intervening era of destruction and repression.

Yahya preserves the text of three royal decrees issued in July–August, September–October, and November–December respectively of 1020 granting favors to the Melkites and other Christians.[462] The last of these provides security for all Christians in Egypt; it came just two months before al-Hakim disappeared. One of the others, for Nicephorus, the new Patriarch of Jerusalem, assured the safety of churches there and in the surrounding areas. The third was for Anba Salmun, who was the head of the monastery at Mount Sinai. He, according to Yahya, was to gain special influence with the caliph.

But there were other signs of al-Hakim's new attitude. About this time when some Muslims complained that the Christians were holding services in their homes and that various of those who had adopted Islam would attend to take the Eucharist, the caliph refused to object to the practice.[463] Nicephorus, who was the child of Byzantine slaves, had been previously a servant in the palace. He had both a son and a daughter. Al-Hakim accepted his request to be made Patriarch. He went to Jerusalem and was consecrated there on 10 July 1020. Anba Salmun had come to al-Hakim the first time to plead for the restoration of the trusts (*waqfs*) that once supported the monks of Mt. Sinai, who were, without them, in dire straits. In return, he said, the monks would pray for the caliph as long as they lived. Al-Hakim accepted and restored the trusts. On Anba Salmun's second visit, he spoke of the destruction of other churches and monasteries, of the seizing of trusts established to maintain them, and the destitution of the monks who had previously lived in them. He was particularly concerned about the monastery of Qusayr, which was to the south of Cairo, near to Hulwan. At one time it was the residence of the Melkite Patriarchs of Alexandria (including Sitt al-Mulk's maternal uncle), but it had been pillaged and torn down ten years earlier. The caliph again granted this request, issuing for the purpose the first of the decrees mentioned above. The text is quite detailed and specific; the principal copy was given to the person in whose favor it was issued (Anba Salmun). It was also properly registered in the various offices of the government, and, most importantly, al-Hakim affixed his motto 'Thanks be to God, Lord of the universe' to it in his own hand. The decree for Nicephorus was the result of his coming to ask for a document in order to protect the Christian community in Jerusalem from threats against them by the local Muslims.

The success of these two pleadings – by Salman and Nicephorus – prompted others. Anba Salmun along with other prelates began to ask, church by church, for a similar concession: permission to rebuild and the restoration of trust properties. The caliph consented in each case, reports Yahya, who claims that his actions then offered encouragement to a party of those who had converted to Islam. They approached him apprehensively but nevertheless determined to argue that they had not left their old religion willingly, whatever the consequences of saying so might bring. The caliph accepted their plea, ordering them at once to resume wearing the *zunnar*, black clothing, identifying crosses and the *ghiyar*. He further commanded the police to protect them thereafter. That opened a flood of others wishing a similar privilege. But some cautioned that it was a ruse, a trick to find out who had accepted Islam in truth and who had merely feigned conversion. Luckily for all, if it was a test, the caliph did not last to see the result. Yahya himself saw in all this good fortune a miracle, a sign of God's favor to the Christians, confirmed by the caliph's decree, a copy of which he includes in his account. Again it was attested by al-Hakim's personal hand-written motto.[464]

Over the final days of his reign, al-Hakim would, claims Yahya, ride on his excursions in the direction of the monastery of Qusayr on his way into the desert. He often met with Anba Salmun and gave him funds and encouragement, personally urging the workers himself to complete the restoration. The caliph spent so much time with Anba Salmun, always granting his requests, that Muslims began to conclude that there was an affinity between them more like that of master and disciple. Al-Hakim's habit of wearing only black wool, as if he were a monk, was taken as evidence of his attachment. However, Yahya's story has its parallel among the Copts. For them the key figure is a monk named Bimin (Poemen). His story comes from Michael, bishop of Tinnis, who was a child at the time. He also mentions the session in which the first of those who reclaimed their former religion were ordered by al-Hakim to put on the *zunnar*, cross and *ghiyar* before being allowed to leave his presence (it so happened that they had come prepared). He continues:

> There was among the number of those who embraced Islam a monk whose name was Poemen who returned to his religion and he begged al-Hakim to empower him to build a monastery outside Fustat in the name of the martyr of Christ, my lord Mercurius, and it is the monastery of Shahran. So he built it and lived in it with his brother monks. Al-Hakim used to come to them many times, and to stay there and to eat of their humble food. All who wanted anything from al-Hakim used to go to the monk Poemen to have him speak about the matter at the time of the caliph's presence at his monastery.[465]

This same Poemen was able to mend relations between the Coptic patriarch and the caliph, leading, Michael implies, to the broader policy that permitted the restoration of churches and the general decree in favor of the Christians. He thus confirms, though less precisely, what Yahya documents.[466]

Michael's account is, even so, on the whole largely hagiographic. He would blame the persecution of the Christians and the destruction of the churches on dissent within the ranks of his own denomination. A poor monk desired to be made a bishop, but he had no money with which to buy that office. He complained loudly against the selling of bishoprics. At one point to silence him he was promised the next available opening. Passed over twice thereafter, he took his case to the caliph and eventually was heard by him. Alarmed by the corruption in the Coptic church, al-Hakim gave an order for the Patriarch's arrest. He was brought to the capital, and there imprisoned. Next, at the caliph's command, the authorities fed him to the lions, only to find that, miraculously, the animals refused to eat him. Suspecting that their keeper had overfed them, al-Hakim insisted the lions be starved and that on the second try the Patriarch be stripped and covered with the blood of a freshly killed lamb. Even so, miracle of miracles, the lions refused once again. Some months later through a ruse the Patriarch escaped and thereafter hid in the monasteries of the desert for the next ten years. The earlier troubles and the imprisonment of the Patriarch would then date approximately to the year 1010, exactly when the destruction of churches began, and they ended in 1020–21, with the help and intervention of Poemen who fortuitously gained influence with al-Hakim, who now became deeply impressed by the strength of Coptic Christianity.

Hagiography aside, there is a noteworthy correspondence between the reports of Michael and Yahya on matters of Christian-government affairs, especially with respect to al-Hakim's actions during the last years of his reign. Nevertheless, it is also odd that each Christian denomination would attribute the turnaround to a monk of theirs whose relationship with the caliph was remarkably similar. Al-Hakim would, on his many rides, visit and converse with these two monks who each thus take on a special role vis-à-vis him and their own communities. But, strange as it may seem, it fits what we know otherwise about his solitary excursions when he went where he pleased and was often quite accessible, even open, to contact of exactly this type. There are, moreover, additional claims about the caliph's coming to visit, his stopping to chat and converse, all a sure sign of his favor as signified by the intimacy of a one on one meeting. A major example comes from Hamza, the Druze prophet, who cites al-Hakim's visitations of a similar kind as evidence that he (God) approved of his (Hamza's) mission.

Al-Hakim's riding in itself was not new to this period. Reports of his wandering at night through the streets and markets go back by then well over a decade to the years 1001 and 1002 at least. Likewise the stories of how he demanded that commerce cease by day with the shops shuttered, and opened at night, over so long a time in all that the inhabitants of the city become quite used to the inversion.[467] They worked by night and slept during the day. Once it happened that the caliph came upon a carpenter busily plying his trade in broad daylight. 'Weren't you ordered not to do this?' he asks. But the man explains. 'When people lived by day this work was done at night. Now that people are active at night, this is when we do the nighttime stuff.' Thereupon al-Hakim, says Ibn Kathir who tells this story, laughed and departed leaving the carpenter alone.[468]

However, as the number of his excursions increased – al-Maqrizi says that he rode from the palace as many as six times a day – stories of encounters with him, many of which we have already noted, multiplied in part based on real events embellished in the telling but also some of outright fiction. Too many accounts from differing sources – Ismaili, Sunni, Melkite, and Coptic – confirm the essential detail that he wandered nearly alone on these outings. That became a point of honor. He could appear in public with little or no escort and yet, although enemies had sworn to kill him, he was not afraid. No one could touch him. Some noted the sheer awe he inspired; others called it fear. The effect on those who encountered him was the same.

Over the final period of his rule, moreover, his appearance changed. Yahya reports that he began to let his hair grow until it reached his shoulders.[469] He cut neither it nor his fingernails.[470] His garment, previously white, was now black wool, with a blue turban now also black.[471] He wore the same clothes for so long without changing them they became fetid with sweat and dust. His must have been quite an image! Imagine on a dark night suddenly seeing the caliph approach, knowing by sight, sound and smell that it was he. No wonder the populace, both the great and the small, came to dread that happening. With this image in mind, Yahya compared him to Daniel's description of King Nabuchadnezzar: '...his body was wet with the dew of heaven till his hair grew as long as eagles' feathers, and his nails were like bird's talons'.[472] But another saw him as a lion, with mane and claws.[473] Whether eagle or lion, it is an image of royalty, not of a poor dervish.

The tales of an encounter with al-Hakim might be broken into categories: some serve to illustrate his accessibility to the common people, others his cruelty or ability to use the awe and fear he engendered to overcome those who otherwise might have caused him harm, and yet more that end with a clever twist, a word or situation turned on its face, as if a joke. The very purpose behind his constant riding was a topic for speculation. Was he spying on his subjects, as some believed? Was it a symptom of a mental illness, as suggested by others?

Certainly having the ruler ride in the open, where he would be accessible to petitioners seeking redress from grievances or simply a favor, constituted a benefit to the lower classes. Reports claim that they flocked to see him, to hand him letters and requests as he rode by, all with the expectation that he might respond on the spot. Often he would write out himself at the time of the encounter what action should follow. His penchant for extreme generosity encouraged many to approach him. It would seem that most received what they wanted and more. A part of the evidence for how serious this situation had become, how frequently he was interrupted on his journeys, is the command he issued in later years that petitions not be brought to him but to the new heir-apparent Ibn Ilyas or the qadi al-Fariqi. Even so he is reported to have spent a good deal of time laughing and talking to commoners. And surely, despite his order, the petitions never ceased to come.

But the other side, his gratuitous cruelty, is also apparent, at least in the stories that have come down to us. One has him pass a man cutting and roasting meat to sell. Al-Hakim takes his own knife and slaughters on the spot one of his grooms and leaves him dead where he fell, near to the Fustat police station, just opposite the butcher, and moves on. So shocked and fearful are the inhabitants of the area they dare not touch or treat the body. Finally the caliph himself provides a sumptuous linen shroud and proper funeral arrangements, complete with a mausoleum built especially for the man.[474] Another of a slightly different variety has him come upon an old man known for contemptible depravity. Al-Hakim says: 'Show me your moon (here meaning butt end)'. The man then reveals his anus, whereupon the caliph orders one of his Sudanese guardsmen to sodomize the fellow in front of everyone. The man pleads for mercy, to be treated less harshly, but al-Hakim only laughs in mockery. The assault lasts for a while before he stops it.[475]

The exact purpose of either story is unclear but both come from Yahya who is far more reliable than many other medieval historians for whom tales like these seem to serve as the base for worse, a deliberate enhancement with exaggeration for effect, either to discredit the Fatimids or to entertain, or both together.

It is useful to find elements of these accounts that match a report from an unconnected source. One author mentions that on his rides al-Hakim would stop to watch a group of Sufis dancing. That appears to be confirmed elsewhere.[476] Another unconfirmed story claims that in 1017 he went out on his donkey and stopped to speak with a man in the candle maker's lane. The two conversed at length and then the caliph invited the fellow to join him. They set off for the Muqattam hills and are gone for a week and then return.[477] The first of these is likely to be factual; the second fanciful.

Yet another story, or better, set of stories about a strikingly similar event related by no less than three unconnected sources, features al-Hakim as a devilish, possibly evil, tempter. Michael, our Coptic author, describes what took place as follows:

> There was constructed for al-Hakim in his palace a marble basin. Water was brought to it by means of a water-wheel flowing into a canal-like channel. On the outside of the basin there was an enclosure of marble on which all kinds of birds were sculpted. He ordered set up in the wall a thin wooden arrow that jutted out with its further extremity reaching as far as the basin ... It was placed high atop the wall, as reported by one who saw it. Al-Hakim then had the public crier proclaim that he who walked out on this arrow and jumped into the basin, falling thus in the water, would be paid 600 dirhams. He caused a number of persons to be tempted by this offer. The lure of dirhams, however, drew a number to walk out, jump and fall on the marble floor, and thus dying in the attempt.[478]

The other versions point to some sort of well, a pool of water at the bottom of a downward sloping circular embankment. The trick was for those who dared to jump out far enough to fall precisely into the water thus avoiding hitting the sides. A miss was fatal. Both Druze and non-Druze sources confirm that something like this happened, the former deducing a special meaning from the event, a lesson taught to mankind by al-Hakim (God), the author of the plan.[479] If so exactly what the caliph thought he was doing is unclear; now it appears to indicate nothing more than a dangerous game ill conceived by a playful tyrant.

Nonetheless, enough of these stories, whether true in all details or not, have a degree of validity to indicate that his actions caused contemporaries to wonder about them in astonishment, particularly at the inconsistency and contradictory character behind them. Here, at this point, we have the testimony of Yahya[480], who, after he recounted several such events, explains all this as being the result of a morbidity in al-Hakim's brain that had given him a kind of melancholia, a corruption of spirit that afflicted him since his youth. He – Yahya could also claim to be a physician – continues his diagnosis:

> The victim [of this illness] imagines astonishing things, and there is no doubt in his mind that he is right in what he imagines about everything he does. It does not prevent him from doing these things, and nothing turns him back. There may be among them one who thinks of himself as a prophet or who often believes that he is God Almighty. Of these people there is outwardly a confusion of speech, but the disturbance in his condition is not revealed to those who see him and talk with him. The suspicion about him disappears at first sight. Sometimes a man's insanity is not apparent in his speech, and these hallucinations and destructive thoughts occur in him about matters that are hidden from the common people. His demeanor among them is that of a wise man; they have a good opinion of him, and their view of him is that he is one of the best people. If they prolonged their examination, they would discover what was concealed from them about their destruction.
>
> This is a picture of the condition of al-Hakim. His deterioration would be clear to whoever had a long association with him. To whomever was distant from him, his actions would be obvious [signs]. One may conclude the truth about this over-powering illness from the convulsions, which happened to him in his youth, from a dry intemperament in his brain. It is the kind of diseased temperament that occurs in melancholics. He needed to be treated with such things as sitting in oil of violets and his body moistened with it. Also, there was the frequency of his insomnia, his passion for pursuing his excursions and his persistent love-madness, which this intemperament causes. Abu Yaʿqub Ishaq ibn Ibrahim ibn Anastas, when he served him, inclined him towards indulgence in drinking liquor (*nabidh*) and listening to songs after he had renounced them and prohibited them to the people. His character was improved, the temperament of his brain was moistened, and his body grew sound. When Abu Yaʿqub died, he reverted to his prohibition against drinking liquor and listening to music; his body returned to its former state, and the damage increased. His state then led to what we have recounted here.[481]

While it is well to remember here that Ibn Anastas, who appears to be behind Yahya's assertion, was himself an unusual character and to recall his death by drowning, that others near to the time adduced a verdict of mental illness, specifically of melancholia – presumably a form of depression – is relatively easy to establish.[482] Evidence of this type does not make this judgment true only that it goes back to observers of that era. It is not an invention of modern historians, although many of them share it. Over time the stories of al-Hakim's actions proliferated in number and variety and equally the explanation of his behavior increasingly settled for the view of it offered here by Yahya.

Note that, as described by this one witness, the disease grew in intensity, seemingly therefore affecting the final period of al-Hakim's rule more than before. Again the judgment of those who lived through it, and were directly touched by what happened, remembered, after he disappeared, the caliph's last days more than the years before.

It would be wrong, however, to accept Yahya's testimony uncritically. He was a contemporary observer but he was also deeply influenced by what had happened to himself and to the Christians. He harbored no love for al-Hakim; it was in his interest to accentuate a negative picture of the caliph by tagging him with madness and mental illness. Yahya likely wished for Muslim rulers more in the mode of al-ʿAziz, tolerant and benign. For the son to have been an obvious exception, incompetent by virtue of an insanity not typical or shared by the other caliphs, suited his view of the matter. In truth, moreover, what he suggests about al-Hakim's condition does not fit nor does it explain more than a tiny portion of his constant activity. He did not cease to run his government nor to monitor the affairs of state, as far as we can tell. If anything he increased his supervision of them, appointing new, and in some ways, more capable men to office.

His announcement that Ibn Ilyas[483] would be his heir appears to us now and to contemporaries then as odd, out of keeping with tradition. Although this man was the great grandson of al-Mahdi, the founding caliph of the Fatimid dynasty, his elevation excluded al-Hakim's own natural son. Nonetheless, Ibn Ilyas, once proclaimed heir apparent assumed a full range of duties as if he were to succeed. Al-Hakim himself mounted the *minbar* and delivered the sermon in which he asked God to bless Ibn Ilyas. Treat him as if he were to me as Aaron was to Moses, he said. Over the years after 1013, the cousin often filled the role of the caliph in public rituals and ceremonies, delivering the sermon, performing the sacrifice, riding in processions wearing the regalia of a caliph. On one occasion he is described as sumptuously adorned astride his horse, whereas, in the same procession, al-Hakim appeared in plain dress riding a donkey. An order at one point decreed that petitions should be handed to him in place of the caliph. Although we lack sufficient information an interpretation of this situation makes of Ibn Ilyas merely a stand-in for the over-burdened caliph, not in reality the person intended for succession. The appointment thus becomes a ruse, a device to relieve al-Hakim of his formal public duties so that he could see to others less obvious to his people.

In 1018, however, he added to the confusion by naming another cousin, al-ʿAbbas b. Shuʿayb, the son of his uncle Abu Hashim, 'Heir designate of the Believers' (*wali ʿahd al-muʾminin*).[484] Ibn Ilyas was merely the 'Heir designate of the Muslims' (*wali ʿahd al-muslimin*). In Ismaili doctrine, and indeed that of many Muslims, the 'believers' (*mu'minun*) form a more exclusive and more important segment of Islamic society than Muslims at large. For Ismailis the 'believers' are themselves – that is, the Ismailis – as opposed to the majority who are mere 'muslims.' Thus, in this sense, Ibn Shuʿayb's title is better than the one of ʿAbd al-Rahim, if in fact a judgment of this kind is relevant. The Druze recognized this distinction and saw, nevertheless, that the facts were the opposite of outward reality.[485] ʿAbd al-Rahim remained, apparently, the favorite of al-Hakim. He had not lost his position. However, in that same year he was sent off to Damascus as its governor.[486] Was he removed from the scene to make way for Ibn Shuʿayb? That appears unlikely. Though seemingly in conflict, both appointments remained in effect and it is hard, if not impossible, to understand what the caliph had in mind. There is no record of Ibn Shuʿayb performing any duties of his office, whatever they might have been.

The ultimate fate of these two men may help explain more about their respective roles. Ibn Ilyas was still in Damascus when al-Hakim went missing. As Sitt al-Mulk began to assert her control over the state, she had him recalled and murdered in Tinnis ostensibly en route to Cairo.[487] Apparently she understood his case as so serious as to require action to end any claim he might have made to the succession. By contrast, she allowed Ibn Shuʿayb simply to renounce his own claim and then permitted him to live out his natural life, even though, when he eventually died a few years later, the historians freely recorded that he had once been heir to the throne. They had not forgotten.[488]

Of all matters that arose during the final years of al-Hakim, none produced effects as long lasting as the advent of the Druze. Since they retain a vital role in the modern Middle East to this day, what occurred in that period, although it happened a thousand years ago, still has meaning and direct relevance in contemporary society. Medieval historians also took note. In their view the Druze, in so far as they worshiped al-Hakim, represent the culmination of his strangeness. It is a heresy gone wild, but one aided and abetted by the caliph himself. Their delusion was his delusion.

As so often the facts surrounding the beginnings of the Druze movement, leaving charges of false belief aside, are difficult to pin down precisely. Although authorities such as al-Maqrizi wanted to describe what happened, the information he and the others could find remained confused and contradictory.[489] Two additional sources therefore become extraordinarily important. They are, first, a treatise by al-Kirmani that he wrote specifically to refute the doctrine of al-Akhram, one of the three principals behind the Druze.[490] A copy made in Fustat at the direct request of the author was dated November 1017, which is likely when it was composed, and, second, the various dated epistles issued by Hamza, the Druze prophet, one each in July 1017 and January 1018, and a series of 11 from May 1019 to September 1020.[491] They are now a part of the *Rasa'il al-hikma*, and are revered by followers of this movement. For the historian they contain the testimony of a witness who not only commented on things he saw but was, as well, a leading participant in the formation of the sect itself.

For most writers the problem was to distinguish among three men who they otherwise knew to have been involved. They were the al-Hasan b. Haydara al-Farghani al-Akhram just mentioned, Abu ʿAbdallah al-Bukhari al-Darazi, who at some point acquired or gave himself the titles *Sayyid al-hadiyin wa hayat al-mustajibin*, and Hamza b. ʿAli b. Ahmad al-Labbad al-Zuzani, also known by the titles *Qa'im al-zaman* and *Hadi al-mustajibin*, the prophet previously cited. Note how easily the latter two might be confused when referred to solely by their titles; each has the term *hadi*, 'guide', and mention of the *mustajibs*, i.e. 'novices'. An even more serious mix-up has the name of the sect derive from al-Darazi, from which comes the word Druze. The common appellation applied to the movement in Arabic was and is al-Daraziyya or al-Duruz. Yet the writings of Hamza are full of contempt for this man, who he says had once joined but later reneged and formed his own group. Al-Darazi is, in these Druze texts, an outcast, the epitome of evil. The true name for the movement itself is al-Muwahhidun, that is, those who uphold strict monotheism.

In the material available from either al-Kirmani or Hamza, who were both present in Egypt at the time, the former is noteworthy for not mentioning either al-Darazi or Hamza, only al-Akhram to whom he addresses his pamphlet, and the latter for including the charges against al-Darazi but making no reference to al-Akhram. In any case but two of Hamza's epistles date to 1017–18, the bulk (11 in all) to 1019–20. It is thus reasonable to assume that al-Akhram was the first to promote those doctrines that subsequently developed in the writings of Hamza into the Druze movement. That means only that he was, in 1017, the most prominent advocate for them, Hamza and al-Darazi having then a minor role.

Unfortunately we possess no statements by either al-Akhram or al-Darazi. However, al-Kirmani offers a review of the teachings of al-Akhram, and, in at least one instance, speaks of this man's associates who support him. The heretical tendencies of al-Akhram, according to this information, range through a catalog of Shiite extremism: the living imam is superior to all prophets and imams of the past; once the true spiritual meanings behind an outward expression is known the literal form can be ignored; the significance of a ritual act is more important than the performance of it and therefore deeds are distinctly inferior to knowledge; knowledge of the inner truth cancels the requirement of works. Al-Kirmani says that the doctrine of al-Akhram and that of his associates makes of al-Hakim the object of worship and that Islamic law, its revelation and the interpretation of it, are silly fables, fluff and stuffing on the basis of which there is no salvation. The ire of al-Kirmani at what he finds grossly unacceptable in all this is obvious but, although he then worked for the head of the Ismaili *daʿwa*, his hands were tied. He comments:

> Were it not that the Commander of the Believers has lowered a curtain of protection over both believer and hypocrite, Muslim and heretic, so that all are equally under it, the response to [your doctrines] would comprise a severe punishment for you, the severing of your aorta and the application of the sword against you. But that is up to God and His guardian [among us, i.e. the imam].[492]

Since January 1007, al-Hakim had insisted that religious doctrine not be subject to dispute and contention, at least not in an open forum. What al-Kirmani indicates does not establish that the caliph supported al-Akhram, merely that the *daʿwa* was forbidden from applying measures against what it saw as heresy that would otherwise require corporal punishment. However, it would have been easy to see it in another way, that al-Hakim deliberately held in check his own *daʿwa* because he was flattered by such extreme devotion. Being the object of worship had its appeal.

If al-Akhram's preaching commenced in 1017, with him as the leading spokesman among those who, in some form or another, advocated the divinity of al-Hakim, al-Darazi and Hamza may have been less prominent associates of his. The two epistles by Hamza that date to 408 suggest as much. Some writers, such as Yahya, claim that al-Darazi arrived in Egypt that year and began to teach similar doctrines. According to the Druze reckoning the Islamic year 408 (1017) is when the mission began. But they insist it ceased entirely during 409 (May 1018-May 1919), which is a year they do not count at all. The chronology of events, however, is not clear, especially as it applies to the relationships among these three. Some authorities put Hamza first, others al-Darazi.

The fate of each is likewise difficult to determine precisely. Al-Maqrizi in his *al-Muqaffa* reports that al-Akhram was honored by the caliph in January 1019 but, while riding with a group to al-Maqs eight days later, a man jumped him, knocking him from his horse and striking him until he died. The crowd then promptly killed that man. Others, however, plundered the home of al-Akhram in Cairo. Meanwhile his body was taken to al-Hakim in a coffin, where it was shrouded and buried. The common people collected the killer's corpse, which they provided with funeral rites, even building a dome over it; and visitors seeking blessings came to it by night and by day. Fourteen days after that, however, they came to find the grave had been opened, the body gone.[493]

The end of al-Darazi may have been connected to a provocation staged by Hamza. That at least is the way the story unfolds in the account of al-Maqrizi and others. The evidence of Hamza's own words, which are quite specific and full of detail in regard to al-Darazi and his followers, suggests a slightly different sequence of events. In June 1019, in the standard version, Hamza dispatched a number of his adherents with a letter to the chief judge at his court in the mosque of Fustat. These men rode their mounts into the mosque while proclaiming the doctrine of their movement, presumably the divinity of al-Hakim. Three confronted the judge handing him a letter that began 'In the name of al-Hakim the Most Merciful', a blasphemy unlikely to be missed by anyone. The people in the mosque and nearby irrupted in loud protest. A riot ensues and three of Hamza's men are killed, the rest flee, pursued by the mob. Those suspected of supporting his doctrine are cut down when and wherever found. Quite upset al-Hakim replaces his police commander in Fustat and has 40 of the locals arrested and executed. Turkish troops and others proceed to al-Darazi's house to seize him. Those in the house resist but the house is destroyed, plundered and 40 of his followers killed. However, he manages to flee. The Turks in full armor march on the palace where they demand that al-Darazi be turned over to them, claiming that this man is one of them and they have the right to deal with him. Word comes out that if they leave and return the next day al-Darazi will be theirs. When they return, instead they are informed that al-Darazi has been killed. And that would be the end of him.

Without confirmation, unfortunately, it is hard to accept this result. Several later writers report that al-Hakim had not executed him but rather sent him to Syria where he continued his mission in the Wadi Taym region. It is there exactly that the Druze were to survive and flourish.

Hamza's testimony corroborates parts of this version. He mentions in an epistle dated two months after the event that he had sent a letter to the judge with 20 of his men, three of whom were killed.[494] In fact he boasts that in spite of 200 armed opponents, the remaining 17 had returned safely and that to avenge the dead al-Hakim executed 100. In another epistle dated four months after the first he writes to the followers of al-Darazi who are in jail. His purpose is to admonish them for having fomented strife.

> I explained to you [previously] that you would destroy yourselves and burn in the fire and that your smoke would reach the good adherents [of our movement]. The morning after we spoke the incident occurred. On that day you were some 500 heavily armed men. You were in the sanctuary. Forty of you were killed. Those fled who fled. Were it not for the mercy of our Lord [al-Hakim] none of you would have escaped. Even so you killed none of the enemy... but your smoke reached us. On the second day, a Thursday, the whole of the army – Easterners, Westerners, Persians and Arabs, mounted and on foot – came after our blood with naphtha, fire, ladders, and wall-piercing battering rams. We had with us only 12, five of whom were unfit for fighting. We killed of them three and wounded many and we defeated them, not, however, with our own power but with that of al-Hakim.[495]

It is not always easy to interpret what Hamza says but he had a much more immediate view of the situation than anyone else who left a record of it and was, moreover, vitally involved. He insists that he had recruited al-Darazi, who should thereafter have been loyal to him. But he is obviously at pains to castigate al-Darazi for not having recognized his exclusive right to lead the movement. Hamza is by his own claim the Imam of the Time (*Imam al-Zaman*) and there can be only one. The similarity in the titles used by the two appears to indicate that al-Darazi, as *Sayyid al-Hadin wa Hayat al-Mustajibin*, promoted himself as the imam, much to the annoyance of Hamza, who insisted that he alone had the right to speak for God (al-Hakim). All others had no knowledge about or understanding of the true reality of the divine presence. Evidently, after breaking with Hamza, al-Darazi went out on his own, quite successfully it appears. Hamza admits, in the passage quoted above, that his followers are vastly outnumbered by those supporting al-Darazi. The ratio is 25 to 1. However high his spiritual status – and his pretensions to the imamate-prophecy – may have been, Hamza was a Persian feltmaker (*labbad*), a tradesman. By contrast al-Darazi was a Turk and that normally at the time meant a soldier, a paid member of an elite corps. Thus it seems likely that, in social standing and wealth, he outranked Hamza, perhaps considerably. Evidently he could attract to his version of the common cause many more than the feltmaker. One key to the viability of the name Druze against the condemnation of the man himself may have depended on the numbers attached to al-Darazi in this early period. A decade later when various parts of the movement came together under the direction of Baha' al-Din al-Muqtana, during a later phase – an era of revival and renewal – the doctrinal foundation was that of Hamza, but sizable numbers of those who joined had once been members of al-Darazi's party, the Daraziyya or Duruz.

By itself Hamza's formulation of the doctrine he advocated is extremely interesting from several points of view, not the least of which is how he turned the teachings of the Ismaili *daʿwa* around, quite consciously altering and, according to him, correcting it. One example may suffice. Hamza conceived of a hierarchy of five spiritual offices to each of which he assigned names, titles and ranks. The five are himself as the Messiah of the Time (*Qa'im al-Zaman*) and the Universal Intellect (*al-ʿAql al-Kulli*), his brother-in-law Isma'il b. Muhammad al-Tamimi, who was the Universal Soul (*al-Nafs al-Kulliyya*), Muhammad b. Wahb al-Qurashi, who was the Logos (*al-Kalima*), Salama b. ʿAbd al-Wahhab al-Samiri, who was the Right Wing, and ʿAli b. Ahmad al-Sammuqi, the Left Wing, who was also known as Shaykh al-Muqtana Baha' al-Din. Hamza has freely adapted for his own purposes names for the elements of the cosmic hierarchy in earlier Ismaili thought, here derived from Neoplatonism. But as Hamza himself confesses, in older doctrine the Logos is always identical with the Universal Intellect. But that is not correct according to him. The truth is as he now explains it: the Logos ranks third, not first.[496]

Obviously many if not most of the adherents of the Druze movement had a background within the Ismaili *daʿwa* and knew its teachings. Some may have studied a broader range of Shiite doctrine as well including those of the radical fringe. Hamza himself reveals a thorough knowledge of earlier phases of al-Hakim's reign[497] and later Druze epistles contain numerous direct references and quotations from the Sessions of Wisdom (*majlis al-hikma*) taught by the heads of the *daʿwa* in his time.

Curiously Hamza not only laid out the hierarchy of his ministers but set over against them another consisting of five evil opponents, the *Didd* (plural *Addad*). They were ʿAbd al-Rahim ibn Ilyas, the Heir Apparent of the Muslims, ʿAbbas ibn Shuʿayb, the Heir Apparent of the Believers, Ibn Abi'l-ʿAwwam, the chief judge, Khatkin al-Dayf, the head of the *daʿwa*, and Abul-Fadl Jaʿfar, the Scholar of the Scholars (*ʿAlim al-ʿulama'*). These men apparently constituted, in his eyes, the establishment responsible for trying to suppress Hamza's revelation. The two sides, one formed by the highest officials of the state, all appointed by al-Hakim, and the other companions and supporters of the man who claimed to speak for al-Hakim and to be his prophet-imam, were engaged in some sort of mutual cursing.

But if the caliph's own government was against Hamza, what evidence is there that al-Hakim approved of him, aided him or otherwise favored what he taught, either secretly or openly? About that Hamza indicates only that a copy of the epistles he issued had been forwarded to the caliph. There is no hint that he had a verbal response, written or oral. A major sign of al-Hakim's acceptance, in his mind – one he notes with special pride – is that during his excursions the caliph would ride by the Mosque of Tibr, just north of Cairo, where Hamza maintained himself and his following, and that he would pause to chat. Hamza would come out of the Mosque and the two would converse alone, one on one. The similarity of Hamza's claim to that of the Melkites and their man Salmun, and to the Copts and the monk Poemen, is striking. One report mentions the same happening with al-Darazi. We can see how Hamza understood his intimate meetings with al-Hakim; what they meant to the caliph is unclear.

Druze epistles by Hamza continue in 1019 and the first nine months of 1020. A report that seems reliable, however, indicates that Hamza left Egypt in the early part of 1020, that he went to Mecca where for a short while he enjoyed the protection of the amir, but that finally he was denounced by pious *mujawirs* for his heresies and soon thereafter killed that same year.[498] A close reading of the epistle from January 1020 appears to suggest that Hamza is communicating with his followers via his sons; he is not present among them. But, if it is true that he died before the end of that year, epistles after that are either not his or are not what they purport to be.

The disturbances associated with the incident involving al-Darazi and Hamza led either directly or indirectly early in 1020 to a greater catastrophe in the looting, rape and burning of Fustat. An accurate account of what happened and in what order may be unattainable; those we have all seem to have been designed to fault al-Hakim as dramatically as possible.[499] The connection with the Druze begins with the caliph's anger at the inhabitants of Fustat, either for not having accepted the doctrine announced to them by Hamza or, more likely, for the actions of the mob in the violence against his followers. Neither appears totally plausible. Supposedly, however, once al-Hakim had suppressed his ire against his Turkish troops, he commenced to issue threats of vengeance aimed at the people of Fustat. According to Yahya, poems and letters attributed to the caliph began to circulate in Fustat. In them he promised that a severe punishment would be visited on the city if its people continued to uphold unacceptable doctrines, to indulge in vices and to oppose him and his policies. So unsettling were the rumors that floated as a result, the government had to issue a special proclamation to calm the situation. Even so another letter, supposedly also by al-Hakim appeared, more disturbing than those earlier.

Finally in March 1020, the caliph armed his Sudanese guards and ordered them with others to Fustat to burn it, seize the women and children and loot the shops and homes of the inhabitants. We have several detailed descriptions of the burning, pillaging, and rape that followed, accounts that stress the atrocity and horror of it, the pain and anguish of the citizens, how they pleaded to be forgiven and for the police to intervene and stop it. In these reports the caliph is depicted as complicit, either directly or by deliberately refusing to take notice.

Other versions claim that al-Hakim was provoked initially by finding near to Fustat on one of his excursions a paper figure of a woman in whose hand was a note that contained a bitter denunciation of him and his forefathers. He retaliated by unleashing a flood of thieves and looters.[500] The people of Fustat, though afraid of who they suspected was behind it, tried to fight back. The conflict intensified, eventually culminating in the destruction of the greater part of the city.

Whatever the actual sequence of events and the culpability of al-Hakim for the disaster, Fustat suffered severely. Eventually, as the strife began to abate, he issued a decree in which he commiserated with the inhabitants for their anguish and loss and said that it had not been done by his order nor had he wished it to happen.

Conspiracy theory is an old preoccupation. It serves to explain what is otherwise obscure or unknown; it is also a tool of polemic, a means to denigrate a political or religious opponent. The last days of al-Hakim were no exception. The lack of solid information about what actually happened provided an opportunity for the invention of several stories that purported to fill the gap. One among them features Sitt al-Mulk as both the capable administrator who stepped in to preserve the dynasty at a moment of weakness and as the person responsible for the death of her brother. Ibn Zafir reports that near the end, as a symptom of his pernicious misrule, al-Hakim began to threaten his highly competent and intelligent sister and to accuse her of having done such vile things nothing like them had occurred before. Although at the start of his reign she had offered him the best advice and he had followed her opinion, at the end he changed, becoming more hostile leading in part to the burning and looting of Fustat. She, according to this account, was one of those who went to him to complain and to try to stop the atrocities. Thereupon his attitude toward her soured, his deference for her seniority disappeared. Instead he castigated her for rumors he had heard about her behavior, things she should not have done. Lately, he said, I have heard reported that men have improperly come to see you in private, that your virginity is now lost. 'I have decided to bring a midwife to examine you. If the matter is as I have heard, I will kill you; if it is not so, I will put you in confinement in prison.' For her part, the account continues, fearing that the dynasty – the dynasty of her own father – was in dire peril and that, if the army should rise up and kill her brother, there would be no possibility of succession by a Fatimid, she resolved to seize the initiative. The caliph's son was already living with her. In extreme secrecy she formed a plan to have al-Hakim assassinated and then to kill those who conspired with her to do it. His elevation of Ibn Ilyas added to her sense of urgency, as did his execution of so many of the elite.

Whether it is true or not that she participated in any such plot, eventually it was she who took control of the government as the disappearance of al-Hakim changed from a brief period of anticipating his possibly imminent return to dawning certainty that he was gone for good. She made sure her nephew received the oath of allegiance from the army and bureaucracy, rank upon rank, until all agreed. The slight few who demurred were done away with; any who remained in doubt came around out of fear of her. But her success also fueled further elaboration of the conspiracy that she actually planned and carried out the murder and concealed his body, although at the same time making sure that some evidence of his death surfaced. Several later medieval historians refused to believe anything of the kind, but strongly anti-Fatimid, eastern (i.e. Abbasid) writers had no reluctance to repeat and embellish such accounts.[501]

Even so, in the record, there are other, simpler accounts of the last time anyone saw al-Hakim. That of Yahya has the ring of truth rather than fiction – a record of what was actually known at the time – in part because it never drifts off in the direction of blame and conspiracy. 'One day,' he says,[502]

> he went out as was his previous habit followed by a young groom in his service known as al-Qarafi. The two made their way far up into the hills where seven Bedouin confronted him and rudely demanded money with rough language, insults and curses. He replied, 'In a place like this I have nothing with me to give you, but I can send you to the head of the treasury al-ʿAmid al-Muhsin Ibn Badis and he will pay you five thousand dirhams.' But they answered, 'It is out of the question that we go to him; he will pay us nothing.' The conversation between them continued until they demanded that he send with them al-Qarafi, the groom, to assure that the payment would be made. Four of the men then went off with al-Qarafi and the three others stayed behind on the path. Those four got the whole sum ordered paid and al-Qarafi went back to look for al-Hakim, but he was slow to return. When he had waited for him in the place where he usually was, he began to be suspicious and he went around the hills seeking him. He bumped into a hermit and inquired of him about al-Hakim, describing what he looked like and also the donkey he had been riding. The man said that he had seen on the path a donkey whose hocks had been slashed. The groom went on to that place where he came upon the hamstrung donkey as had been described and saw it for himself. The Lady, sister of al-Hakim, ordered all the commanders, military officers and other people to ride into the desert to find out what had become of the caliph. They went to the monastery of Qusayr and searched it lest he was hiding there. They searched also all the places at which he was likely to have stopped, but found no trace of him. Later they came upon the woolen cloak that he had been wearing on the side of the mountain. It had been lacerated with the thrust of a knife and showed evidence of bloody wounds. Still his body was not found. Most people then concluded that the three Bedouin who had not

> gone with their companions who went with the groom al-Qarafi to get the money for them, had gone back to al-Hakim, had killed him. They had buried him, and then removed all evidence of the grave.

As Yahya indicates, the majority of observers decided that al-Hakim had been murdered and that, therefore, the succession could proceed validly. With Sitt al-Mulk acting as regent for her nephew al-Zahir and soon firmly in control, she immediately commenced to re-establish a sense of stability and continuity. The eccentricities of the former reign began to fade, to be replaced by the earlier traditions of the dynasty characterized by a carefully balanced policy of accommodation. Gradually, Sunnis and non-Ismaili Muslims, Christians and Jews regained the status and protections accorded them in the tolerant days of al-ʿAziz. Women re-entered the marketplace. Ismailis breathed easier once the transition to a new imam took hold and appeared to offer no break with the past. Any challenge to the elevation of al-Zahir was swept away smoothly and cleanly and all traces of an alternate succession were soon forgotten by them.

Nonetheless, the end of al-Hakim remained in part an unresolved mystery. Had he really died? Absent his body some doubt inevitably persisted. Evidence of how perplexed the authorities were suggests that even they harbored reservations on that score. Could, for example, it be that he simply grew tired of being the caliph, an office that demanded his attention at all times, even, it seems, on his solitary outings into the desert. Perhaps he decided to ride off and not return, leaving behind his former public life to become a wandering mendicant. His tendency toward an increasingly ascetic habit might have led him in that direction naturally. In 1021 he merely took the final step. Was he then still alive and might he even yet return? The Druze add to these speculations by noting that, as God, what had been al-Hakim simply reverted to His true uniquely divine form, the one transcendent unreachable almighty being. That the caliph's death could not be proven was definitive evidence, in their view, that he was not, and had not been, human. By the end others might have begun to wonder about that as well.

9

Afterlife and Epilogue

Al-Hakim rode off on his last known excursion barely months beyond the 400th anniversary of the Prophet's death. Muhammad departed this earthly realm in the 11th year of the Islamic calendar. This caliph, his successor, disappeared exactly four centuries later in the year 411. Was that merely a coincidence?

In the period leading up to that very year, there were many who anticipated the possibility of such a correspondence. One among them, most significantly, was the Ismaili *daʿi* al-Kirmani whose expectations for that precise moment anticipated great events, a messianic triumph in which all the enemies of the Fatimid line would fall, leaving al-Hakim alone at the summit of a universal Islamic empire, governed once again by pure righteousness and divine authority. Surely the caliph himself was likewise aware of the importance of the year 411. But did he purposely act on it? Could he have deliberately chosen the timing of his disappearance to coincide somehow? Or, failing the expected triumph, did he select instead an absence, as a kind of punishment for his wayward subjects who had fallen short in their zeal for him, who had not brought about this ultimate victory, preventing thus his and their reward in the here and now? He might also have simply wanted to leave behind the crushing responsibilities of his high office. The trajectory of his increasingly ascetic behavior suggests this latter possibility. Clearly, barring firm evidence of his death, such as the discovery of his body, alternate scenarios remained in play. Even though the Fatimid dynastic establishment, led by Sitt al-Mulk, had determined to carry on by elevating al-Zahir to the caliphate and vigorously suppressing all sentiment to the contrary, there are in the record too many reports, first of individuals who refused to acknowledge the succession pending final news of al-Hakim, and then later of claims of his actually having reappeared. The situation was, and would remain for years to come, anything but settled despite the wishes of Sitt al-Mulk and her party. Her people had time and force on their side, and yet even so, as belief in al-Hakim's expected return eventually subsided, the myth and legend surrounding what he had been about and what it had meant persisted and grew. The extraordinary world he had created around himself lived on, though less and less in fact but more and more in fiction. Ismailis normally remember their imams, recite each of their names and rehearse their accomplishments with fervent devotion; that should not be surprising. However, the fate of al-Hakim was unlike any of the others, both in the immediate aftermath of his reign and in the memories it engendered in the population at large.

By the end in 411/1021, al-Hakim had already lived through several key messianic moments.[503] He was caliph for the crucial era of chiliastic expectation connected to the close of the first Christian millennium. However, whatever the year 1000 might have meant to those Christians who observed it, it meant little to the Muslims, Jews and even many Christians who followed a different calendar. Moreover, al-Hakim was at the time only 15 and still under the careful control of Barjawan. More significant was the year 400 of the Islamic era, which came ten lunar years later. The turn of a century raised hopes among the Muslims of the coming of a renewer, a person who could and would reform religious doctrine and observance, bringing it back once again to what it had been in the days of the Prophet. A belief of this type occurred widely. The Fatimid caliphate was, in the year 400/1009, at the height of its power and success; its adherents and supporters might well have anticipated even better, a total victory and triumph. Al-Hakim, the reigning imam, was surely, accordingly, the person chosen to do it. Perhaps he believed as much himself, that he was the culmination of his line, the one among them destined for the final restoration of prophetic rule over all the lands of Islam.

Can his tendency toward asceticism, for example, be traced back to this year 1009? Note that his order for the destruction of the Church of the Holy Sepulcre caused it to fall that year. Did he choose the timing to coincide? Could the changes in his demeanor, his abandoning of royal pomp with its elaborate costumes and finery, his insistence on riding a donkey – itself a sign of messianism – his infliction of hardship on the Christians and Jews possibly to encourage their conversion, have been deliberate and in accord with a plan conceived to implement reforms associated with the turn of the Islamic century?

In truth, although expectations surrounding each possibility added to the aura of al-Hakim and his reign, they proved of slight consequence. As the years 390/1000 and 400/1009 came and went, whatever meaning they once possessed faded, to be turned over in anticipation of the next and future date. Al-Kirmani wrote about the great triumph of 411 well before it was to happen. When the time arrived, he was no longer in Egypt. Yet, if the news of the caliph's disappearance reached him, he must have surely realized that his prediction – as would have been true of the many others who shared with him in it – was not to happen. Previous hopes that had been bound up with al-Hakim were to result, it seems, in disappointment.

Nonetheless, for al-Kirmani, the imamate as he had described it continued. What one imam fails to accomplish, the next one may achieve; the line moves forward. Al-Kirmani himself foresaw many, many imams to come, each bringing the same possibility of the ultimate triumph that eluded al-Hakim. He thus upheld an old Shiite doctrine about the end of one person's imamate and its replacement by another. The death of the caliph is final: the king is dead, long live the king. The appeal, the *daʿwa*, in the name of one ends and that of his successor begins. There was even a technical Arabic term for such a doctrine: *qatʿiyya*, meaning the 'cutting off', 'ending', or 'cessation', here in reference to the reign of an imam-caliph.

Such a term served primarily to counter its opposite, the Arabic *waqfiyya*, which means in this instance 'suspension in place'. It is a doctrine upholding the persistence of a given imamate as not having ended, typically by the claim that such and such an imam has not really died but has instead gone into hiding or some form of occultation. Therefore his authority continues. As long as he lives, no other imam can replace him. In effect the line of succession has been suspended. The best known of several examples like this is that maintained by the Twelver Shiites both now and then. For them the imam of the present, even after the passage of a millennium, is the same person who went into occultation in the ninth century. The line of imams thus 'stopped' with him and he therefore remains today, as he was then, the supreme religious leader. No one can or will succeed him.

Claims of this latter type arose frequently enough in the early history of the Shiites that each and every succession had to take the possibility into account, not normally out of fear of serious dissent, but to preclude any tendency in that direction and to establish quickly and efficiently the full authority of the new ruler. A few adherents of the eighth-century imam Jaʿfar al-Sadiq insisted, for example, that he had not died but was alive and living on an island in an ocean far to the west. Allowing claimants to argue that the previous imam was not dead, but rather in occultation, either temporarily or permanently, created a challenge to the ongoing rule of the dynasty. Imagine then what could arise in a situation where the imam had, in fact, disappeared, where even the government, much as it might want to, could not prove conclusively that he had died.

There were therefore two possibilities the new caliph and his aunt could not easily control. One was the belief that al-Hakim has simply taken a long vacation, that he had found a situation in which he could isolate himself and relax anonymously for a time, and that eventually he would reappear to reclaim the caliphate. In Ismaili theory, as indeed in most Shiite doctrine, an imam cannot be deposed by humans. His office is beholden only to God, who thus is the sole determiner of the imam's fate. If al-Hakim were still alive, no matter his state and condition, he remained caliph even in seclusion. Evidence – incontrovertible evidence – that he was not dead would automatically invalidate the elevation of his son. At any moment he could reveal himself and justly resume his former role.

Curiously the old Shiite notion of a prolonged occultation, the Arabic term for it is *ghayba*, does not seem to have entered the discussion in the case of al-Hakim though surely his disappearance fit and a doctrine of this type would have been most appropriate. Instead those who refused to consider him dead actually hoped he would walk back in from his desert wanderings and announce himself. The mystery of his whereabouts was more mundane than theological.

For the Druze, however, the matter involved theology pure and simple. Therefore the second tendency, one also beyond the control of Sitt al-Mulk, was the doctrine that al-Hakim had not been human but rather God and that his disappearance indicated God's resumption of His transcendent, ineffable form. The caliph had not died; he had merely ceased to reveal himself to humans.

Druze theology, as expressed in the earliest writings of its masters, particularly Hamza, its prophet, suggests both a profound degree of intellectual sophistication and yet also an earthly simplicity that often seems radically at odds with its basic inspiration. The authors of the Druze *Epistles of Wisdom*, which is our primary source – most often our only source – for Druze thinking, knew quite well the teachings of al-Hakim's *daʿis*, paramount among whom was al-Kirmani. This *daʿi* in turn drew on his predecessors in the mission of the *daʿwa*. The Ismailis advocated a theology that considers God as so beyond the grasp of either the senses or of the intellect, He cannot be known by methods available to humans, with the exception of the prophets and others blessed with divine inspiration. To insure against contaminating the notion of God, one prominent writer before al-Kirmani advocated use of negations. In speaking of God, he said, we are to deny that He is any of the things humans are. God is not in a place, not in a time, not describable, not in a relation to other things. But, although an essential first step, such a process of negation is not enough. We must follow the first set of denials with a second: God is *not* not in a place, *not* not in a time, *not* not describable, *not* not in a relationship to other things. Al-Kirmani accepted this principle and added to it the logical conclusion that such a method would have removed God totally from human consciousness. Reasoning cannot apprehend God as He really is; He is not subject to intellectual inquiry or its processes. Al-Kirmani realized that the God humans worship and speak about is merely an intellectual figure, an image in our minds, but that is not God as He truly is at all. God is so utterly dissimilar to us, so completely unique in His being, we have no way to fathom what He is. Nor, of course, a means of communicating with Him. We worship something we believe is God, but that is not actually Him.

Hamza, and his colleagues al-Tamimi and al-Muqtana, who are the only representatives of the Druze position whose writings survive – it is their theology we can study – saw the dark side of al-Kirmani's position, with its stark divorcing of God from human society, leaving a gap of utter and total separation. How then would humans know anything of how they had been made, who created them, and in what way they are obligated to Him? God on His part might want to instruct His creatures and teach them the duty they owed to Him. However, the way from Him to them or them to Him was insurmountably blocked. In order to bridge the vast gulf between Him and His subjects, as a mercy from Him, He has chosen to assume, on occasion, the physical form of a human in which and through which to provide the required guidance. As these Druze writers explain, it makes good sense, moreover, that God would select for such a purpose, not a humble nobody, but a royal, a king or caliph. As He has done before in previous situations in earlier times, He now takes up the personage of al-Hakim, becoming human by using this caliph's form. Al-Hakim henceforth is not a human being; he has no father or mother, no son or daughter. According to one reading of the Druze texts that condition may have begun, by their reckoning, in the year 1009.

In general outline Druze theology bears a striking resemblance to some forms of Christianity. Just as Christians insist that they are strict monotheists despite believing in the trinity, with Jesus as, in one respect, human although also God, so do the Druze who technically should be called the Monotheists, *al-Muwahhidun* in Arabic, even though they maintain that God appeared in human form in the person of al-Hakim. They see no conflict with their monotheism in such an idea.

The God-caliph al-Hakim, whose purpose was to instruct, was nevertheless, even though at last available in human form, hard to understand. He remained unpredictable and difficult to fathom, teaching by the issuing of decrees, rules and items of legislation, by actions, by example, the real import of which was unclear to ordinary folk. Comprehension of His messages, what they mean and imply, required prophetic interpretation. That was the job of Hamza. Al-Hakim's inscrutable actions and policies, his inexplicable alterations of behavior and mood, and unprecedented attempts to impose a new order through laws and regulations, all have a special meaning revealed solely to Hamza, who alone could explain them to those who followed him, those who have accepted the reality of the situation in which al-Hakim is God Himself. With the timely disappearance of al-Hakim, Hamza's case looked as if it might have proof of his claim. God could not have died. But, despairing of humans ever realizing the truth, He had retired to His true self, leaving them to flounder in their misguided ingratitude.

By then, if we accept our best evidence, most of those involved in the original Druze movement were dead, including Hamza. The new ruler sought immediately to eradicate any trace of the Druze doctrine, relentlessly pursuing its adherents and exterminating them wherever they were found to survive. All who had once upheld the divinity of al-Hakim now hid, or migrated toward safer quarters. For seven years nothing more exists in the Druze record itself. Finally, al-Muqtana, the sole remaining member of the hierarchy of five ranks recognized by Hamza, announced that he had been instructed to revive the mission and he began to issue his own epistles, now in a steady stream. He hoped to rescue the teachings of his master and reaffirm the meaning of the events in Egypt when al-Hakim/God was there. It is clear from what he wrote that his task was perilous, with the pockets of loyal Druze scattered and always in grave danger, both from the government and its agents and from dissent within the small Druze communities. Nonetheless, in large measure, he succeeded. He reconstituted the movement, drew it into a more defensible position, offered it a viable written body of doctrine, and bequeathed it a chance to survive amid a climate of implacable hostility. It is, even so, a matter of astonishment that the Druze are with us today, a thousand years after the last appearance of al-Hakim. Few movements like it endure anywhere near as long.

The former option, that al-Hakim had simply gone away temporarily and could return at any time, engendered a series of reports about one or more individuals who in later years proffered just such a claim for themselves. A key piece of evidence in each case was the close physical resemblance of the man to al-Hakim. Already during the reign itself, toward the end, Yahya reports[504] that one man arrived in Egypt coming he said from Acre. He wore the costume of the descendants of ʿAli and he set himself up near to the palace selling pens and ink. He so resembled the caliph, al-Hakim himself became curious and stopped to query the fellow about it. The man then insisted that he was al-Hakim's brother, the son of a concubine made pregnant by al-ʿAziz but then evicted from the palace. Thereafter al-Hakim would from time to time ride by and stop to chat, giving the fellow presents and enough to provide for his subsistence. The Egyptians took to calling this man 'the Double' because he looked so much like the caliph. He remained where he had first settled living as he had until the end of the reign. The new caliph had him arrested and imprisoned. Once al-Zahir visited the fellow to see for himself the resemblance but the man spoke to him so rudely, addressing him ungraciously as the 'son of my brother', that he was returned to prison cell and there he died a few days later.

This episode illustrates first that a great many people had a clear image of what al-Hakim looked like. His double, either a version of himself or his likeness, might appear and that person could make a claim to be him successfully enough to fool a goodly number.

Another incident provides evidence of a second option. In the year 1024 – four years after al-Hakim's disappearance – a man known by the name Ahmad b. Tatawwa, a Kutama Berber, was apprehended by the authorities. He showed signs of having been traveling and his hair had been allowed to grow quite long. He said that he had just arrived from Kufa, in the east, and that he had been there in the company of al-Hakim, the imam, who had sent him back to the people to see how they were faring. The authorities issued an order that he be hung and so he was.[505] Still, although the governing powers were in no mood to investigate the situation further, could what this man reported have been true? That al-Hakim had departed Egypt and now resided somewhere in the east?

Yet another story comes from the Copts, from the *History of the Patriarchs*, itself an odd mixture of hagiography and the occasional fact. Even so it cannot be easily dismissed and the case in this instance is too curious not to repeat. Bishop Michael, who is the author here, reports[506] that, from the moment of his disappearance through to the end of his son's reign, the people continued to say that al-Hakim was still alive. Many were those, he adds, who used to adorn themselves in the same manner as he used to do and claim 'I am al-Hakim.' Dressed so and claiming to be him allowed them to pass among the gullible and collect money from them. One of the more successful at it was a man from Shubra Kilsa called Shurut, a former Christian who had embraced Islam. He was also learned in the magical arts. He resembled al-Hakim, according to people who saw him, even in his speech, although he was admittedly a little taller. He referred to himself as Abu'l-'Arab and a number of individuals followed him, thereby becoming his disciples. His game was to send letters to the wealthy seeking money by explaining that he would reimburse them when he should return to his throne. Those who met him and said to him 'You are our lord the king' he would strike and say 'Watch out for your head [lest you lose it]!' This fellow kept this up for 20 years living undercover in Fustat. He lasted so long the people began to believe that he was actually al-Hakim, hiding thus because of some secret affair known only to himself.

That went on until the time of al-Zahir's son al-Mustansir, when the pretender left for Buhayra in the Nile Delta, there to reside for two years with the Bedouin Banu Qurra in a tent pitched especially for him. Pretending that he was a prophet, he wore miserable garments as if an ascetic, although he gave the Bedouin fine clothes and weapons. When they asked him why, he answered, so as to elude the end I fear. People in the region used to go to see him, prostrating themselves before him and addressing him as if he were a king or caliph. He attempted to stop them lest news of it spread too widely. However reports of it soon reached the capital causing an uproar there. Shurut knew enough to flee. Where he went next is not known, although Michael admits that a later Coptic Patriarch once received a letter from him and that the latter responded by sending the fellow money. Apparently a scam based on the claim to be al-Hakim, as in this case, retained its ability to deceive long, long after anyone had last laid eyes on the man himself.

Yet one more case features the appearance in the year 1042 in Cairo of a man who called himself either Sakin, according to some reports,[507] or Sulayman, in another version of his story.[508] He resembled al-Hakim and in fact claimed to be al-Hakim. His agents (*da'is*) had been spread in the land in secret. He went to the palace at a moment when it was devoid of troops and announced to the servants in it: 'Say that this is al-Hakim'. The keeper of the gateway promptly became alarmed and a commotion ensued. The fellow was then arrested and crucified. His associates were likewise seized and killed, among them Muhammad b. ʻAni, a Kutama Berber, who had been one of the man's *daʻis*. This information comes from al-Maqrizi. Al-Nuwayri, another historian from the Mamluk era, adds to it that there was in Fustat a group of people who believed that al-Hakim was still alive although in occultation. Al-Nuwayri's source comments here that this group has persisted until our time. They swear oaths in matters of theirs by saying: 'By the truth of the occultation of al-Hakim.' But they do not, of course, reveal this to everyone. When, in this year, this man appeared, those who continued to believe in al-Hakim's occultation rallied to him and all of them marched on the palace in an attempt to enter him into it. People were caught by surprise and the matter soon resulted in fighting between the party of the pretender and the supporters of the dynasty. The wazir arrived shortly and the whole group was apprehended, crucified alive and riddled with arrows until all were dead.

The fifteenth-century Ismaili historian Idris ʻImad al-Din provides his own account of this event and it differs in a few interesting details.[509] He seems to blame Ibn ʻAni as much as Sakin, although it was the latter who looked like al-Hakim. He also rode a donkey and dressed in the manner of al-Hakim. Idris says nothing about the persistence of a group who continued to deny the death of al-Hakim. The attempt to enter the palace involved these two only. They tried a gateway that the caliph had never used and that alerted the servants who jumped both men. The latter then resorted to magical tricks to escape. However, the wazir ordered them both thrown into the Nile and there they perished. 'God thus provided protection against their evil, rendered vain their sorcery, and caused their tricks to be futile,' comments Idris.

All this is enough to illustrate the difficulties facing Sitt al-Mulk when she assumed the role of savior of the dynasty by having her nephew proclaimed imam and caliph. A believable report says that she had already accepted responsibility for the future al-Zahir and his mother, both of whom had left the main palace and moved in with her toward the end. About this wife of al-Hakim, we know little. Al-Maqrizi relates the information that she was by name Amina and was the daughter of ʻAbdallah the second son of al-Muʻizz.[510] If so she had to have been born in 974 or earlier, the year of this son's death. She would have been at least 11 years older than al-Hakim. And since al-Zahir was born in 1005, she would have been 30 or more at the time, not old by modern standards but perhaps so according to notions prevailing in the eleventh century.

Sitt al-Mulk herself was already over 50 when her brother disappeared.[511] Still clearly, although the years of his rule may have been difficult for her, she obviously retained her authority and sense of command. She knew that, once the declaration of al-Zahir's caliphate was made public, the government could tolerate no doubts or reservations concerning the death of al-Hakim. During one of the ceremonies for the swearing of allegiance to al-Zahir, most of those present readily acquiesced, all that is, except a Turkish junior officer who had previously been the person to carry the caliph's spear ahead of him in processions. When confronted he said: 'I will not swear the oath of allegiance until I learn what happened to my master.' The authorities then grabbed him, threw him down on his face and dragged him to the river and threw him in, there to drown. And, says al-Maqrizi, 'fear spread thereafter accordingly.'

The hand of Sitt al-Mulk was certainly behind what happened even if she acted through others. The government instituted a rigorous policy designed to exclude any occurrence of resistance of this type or any suggestion that al-Hakim might still be alive. Partly to insure that it did not, she assumed the position of regent, although her nephew was already 16. She ruled thereafter so effectively that, when she died two years later, on 5 February 1023, the obituary notices for her took special note that, although a woman, she had been a patron to men.[512]

Two of her notable acts in the first days of the new regime were the executions of the former heir apparent Ibn Ilyas and Husayn b. ʿAli Ibn Dawwas, the Kutama amir whom she had relied on to perform the public functions necessary to secure the oaths of allegiance from key segments of the military. According to al-Maqrizi, she initially favored Ibn Dawwas, granting him wealth and power along with responsibility for the administration of the state. But, almost without warning, she soon arranged that the guard whose special role it had been to carry out executions on the orders of their master – the caliph – cut down Ibn Dawwas. On her command, their leader, a Sicilian named Nasim, confronted him when he appeared in public, saying aloud to those present: 'O slaves of our lord, the Commander of the Believers declares to you that this man is the murderer of your lord al-Hakim.' He then raised his sword and ordered the guard he commanded to kill Ibn Dawwas. Among the dead man's possessions they discovered in a box the knife that al-Hakim had carried in his sleeve. Presumably Ibn Dawwas acquired it when he murdered the caliph.[513] How Sitt al-Mulk had come to know about all this instantly became a matter of intense speculation. Anti-Fatimid historians in the east thought they had the obvious answer: she was herself a co-conspirator and getting rid of Ibn Dawwas was a means to cover her tracks.

The oldest version of the 'eastern' account comes from the Baghdad historian Hilal al-Sabi', who died in 1056, but it was picked up and repeated by many others from medieval times to the present. Although Ibn Taghri Birdi was himself Egyptian, he strongly preferred and often copied the Baghdad line. In this case he offers the most elaborate version,[514] one he says he has taken directly from al-Sabi'.

It commences by noting Sitt al-Mulk's keen intelligence and resolution, that she tried to warn her brother that his actions were about to ruin the dynasty, and that she had heard rumors of a coup in the making. He is said to have responded with the threat, noted earlier, about his intent to have her virginity examined and consequently her realizing that he would destroy her. Al-Sabi' then brings in Ibn Dawwas, the Kutama chieftain. This man so feared al-Hakim, he refused to enter the palace. He served the caliph but only on his horse in public. Confronted by al-Hakim he explained that he had served faithfully but that he now felt in his soul that the caliph intended to kill him. He is reported to have said: 'I will expend myself to the utmost of my ability for you but you have no need for my presence in your palace.' ... 'If you should intend to do me evil, kill me in my home among my family and then my children can bury and care for me; I prefer that over your killing me in your palace and throwing me out where my flesh will be eaten by the dogs.' Al-Hakim is said to have laughed at this answer and let the man be. However, it is quite reasonable to assume that Ibn Dawwas was not at all reassured.

Next Sitt al-Mulk sends to Ibn Dawwas one of her most trusted private servants to say: 'I have a matter for you concerning which it is necessary for us to meet. Either you adopt a disguise and come to me at night, or I will do the same.' He replies: 'I am your servant and under your command.' So she goes to his house at night herself in disguise. No one else accompanies her. When she enters, he stands and then kisses the ground in front of her several times and then stands again for service. She orders him to sit. They are alone. She says: 'O Sayf al-Dawla [calling him by his title], I have come about a matter that concerns the security of me, and you, and the Muslims. In it you will find great good fortune. I need your assistance in this matter.' He says: 'I am your servant.' She then takes from him an oath and covenant and says to him: 'You understand what my brother intends in your regard and that, when he is able, he will do away with you. It is the same with me. We are in the gravest of danger. Added to that is his proclamation of his claim to be divine and his tearing apart the sacred law, the law of his ancestors. His crimes have multiplied. I am fearful that the Muslims will rise up and kill him and kill us with him and this dynasty will end most disgracefully.' Ibn Dawwas says: 'What you say is true, O mistress of ours. What's to be done?' She answers: 'Kill him and be delivered from him. Once we have accomplished that, we will raise his son in his place and we will distribute monies. You will yourself become master of his army and his administration, the leader of the state and the one who commands it. I am a woman behind a veil; I have no desire except to be safe from him and that I live among you protected from humiliation.' Then she offered him vast land grants, promises of money, honors, and elaborate processions. At that point he says: 'Command me as you wish.' She replies: 'I want two servants of yours that you trust with your secrets and can rely for your most important matters.' He produces two servants that he characterizes as quite clever. She takes an oath from them and gives them a thousand dinars with an order for clothes, grants, riding mounts and other things. She says to the pair: 'I want you to climb tomorrow up the mountain. It will be the time of al-Hakim's riding and he will be alone, no one remaining with him except al-Qarafi the groom. Perhaps he will dismiss him and enter among the people by himself. At that rush him and slay him, and kill also al-Qarafi and the boy if both are with him.' He gives them two daggers of Maghribi manufacture, one of which is called 'Yafurat', both of them tipped with points like those of a scalpel for cupping. Having set and determined what was to happen next, she returns to her palace.

Not content with the story so far, al-Sabi' now reveals what al-Hakim was up to at that very moment. In studying the heavens and his horoscope, the caliph learns that his life is about to be cut short, although, if he were to make it through the night, he would live to be over 80. Still he is reluctant not to ride. That same night he tells his own mother what might happen and he warns her against Sitt al-Mulk and provides a large sum should something bad come to pass. She begs him for her sake not to go out. He says he will do as she says. However, toward the last third of the night, he decides otherwise and mounts his donkey to set off. The sister is watching from her palace, which is just opposite his; if and when he rides, she knows it. Passing out al-Hakim sends back the captain of the guard and continues on with al-Qarafi and the boy.

Next comes the incident with the Banu Qurra and his sending the groom back with them. As morning approaches, the two servants, now described as Sudanese blacks, jump him and throw him to the ground. He shouts: 'Woe to you both, what are you doing?' They finish killing him, cutting him in pieces and stuff all in a bag. They slaughter the boy as well and carry al-Hakim's corpse off to Ibn Dawwas after having hobbled the donkey. With the two servants, Ibn Dawwas takes the body to Sitt al-Mulk. They bury it in her house and conceal the whole affair. She then rewards Ibn Dawwas and the two servants richly.

Note in all of this how intimate our historian is with the details of private conversations, details of exactly what was said between Sitt al-Mulk and Ibn Dawwas and between al-Hakim and his mother when no one was listening except the two who spoke to each other. Al-Sabi' had to have been a fly on the wall. He can have heard what was said no other way. The only other possibility is that he made it all up. And that is the most likely. If so then the charge of Sitt al-Mulk's complicity rests on a fabrication and is a pure fiction put into circulation by pro-Abbasid writers as a way to defame the Fatimids.

On the other side of the issue, among those who resolutely insisted on the death of al-Hakim, stories of yet another kind circulated. One reported by al-Musabbihi cites a rebellion in Upper Egypt in which the instigator, once captured, claimed that he had himself killed al-Hakim. He produced what he said was a piece of skin from the caliph's head along with bit of the kerchief he was wearing. Here is the report:

> In that month [April 1024], news arrived concerning the rebel who had risen in Upper Egypt that [the commander] Haydara b. 'Aqabayan had not rested until he had this man in hand. The rebel was a member of the Hasanid nobility. He was interrogated and he confirmed that it was he who had killed al-Hakim bi-Amr Allah along with four other individuals who thereafter had scattered to different lands. One of them had gone to Barqa; another to Iraq. This fellow revealed to Haydara a piece of the skin from al-Hakim's head and a section of the kerchief that was on him. Haydara then asked: 'Why did you kill him?' He answer: 'Out of zeal for God and for Islam!' 'And how did you kill him?' He took out a knife and plunged it into his own heart saying, 'This is how I killed him!' Haydara cut off his head and sent it to the caliph along with the items that were found with him.[515]

Al-Maqrizi, who repeats this same story, appends to it in his *Khitat* the following judgment: 'This is the correct version of the killing of al-Hakim, not that which is related by the Easterners in their books which has his sister murder him.'[516] The soundness of al-Maqrizi's verdict in this case seems apt and judicious. On this issue there is little or no reason to trust al-Sabi', or Ibn Taghri Birdi who followed him.

*

In the afterlife of al-Hakim, the further we move from the era of his actual rule, the less real he becomes. His religious supporters continue to revere him with a slight, although distinct, tendency to hagiography. But the opposition, and those who suffered under him, recalled his time quite selectively. In remembering him, exaggeration and hostility are not necessarily the dominant motives of those who decided to write about him. Instead a kind of fiction takes over in which the real if bizarre events that actually happened yield to outright fable. Even among those who claim to be partisans of accuracy – among them many modern historians – stories about al-Hakim persist regardless of whether they reflect the best evidence or not. His times were indeed extraordinary, full of unheard of incidents; and the imaginary narrative later concocted to account for them must therefore be, it seems, even stranger.

A particularly appropriate example comes from an otherwise relatively sound and sober Mamluk historian, Ibn al-Dawadari. At the close of his depiction of the reign of al-Hakim, this man cannot resist adding the following tale – apparently one he personally favored – as his last word on the caliph.

The Treasure of the Bear

Muhammad b. ʿAbd al-Razzaq reports in his book called *The Solution to the Symbols in the Science of Treasures* (*Hall al-rumuz fi ʿilm al-kunuz*) that there was in Egypt during the caliphate of al-Hakim, the ʿUbaydite, a butcher named Wardan. A beautiful woman used to come to him each day, wish him good morning and give him a number of golden dinars, for which she would take from him lamb meat. She had him divide it into two pieces, which she took away carried by a porter in his basket. This situation continued in the same manner for some length of time. One day Wardan thought about the case of this woman and he brought out the gold he had been collecting from her. He noticed that all of them were of a very old minting and that he could not understand what was written on them. He began to be preoccupied with her and that she seemed to come without fail. He got together with the porter who carried the lamb for her and asked him about her situation. 'By God,' he replied, 'O master, I am puzzled about this strange woman. That is because when she has me carry the lamb away from you, she goes with me to a monk in the Qasr al-Shamʿ. There she gives him two dinars and takes from him two flagons of wine. She gives him another dinar, which he weighs out for her as 20 dirhams. She is in need of ten dirhams for fruit, sweets, wax, a little bread, and necessities for cooking such as green vegetables, rice and firewood. She has me carry all that to the edge of the Garden of the Wazir up close to the mountain. Then she ties tightly over my eyes two bandages and takes me by the hand, walking with me for about an hour over rough terrain. I place the basket on a large boulder and take away from there a basket that is empty. She returns with me to the spot where she bound my eyes, looses the bandages and gives me the ten dirhams. She says to me: 'Don't cut off the means of your livelihood.' When Wardan heard that it convinced him that she would continue to arrive without fail. He said to the porter: 'O brother, by God, she spoke the truth; you will not lose your means of livelihood. We will collect from her our due. Take what is with you.'

Thereupon Wardan began to prepare for the moment when she would come to him again and collect the lamb meat as was her habit and leave. Wardan left his boy in the shop and followed her taking special care that she would not notice him as she completed the rest of her shopping and departed Fustat. All the while he was following in secret. When she bound the eyes of the porter and led him onward, he continued to follow them until they came to that large boulder. Wardan hid behind another boulder until she delivered the porter to his place. She returned and carried away the contents of the basket. At that he lost track of her. Wardan rushed over to the boulder on which the basket had been sitting and found to the side of it a passage into a tunnel with a stairway going down. He descended the stairs into a dark chamber at the further end of which a light shone. He walked on until he came to that light and found on his right the door to a large lighted room, quite beautiful, without finding out how that light came into it. He sat at the edge of that door in the darkness observing the interior of the room.

At once he saw in the center of the room a black bear, a beast of the largest variety. And the woman had taken a piece of the lamb and cut from it the choicest portion of about four pounds. She threw the rest of the piece to the bear. He pounced on it until he finished it and he began to crunch the bones as if they were mere trifles. Then the woman hung up a portion and cooked that piece she had cut from the part she threw to the bear. Afterward she suspended the other part on a hook attached under a spot where the wind played with it, though it was not apparent from where it came. When her food was roasted, she put it into a glazed bowl of great value. Then she ate her fill and removed the rest. Then she spread out those fruits and sweets and poured the wine into an embossed crystal vessel with gems such as to take away sight. She drank and turned to water the bear.

He sipped up all that she gave him, so much that he consumed one whole flagon. She stood up and removed her trousers and turned over. The bear came over to her and mounted her once and jumped up and then began again, only to jump up once more and begin yet again for ten more times in a row. It went on, he using her and her him until they toppled over in place and fell down, he on top of her, as if dead and she likewise.

Wardan said to himself: 'Why am I sitting here? What happens if this bear wakes up and sees me and then cuts me into pieces?' So he drew out of his waistband a knife so sharp it reaches bone before flesh, which the butchers know as *al-Dabiha*, and he set about slaughtering the bear by plunging the knife into it. Then he cut its head from its body. As he did, the bear let out a snort like the head of a cow only louder. The woman woke as if crazy when she heard the snort. She looked at Wardan standing over the corpse of the bear with a knife in his hand. She then noticed the bear, its head separated from its body. She uttered a cry so anguished her soul almost overflowed. She said: 'Could it be Wardan who has done that, surely it is so'. So Wardan said to her: 'O harlot, what dragged you into this situation? Is the world devoid of men?' She replied: 'O Wardan, all this was written and destined to happen. My life has run its course; kill me as you have slaughtered this bear. For me there is no more life after this in this world.' Wardan said: 'Fear God, almighty and glorious, and turn to God for repentance. I will marry you properly and we will live out our lives on the treasure of this place. God will turn our end into good.' She said: 'O Wardan, don't trouble yourself. Slaughter me and don't tarry. If it were anyone but you among the whole of God's creation, this would not have come to pass. If you will not do as I command you do, I will destroy you. But if you do it, you will save yourself along with all of this treasure.' He answered: 'And what is in your power to do to me?' She went up to the surface in the middle of that place in which there was a bit of water and spoke words over it. Water then gushed from the sides of the place and instantly rose up to the level of an anklet. She said: 'Wardan, catch hold of yourself and slaughter me as I ordered you to do; otherwise you will perish by drowning.' Wardan replied: 'Stay, woman, and I will do as you commanded.'

She spoke words again and the water returned to where it had been. She said: 'Now to it, Wardan! Do to me what you did to the bear!' Once upon her he grabbed her cloak and slew her, leaving her at the side of the bear.

Then he gathered as much of the pearls, gems and gold as he could carry, carting them away in the basket of the porter, covered over with his garment. He set out. When he arrived at the gate of Fustat, ten members of the guard force jumped him and said to him: 'Wardan, don't be frightened, but answer al-Hakim.' They went with him to present him to al-Hakim who, when he saw him, said to him: 'Wardan, did you slaughter the bear and the harlot?' Wardan confessed to it and said: 'Yes, O Commander of the Believers.' The caliph said: 'Show me your basket.' He looked in and then covered it as it had been and said: 'O Wardan, this basket is your share. No one will interfere with it, but now go with me and surrender the treasure.'

At that he mounted his donkey and Wardan accompanied him to the treasure. Wardan said: 'O Commander of the Believers, go down and see it and look at what a horrifying creature this bear was.' Al-Hakim replied: 'O how wrong, Wardan, do not believe you saw either a bear or a woman. Those two were as wardens of this treasure until it became possible for you to take it. Opening it depended on you; no one else other than you had the ability to descend to it. Go down now and bring up all that is there. Do not resist the master of the throne.' Wardan reports: 'So I went down and found no trace of either the bear or the woman and no sign of blood.'

After that Wardan retrieved from it the riches, gems and money that were there and surrendered all of that to al-Hakim, who carried it away to his observatory on a mound overlooking the Birkat al-Juyush. There he placed it in the treasury that al-Hakim had constructed. He marked it as his own. And so it remained in the observatory. But only God knows for sure!

Next he gave Wardan that basket and issued an order that no one was to interfere with him. Wardan built with it all of the markets in Fustat known as the Market of Wardan (*Suq Wardan*), but again about that God only knows![517]

This fantasy offers no evidence of a true connection to the real al-Hakim and it tells us little or nothing about him. Yet it surely indicates, even so, how his name and fame had entered the realm of fabulous legend already only a few centuries after his time. Avid readers of the *Arabian Nights* might have recognized this tale of Wardan, the Butcher, which appears there as well. Both versions are remarkably similar, although not exactly the same, and we must assume that the story itself circulated in the period just prior to Ibn Taghri Birdi in, among other places perhaps, the source he mentions (although we know no more about such a work!) and was about then – the late thirteenth/early fourteenth century – also adopted and adapted to fit the requirements of the frame-story of the *Arabian Nights*.

Some translations of the latter distort the story beyond easy recognition. Richard Burton's is, however, well worth consulting, even though he insists that al-Hakim could not be *the* al-Hakim who had been associated with the Druze – a silly claim that reveals Burton's lack of knowledge of history.[518] Ibn Taghri Birdi obviously knew better. Burton's ability to translate is another matter and the critical racy bit at the center of the story is worth quoting in his famously uncensored version. Although his English might now seem quaintly archaic, it faithfully reflects the Arabic[519] of the *Arabian Nights*.

> And as soon as she was heated with wine, she put off her petticoat-trousers and lay down on her back; whereupon the bear rose and came up to her and stroked her, whilst she gave him the best of what belongeth to the sons of Adam till he had made an end, when he sat down and rested. Presently, he sprang upon her and rogered her again; and when he ended he again sat down to rest; and he ceased not so doing till he had futtered her ten times and they both fell to the ground in a fainting-fit and lay without motion. Then quoth I to myself [here the butcher is speaking], 'Now is my opportunity,' and taking a knife I had with me, that would cut bones before flesh, went down to them and found them motionless, not a muscle of them moving for their hard swinking and swiving.[520]

Despite Burton's expressed judgment to the contrary, both versions most certainly bring in, at the end, the Fatimid caliph al-Hakim. It is he who claims the greatest portion of the treasure. However, it is a role almost any ruler might have played; there is no intrinsic reason for it to belong to him specifically.

In the modern use of al-Hakim such accidental connections, which exist as well in several other medieval stories that build on his fame but without a necessary relevance, would be lost on an audience that no longer remembered him either directly or indirectly. The best known of these is the 'Tale of the Caliph Hakim' by the nineteenth-century French poet and author Gérard de Nerval – itself a small masterpiece of French literature. Although first issued separately in 1847, it eventually appeared as one of many component pieces of the same author's *Journey to the Orient* (*Voyage en Orient*) of 1851. Nerval himself visited the east – Cairo, Beirut, Istanbul – in 1843, and he frames his account in the first person even though most, if not all, of what he reports is highly embellished to the point of pure fiction. And the tales embedded here and there in this work are surely to be taken as exactly that.

Although set in the semi-real world of the orient, they are figments of the imagination, inventions of a mind given to poetry and fantasy, based less on historical fact than on the personal preoccupations of the man who created them.

Nerval's story of al-Hakim comes to him, he claims, from a Druze shaykh he encountered in Lebanon. It is thus not, in the internal logic of the book, his own but someone else's. Nerval nonetheless admits there that he has himself read several of the important sources, among them the writings of al-Maqrizi and al-Nuwayri, both of which he could have easily found in the work of the French orientalist Silvestre de Sacy. The latter's two volumes *Exposé de la religion des Druzes*, which commences with a biography of al-Hakim, was published in 1838, just five years prior to Nerval's trip to the east. Therefore, there seems little reason to doubt that Nerval possessed fairly accurate information about the caliph. That he chose in large part to ignore most of it betrays his novelist's instinct for wild flights of imagination, much of which we now recognize as personal to him, and that makes his tale less about al-Hakim than the author. He adopted the caliph as his own, a vision of himself in the person of the most unusual ruler of the Islamic east. Yet, many elements of Nerval's account – purported madness and insanity for example – exist in the lives of both the Fatimid caliph and the French poet. The latter's bouts of mental illness and confinement institutionally were transferred into the story. However, quite in contrast to the story of Wardan, Nerval's al-Hakim arrays the real as a tool of authenticity: Barjawan becomes the evil wazir Argevan, Sitt al-Mulk is Setalmulc, al-Hakim's sister and the object of both his and his double Yousouf's passionate and lustful affections. There are many more details in the story that derive from the real world. But a central player is hashish, which although said to be the origin of the word assassins, suggesting the later Nizari Ismailis, is out of place at the time of al-Hakim. It was, however, an interest of Nerval and his friends.

At a key point al-Hakim, as had become his wont, sets off disguised as a simple fellah for his favorite hashish den, run by Sabeens and frequented by his friend Yousouf, the man who had introduced him to the intoxication of hemp. He is there drifting into visions of his own potentially divine being when the police raid the place, arresting all those found to be in it. Al-Hakim protests that, as the caliph, they have no right to seize him. The head of the police force then announces that this man – pointing to the caliph, who is obviously only a lowly farmer – must be mad and they drag him off to the insane asylum. Once inside he is trapped. If he continues to insist that he is al-Hakim, they will assume he is crazy. If he ceases to protest, he loses his identity and may not gain his freedom in any case. Nerval's al-Hakim also occasionally believes that he is God. In the asylum, however, there are already several gods and not a few caliphs, along with the king of the rebel geniis and Adam, among others. The physician in charge has with him during his rounds the illustrious philosopher Ibn Sina (Avicenna), who lived at the time of the real al-Hakim but certainly never in his life came anywhere close to Cairo. Nevertheless the blend of reality and fiction serves the author's literary purpose well. His Hakem is a marvelous creation, a mix of history and fantasy, at once entertaining and profoundly insightful, showing what an unrestrained poetic fancy might make out of the few facts we can know with any certainty. We appreciate Nerval, the artist, without confusing hopefully his vision of the enigmatic caliph with what is true about him historically, even while we understand that there is also a poetic truth that has its own standards and that it might not follow the same rules.

Another quite interesting example of the use of al-Hakim appears in a more recent award-winning novel by the Moroccan philosopher-poet Bensalem Himmich. Its title in Arabic *Majnun al-hukm* is difficult to translate precisely but suggests 'insane authority' or the 'rule of the madman'. First published in 1989, it has already been translated into Spanish, French and most recently English, the latter under the title *The Theocrat*.[521] Himmich conjures a lengthy intimate portrait of al-Hakim starting from authentic quotations of the medieval sources. In fact a good many of the most important statements by the Arabic authorities that have a place earlier in this book are also a part of his narrative. Although medieval opinion about this caliph was not necessarily either apt or just, use of the very words of authors such as Yahya of Antioch, al-Maqrizi, Ibn Taghri Birdi, Ibn al-Athir, al-Kirmani, Sibt Ibn al-Jawzi – who are after all our sources as well as his – lend the novel the air of having a firm grounding in fact. It, moreover, connects its language to the classical Arabic of these writers. Himmich then adds to them his own novelist's inspiration, using what he calls 'historical imagination' to envision the world around the man himself: who he was, what did he think, what did he say, what were the words his devotees recorded on his behalf, including his decrees, proclamations, and pronouncements, some of which are authentic and some invented. In sections Himmich seizes upon a small incident or report and greatly expands it: punishment by sodomy becomes in his hands a full tale of the unfortunately grotesque slave Masʿud whose job was to inflict personally such a penalty when it was called for. The largest single piece in the book is a long account of the rebellion of Abu Rakwa, which occupies just over a third of it. Although the meaning of much of the novel is unclear, and is perhaps deliberately and openly ambiguous, this part may represent to the author the hope of a popular political and religious answer for the personal excesses of the main character. However, the novel ends with the death of Sitt al-Mulk and the reign of al-Zahir wherein, to quote the English translation (the Arabic in turn cites al-Maqrizi):

> Just one year after Sitt al-Mulk's death, the Egyptians, now ruled by al-Zahir ... set about ridding themselves of all their suppressed anxieties and erasing for ever their fears and constraints. In so doing they exceeded all limits. ... al-Zahir started drinking wine and allowed the people to do likewise, to listen to singing, to drink beer, eat *mulukhiyya* and various types of fish. People spent a lot of time on amusements.
>
> Al-Zahir died in the second half of Sha'ban in A.H. 427.... His caliphate had lasted for 15 years.... He loved entertainments and was very fond of singing. In his time people in Egypt were very chic and hired singers and dancers. The whole thing reached unprecedented proportions.[522]

It seems that freedom can have its excesses as well.

Finally, the following poem appeared in *The New Yorker* on 10 June 1996[523]:

The Caliph

The wily and flamboyant Fatimid, the
intricate Caligula of God, the
neurasthenic delegate of prophets (may
God pray for them!), forbad all women
to wear shoes. He barred the cobblers from
tapping their lasts or battering their little anvils;
only poor prosodists could mime their hammer-taps.
This, before he vaporized in the mauve
and umber desert of the air: al-Hakim,
defender of the devious
ambiguity of the Godhead, His penchant for
bagatelles, Creator of the paradox
of sharks and swans, Draconian Comedian!

He placed an interdict on
lamentation. He forbad all women to
weep at funerals, rescinded ululations,
and so each black cortège
wound through the lanes of Cairo voicelessly.
Even sorrow is too great a liberty,
since it inhabits memory, citadel
beyond the fists of despots, or of God.

And sometimes, in the pitch-light of the bazaar,
God's shadow baited bears or egged men on
to braggadocio or fisticuffs, or spied upon
their most secretive gestures, their least,
askance innuendos, their cupped whisperings,
till, surrogate, he evanesced on the Muqattam Hills
one evening, leaving only slivered veils behind.

Perhaps only the forbidden know
the unshod deprivations of the dead,
and perhaps only children who've just learned to walk
savor the nakedness of heels and soles.
Perhaps only the mad
value the little freedom of the shoes.

The author in this instance is Eric Ormsby, a highly respected authority on al-Ghazzali and other Islamic thinkers. He is also most recently Senior Research Fellow at the Institute of Ismaili Studies in London. Even so, in his other life as a poet, like de Nerval before him, he too imagines an al-Hakim that is perhaps more of a fiction than a reality; the lure of the caliph's extravagant legend, as it has done for many others, outweighs the more mundane but unbalanced, uncritical and surely incomplete historical record, although even that is, as we have seen, already strange enough.

Notes

Chapter One: Writing the Biography of an Enigma

1 Yaḥyā b. Saʿīd al-Anṭākī, *Taʾrīkh*, ed. I. Kratchkovsky with French trans. by A. Vasiliev, *Patrologica Orientalia* 18 (1924): 699–833 and 23 (1932): 347–520; part III, ed. Kratchkovsky, French trans. by F. Micheau and G. Troupeau, Patrologica *Orientalia* 47 (1997): 373–559, ed. by ʿUmar ʿAbd al-Salam Tadmuri (Ṭarabilis, Lubnan, 1990); Tāqī al-Dīn al-Maqrīzī, *Ittiʿāẓ al-hunafāʾ bi-akhbār al-aʾimma al-fāṭimiyyīn al-khulafāʾ*, vol. I, ed. Jamāl al-Dīn al-Shayyāl and vols. II–III, ed. Muḥammad Ḥilmi Muḥammad Aḥmad (Cairo, 1967–1973), new edition by Ayman Fuad Sayyid (forthcoming); *Taʾrīkh baṭārikat al-kanīsa al-miṣriyya (History of the Patriarchs of the Coptic Church of Alexandria)*, also called *Siyar al-bayʿa al-muqaddasa*, ed. with English translation Y. ʿAbd al-Masīḥ, A.S. ʿAṭiya, Uswald Burmester and A. Khāṭir (Cairo, 1959–68).

2 See in general Paul E. Walker, *Fatimid History and Its Sources* (London, 2002), Farhad Daftary, *Ismaili Literature: A Bibliography of Sources and Studies* (London, 2004), and Ismail Poonawala, *Biobibliography of Ismaʿili Literature* (Malibu, CA, 1977).

3 *Chiliastische Erwartungen und die Versuchung der Göttlichkeit. Der Khalif al-Hākim (386–411), Abhandlungen der Heidelberger Akademie der Wissenschaften, Philosophisch-Historische Klasse*, 1977. 2 Abhandlung.

4 'Der Treuhänder Gottes: Die Edikte des Kalifen al-Ḥākim,' *Der Islam* 63 (1986): 11–72.

5 *Damas et la Syrie sous la domination fatimide* (359–468/969–1076 2 vols. (Damascus, 1986 and 1989), part three.

6 *La Quiétude de l'Intellect: Néoplatonisme et gnose ismaélienne dans l'oeuvre de Hamid ad-Din al-Kirmani* (Xe/XIe s.) (Leuven, 1995).

Chapter Two: The Father, The Dynasty, Childhood and Regency

7 On the death of al-ʿAziz and the accession of al-Hakim, the principal source is the *Ittiʿāẓ* 1: 291–92; 2: 3–4.

8 Ibn Khallikān, *Wafayāt al-aʿyān*, ed. Iḥsān ʿAbbās, 8 vols. (Beirut, 1968), Eng. trans. M. de Slane, 4 vols. (Paris, 1842-71) 5: 375-76, trs. 3: 529; Ayman Fuad Sayyid, 'Nuṣūṣ ḍaʾīʿa min Akhbār Miṣr li-l-Musabbiḥī,' *Annales Islamologiques* 17 (1981): 1–54, p. 18.

9 *Ittiʿāẓ*, 2: 3.

10 Jamāl al-Dīn ʿAli Ibn Ẓāfir, *Akhbār al-duwal al-munqaṭiʿa*, ed. André Ferré (Cairo, 1972), p. 43; Shihāb al-Dīn Aḥmad al-Nuwayrī, *Nihāyat al-arab fī funūn al-adab: al-Juzʾ al-thāmin waʾl-ʿishrūn*, ed. Muḥammad Muḥammad Amīn and Muḥammad Ḥilmī Muḥammad Aḥmad (Cairo, 1992) 28: 167.

11 *History of the Patriarchs*, Ar. 113, trs. 170–71.

12 Yaḥyā, Tadmuri ed., 95, 113, 203, 248, 249, 273, 282, 283, 371, 372, 463–4.

13 *Ittiʿāẓ*, 2: 288-89.

14 Yaḥyā, Tad. ed., p. 290. See also Idrīs 'Imād al-Dīn [*ʿUyūn al-akhbār, al-sabʿ al-sādis*, ed. Muṣṭafā Ghālib (Beirut, 1984), p. 257] who mentions al-Hakim's mother and sister at the time of Barjawan's killing.

15 *Historiarum libri quinque*, ed. and trans. John France (Oxford, 1989), 136–37.

16 *History of Deeds Done Beyond the Sea*, trs. E.A. Babcock, 2 vols. (New York, 1943), pp. 66–67.

17 *Ittiʿāẓ*, 1: 236; *Khiṭaṭ* (*al-maʿrūf biʾl-mawāʿiẓ waʾl-iʿtibār biʾdhikr al-khiṭaṭ waʾl-āthār*), ed. Ayman Fuad Sayyid, 5 vols. (London, 2002–04), 4: 288.

18 Abū Bakr b. ʿAbdallāh b. Aybak Ibn al-Dāwādarī, *Kanz al-durar wa jāmiʿ al-ghurar*, part six, *al-Durra al-muḍiyya fī akhbār al-dawla al-fāṭimiyya*, ed. S. al-Munajjid (Cairo, 1961), 6: 236; *Ittiʿāẓ, 2: 289; Khiṭaṭ* 4:288.

19 *Kitāb al-Dhakhāʾir waʾl-tuḥaf*, ed. Muḥammad Ḥamīd Allah (Kuwayt, 1950), Eng. trans. Ghāda al-Ḥijjāwi al-Qaddūmī, *Book of Gifts and Rarities (Kitāb al-Hadāyā wa al-Tuḥaf)* (Cambridge, MA, 1996), para. #355 (Rashida) and #357 (ʿAbda), Arabic 241–42, Eng. pp. 223–24; *Khiṭaṭ*, 2: 373–74.

20 *Book of Gifts*, para. #354, Arabic 240, Eng. 222–23.

21 These figures derive from information supplied by al-Maqrīzī in the *Ittiʿāẓ*.

22 On this succession see Walker, 'Succession to Rule in the Shiite Caliphate,' *Journal of the American Research Center in Egypt* 32 (1995), pp. 239–264, pp. 245–46. Reprinted in *Fatimid History and Ismaili Doctrine* (Ashgate/Variorum, 2008), no. II.

23 *Itti'āẓ*, 1: 291.
24 Ibn al-Dawādārī, 6: 257.
25 *Itti'āẓ*, 1: 272.
26 *Itti'āẓ*, 1: 278–79.
27 *Itti'āẓ* 1: 279.
28 Ibn Ẓāfir, 43; Nuwayrī, 28: 167.
29 *Itti'āẓ*, 1: 279.
30 *Itti'āẓ*, 1: 281.
31 *Itti'āẓ*, 1: 282.
32 *Itti'āẓ*, 1: 283.
33 *Itti'āẓ*, 1: 283.
34 *Itti'āẓ*, 1: 283–4.
35 *Itti'āẓ*, 1: 288.
36 *Itti'āẓ*, 1: 289.
37 *Itti'āẓ*, 2: 4.
38 *Itti'āẓ*, 2: 4; Yaḥyā, Tad. ed., 237–38.
39 On Ibn 'Ammar see in addition, al-Maqrīzī's *Kitāb al-Muqaffā al-kabir*, ed. M. al-Ya'lāwī, 8 vols. (Beirut, 1991), bio. #1204, 3: 433–41.
40 Halm, *Das Reich des Mahdi: Der Aufstieg der Fatimiden* (Munich, 1991), English trans. M. Bonner, *The Empire of the Mahdi: The Rise of the Fatimids* (Leiden, 1996), pp. 359-60, trs. 405–06.
41 *Itti'āẓ*, 2: 5.
42 *Itti'āẓ*, 2: 5.
43 *Itti'āẓ*, 2: 7.
44 *Itti'āẓ*, 2: 5–6.
45 Arrested on 20 January 997; hung on 30th: Yaḥyā, Tad. ed., p. 238: *Itti'āẓ*, 2: 8; Nuwayrī, 28: 168–69; *Khiṭaṭ*, 3: 620–22.
46 On Ibn 'Ammar's actions against Manjutakin and his favorable treatment of the Kutama, see *Itti'āẓ*, 2: 10–13; Nuwayrī, 28: 170–71.
47 Nuwayrī, 28: 171–72.
48 Abu'l-Qāsim 'Ali Ibn al-Ṣayrafī, *al-Ishāra ilā man nāla al-wizāra*, ed. Ayman Fuad Sayyid (Cairo, 1990), p. 57, mentions a letter sent to Ibn 'Ammar's uncle to explain the errors of the nephew.
49 On Ibn 'Ammar, see in addition to the *Itti'āẓ*, *Muqaffā* (#1204), 3: 433–41.
50 *Itti'āẓ*, 2: 13. On Barjawan see also Maqrīzī's *Muqaffā*, (#1015), 1: 572–75; Abu Ya'lā Ḥamza Ibn al-Qalānisī, *Dhayl ta'rīkh Dimashq*, ed. H. F. Amedroz (Leiden and Beirut, 1908), pp. 44–56.
51 'Izz al-Dīn Abu'l-Ḥasan 'Alī Ibn al-Athīr, *al-Kāmil fi'l-ta'rīkh*, ed. C. J. Tornberg (Leiden, 1867; reprinted Beirut, 1965–67), 9: 118–23.

52 *Itti'āẓ*, 2: 13–14.

53 *Itti'āẓ*, 2: 14–15.

54 Sitt al-Mulk's gifts on this occasion are listed in the *Khiṭaṭ* 2: 499, with information from *al-Dhakhā'ir wa'l-tuḥaf*, Book of Gifts (para. #78). See also *Itti'āẓ*, 2: 15.

55 *Itti'āẓ*, 2: 18.

56 *Itti'āẓ*, 2: 16.

57 *Itti'āẓ*, 2: 17.

58 *Itti'āẓ*, 2: 17.

59 *Itti'āẓ*, 2: 18–19 and chapter 6 below.

60 *Itti'āẓ*, 2: 20.

61 *Itti'āẓ*, 2: 21–3. See also the biography of him by Ibn Ḥajar al-'Asqalānī in *Raf' al-iṣr 'an quḍāt Miṣr*, ed. 'Alī Muḥammad 'Umar (Cairo, 1998), pp. 422–26.

62 *Itti'āẓ*, 2: 23.

63 *Itti'āẓ*, 2: 25-29; Idrīs, 253–57; Nuwayrī, 28: 174–75.

64 *Itti'āẓ*, 2: 26.

65 For example, Yaḥyā, Tad. ed., p. 463.

66 *Khiṭaṭ* 3: 9.

67 *Itti'āẓ*, 2: 26; *Book of Gifts*, para. #338 (p. 218).

68 The version that has Barjawan call his master the 'gecko' comes from the generally unreliable Coptic *History of the Patriarchs*, Arabic, p. 121 (f149r), Eng. 183. However note the reverse – that it was al-Hakim who called Barjawan the 'gecko' – which is stated clearly by Maqrīzī in his biography of Barjawan (*Muqaffā*, vol. 2, p. 575), a fact already recognized by Silvestre de Sacy in his *Chrestomathie arabe*, (Paris, 1826–27), vol. 1, p. 131, who there provides both versions.

69 *Itti'āẓ*, 2: 26.

70 *Itti'āẓ*, 2: 26.

71 *Itti'āẓ*, 2: 27–29.

72 *Itti'āẓ*, 2: 29.

Chapter Three: al-Maqrizi's Chronicle of the Middle Years

73 *Itti'āẓ*, 2: 20.

74 All of the quoted material in this chapter follows closely the Arabic text of al-Maqrīzī (pp. 3–123), which is itself arranged in a strict chronological

order year by year. Passages are therefore easily identified accordingly and there seems to be no need to cite them additionally in the notes.

75 Cf. *Khiṭaṭ*, 3: 621, also the same for his killing.

76 Cf. *Khiṭaṭ*, 1: 579.

77 From here see version in *Khiṭaṭ*, 3: 39–43.

78 On Jaysh see Ibn al-Athīr, 9: 119–23.

79 For Yanis here and in the previous chapter see *Khiṭaṭ*, 3: 46.

80 Version in ʿAlī b. Mūsā al-Maghribī Ibn Saʿīd, *al-Nujūm al-zāhira fī ḥulā ḥaḍrat al-Qāhira, al-qism al-khāṣṣ bi'l-Qāhira min Kitāb al-Mughrib fī ḥulā al-Maghrib*, ed. Ḥusayn Naṣṣār (Cairo, 1970), p. 60.

81 391 (= December 1000 – November 1001).

82 Version in Nuwayrī, 28: 176.

83 Similar paragraph in *Khiṭaṭ*, 3: 358-59.

84 392 (= November 1001 – November 1002).

85 Nuwayrī, 28: 177; *Khiṭaṭ*, 4: 110 (in the year 393).

86 394 (October 1003–October 1004)

87 For an account of the reason, see Ibn Saʿīd, p. 71.

88 The Arabic reads here 'the 12th' which was not a Thursday and would place this event prior to his appointment. It therefore must be the following Thursday which is the 22nd.

89 395 (October 1004–October 1005)

90 *Khiṭaṭ*, 3: 359.

91 It is essential to read this passage as it appears in *Khiṭaṭ* 3: 59–61.

92 *Khiṭaṭ*, 3: 37.

93 *Khiṭaṭ*, 3: 37.

94 The *bayazara*, the *fahhadin*, and the *hajjalin*, keepers respectively of hawks, large cats (lynx and lions) and small game birds.

95 *Khiṭaṭ*, 2: 502–04.

96 Version Ibn Saʿīd, p. 61.

97 Version Ibn Saʿīd, p. 61.

98 The better text is in the *Khiṭaṭ*, 3: 60–61.

99 This story is likely out of place in 395; there is a version in Ibn Saʿīd, p. 71.

100 396 (October 1005–September 1006).

101 397 (September 1006–September 1007).

102 398 (September 1007–September 1008).

103 *Khiṭaṭ*, 1: 715.
104 Saqr might be read Suqayr. See the version of this passage in Ibn Saʿīd, p. 62. The ultimate source here is the *Balashkar al-'udaba'* of al-Ruzbari.
105 399 (September 1008–August 1009).
106 Version Ibn Saʿīd, p. 61.
107 Cf. *Khiṭaṭ*, 4: 1047.
108 Slightly different report in Ibn Saʿīd, p. 72.
109 400 (August 1009–August 1010).
110 Cf. *Khiṭaṭ*, 4: 904.
111 *Khiṭaṭ*, 4: 84.
112 401 (August 1010–August 1011).
113 Khitat, 4: 84.
114 Nuwayrī, 28: 189.
115 For another version and some explanation of terms see *Book of Gifts* (*K. al-Hadāyā wa al-Tuḥaf*), trans. para. #339.
116 402 (August 1011–July 1012).
117 *Khiṭaṭ*, 1: 724.
118 *Khiṭaṭ*, 4: 394.
119 403 (July 1012–July 1013).
120 Ṣayrafī, p. 59 & note.
121 Cf. Nuwayrī, 28: 191.
122 Another version Nuwayrī, 28: 192.
123 404 (July 1013–July 1014).
124 Cf. Ibn al-Dawādārī, 6: 288.
125 Better version *Khiṭaṭ*, 4: 182–83.
126 Version Nuwayrī, 28: 192–93 with details of exceptions.
127 405 (July 1014–June 1015).
128 *Khiṭaṭ*, 3: 359.
129 *Khiṭaṭ*, 4: 175.
130 Ibn Saʿīd (p. 65) adds 'and the spot was marked by a stone.'
131 Ibn Saʿīd, p. 66.
132 406 (June 1015–June 1016).
133 Ibn al-Dawādārī, 6: 291; *Khiṭaṭ*, 2: 326.
134 Ṣayrafī, pp. 62–3 with more information

Chapter Four: The Institutions of His Rule

135 He was granted the formal title on 19 April 979: Ṣayrafī, p. 49; Ibn Ẓāfir, p. 38.

136 The full text is in Ibn al-Qalānisī, pp. 80–83.

137 The head of the chancery in the late Fatimid period, Ibn al-Ṣayrafī, composed a succinct history of the wazirate prior to his time, which he called *Advice to He Who Obtains the Rank of Wazir* (*al-Ishāra ilā man nāla al-wazāra*) and he included most of those who had occupied the lesser office of *wasita*. In it he provides a few important details about appointees in the era of al-Hakim.

138 Ibn al-Qalānisī, pp. 58–60; Ṣayrafī, p. 58; *Ittiʿāẓ*, 2: 44 (under the wrong year); *Khiṭaṭ*, 3: 89.

139 He was executed on 10 June 1003: *Khiṭaṭ*, 3: 89; *Muqaffā*, (#2791) 3: 324.

140 *Khiṭaṭ*, 3: 41, 524; 4: 140, 141; Yaḥyā, pp. 280–81, 284, 285; *Ittiʿāẓ*, 2: 81, 83.

141 Yaḥyā, Tad. ed., p. 286.

142 Yaḥyā, Tad. ed., p. 294; Ṣayrafī, p. 59.

143 *Ittiʿāẓ* 2: 94; Ṣayrafī, pp. 59–61; Yaḥyā, p. 310, ed./trs. 386–87.

144 *Khiṭaṭ*, 4: 145, 712–13.

145 Ṣayrafī, pp. 61.

146 Yaḥyā, p. 312–13, ed./trs. 388–89.

147 Ṣayrafī, pp. 61-62; Yaḥyā, p. 313, ed./trs. 388–89.

148 Ṣayrafī, pp. 62–63; Yaḥyā, p. 333, ed./trs. 414–15.

149 Ṣayrafī, p. 64.

150 Ṣayrafī, p. 64; Yaḥyā, p. 334, ed./trs. 414–15.

151 Ṣayrafī, p. 65.

152 *Ittiʿāẓ* 2: 42.

153 On Ghabn, see Yaḥyā, p. 309, ed./trs. 384–86; Ibn Saʿīd, p. 63; *Khiṭaṭ*, 4: 182–84.

154 On the Fatimid judiciary see Walker, 'The Relationship between Chief Qadi and Chief Daʿi under the Fatimids' in G. Kraemer and S. Schmidtke, eds. *Religious Authority in Middle Eastern Islam* (Leiden: Brill, 2006), 70–94. For the era of al-Hakim, Walker, 'The Ismaili Daʿwa in the Reign of the Fatimid Caliph al-Hakim,' *JARCE* 30 (1993): 161–182, reprinted in *Fatimid History and Ismaili Doctrine*; Richard Gottheil, 'A Distinguished Family of Fatimide Cadis (al-Nuʿman) in the Tenth Century,' *Journal of the American Oriental Society* 27 (1906): 217–296.

155 *Ittiʿāẓ*, 2: 21.

156 *Raf' al-iṣr*, (#221) pp. 422-26; *Muqaffā*, (#3444) 7: 347–53.

157 *Itti'āẓ* 2: 21–23.

158 *Itti'āẓ*, 2: 59.

159 *Itti'āẓ*, 2: 23

160 *Itti'āẓ*, 2: 23. On him see in addition to sources already cited, *Muqaffā* (#1253) 3: 620–31; *Khiṭaṭ*, 3: 39–43.

161 *Itti'āẓ*, 2: 24.

162 Taken from Shihāb al-Dīn Aḥmad al-Qalqashandī, *Ṣubḥ al-a'shā fī ṣinā'at al-inshā'* (Cairo, 1912-1938), 10: 384–88.

163 *Itti'āẓ*, 2: 49.

164 *Itti'āẓ*, 2: 49–50.

165 *Itti'āẓ*, 2: 37, 40.

166 *Itti'āẓ* 2: 40.

167 *Itti'āẓ*, 2: 50.

168 *Itti'āẓ*, 2: 50.

169 *Itti'āẓ*, 2: 49, 59; Nuwayrī, 28: 180; Ibn Sa'īd, p. 71.

170 On this episode see chapter six below.

171 *Itti'āẓ*, 2: 106–07.

172 *Itti'āẓ*, 2: 108–09. On the date Ibn Ẓāfir, p. 62; Yaḥyā, Tad. ed., p. 312.

173 Why this judge was excluded from responsibility for Palestine and with it Jerusalem is not clear. The judge there was the Sharif Abu Talib al-Hasan b. Ja'far, who was known as Ibn Bint Ziri (See Abū 'Abdallāh Muḥammad b. 'Alī Ibn Ḥammād al-Ṣanhājī (also Ibn Ḥamādu), *Histoire des Rois 'Obaïdides (Akhbār mulūk banī 'ubayd wa sīratihum)*, ed. and trans. M. Vonderheyden (Algiers and Paris, 1927), Ar. 57, French 86). Perhaps he had some special claim on the position, a condition recognized by the caliph.

174 Ibn Athīr, 9: 223, adds to these cities al-Kufa and claims there were others as well.

175 Abu'l-Faraj 'Abd al-Raḥmān Ibn al-Jawzī, *al-Muntaẓam fī ta'rīkh al-mulūk wa'l-umam* (Haydarabad, 1939) 7: 248–51; Jamāl al-Dīn Abu'l-Maḥāsin Ibn Taghrī Birdī, *al-Nujūm al-zāhira fī mulūk Miṣr wa'l-Qāhira* (Cairo, 1929-49; Cairo, 1963–71) 4: 224–27; Nuwayrī, 28: 190; *Itti'āẓ*, 2: 88; Ibn al-Athīr, 9: 223; Heinz Halm, *Die Kalifen von Kairo: Die Fatimiden in Ägypten 973–1074* (Munich, 2003), p. 275.

176 On this office in the earliest Fatimid period, see Wilferd Madelung, 'Ḥamdān Qarmaṭ and the Dā'ī Abū 'Alī,' *Proceedings of the 17th Congress of the UEAI* [Union Européenne des arabisants et islamisants], (St. Petersburg, 1997), pp. 115–24.

177 See Walker, 'The Relationship between Chief Qadi and Chief *Da'i* under the Fatimids', 70–94.

178 The Arabic reads here 'the 12th' which was not a Thursday and would place this event prior to his appointment. It therefore must be the following Thursday which is the 22nd.

179 *Itti'āẓ*, 2: 50.

180 Ed. by W. Ivanow in *Majallat Kulliyat al-ādāb* of the Egyptian University 4 (1936): 93–107; Eng. trans. by Ivanow in *Rise of the Fatimids* (London, 1942).

181 Ed. with an Eng. trans. by Arzina Lalani (London, I.B. Tauris, 2008).

182 On this event and the role of the *da'wa* during the reign of al-Hakim in general, see Walker, 'Ismaili Da'wa in the Reign of the Fatimid Caliph al-Ḥākim', and Walker, 'In Praise of al-Ḥākim": Greek Elements in Ismaili Writings on the Imamate' in Emma Gannagé, *et al* eds. *The Greek Strand in Islamic Political Thought: Proceedings of the Conference at the Institute for Advanced Study, Princeton, 16–27 June 2003* (special issue of *Mélanges de l'Université Saint-Joseph*, 57 (2004): 367–392. Both articles appear also in *Fatimid History and Ismaili Doctrine.*

183 A literal translation of the full title is *The Sufficiently Concise Summation of the Rules for the Comportment of the Ranks and the Requirements for the Rightly Guiding Da'wa.*

184 For those by 'Abd al-'Aziz, see *Rasa'il al-hikma* (Beirut, 1984), no. 70 (p. 605), citing his 117th and 129th *majlis*, and no. 74 (p. 670 and 674), citing his 110th, 125th and 126th *majlis*. For al-Fariqi, see *Rasa'il* no. 42 (p. 331), citing the 144th, no. 69 (p. 589), citing his 140th, and no. 74 (p. 669), citing his 7th *majlis*.

185 *Itti'āẓ*, 2: 68. See Walker, 'Ismaili Da'wa', p. 173.

186 *Itti'āẓ*, 2: 82. See Walker, 'Ismaili Da'wa,' pp. 175–76

187 *Itti'āẓ*, 2: 85. Note correct reading is '*al-najwa*.'

188 *Itti'āẓ*, 2: 86.

189 On this man see Walker, 'Another Family of Fatimid Chief Qādīs: The al-Fāriqīs,' *Journal of Druse Studies.* Vol. 1, no. 1 (2000): 49–69. Also in *Fatimid History and Ismaili Doctrine.*

190 *Itti'āẓ*, 2: 103.

191 Yaḥyā, Tad. ed., p. 314, ed./trs. 390–91. Note that Yaḥyā includes this information directly after his account of events in 405 when the office of *wasita* was likewise vacant and when al-Hakim ran the government on his own. That report states in part, 'he continued without a *wasita* for a

period of four months [beginning Shawwal 405]. The employees of the various bureaus began to enter themselves into his presence and to seek of him whatever they required and he would order them in each of these matters as he wished.'

192 al-Maqrīzī's entry for 405 is relatively detailed yet it does not mention either the restoration of the *majlis* or Khatkin's appointment. On the question of the dates here see Walker, 'Ismaili Daʿwa,' pp. 176–79.

193 Edition of Ghalib in *Majmūʿa*, p. 20; Walker, 'Ismaili Daʿwa', Variorum, III, p. 34.

194 *Ittiʿāẓ*, 3: 335–44.

195 Ibn al-Ṣayrafī (Ṣayrafī), *al-Qānūn dīwān al-rasāʾil*, ed. ʿAli Bahjat (Cairo, 1905); ed. Ayman Fuad Sayyid (Cairo, 1990), French trans. Massé, 'Code de la chancellerie d'état,' *Bulletin de l'Institut Français d'Archéologie Orientale* 11 (1914): 65–120.

196 Nāṣir b. Khusraw's *Book of Travels (Safarnāma): a parallel Persian-English text*, ed. and trs. Wheeler M. Thackston (Costa Mesa, CA, 2001), pp. 62–63.

197 On the construction and layout of Cairo as well as the palace within it, see Ayman Fuad Sayyid, *La Capitale de l'Egypte jusqu'à l'époque fatimide (al-Qâhira et al-Fustât)-Essai de reconstitution topographique* (Beirut and Stuttgart, 1998), particularly chapter seven 'Les Palais fatimides', pp. 209–326.

198 *Book of Travels*, pp. 58–59.

199 *Khiṭaṭ*, 3: 111.

200 Ibn Saʿīd, p. 63.

201 On the ceremonies connected to the yearly festivals (*ʿids*), see Walker, *Orations of the Caliphs: Festival Sermons of the Fatimid Imams* (London, I.B. Tauris, 2008), and on Fatimid ceremonies in general Paula Sanders, *Ritual, Politics and the City in Fatimid Cairo* (Albany, 1994).

202 *Ittiʿāẓ*, 2: 58.

203 The account by al-Musabbiḥī of the ceremonies he personally attended under al-Zahir have been translated by Walker in his *Orations of the Caliphs*.

204 *Khiṭaṭ*, 2: 539; Bulaq ed., 1: 470.

205 Ibn al-Jawzī 7: 230–31.

206 See in general Walker, 'Fatimid Institutions of Learning,' *JARCE* 34 (1997): 179–200, reprinted in *Fatimid History and Ismaili Doctrine*.

207 For his favorable comments see the introduction to his *Rāḥat al-ʿaql* (ed. M. Kāmil Ḥusayn and M. Ḥilmī. Cairo, 1953), pp. 22–23; for criticism see his *Kitāb al-Riyāḍ* (ed. Aref Tamer, Beirut, 1960).

208 *Khiṭaṭ*, 4: 96–99; Ibn ʿAbd al-Ẓāhir, *al-Rawḍa al-bahiyya al-zāhira fī khiṭaṭ al-muʿizziyya al-qahira*, ed. Ayman Fuad Sayyid (Cairo, 1996), pp. 143–50.

209 On this mosque see Nuwayrī, 28: 176–77; Yaḥyā, Tad. ed., pp. 252–53; *Khiṭaṭ*, 4: 126–29.

210 *Khiṭaṭ*, 4: 130–31.

211 *Khiṭaṭ*, 4: 107–112; Ibn al-Dawādārī, 6: 286.

212 Ibn ʿAbd al-Ẓāhir, p. 68.

213 *Khiṭaṭ*, 4: 887.

214 Ibn al-Dawādārī, 6: 261; *Khiṭaṭ*, 4: 21.

215 *Ittiʿāẓ*, 2: 96.

216 *Khiṭaṭ*, 4: 74.

217 *Ittiʿāẓ*, 2: 49 and 100.

218 *Ittiʿāẓ*, 2: 56–57; *Khiṭaṭ*, 2: 502-03; Nuwayrī, 28: 179. On this institution see Walker, 'Fatimid Institutions of Learning,' pp. 189–93, Variorum reprint item no. I, pp. 20–28, and the additional references provided there.

219 Ibn Taghrī Birdī, 4: 222–23.

220 *Ittiʿāẓ*, 2: 56; *Khiṭaṭ*, 2: 503; Ibn Saʿīd, p. 60; Yaḥyā, Tad. ed., pp. 258–59; Walker, 'Institutions of Learning', p. 189, reprint pp. 20–21.

221 Yaḥyā, Tad. ed., pp. 258–59.

222 *Ittiʿāẓ*, 2: 80; *Muqaffā* (#1095) 3: 73–74; Ibn Khallikān, 3: 223–24; Ibn al-Jawzī, 7: 291–92.

223 *Khiṭaṭ*, 2: 503.

224 *Rafʿ al-iṣr*, old ed. 1: 102

225 Walker, 'Institutions of Learning', pp. 193–97, reprint, no. I, pp. 28–35.

226 Ibn Khallikān, 3: 430, trs. 2: 365.

227 Ibn Khallikān, 3: 430, trs. 2: 365–66.

228 Idrīs, the 15th-century Ismaili author, notes this fact with pride: *'Uyūn al-akhbār*, pp. 295–300.

229 *Ittiʿāẓ*, 2: 80; Nuwayrī, 28: 184.

230 Nuwayrī, 28: 177-78; Ibn Saʿīd, p. 69.

231 *Ittiʿāẓ*, 2: 100.

232 Abu'l-ʿAbbās Aḥmad Ibn ʿIdhārī al-Marrākushī, *al-Bayān al-mughrib fī akhbār al-Andalus wa'l-Maghrib*, vol. 1, ed. G. S. Colin and É. Lévi-Provençal (Beirut, 1948), p. 256, gives the names of three other astrologers that were executed by al-Hakim: al-Bakri, Ibn Kharita, and Ibn al-Ghazi al-Munajjim.

233 Ibn Saʿīd, p. 68.

234 *Itti'āẓ*, 2: 31; Nuwayrī, 28: 185.

235 *Itti'āẓ*, 2: 73; Ibn Sa'īd, p. 62.

236 *Itti'āẓ*, 2: 73.

Chapter Five: Friends and Rebels

237 Ibn Sa'īd, pp. 57, 70; *Itti'āẓ*, 2: 47. See also Bianquis, *Syrie*, pp. 270–71.

238 *Itti'āẓ*, 2: 59

239 See Bianquis, *Syrie*, pp. 270–71.

240 Ibn Sa'īd, p. 55.

241 Ibn Sa'īd, p. 67.

242 A long list of names of those executed could be compiled from various sources including the *Itti'āẓ* where the information comes up in the entries for each separate year. Ibn Sa'īd, by contrast, seems to specialize in collecting reports of this kind; see pp. 57–59, 67, 69–70. As another example Yaḥyā adds (p. 258 of his *History*) that in the Islamic year 397 al-Hakim had all those in jail killed.

243 *Itti'āẓ*, 2: 55–56; *Khiṭaṭ*, 3: 60.

244 *Itti'āẓ*, 2: 57–8.

245 Ibn Ḥajar, *Raf' al-iṣr*, bio. of 'Abd al-'Aziz; Ayman Fuad Sayyid, 'Nuṣūṣ', *AI* (1981), pp. 24–5.

246 *Itti'āẓ*, 2: 70.

247 *Itti'āẓ*, 2: 70.

248 Yaḥyā, pp. 330-32, ed/trs. 411–12.

249 The details that follow here come principally from the *Itti'āẓ*. On Husayn see also *Muqaffā*, (#1228) 3: 495–97.

250 Idrīs, pp. 276–80; Yaḥyā, Tad. ed., pp. 284–85.

251 There is a copy of the text in Idrīs's *'Uyūn al-akhbār*, 6: 276–80.

252 *Itti'āẓ*, 2: 84.

253 *Itti'āẓ*, 2: 85.

254 *Itti'āẓ*, 2: 86–7; Yaḥyā, Tad. ed., pp. 287–88.

255 Yaḥyā, Tad. ed., pp. 287–88; Ibn Sa'īd, pp. 72–3; *Muqaffā*, (#1069), 3: 33–34; Bianquis, *Syrie*, p. 289.

256 *Itti'āẓ*, 2: 98.

257 On this man and his rebellion see the following: Nuwayrī, 28: 173–74; *Muqaffā*, (#1230), 3: 498–500; Ibn al-Qalānisī, pp. 50-51; Yaḥyā, Tad. ed., pp. 240–41 and note no. 8; Ibn Sa'īd, p. 69; Ibn al-Athīr, 9: 120; *Itti'āẓ*, 2:19; Assaad, pp. 60–61.

258 The most important are *Itti'āẓ*, 2: 60–66; Ibn al-Athīr, 9: 197–203; Nuwayrī, 28: 180–85; Ibn 'Idhārī, pp. 257–58; Ibn al-Qalānisī, pp. 64-66; Ibn al-Jawzī, 7: 233–34; Yaḥyā, Tad. ed., pp. 259–68; Idrīs, pp. 259–72; Ibn Taghrī Birdī, 4: 215–17, 221; Ibn Ẓāfir, pp. 44–48. See also Jorge Aguade, 'Abu Rakwa' *Actas del IV Coloquio Hispano-Tunecino* (Palma de Mallorca, 1979) (Madrid, 1983), pp. 9–27, which is the most comprehensive modern study of it.

259 Ibn Ẓāfir, pp. 44–48.

260 Ibn Ẓāfir, p. 45.

261 Ibn Sa'īd, p. 57.

262 *Itti'āẓ*, 2: 65-66.

263 *Itti'āẓ*, 2: 66.

264 Ibn Taghrī Birdī, 4: 215-17; Ibn Ẓāfir, p. 47.

265 *Itti'āẓ*, 2: 61.

266 F. Richard Stephenson and David A. Green, *Historical Supernovae and Their Remnants.* (Oxford: Clarendon Press, 2002), chapter 9, 'The SN of ad 1006,' pp. 150–74.

267 Ibn Ẓāfir, p. 48.

268 *Itti'āẓ*, 2: 66.

269 The main sources are, in addition to the *Itti'āẓ*, Ibn 'Idhārī, pp. 259–60; Ibn Ẓāfir, pp. 48-50; Nuwayrī, 28: 185–88; Yaḥyā, Tad. ed., pp. 290–92; Ibn al-Jawzī, 7: 164; Ibn al-Qalānisī 60–64; Idrīs, pp. 273–76, *Khiṭaṭ*, 3: 524–27; *Muqaffā*, (#1176), 3: 350–53.

270 On the Jarrahids in general, see Marius Canard, 'Djarrahids' in the *Encyclopedia of Islam* (2nd edition).

271 On the family see Ibn Khallikān, 1: 428–33, trs. 1: 450-56; Ibn Ẓāfir, pp. 48–50; Bianquis, *Syrie*, p. 290 & note 1.

272 Ibn Sa'īd, pp. 57–8; *Muqaffā*, (#2140), 5: 592.

273 Ibn al-Qalānisī, pp. 62–63.

274 On this man and his career see 'al-Maghribi' by P. Smoor in the *EI2*; 'al-Wazir al-Maghribi' in *Muqaffā*, (#1246), 3: 536–60; Ibn Khallikān, (#193) 2: 172–77.

275 Yaḥyā, Tad. ed., pp. 305–09.

276 Abu'l-Fawāris, *al-Risāla fi'l-imāma*, ed. and trans. S. Makarem in *The Political Doctrine of the Ismailis* (Delmar, NY, 1977).

277 al-Naysābūrī, *Kitāb Ithbāt al-imāma*, ed. Arzina Lalani (London: I.B. Tauris (forthcoming); ed. M. Ghalib (Beirut, 1984).

278 On him in general see Walker, *Hamīd al-Dīn al-Kirmānī: Ismaili Thought in the Age of al-Ḥākim* (London, 1999).

279 al-Kirmānī, *al-Maṣābīh fī ithbāt al-imāma*, ed. and trans. Paul E. Walker in *Master of the Age: An Islamic Treatise on the Necessity of the Imamate* (London, I.B. Tauris, 2007).
280 *Master of the Age*, pp. 122–24.
281 *Master of the Age*, p. 126.

Chapter Six: Social Reform and Legislation

282 For a full treatment of this subject see Michael Cook, *Commanding Right and Forbidding Wrong in Islamic Thought* (Cambridge, 2000).
283 *Itti'āẓ*, 2: 54.
284 Wilferd Madelung, 'The Religious Policy of the Fatimids toward their Sunnī Subjects in the Maghrib,' in Barrucand, ed., *L'Égypte fatimide*, pp. 97–104; and Madelung and Paul Walker, *The Advent of the Fatimids: A Contemporary Shī'ī Witness* (London, 2000).
285 Qāḍī al-Nu'mān, *Pillars of Islam*, Eng. trs. Fyzee and Poonawala, 2 vols (Oxford, 2002 and 2004), 1: 265.
286 *Pillars*, 1: 265.
287 *Khiṭaṭ*, 4: 84.
288 *Itti'āẓ*, 2: 39.
289 *Itti'āẓ*, 2: 49.
290 *Itti'āẓ* 2: 67.
291 *Itti'āẓ*, 2: 69.
292 *Itti'āẓ*, 2: 78.
293 See also the comments of Idrīs, p. 293.
294 *Itti'āẓ*, 2: 98.
295 Walker, *Ḥamīd al-Dīn al-Kirmānī*, p. 38 and references there to the manuscript of this unpublished work.
296 *Itti'āẓ*, 2: 80.
297 Ibn Sa'īd, p. 72.
298 On this type of prayer, which is considered an unacceptable innovation by some, see 'Kunut' by A. J. Wensinck in the *EI2*.
299 *Itti'āẓ*, 2: 82; Yaḥyā, Tad. ed., p. 286.
300 *Itti'āẓ*, 2: 86.
301 *Itti'āẓ*, 2: 98.
302 *Itti'āẓ*, 2: 100.
303 *Itti'āẓ*, 2: 38.

304 A. Ghouchani and C. Adle, 'A Sphero-conical Vessal as Fuqqa'a or gourd for Beer,' *Muqarnas* 9 (1992): 72–92.

305 *Pillars*, 2: 115.

306 *Itti'āẓ*, 2: 54.

307 *Itti'āẓ*, 2: 69.

308 *Itti'āẓ*, 2: 76.

309 *Itti'āẓ*, 2: 77.

310 *Itti'āẓ*, 2: 81.

311 *Itti'āẓ*, 2: 83.

312 *Itti'āẓ*, 2: 86, 87.

313 *Itti'āẓ*, 2: 89.

314 *Itti'āẓ*, 2: 89.

315 *Itti'āẓ*, 2: 90.

316 *Itti'āẓ*, 2: 91.

317 *Itti'āẓ*, 2: 91.

318 *Itti'āẓ*, 2: 93.

319 *Itti'āẓ*, 2: 95.

320 Ibn al-Dawādārī, 6: 280-81. Another version has the caliph himself come upon the man, pose the same question, laugh at the irony of the fellow's answer, and then forgive him.

321 *Itti'āẓ*, 2: 53.

322 *Itti'āẓ*, 2: 53.

323 Nuwayrī, 28: 178; *Itti'āẓ*, 2: 81.

324 *Pillars*, 2: 103.

325 *Pillars*, 2: 94.

326 *Itti'āẓ*, 2: 53-4.

327 *Itti'āẓ*, 2: 69.

328 *Itti'āẓ*, 2: 77.

329 *Itti'āẓ*, 2: 81.

330 *Itti'āẓ*, 2: 86.

331 *Itti'āẓ*, 2: 90.

332 *Itti'āẓ*, 2: 91.

333 *Itti'āẓ*, 2: 90.

334 *Itti'āẓ*, 2: 95.

335 *Itti'āẓ*, 2: 103.

336 *Itti'āẓ*, 2: 38.

337 *Itti'āẓ*, 2: 53.

338 *Itti'āẓ*, 2: 76.
339 *Itti'āẓ*, 2: 76.
340 *Itti'āẓ*, 2: 77.
341 *Itti'āẓ*, 2: 86–8.
342 *Itti'āẓ*, 2: 81.
343 *Itti'āẓ*, 2: 95.
344 *Itti'āẓ*, 2: 102–03.
345 *Itti'āẓ*, 2: 103–04.
346 *Itti'āẓ*, 2: 110.
347 On this episode see above pp. 116–17; Ibn al-Jawzī, 7: 268–70.
348 Yaḥyā, Tad. ed., p. 307.
349 Ibn Sa'īd, p. 64.
350 Ibn al-Dawādārī, 6: 258.
351 *Itti'āẓ*, 2: 53, 54.
352 *Itti'āẓ* 2: 69.
353 *Itti'āẓ*, 2: 76.
354 *Itti'āẓ*, 2: 53.
355 *Itti'āẓ*, 2: 91.
356 *Itti'āẓ*, 2: 91.
357 *Itti'āẓ*, 2: 79.
358 *Itti'āẓ*, 2: 87.
359 *Itti'āẓ*, 2: 89.
360 *Itti'āẓ*, 2: 90.
361 *Itti'āẓ*, 2: 94.
362 *Pillars* 2: 192.
363 *Itti'āẓ*, 2: 56.
364 *Itti'āẓ*, 2: 103.
365 Ibn al-Dawādārī, 6: 258.
366 *Itti'āẓ*, 2: 53.
367 *Itti'āẓ*, 2: 53.
368 *Itti'āẓ*, 2: 54–5.
369 *Itti'āẓ*, 2: 44.
370 *Itti'āẓ*, 2: 44, 45; Yaḥyā, Tad. ed., p. 252.
371 Sadik A. Assaad, *The Reign of al-Hakim bi amr Allah (386/996-411/1021): A Political Study* (Beirut, 1974), 93–107, notes this explanation and some others.
372 Yaḥyā, Tad. ed., pp. 249–50.
373 *Itti'āẓ*, 2: 71.

374 *Itti'āẓ*, 2: 74–5.
375 *Itti'āẓ*, 2: 76.
376 *Itti'āẓ*, 2: 86.
377 Yaḥyā, Tad. ed., p. 289.
378 *Itti'āẓ*, 2: 89.
379 Yaḥyā, Tad. ed., pp. 281–82.
380 *Khiṭaṭ*, 4: 1030.
381 Yaḥyā, Tad. ed., p. 282–83.
382 *Itti'āẓ*, 2: 93–4.
383 *Itti'āẓ*, 2: 94–5.
384 *Itti'āẓ*, 2: 100.
385 See Yaḥyā, Tad. ed., pp. 295-99; *History of the Patriarchs*, trs. pp. 191–92.
386 *Itti'āẓ*, 2: 48.
387 *Itti'āẓ*, 2: 79; *Khiṭaṭ*, 4: 940; Yaḥyā, Tad. ed., p. 253; Ibn al-Dawādārī, 6: 269; Nuwayrī, 28: 185.
388 Yaḥyā, Tad. ed., p. 253.
389 *Itti'āẓ*, 2: 79.
390 The best general study of this incident is Marius Canard's 'La Destruction de l'Eglise de la Résurrection par le calife Hâkim et l'histoire de la descente du feu sacré,' *Byzantion* 35(1955): 16-43, reprinted in *Byzance et les musulmans*, item XX.
391 Ibn al-Qalānisī, pp. 66–68; Nuwayrī, 28: 184; Ibn al-Jawzī, 7: 239-40; *History of the Patriarchs*, trs. pp. 193–4; Ibn al-Athīr, 9: 208–09, all with variations.
392 *Itti'āẓ*, 2: 74–5.
393 *Itti'āẓ*, 2: 75.
394 A good example from a slightly later period can be found in the *Book of Gifts*, para. #86, pp. 110–11; Arabic pp. 77-78.
395 P. 66.
396 *Itti'āẓ*, 2: 75.
397 *Itti'āẓ*, 2: 94–5.
398 The most complete listing is in Yaḥyā, Tad. ed., pp. 278, 279–80, 282–83.
399 *Khiṭaṭ*, 4: 1007–09.
400 *Khiṭaṭ*, 4: 1007–09.
401 *Itti'āẓ*, 2: 100.
402 See chapter eight below.
403 *History of the Patriarchs*, trs. pp. 204–08.
404 *Itti'āẓ*, 2: 35.
405 *Itti'āẓ*, 2: 39-40; *Book of Gifts*, para. #173, pp. 163–64.

406 *Itti'āẓ*, 2: 30–31.
407 *Itti'āẓ*, 2: 48.
408 *Itti'āẓ*, 2: 96.
409 *Itti'āẓ*, 2: 97.
410 Yaḥyā, Tad. ed., pp. 339–41.
411 *Itti'āẓ*, 2: 78.
412 *Itti'āẓ*, 2: 58.
413 *Itti'āẓ*, 2: 69.
414 'Maks' by W. Björkman in the *EI2*.
415 *Itti'āẓ*, 2: 15, 2: 74, 2: 87, 2: 93, 2: 102 and 2: 102 respectively.
416 *Itti'āẓ*, 2: 79.

Chapter Seven: Foreign Affairs

417 Ibn al-Jawzī, 7: 248–51; Ibn Taghrī Birdī, 4: 224–27; Nuwayrī, 28: 190; *Itti'āẓ*, 2: 88; Ibn Athīr, 9: 223; Halm, *Die Kalifen*, p. 275.
418 See also Adam Metz, The *Renaissance of Islam*, trs. Salahuddin Khuda Bukhsh and D.S. Margoliouth (Patna, 1937), p. 325.
419 The explanation provided by Sunni historians for Qirwāsh's rather quick reversal is that of Nuwayrī (28: 190): 'In the year 401, the *da'wa* for al-Ḥākim was established in al-Madā'in, which lies half a stage from Baghdad. The *khuṭba* was also said for him in the Iraqi cities of al-Anbar and Qasr ibn Hubayra because of Qirwāsh's having accepted allegiance to him and having revealed his own Shiism. That was in the days of the Abbasid caliph al-Qādir.'
420 We are confident that this is a verbatim copy of what the *khuṭba* actually said because Ibn al-Jawzī makes that claim and because it preserves all the parts normally included in a double *khutba*.
421 This is a reference to those imams in the Ismaili line – usually said to be three – between Muḥammad b. Ismā'īl b. Ja'far al-Ṣādiq and al-Mahdī who went into hiding to avoid Abbasid persecution.
422 Ibn al-Jawzī, 7: 236; Ibn Taghrī Birdī, 4: 229–31.
423 Ibn al-Jawzī, 7: 262; Ibn Taghrī Birdī, 4: 232.
424 Ibn al-Athīr, 9: 122; Ibn al-Qalānisī, pp. 54–55.
425 Yaḥyā, Tad. ed., pp. 248, 273, 389.
426 *Itti'āẓ*, 2: 39–40.
427 *Itti'āẓ*, 2: 99.
428 *Itti'āẓ*, 2: 101.

429 *Ittiʿāẓ*, 2 107-08.

430 On the *baqṭ* and its history see Heinz Halm, 'Der nubische baqṭ,' in U. Vermeulen and D. De Smet, eds, *Egypt and Syria in the Fatimid, Ayyubid and Mamluk Eras*, II, pp. 63–103.

431 The incoming letter has the date Shawwal 390 and al-Ḥākim's reply the 10th of Dhu'l-Qaʿda 391. Idrīs, *ʿUyūn al-akhbār*, 6: 300–02; Husayn Hamdani, *al-Sulayhiyyūn wa'l-ḥaraka al-fāṭimiyya fi'l-Yaman* (Cairo, 1955), p. 301, appendix 1; Assaad, pp. 125–26.

432 Ibn al-Jawzī, 7: 246. See also Ibn Taghrī Birdī, 4: 222 and Ibn al-Athīr, 9: 219.

433 *al-Rawḍa al-bahiyya al-zāhira fi Khiṭaṭ al-muʿizziyya al-qāhira*, ed. Ayman Fuad Sayyid (Cairo, 1996), p. 40. Virtually the same information appears in al-Maqrīzī's *Khiṭaṭ*, 2: 485.

434 *ʿUyūn al-akhbār*, 6: 288. Idrīs assigns the event to the year 410 which must be a mistake for 400 and credits his information to al-Sharīf al-Ḥimyarī al-Ḥusaynī's *Kitāb al-maʿrūf bi-Kanz al-akhbār fi'l-siyar wa'l-akhbār*.

435 The incident is mentioned in his as yet unpublished *Tanbīh al-hādī wa'l-mustahdī* (p. 234 of ms. #723 belonging to the Institute of Ismaili Studies, London).

436 On this claim and the various versions of it, see the study by Yusuf Ragib, 'Un Épisode obscur d'histoire fatimide,' *Studia Islamica* 48 (1978), pp. 125–32. See also Shaun Marmon, *Eunuchs and Sacred Boundaries in Islamic Societies* (New York, 1995), pp. 35–38.

437 On this family see 'Kalbid' by U. Rizzitano in the *EI2*.

438 *Ittiʿāẓ*, 2: 99; Yaḥyā, Tad. ed., pp. 339–41.

439 *Muqaffā*, (#1087) 3: 66–67.

440 *Ittiʿāẓ*, 1: 263.

441 *Ittiʿāẓ*, 1: 237–38.

442 Ibn ʿIdhārī, p. 259.

443 Ibn ʿIdhārī, p. 260.

444 *Ittiʿāẓ*, 2: 101.

445 On this Zirid ruler see 'al-Muʿizz b. Badis' by M. Talbi in the *EI2*.

446 Ibn al-Athīr, 9: 294–95; Ibn ʿIdhārī, pp. 268–70.

447 *Ittiʿāẓ*, 2: 278–79.

448 Ibn ʿIdhārī, pp. 248–49.

449 *Muqaffā*, (#304) 1: 256–58.

450 Ibn ʿIdhārī, p. 249.

451 *Ittiʿāẓ*, 2: 43.

452 Ibn ʿIdhārī, p. 259; *Ittiʿāẓ*, 2: 99.
453 Ibn ʿIdhārī, pp. 360–61.
454 *Ittiʿāẓ*, 2: 111.
455 *Ittiʿāẓ*, 2: 111.
456 Ibn ʿIdhārī, p. 261.
457 Ibn ʿIdhārī, pp. 261, 268–70; *Ittiʿāẓ*, 2: 115.
458 For a complete analysis of Fatimid policy in Syria see Bianquis, *Damas et la Syrie sous la domination fatimide*, most especially part two 'La Mainmise fatimide' and part three 'Le Syrie sous la règne personnel d'al-Hakim' (pp. 175–387).

Chapter Eight: The Final Seven Years

459 Druze epistle no. 41 – the first by al-Muqtanā – pp. 309–19, esp. 317, 319.
460 On this event see in addition to the *Ittiʿāẓ*, *Khiṭaṭ*, 4: 183; Yaḥyā, p. 310, ed./tr. 386-87; Ibn ʿIdhārī, p. 276.
461 Confirmed by Ibn al-Dawādārī, 6: 298.
462 Yaḥyā, pp. 352–59, ed./tr. 432–43.
463 Yaḥyā, pp. 432–33; confirmed by Michael, *History of the Patriarchs*, p. 135, trs. 205.
464 The source here is Yaḥyā, but the event is confirmed by Michael in *History of the Patriarchs*, p. 137, trs. 208.
465 *History of the Patriarchs*, p. 135, trs. 205.
466 *History of the Patriarchs*, p. 137, trs. 208.
467 Yaḥyā, Tad. ed., p. 250.
468 The story is quoted by the editor in note 9 to Yaḥyā, Tad. ed., p. 251.
469 Yaḥyā, Tad. ed., pp. 300–01, traces the changes back to the Islamic year 403.
470 Yaḥyā, p. 330, ed./trs. 408–09.
471 Druze epistle no. 11, p. 101.
472 Yaḥyā, ed/tr, 410-11. The reference in Daniel is 4: 33.
473 *History of the Patriarchs*, trs. pp. 186–87.
474 Yaḥyā, ed/trs. pp. 386–87.
475 Yaḥyā, p. 329, ed/tr, 408–09.
476 Druze epistle no. 11 (p. 107); Ibn Saʿīd, p. 59.
477 Ibn al-Dawādārī, 6: 294.
478 *History of the Patriarchs*, p. 126, trs. 191.
479 Druze epistle no. 17, pp. 107-08; *Khiṭaṭ*, 4: 906.

480 Yaḥyā, pp. 330–32, ed./trs. 410–13.

481 Translation based on that of Michael Dols in his *Majnūn: The Madman in Medieval Islamic Society* (Oxford, 1992), pp. 150–51. See also his discussion of the context and meaning, pp. 145–52.

482 Nuwayrī, for example, uses the same word, *al-mankhuliya* (28: 176). He claims the illness commenced in 1003.

483 On Ibn Ilyas, see *Itti'āẓ*, 2: 97, 98, 99, 100–101, 104, 106, 114, 116; Ibn Sa'īd, pp. 64, 65; Yaḥyā, Tad. ed., p. 306. For examples of coins and tiraz with his name as heir apparent, see Ayman Fuad Sayyid's note p. 64 of his edition of al-Ṣayrafī. The Druze epistle no. 35 (p. 257) contains an example of how those texts cite Ibn Ilyas.

484 Yaḥyā, pp. 333–34, ed./trs. 414–15.

485 For the Druze discussion of this matter, see the *Rasā'il al-ḥikma*, epistle no. 17, 'Risālat al-tanzīh' (Beirut, 1986), pp. 189–91. Also no. 18 (p. 200), no. 35 (p. 257), and no. 74 (pp. 672–73).

486 Yaḥyā, pp. 349–52, ed./trs. 428–33; Nuwayrī, 28: 193.

487 Yaḥyā, pp. 368-70, ed./trs. 448–51; *Itti'āẓ*, 2: 116.

488 On his appointment, see Yaḥyā, pp. 333–34, ed./trs. 414–15. His death notice is in the *Itti'āẓ*, 2: 173, under the entry for the year 415 (18 December 1024) and it says explicitly 'The amir Abū Hāshim al-'Abbās b. Shu'ayb b. Da'ūd b. 'Abdallāh al-Mahdī who had been the *walī 'ahd al-mu'minīn.*' The corresponding passage in al-Musabbiḥī, *al-Juz' al-arba'ūn min Akhbār miṣr*, edited by A. F. Sayyid and Th. Bianquis (Cairo, 1978), 105 is slightly corrupt: for Sa'īd, read Shu'ayb (as in the index). Al-Musabbiḥī also calls him *walī 'ahd amīr al-mu'minīn* in this context, which clouds the issue somewhat. See as well *Itti'āẓ*, 2: 183–84, where al-Maqrīzī remarks that, at the beginning of al-Ẓāhir's reign, the affairs of the nation were in the hands of his aunt and that 'it was she who made sure the caliphate came to him instead of to the *wali 'ahd* Abū Hāshim al-'Abbās.' Ibn Shu'ayb was subsequently forced to pledge allegiance to al-Ẓāhir with a sword hanging over him. The *Khiṭaṭ* (4: 859) contains an entry on the 'Masjid of the wali 'ahd al-mu'minīn', who was this same Abū Hāshim al-'Abbās ibn Shu'ayb.

489 *Itti'āẓ*, 2: 113; *Muqaffā*, bio. #846 (al-Darazī) 1: 306–09, bio. #1277 (Ḥamza) 3: 659–62, bio. #1182 (al-Akhram) 3: 361–62; Yaḥyā, pp. 334–39, 339–40, 342–50, ed./trs. 414–19, 420–29; Ibn Ẓāfir, pp. 51–54; *History of the Patriarchs*, p. 124, trs. 187–88. See also the modern studies of David R. Bryer, 'The Origins of the Druze Religion,' *Der Islam 52* (1975): 47-84 and

239-264; *Der Islam* 53 (1976): 5–27; M. G. S. Hodgson, 'al-Darazi and Hamza in the Origins of the Druze Religion,' *JAOS* 82 (1962): 5–20; and A. I. Silvestre de Sacy, *Exposé de la religion des Druzes* (Paris, 1838; reprint Paris, 1964).

490 al-Risāla al-wāʻiza, ed. M. Kamil Husayn in *Majallat Kulliyyat al-Adab, Jami'at Fu'ad al-Awwal*, 14 (1952) pp. 1–29; ed. M. Ghalib in *Majmūʻa*, pp. 134–47.

491 They are nos. 6, 7, 9, 28, 10, 16, 12, 17, 13, 19, 21, 22, 24 respectively.

492 Ghalib ed., p. 146.

493 Bio. #1182.

494 Druze epistle no. 17, p. 178.

495 Druze epistle no. 19, p. 203.

496 Druze epistle no. 13, p. 144.

497 See, for example, epistle no. 12, in which Ḥamza discusses Barjawān, Ibn ʻAmmār, Abū Rakwa, and Mufarrij.

498 On his death see H. Halm, 'Der Tod Ḥamzas, des Begründers der drusischen Religion,' in U. Vermeulen and D. De Smet, eds, *Egypt and Syria in the Fatimid, Ayyubid and Mamluk Eras*, II, pp. 105-113

499 The principal sources are Ibn Taghrī Birdī, 4: 180-83; Ibn al-Dawādārī, 6: 298; Yaḥyā, pp. 345–48, ed./trs. 424–29; Nuwayrī, 28: 193–94; Ibn Ẓāfir, pp. 54–57. Note that in his *Khiṭaṭ*, 3: 337, al-Maqrīzī reports that al-Musabbiḥī mentioned the burning of Fustat, a fact not covered in the *Ittiʻāẓ*, but which suggests that solid contemporary information was once available about this incident. See also Ayman Fuad Sayyid, *Capitale*, pp. 614–16.

500 Ibn Taghrī Birdī, 4: 180–83.

501 See for example Ibn Ẓāfir pp. 57–59; Ibn al-Jawzī, 7: 297–300; Ibn Taghrī Birdī, 4: 190–92.

502 Yaḥyā, pp. 359–61, ed./trs. 444–45.

Chapter Nine: Afterlife and Epilogue

503 For a complete analysis of the possibilities, see Van Ess, *Chiliastische Erwartungen*.

504 Yaḥyā, pp. 332–33, ed./trs. 412–13.

505 al-Musabbiḥī, *Akhbār miṣr*, p. 91.

506 *History of the Patriarchs*, pp. 137–38, trs. 209–10

507 Nuwayrī, 28: 213–14; Ibn al-Athīr, 9: 513.

508 *Ittiʻāẓ*, 2: 189.

509 *'Uyūn al-akhbār*, 6: 328.

510 *Itti'āẓ*, 2: 124.

511 She was born in the Maghrib in 970.

512 Ibn 'Idhārī, p. 271; Nuwayrī, 28: 205. On three of the key historical problems connected to her life, see the study by Heinz Halm, 'Le destin de la Princesse Sitt al-Mulk,' in Barrucand, ed., *L'Égypte fatimide*, pp. 69–72.

513 *Itti'āẓ* 2: 125-28; Ibn 'Idhārī, p. 271.

514 Ibn Taghrī Birdī, 4: 185-90.

515 al-Musabbiḥī, *Akhbar Misr*, pp. 27-28.

516 *Khiṭaṭ*, 4: 146.

517 Ibn al-Dawādārī, 6: 302-08.

518 See his note 1, p. 296.

519 *The Alif Laila or Book of the Thousand Nights and One Night*, edition of the Arabic by W. H. Macnaghten, 4 vols. (Calcutta, 1839), 2: 312–16.

520 Burton trs., pp. 293–97 (nights nos. 353–55).

521 By Mohamed Saad Eddine El Yamani in French as *Le Calife de l'epouvante: Roman* (1999), in Spanish by Federico Arbós as *El loco del poder* (Madrid, 1996), and the English translation of Roger Allen (Cairo: AUC Press, 2005).

522 2nd edition of the Arabic (Rabat, 1998) pp. 243–44; Eng. p. 202.

523 The author Eric Ormsby published it also in a collection of his poems called *For A Modest God: new and selected poems* (New York: Grove Press, 1997, pp. 30–31).

Bibliography

Abu'l-Fawāris, 'al-Risāla fi'l-imāma,' ed. and trans. S. Makarem in *The Political Doctrine of the Ismailis*. Delmar, NY, 1977

Aguade, Jorge, 'Abu Rakwa' *Actas del IV Coloquio Hispano-Tunecino* (Palma de Mallorca, 1979) (Madrid, 1983), pp. 9–27.

Alif Laila or Book of the Thousand Nights and One Night, edition of the Arabic by W. H. Macnaghten, 4 vols. Calcutta, 1839.

Assaad, Sadik A., *The Reign of al-Hakim bi amr Allah (386/996–411/1021): A Political Study*. Beirut, 1974.

Bianquis, Thierry, *Damas et la Syrie sous la domination fatimide (359–468/969–1076)*. 2 vols. Damascus, 1986 and 1989.

——, ''Abd al-Gani ibn Saʿid, un savant sunnite au service des Fatimides,' *Actes XXIX C.I.O.* [Etudes Arabes et Islamiques I, Histoire et Civilisation I] (1975): 39–47.

——, 'Al-Ḥākim bi amr Allāh ou la folie de l'unité chez un souverain fatimide,' *Les Africains*. Vol. 11 (Paris, 1977), pp. 107–133. (sous la direction de Charles-Andre Julian et al., Les editions du Jaquar, new ed. 1990).

Book of Gifts and Rarities, see *Kitāb al-Dhakhā'ir wa'l-tuḥaf.*

Bouthoul, Betty, *Le calife Hakim: Dieu de l'an mille*. Sagittaire, 1950.

Bryer, David R., 'The Origins of the Druze Religion,' *Der Islam* 52 (1975): 47–84 and 239–264; *Der Islam* 53 (1976): 5–27.

Burton, Richard, *Book of The Thousand Nights and a Night*. 10 vols. 1885.

Canard, Marius, 'La Destruction de l'Eglise de la Résurrection par le calife Hâkim et l'histoire de la descente du feu sacré,' *Byzantion* 35 (1955): 16–43, reprinted in *Byzance et les musulmans*, item XX.

Cook, Michael, *Commanding Right and Forbidding Wrong in Islamic Thought*. Cambridge, 2000.

Daftary, Farhad, *The Ismāʿīlīs: Their History and Doctrines*. Cambridge, 1990.

——, *Ismaili Literature: A Bibliography of Sources and Studies*. London, I.B.Tauris, 2004.

——, *A Short History of the Ismailis: Traditions of a Muslim Community*. Princeton, 1998

de Nerval, Gérard, *Voyage en Orient*. 1851

De Smet, D., 'Les interdictions alimentaires du calife fatimide al-Ḥākim: marques de folie ou announce d'un règne messianique?' in U. Vermeulen and D. De Smet, eds, *Egypt and Syria in the Fatimid, Ayyubid and Mamluk Eras*, I, pp. 53–70.

——, *La Quiétude de l'Intellect: Néoplatonisme et gnose ismaélienne dans l'oeuvre de Ḥamīd ad-Dīn al-Kirmānī (Xe/XIe s.)*. Leuven, 1995.

Dols, Michael W., *Majnūn: The Madman in Medieval Islamic Society*. Oxford, 1992.

Ghouchani, A., and C. Adle, 'A Sphero-Conical Vessel as Fuqqa'a, or a Gourd for 'Beer',' *Muqarnas* 9 (1992): 72–92.

Glaber, Rodulfus, *Historiarum libri quinque*, ed. and trans. John France. Oxford, 1989.

Gottheil, Richard, 'A Distinguished Family of Fatimide Cadis (al-Nuʿman) in the Tenth Century,' *Journal of the American Oriental Society 27* (1906): 217–296

Halm, Heinz, 'Der nubische baqṭ,' in U. Vermeulen and D. De Smet, eds, *Egypt and Syria in the Fatimid, Ayyubid and Mamluk Eras*, II, pp. 63–103.

——, 'Der Tod Ḥamzas, des Begründers der drusischen Religion,' in U. Vermeulen and D. De Smet, eds, *Egypt and Syria in the Fatimid, Ayyubid and Mamluk Eras*, II, pp. 105–113.

——, 'Der Treuhänder Gottes: Die Edikte des Kalifen al-Ḥākim,' *Der Islam* 63 (1986): 11–72.

——, 'Sitt al-Mulk,' *EI2*.

——, *Das Reich des Mahdi: Der Aufstieg der Fatimiden*. Munich, 1991. English trans. M. Bonner, *The Empire of the Mahdi: The Rise of the Fatimids*. Leiden, 1996.

——, *Die Kalifen von Kairo: Die Fatimiden in Ägypten, 973–1074*. Munich, 2003.

——, 'Le destin de la Princesse Sitt al-Mulk,' in Barrucand, ed., *L'Égypte fatimide*, pp. 69–72.

Hamdani, Husayn F., *al-Ṣulayḥiyyūn wa'l-ḥaraka al-fāṭimiyya fi'l-Yaman*. Cairo, 1955.

Himmisch, Bensalem, *Majnūn al-ḥukm*. 2nd ed. Rabāṭ, 1998. Eng. trans. Roger Allen, *The Theocrat*. Cairo, AUC Press, 2005; French trans. Mohamed Saad Edddine El Yamani, *Calife de l'épouvante: roman*, Le Serpent à Plumes, 1999; Spanish trans. Federico Arbós, *El loco del poder*. Madrid, 1996.

Hodgson, M. G. S., 'al-Darazi and Hamza in the Origins of the Druze Religion,' *Journal of the American Oriental Society* 82 (1962): 5–20.

Ibn ʿAbd al-Ẓāhir, *al-Rawḍa al-bahiyya al-zāhira fī khiṭaṭ al-muʿizziyya al-qāhira.* Ed. Ayman Fuad Sayyid. Cairo, 1996.

Ibn al-Athīr, ʿIzz al-Dīn Abu'l-Ḥasan ʿAlī, *al-Kāmil fi'l-taʾrīkh.* Ed. C. J. Tornberg. Leiden, 1867; reprinted Beirut, 1965–67.

Ibn al-Dawādārī, Abū Bakr b. ʿAbdallāh, *Kanz al-durar wa jāmiʿ al-ghurar*, part six, *al-Durra al-muḍiyya fī akhbār al-dawla al-fāṭimiyya.* Ed. S. al-Munajjid. Cairo, 1961.

Ibn Ḥajar al-ʿAsqalānī, *Rafʿ al-iṣr ʿan quḍāt Miṣr.* Ed. ʿAlī Muḥammad ʿUmar. Cairo, 1998.

Ibn Ḥammād, Abū ʿAbdallāh Muḥammad b. ʿAlī al-Ṣanhājī (also Ibn Ḥamādu), *Histoire des Rois 'Obaïdides (Akhbār mulūk banī ʿubayd wa sīratihum).* Ed. and trans. M. Vonderheyden. Algiers and Paris, 1927.

Ibn ʿIdhārī, Abu'l-ʿAbbās Aḥmad al-Marrākushī, *al-Bayān al-mughrib fī akhbār al-Andalus wa'l-Maghrib.* Vol. 1, ed. G. S. Colin and É. Lévi-Provençal. Beirut, 1948.

Ibn al-Jawzī, Abu'l-Faraj ʿAbd al-Raḥmān, *al-Muntaẓam fī taʾrīkh al-mulūk wa'l-umam.* Haydarabad, 1939.

Ibn Khallikān, Aḥmad, *Wafayāt al-aʿyān.* Ed. Iḥsān ʿAbbās. 8 vols. Beirut, 1968. Eng. trans. M. de Slane. 4 vols. Paris, 1842–71.

Ibn al-Qalānisī, Abū Yaʿlā Ḥamza, *Dhayl taʾrīkh Dimashq.* Ed. H. F. Amedroz. Leiden and Beirut, 1908.

Ibn Saʿīd, ʿAlī b. Mūsā al-Maghribī, *al-Nujūm al-zāhira fī ḥulā ḥaḍrat al-Qāhira, al-qism al-khāṣṣ bi'l-Qāhira min Kitāb al-Mughrib fī ḥulā al-Maghrib.* Ed. Ḥusayn Naṣṣār. Cairo, 1970.

Ibn al-Ṣayrafī, Abu'l-Qāsim ʿAlī, *al-Ishāra ilā man nāla al-wizāra.* Ed. Ayman Fuad Sayyid. Cairo, 1990.

——, *al-Qānūn dīwān al-rasāʾil.* Ed. Ayman Fuad Sayyid (Cairo, 1990), French trans. Massé, 'Code de la chancellerie d'état,' *Bulletin de l'Institut français d'archéologie orientale* 11 (1914): 65–120.

Ibn Taghrī Birdī, Jamāl al-Dīn Abu'l-Maḥāsin, *al-Nujūm al-zāhira fī mulūk Miṣr wa'l-Qāhira.* Cairo, 1929-49; Cairo, 1963–71.

Ibn Ẓāfir, Jamāl al-Dīn ʿAlī, *Akhbār al-duwal al-munqaṭiʿa.* Ed. André Ferré. Cairo, 1972.

Idrīs ʿImād al-Dīn, *ʿUyūn al-akhbār.* Ed. M. al-Yaʿlāwī as *Taʾrīkh al-khulafāʾ al-fāṭimiyyīn bi'l-maghrib: al-qism al-khāṣṣ min Kitāb ʿuyūn al-akhbār.* Beirut, 1985.

——, *ʿUyūn al-akhbār, al-sabʿ al-sādis.* Ed. Muṣṭafā Ghālib. Beirut, 1984.

ʿInān, Muḥammad ʿAbdallāh, *al-Ḥākim bi-Amr Allāh wa asrār al-daʿwa al-fāṭimiyya*. Cairo, 1959.

Irwin, Robert, *The Arabian Nights: A Companion*. London, 2004.

Ivanow, W., *Ismaili Literature: A Bibliographical Survey*. Tehran, 1963.

——, *Ismaili Tradition Concerning the Rise of the Fatimids*. London, 1942.

Jabrīl, Muḥammad, *Mā dhakarahu ruwāt al-akhbār ʿan sīrat amīr al-muʾminīn al-Ḥākim bi-amr Allāh*. Dār al-Hilāl, 2003.

al-Kirmanī, Ḥamīd al-Dīn, *al-Maṣābīḥ fī ithbāt al-imāma*, in Walker, *Master of the Age: An Islamic Treatise on the Necessity of the Imamate*, with a critical edition of the Arabic text of Ḥamīd al-Dīn al-Kirmānī's *al-Maṣābīḥ fī ithbāt al-imāma (Lights to Illuminate the Proof of the Imamate)*, full translation, introduction and notes. London: I.B.Tauris, 2007.

——, *al-Risāla al-wāʿiẓa*. Ed. M. Kāmil Ḥusayn, in *Majallat Kulliyyat al-adāb, Jāmiʿa Fuʾad al-Awwal*, 14 (1952): 1–29; ed. Ghālib in *Majmūʿat rasāʾil*, 134–47;

——, *al-al-Risāla al-durriyya fī maʿnā al-tawḥīd*. Ed. M.K. Husayn, Cairo, 1952; ed. M. Ghālib in *Majmūʿat rasāʾil*, pp. 19–26.

——, *Kitāb al-Riyāḍ*. Ed. Aref Tamer. Beirut, 1960.

——, *Kitāb Maʿāṣim al-hudā wa'l-iṣāba fī tafḍīl ʿAlī ʿalā al-ṣaḥāba*, mss. D(724), The Institute of Ismaili Studies, London.

——, *Kitāb Rāḥat al-ʿaql*. Ed. M. Kāmil Ḥusayn and M. Ḥilmī. Cairo, 1953.

——, *Kitāb Tanbīh al-hādī wa'l-mustahdī*, Ms. D(723), The Institute for Ismaili Studies, London; Ms. Fyzee Collection, Bombay University Library, no. 57 (Goriawala).

——, *Majmūʿat rasāʾil al-Kirmānī*. Ed. M. Ghālib. Beirut, 1987. (Contains *al-Durriyya, al-Nuẓum, al-Raḍiyya, al-Muḍīʾa, al-Lāzima, al-Rawḍa, al-Zāhira, al-Ḥāwiya, Mabāsim, al-Wāʿiẓa, al-Kāfiya*).

——, *Risālat mabāsim al-bishārāt*, in Husayn, *Ṭāʾifat al-durūz*, pp. 52–71; in Ghālib, *al-Ḥaraka al-bāṭiniyya fi'l-islām*, pp. 205–33; and in *Majmūʿat rasāʾil al-Kirmānī*, pp. 113–33.

Kitāb al-Dhakhāʾir wa'l-tuḥaf. Ed. Muḥammad Ḥamīd Allāh. Kuwayt, 1950. Eng. trans. Ghāda al-Ḥijjāwī al-Qaddūmī, *Book of Gifts and Rarities (Kitāb al-Hadāyā wa al-Tuḥaf)*. Cambridge, MA, 1996.

Lewis, Bernard, 'Bardjawān', *EI2*.

Madelung, Wilferd, 'Ḥamdān Qarmaṭ and the Dāʿī Abū ʿAlī,' *Proceedings of the 17th Congress of the UEAI* [Union Européenne des arabisants et islamisants], (St. Petersburg, 1997), pp. 115–24.

——, 'Notes on Non-Ismāʿīlī Shiism in the Maghrib,' *Studia Islamica* 44 (1976): 87–97.

——, 'The Religious Policy of the Fatimids toward their Sunnī Subjects in the Maghrib,' in Barrucand, ed., *L'Égypte fatimide*, pp. 97–104.

Madelung, Wilferd, and Paul E. Walker, *The Advent of the Fatimids: A Contemporary Shīʿī Witness*. London, I.B.Tauris, 2000.

Mājid (Magued), ʿAbd al-Munʿim, *al-Ḥākim bi-Amr Allāh al-khalīfa al-muftarā ʿalayh*. Cairo, 1959, 1982

Makarem, Sami Nasib, *The Political Doctrine of the Ismāʿīlīs* (The Imamate): *An Edition and Translation, with Introduction and Notes, of Abū l-Fawāris Aḥmad ibn Yaʿqūb's* ar-Risāla fī l-Imāma. Delmar, New York, 1977.

——, 'Al-Ḥākim bi-Amrillāh's Appointment of His Successors,' *Abḥāth* 23 (1970): 319–24.

al-Maqrīzī, Tāqī al-Dīn Abu'l-ʿAbbās Aḥmad, *Ighāthat al-umma bi-kashf al-ghumma*. Ed. Muḥammad Muṣṭafā Ziyāda and J. al-Shayyāl. Cairo, 1957; French trans. G. Wiet 'Le traité des famines de maqrīzī,' *JESHO* 5 (1961): 1–90; Eng. trans. A. Allouche, *Mamlūk Economics: A Study and Translation of al-Maqrīzī's Ighāthah*. Salt Lake City, 1994.

——, *al-Khiṭaṭ (al-maʿrūf bi'l-mawāʿiẓ wa'l-iʿtibār bi'dhikr al-khiṭaṭ wa'l-āthār)*, 2 vols. Bulaq, 1853; ed. Ayman Fuad Sayyid, 5 vols. London, 2002–04. Unless so noted all references are to this later edition.

——, *Ittiʿāẓ al-ḥunafāʾ bi-akhbār al-aʾimma al-fāṭimiyyīn al-khulafāʾ*. Vol. I, ed. Jamāl al-Dīn al-Shayyāl and vols. II–III, ed. Muḥammad Ḥilmī Muḥammad Aḥmad. Cairo, 1967–1973.

——, *Kitāb al-Muqaffā al-kabīr*. Ed. M. al-Yaʿlāwī. 8 vols. Beirut, 1991.

Marmon, Shaun, *Eunuchs and Sacred Boundaries in Islamic Societies*. New York, 1995.

Mernissi, Fatima, *The Forgotten Queens of Islam*. Trans. M. J. Lakeland. Minneapolis, 1993.

Metz, Adam, *The Renaissance of Islam*, trs. Salahuddin Khuda Bukhsh and D. S. Margoliouth. Patna, 1937.

al-Musabbiḥī, al-Mukhtār, *al-Juzʾ al-arbaʿūn min Akhbār Miṣr*. Pt. 1 (historical section), ed. Ayman Fuad Sayyid and Th. Bianquis. Cairo, 1978.

Nāṣir b. Khusraw, *Nāṣir-i Khusraw's Book of Travels [Safarnāma]*. Persian text and Engl. trans. W. M. Thackston Jr. Costa Mesa, CA, Mazda, 2001.

al-Naysābūrī, Aḥmad, *Istitār al-imām*, ed. W. Ivanov in *Bulletin of the Faculty of Arts, University of Egypt* 4, part 2 (1936): 93–107, Eng. trans. by Ivanov in *Ismaili Tradition Concerning the Rise of the Fatimids*, pp. 157–183.

——, *Kitāb Ithbāt al-imāma*. Ed. Arzina Lalani, London: I.B.Tauris (forthcoming); ed. M. Ghalib. Beirut, 1984.

——, *Risāla al-mūjaza al-kāfiya fī ādāb al-du'āt* in Ḥātim b. Ibrāhīm al-Ḥāimdī's *Tuḥfat al-qulūb wa furjat al-makrūb*. Ed. Abbas Hamdani. London, I.B.Tauris (forthcoming).

al-Nuwayrī, Shihāb al-Dīn Aḥmad, *Nihāyat al-arab fī funūn al-adab: al-Juz' al-thāmin wa'l-'ishrūn*. Ed. Muḥammad Muḥammad Amīn and Muḥammad Ḥilmī Muḥammad Aḥmad. Cairo, 1992.

Ormsby, Eric, 'The Caliph,' *The New Yorker*, June 10, 1996.

——, *For A Modest God: new and selected poems*. New York: Grove Press, 1997.

Poonawala, Ismail K., *Biobibliography of Ismā'īlī Literature*. Malibu, CA, 1977.

Qāḍī al-Nu'mān, *Da'ā'im al-islām*. Ed. A. A. A. Fyzee. Cairo, 1951–61; Eng. trs. Fyzee and Poonawala as *The Pillars of Islam*, 2 vols Oxford, 2002 and 2004.

al-Qalqashandī, Shihāb al-Dīn Aḥmad, *Ṣubḥ al-a'shā fī ṣinā'at al-inshā'*. Cairo, 1912–1938.

Rāghib, Yūsuf, 'Un épisode obscur d'histoire fatimide,' *Studia Islamica* 48 (1978): 125–132.

Rasā'il al-ḥikma, Druze epistles, Beirut edition; epistles nos. 1–40, ed. Daniel De Smet. Leuven, Peeters, 2007.

Sanders, Paula, *Ritual, Politics and the City in Fatimid Cairo*. Albany, 1994.

Ṣayrafī, see Ibn al-Ṣayrafī

Sayyid, Ayman Fuad, 'Nuṣūṣ ḍā'i'a min Akhbār Miṣr li-l-Musabbiḥī,' *Annales islamologiques* 17 (1981): 1–54.

——, *al-Dawla al-fāṭimiyya fī Miṣr: tafsīr jadīd*. 2nd edition, Cairo, 2000.

——, *La Capitale de l'Egypte jusqu'à l'époque fatimide (al-Qâhira et al-Fustât) - Essai de reconstitution topographique*. Beirut and Stuttgart, 1998.

Silvestre de Sacy, Antoine Isaac, *Chrestomathie arabe*. Paris, 1826–27.

——, *Esposé de la religion des druzes, tiré des livres religieux de cette secte et précédé de la vie du khalife Hakem-Biamr-Allah*. 2 vols. Paris, 1838.

Stephenson, F. Richard, and David A. Green, *Historical Supernovae and Their Remnants*. Oxford: Clarendon Press, 2002. (esp. chapter 9, 'The SN of ad 1006,' pp. 150–74).

Ta'rīkh baṭārikat al-kanīsa al-miṣriyya (History of the Patriarchs of the Coptic Church of Alexandria, also called *Siyar al-bay'a al-muqaddasa)*. Ed. and trans. Y. 'Abd al-Masīḥ, A. S. 'Aṭiya, Uswald Burmester and A. Khāṭir. Cairo, 1959–68.

Van Ess, Josef, *Chiliastische Erwartungen und die Versuchung der Göttlichkeit. Der Khalif al-Hākim (386–411), Abhandlungen der Heidelberger Akademie der Wissenschaften*, Philosophisch-Historische Klasse, 1977. 2 Abhandlung.

——, 'Biobibliographische Notizen zur islamischen Theologie,' *Die Welt des Orients* 9 (1977/78): 255–61.

Van Nieuwenhuyse, Stijn, 'The Uprising of Abū Rakwa and the Bedouins Against the Fāṭimids,' *Acta Orientalia Belgica* 17 (2003): 245–64.

Van Reeth, J. M. F., *'Al-Qumāma et le Qā'im* de 400 AH: le trucage de la lampe sur le tombeau du Christ,' in U. Vermeulen and D. De Smet, eds, *Egypt and Syria in the Fatimid, Ayyubid and Mamluk Eras*, II (Leuven, 1995), pp. 171–90

Walker, Paul E., *The Advent of the Fatimid*, see Madelung, Wilferd.

——, 'Another Family of Fatimid Chief Qāḍīs: The al-Fāriqīs,' *Journal of Druse Studies*, vol. 1, no. 1; reprinted in *Fatimid History and Ismaili Doctrine*. Ashgate, Variorum, 2008.

——, *Abū Ya'qūb al-Sijistānī: Intellectual Missionary*. London, I.B.Tauris, 1996.

——, *Early Philosophical Shiism: the Ismaili Neoplatonism of Abū Ya'qūb al-Sijistānī*. Cambridge, 1993.

——, *Exploring an Islamic Empire: Fatimid History and Its Sources*. London: I.B.Tauris, 2002.

——, *Fatimid History and Ismaili Doctrine*. Ashgate, Variorum, 2008.

——, 'Fatimid Institutions of Learning,' *Journal of the American Research Center in Egypt (JARCE)* 34 (1997): 179–200; reprinted in *Fatimid History and Ismaili Doctrine*. Ashgate, Variorum, 2008.

——, *Ḥamīd al-Dīn al-Kirmānī: Ismaili Thought in the Age of al-Ḥākim*. London, I.B.Tauris, 1999.

——, ''In Praise of al-Ḥākim': Greek Elements in Ismaili Writings on the Imamate,' in Emma Gannagé, et al eds. *The Greek Strand in Islamic Political Thought: Proceedings of the Conference at the Institute for Advanced Study, Princeton, 16–27 June 2003* (special issue of *Mélanges de l'Université Saint-Joseph*, vol. 57 (2004), pp. 367–392.; reprinted in *Fatimid History and Ismaili Doctrine*. Ashgate, Variorum, 2008.

——, 'The Ismaili Da'wa in the Reign of the Fatimid Caliph al-Ḥākim,' *JARCE* 30 (1993): 160–182; reprinted in *Fatimid History and Ismaili Doctrine*. Ashgate, Variorum, 2008.

——, *Master of the Age: An Islamic Treatise on the Necessity of the Imamate*. London: I.B.Tauris, 2007.

——, *Orations of the Fatimid Caliphs: Festival Sermons of the Ismaili Imams*. London, I.B.Tauris, 2009.

——, 'The Relationship between Chief Qadi and Chief Dā'ī under the Fatimids' in G. Kraemer and S. Schmidtke, eds. *Religious Authority in Middle Eastern Islam* (Leiden: Brill, 2006), 70–94.

——, 'Succession to Rule in the Shiite Caliphate,' *JARCE* 32 (1995): 239–264; reprinted in *Fatimid History and Ismaili Doctrine*. Ashgate, Variorum, 2008.

William of Tyre, *History of Deeds Done Beyond the Sea*, trans. E. A. Babcock, 2 vols. New York, 1943.

Yaḥyā b. Saʿīd al-Anṭākī, *Taʾrīkh*. Ed. ʿUmar ʿAbd al-Salām Tadmūrī. Ṭarābilis, Lubnān, 1990; ed. I. Kratchkovsky with French trans. A. Vasiliev, Patrologica *Orientalia* 18 (1924): 699–833 and 23 (1932): 347–520, part III, ed. Kratchkovsky, French trans. F. Micheau and G. Troupeau, *Patrologica Orientalia* 47 (1997): 373–559. Citations are normally first to the Tadmūrī edition and second to the French translation and its parallel Arabic.

Index

www.ingramcontent.com/pod-product-compliance
Lightning Source LLC
Chambersburg PA
CBHW071708120626
46550CB00001B/146
9789774165689